WITHDRAWN

HARVARD LIBRARY

WITHDRAWN

END-TIMERS

Three Thousand Years of Waiting for Judgment Day

Martin Ballard

PRAEGER

AN IMPRINT OF ABC-CLIO, LLC
Santa Barbara, California • Denver, Colorado • Oxford, England

Copyright 2011 by Martin Ballard

All rights reserved. No part of this publication may be reproduced, stored in a retrieval system, or transmitted, in any form or by any means, electronic, mechanical, photocopying, recording, or otherwise, except for the inclusion of brief quotations in a review, without prior permission in writing from the publisher.

Library of Congress Cataloging-in-Publication Data

Ballard, Martin.
　End-timers : three thousand years of waiting for Judgment Day / Martin Ballard.
　　p. cm.
　Includes bibliographical references (p.　) and index.
　ISBN 978–0–313–38428–8 (cloth : alk. paper) — ISBN 978–0–313–38429–5 (ebook)
1. End of the world. 2. Eschatology. I. Title.
BL503.B35　2011
202'.3—dc23　　　　　　2011026022

ISBN: 978–0–313–38428–8
EISBN: 978–0–313–38429–5

15　14　13　12　11　　1　2　3　4　5

This book is also available on the World Wide Web as an eBook.
Visit www.abc-clio.com for details.

Praeger
An Imprint of ABC-CLIO, LLC

ABC-CLIO, LLC
130 Cremona Drive, P.O. Box 1911
Santa Barbara, California 93116-1911

This book is printed on acid-free paper ∞

Manufactured in the United States of America

Unless otherwise noted, Scripture quotations are from *New Revised Standard Version Bible*, Copyright © 1989 National Council of the Churches of Christ in the United States of America. Used by permission. All rights reserved.

Qur'an quotations are drawn from the On-line Quran Project (http:/al-quran.info/?x = y), which bases English text on *The Holy Qur'an—Text, Translation and Commentary*, trans. Abdullah Yusuf Ali (Lahore, Cairo, and Riyadh) 1938.

Contents

Preface		v
Acknowledgments		ix
1	Fighting the Dragon of Chaos: Beginnings	1
2	David's Righteous Branch: The Jewish End-Time	9
3	The Secret of the Kingdom: The Christian End-Time	25
4	The Book Shall Be Laid Down: The Islamic End-Time	43
5	The Day of Antichrist Approaches: Europe before 1346	61
6	Do Not Let Your Sword Cool: Plague and Reformation	81
7	Everything That Is Hidden Is Found: Mystics and Explorers	99
8	Before the End of the World Come: A Messianic Century	111
9	In the Hands of an Angry God: End-Timers in Conflict	133
10	When the Master Comes: Messiah and Mahdi	151

11	No Other Goal than Palestine: Zionists and Politicians	165
12	Signs of the Times: A Troubled World	181
Notes		207
Select Bibliography		227
Index		243

Preface

Norman Cohn's *The Pursuit of the Millennium: Revolutionary Millenarians and Mystical Anarchists of the Middle Ages*[1] still holds its place high on *The Times Literary Supplement*'s list of the most influential books. While German scholars had taken an interest in medieval sects for decades, this work opened up millennial studies to English readers. But Cohn was aiming for more. Born into a mixed Jewish and Catholic family, he had lost relatives to the Holocaust and, in the immediate postwar years, served in the British army in Vienna, where he was surrounded by evidence of Nazi and Stalinist oppression. When he came to concentrate on medieval history, he made a link between twentieth-century suffering and the persecution of heretics, witches, and Jews during those early troubled centuries. While the depth of Cohn's scholarship has never been in question, some of his emphases and conclusions have aroused debate. Medieval historians, in particular, question the way he presents a stark dichotomy between apocalyptic sects and the Augustinian Catholic mainstream. They insist that terror of the apocalypse and descent into hell pervade all areas of medieval society. This can be illustrated by literary works from Dante and Chaucer, from passion plays, and from the doom paintings that loomed down from so many church walls.

Cohn's later regression into antiquity appears to have been motivated by Old Testament scholars' stubborn refusal to acknowledge how much postexile apocalypticism drew inspiration from the older Aryan prophet Zarathustra (Zoroaster). Cohn's *Cosmos, Chaos and the World to Come: The Ancient Roots of Apocalyptic Faith*[2] was approved by veteran Persian scholar Mary Boyce, who was the world expert in this area. It therefore comes as a surprise that—at least by the evidence of mainstream scholars' book lists—Boyce's works remain little read. In common with Cohn, I find the evidence for Zoroastrian influence very compelling.

It has long been accepted that no sharp distinction can be drawn between political and ecclesiastical history of Europe before the time of the European

Enlightenment. Then, in about 1660 (after even Norman Cohn has lost interest in the subject), the secular and sacred narratives sharply diverge. While works by twelfth-century abbot Joachim of Fiore have been closely scrutinized by major scholars, nineteenth-century John Nelson Darby awaits an interpreter. Yet it was he who laid the foundations of the "dispensational" theology that now enthralls millions of evangelical Christians across America and the wider world. Darby's works may appear bizarre—even alarming—to the liberal-minded reader. It may stretch credulity that—four centuries after Galileo—apparently well-educated people could seriously expect to be "raptured" through the sky to the heavens, while hundreds of millions are dying on the battlefield of Armageddon below. Again, it is Norman Cohn who delivers the warning:

There are times, when this underworld emerges from the depths and suddenly fascinates, captures and dominates multitudes of usually sane and responsible people who thereupon take leave of sanity and responsibility. And it occasionally happens that this underworld becomes a political power and changes the course of history.[3]

This book is neither a defense of nor an evangelical attack on end-time belief. It attempts provide an overview of an intimidating mass of historical and theological scholarship, most of which which lies outside the scope of students and general reader. Cohn interpreted apocalayptic patterns in the light of events that dominated the mid twentieth century; I am alarmed by the challenges that face humanity in the early twenty first. Without offering solutions, the later chapter seek to disentangle some of the stubborn issues that currently threaten peace across the Middle East and beyond.

Basic terms need some explanation:

- *Eschatology* is derived from the Greek word *eschatos* (*last*); this is the study of the last things. As a theological discipline, it starts from no assumption over how the end will come or what characteristics it may have.
- *Apocalypse* is the Greek word for *revealing*, or *revelation*. While some Old Testament scholars insist that this word should never be used outside the context of a direct revelation of heaven, it is more generally used to describe any sudden eruption of the Last Things.
- The *Messiah* or anointed one (in Christianity also *Christ*; in Islam, *Mahdi*) is the redeemer figure who will come to save the world.
- *Millennium/Millennialism*: At its narrowest interpretation (*chiliasm*), this is the thousand-year period when the Messiah will return in bodily presence to rule the earth. Interpreted more broadly, the term can also encompass the practice of dividing time into eras or dispensations. Millennial periods can be variable and need not last a literal thousand years.

While *eschatology* and *chiliasm* remain technical terms, the others have escaped from theological jargon into general speech, where scholars lose control of usage. Picking up a wide range of meanings and overtones, the words can describe any kind of final, violent, or doom-laden event. In practice, *apocalyptic* and *millennial* are often used as synonyms. Since sources like the *Book of Revelation* move freely between different visions of the end-time, even scholars can find it impossible to keep language precise.

More abstruse Christian terminology of the nineteenth and early twentieth centuries will be explained, where necessary, within the text.

It is a privilege to live within range of the magnificent research resources provided by the Cambridge University Library, along with departmental and college libraries and special collections. However, over the sound of grinding axes, the Internet now offers access to much otherwise unavailable information. This resource provides easy access to analytical articles (which may or may not be as tightly researched as those in learned journals), to exchanges of argument—or even abuse—and a mass of information on the most improbable subjects. Many valuable primary sources can now be accessed at a the click of a mouse and internet references provide the necessary link for the majority of readers, who do not live within range of a Deposit Library.

Acknowledgments

My thanks are due to librarian and mission expert Terry Barringer, who has now supported me through many years and two books; also for helpful contributions and advice of my Arabist grandson Ed Ballard. Also to my wife Eva and daughter Alison for their endless patience, good humor, advice, and support.

— 1 —

Fighting the Dragon of Chaos: Beginnings

Although 4,000 years is no more than a fraction of the 70,000 that have passed since the first members of species *homo sapiens* followed a circuitous route into Asia from the African plain, virtually all recorded history is compressed within that period. By 2000 BCE, both settled agriculture and urban living were well established in Egypt, Mesopotamia, China, and the Indus Valley. Beyond these early centers of civilization, bronze-working skills had already been widely mastered, while pastoralists had tamed horses and knew how to support mobile communities on the products of living as well as dead animals. Freed at last from the daily struggle for survival, potters and scribes could focus on developing specialized skills that supplied a whole community's needs. Soon, the earliest trading contact for the exchange of products and natural resources had been opened between different centers of that elusive condition that would become known as civilization

Progress brought problems. The hunter-gatherer life style might have been a struggle, but it is thought that communities generally lived in some kind of peace[1] and a measure of social equality. With growing prosperity, urban dwellers now needed to protect their produce in granaries and their houses behind stone city walls, and even nomadic communities became exposed to attack by marauding bands of animal thieves. In this new world, communities needed to recruit powerful fighters who could be relied on to protect their hard-won property. Holding a near monopoly of advanced weapons, these warriors lost no time in establishing their position as a privileged and wealthy ruling class.

Still, human protection was not enough. Out of the multitude of available deities, city-states would select one as their own and lavish whatever wealth they could afford on temples, ceremonies, and sacrifices designed to ensure that this special guardian remained on their side. Since any failure in ritual could bring disaster on the whole community, these rites needed to be preformed by a specialist class of priests, who then allied themselves with the rulers and assumed responsibility for upholding the unequal social order. Under their supervision, craft-workers, pastoralists and farm laborers, women and men, slave and free, were kept in their divinely ordered place within the hierarchal structure. By this time the ruler—be it king, queen, or pharaoh—had acquired responsibility for keeping chaos in its place and making the rain fall.

With food sources and boundaries secure, the more privileged members of society could now indulge in cosmic speculation. Whether arrived at independently or through interchange of ideas, proto-philosophers in the two ancient civilizations of Egypt and Sumer reached similar conclusions about the world in which they lived. Above their heads they saw the sky's great arch, from which stars—mainly static, but with a few wanderers—shone at night. Since these heavens gave much-needed rain, it followed that "upper waters" were held in place behind a solid firmament. The flat earth, in turn, sat above the "lower waters." People could see how the great rivers, beside which they built their civilizations, were fed by fresh water from subterranean springs, but they lived in fear that this life-giving resource would be overwhelmed by the salty oceans, which represented the state of chaos out of which the ordered world had emerged.

Since fresh and salt waters needed to be kept apart, the underworld could only be seen as a place of endless conflict. Priests from both civilizations told how powerful gods struggled to keep chaos at bay. According to Babylonian legend, warrior deity Marduk (Ashur in Assyria) descended into the nether world to fight the dragon of chaos. For their part, Egyptians told how the sun god Ra drove his chariot across the heavens by day before plunging into the underworld to wage a nightly a battle with an equally evil serpent. The chariot's re-emergence at dawn provided assurance that the forces of order had triumphed once again. Since sickness and death were also caused by demon possession, it was a matter of the greatest urgency for every individual that pharaoh and priests should perform their sacred duties with the greatest possible diligence.

Both Sumerians and Egyptians believed that the gods lived in the heavens, while evil spirits inhabited the lower world. After death, men and women could only look forward to a bleak existence in an underground "abode of the dead," where they would live in darkness and eat dirt and dust. Israelites and Greeks would later share this vision of a land of sorrows, which they respectively called Sheol and Hades. Behind the Greek fable that told how Persephone descended into the underworld in autumn and reappeared in spring lies the Sumerian myth of how the goddess Inanna (Ishtar) visited her sister Ereshkegal, who was queen of the underworld. Both stories tell of death and rebirth—of winter, spring, and fertility. Inanna's lament describes the sense of loss and desolation that all humans would experience in that bleak underworld.

> I eat clay for bread, I drink muddy water for beer
> I have to weep for young men forced to abandon their sweethearts
> I have to weep for girls wrenched from their lovers' laps
> For the infant I have to weep, expelled before its turn.[2]

A few fortunate Egyptians could anticipate a brighter fate. On his death, every pharaoh would take his place in Ra's boat, where he would continue his earthly task of keeping chaos at bay. A few favored nobles might also be received into a resting place with the gods. Their Sumerian counterparts found immortality more elusive. The Epic of Gilgamesh—the world's most ancient poem—tells how the King of Uruk took up a fruitless search for immortality. In the end, he could only accept the advice offered by Siduri, the woman wine-bearer.

> You will never find the life for which you are looking.
> When the gods created man they allotted him death,
> but life they kept in their own keeping.
> As for you Gilgamesh, fill your body with good things,
> Day and night, night and day,
> Dance and be merry, feast and rejoice ...
> Make your wife happy in your embrace;
> For this too is the lot of man.[3]

Even as a king, Gilgamesh could see no hope for the future. In order to get any glimpse of paradise, he needed to look backward to a mythical golden age when "there being no snakes, no scorpions, no hyenas, no lions, no dogs, no wolves, neither fear nor terror; humanity had no enemy."[4] In his epic, Gilgamesh told of a huge event, near the beginning of time, that had shaped the history of the world. After creation was complete, air god Enlil supervised the creation of human beings from the womb of the mother goddess. Although not immortal, those early humans could live to huge old age, as they assisted the gods by helping out with all the thankless tasks of daily life.

When gods began to complain that these humans were polluting the earth and breeding too fast, the issue was discussed in the divine council. "The noise of mankind has become too much," complained Enlil. "I am losing sleep over the racket."[5] After these irritating humans had survived a series of divinely inflicted disasters, Enlil finally loosed the upper waters in a great flood, which arrived "like a wild ass screaming in the wind." Seriously alarmed that there would henceforth be no human servants to do his dirty work, water god Ea secretly advised the virtuous Atra-Hasis to build a boat, which had to be large enough to accommodate samples of all animal species. When the waters subsided, Atra-Hasis' ark finally came to rest on a mountain summit, where he offered a sacrifice to the gods and—alone of all humankind—he received the gift of eternal life.

Storytellers and scribes were not concerned whether Gilgamesh was a historical figure any more than whether any particular pharaoh had fought the battles for which his tomb narrative gave him credit. The essence of ancient myth lay not in historical veracity but in the timeless message that lay behind the narrative. Flood myths would later spread across Middle Eastern cultures, of which one found a place in the Book of Genesis. In modern times, some scholars would ask whether these tales might have arisen independently out of the folk memory of a real flood, which is thought to have happened when, at some time in the fifth millennium BCE, the Mediterranean broke through the Hellespont to inundate large areas of country around the Black Sea. Ancient Mesopotamian storytellers would surely have been amazed that their literal-minded descendants could so signally fail to grasp the narrative's hidden mythic meaning.

*

It has long been recognized that similarities of vocabulary and grammatical structure in languages spoken across huge areas from Western Europe to the Indian subcontinent indicate that, at some time in the past, they had all branched off from a single parent stem. By linguistic analysis, scholars focused attention on a people, known from antiquity as Aryan, who lived on the steppes of southern Asia, somewhere near the Black and Caspian Seas, in the third millennium BCE. Archaeologists find them a deeply frustrating people. These illiterate nomads lived on the move, passing devotional hymns down the generations by word of mouth, leaving no temples or palaces, pottery, or carving. Modern genetic testing has, however, confirmed that the linguists' theories on a common Aryan origin are based on solid foundations. The Asian steppes will only support a sparse population and these Aryans were probably pushed from their homes—toward the west, east, and south—by overpopulation, hunger, and tribal warfare. Unlike the Moguls of later times, they left no apparent trails of devastation in their wake, but they did carry their language, social structure, gods, hymns, and fables into very distant lands.

Those Aryans who moved towards the west, into an area that would later be known as Europe, found no mountain barrier or advanced civilization that lay across their line of progress. Little is known of these migrations beyond the fact that they bequeathed versions of their speech that would divide into the Greco-Roman, Celtic, and Germanic language families that—barring small enclaves in Georgia and northern Spain—would dominate the continent. Myths and fables from areas as far apart as Scandinavia, Greece, and Russia show evidence of a common Aryan origin. In about 800 BCE, early Greek poet Hesiod wrote of the community of gods, chaos, and the creation of the world.

Now Iapetus took to wife the neat-ankled maid Clymene, daughter of Ocean, and went up with her into one bed. And she bare him a stout-hearted son, Atlas ... And Atlas through hard constraint upholds the wide heaven with unwearying head and arms, standing at the borders of the earth before the clear-voiced Hesperides; for this lot wise Zeus assigned to him.[6]

It is believed that, in around 1800 BCE, bands of Aryans arrived in northwest India by way of Afghanistan and the mountains of the Hindu Kush at just the time when the early Indus valley civilization was sliding into in terminal decline. The invasion may or may not have been violent, but genetic research has established that the newcomers managed to gain control of the upper castes of north Indian society, leaving the indigenous people to populate the lower castes.[7] Aryan priests codified the ancient traditions into a collection of sacred hymns known as the *Rig Veda*, which would be passed down with astonishing accuracy by word of mouth, before being finally committed to writing many centuries later. These invocations and praises to the gods offer no treatise on morality and no divine revelation. They recount the old story of how the dragon of chaos was dismembered and primal darkness transformed "into a world with divisions, spheres, realms, numbers, a world of light, symbol of consciousness emerging from the unconscious."[8] From these chants, scholars have reconstructed the Aryan practices and beliefs as they had once been on the Asian steppes, the multitude of nature deities of earth, sun, water, fire, and wind, the water used in libations and holy fires that burned in every home. Although the early Vedas contain no insights into End-Time events, they did reach after more abstract concepts of eternity by linking the words *breath* and *wind* and imagining a universe that had been constructed out the body of primal man. Venerating ancestors as integral parts of their cosmos, they still looked forward to the time when their own bodies would blend with the waters to provide food for plants.[9] But cultural influences moved in both directions. On the one side, Indo-European languages would ultimately be spoken across Pakistan and Bangladesh and by more than 70 percent of Indians. On the other side, it can already be detected in the *Vedas* that indigenous concepts of life and death and the nature of time would ultimately triumph over the thought patterns that the Aryans had brought with them. Western history has traditionally been perceived as a straight line, which progresses from a specific moment of creation, toward some kind of End-Time event. In the subcontinent, in contrast, the Indo-Aryans absorbed the Eastern vision of a universe that is in constant motion, in which time follows an immense circular process before starting again after the wheel has turned full circle. Although apocalyptic movements have emerged within Eastern faiths (as in cults connected with creator and destroyer god Siva and his blood-stained consort the goddess Kali), End-Time beliefs generally sit uneasily within the Eastern tradition.

*

The Zoroastrian faith has been described as a "shadowy presence" spread across the ancient world. For many years, scholars argued over the date when the prophet Zarathustra (Zoroaster in the later Greek form) is supposed to have lived, with estimates widely separated over some 900 years, between 1500 and 600 BCE. It is now widely believed that he was a historical figure who may have taken part in the third Aryan migration into western Persia (Iran) in about 1200 to 1100 BCE. Probably born into the Aryan priesthood, he inherited his ancestors' belief in a single supreme god, Ohrmazd, who was supported by a variety of lesser nature divinities. At the age of 30, Zarathustra found himself in the presence of a shining being, the one all-wise, wholly good, just, and uncreated god Ahura Mazda. Originally perhaps a younger god who supplanted his senior

Ohrmazd, in later Zoroastrian tradition, the two names would interchangeably represent the supreme Lord, who presided over Creation and would control the Last Things. Describing Ahura Mazda as the "one who set chaos in order," Zarathustra described how he had created a regular world, which was as perfectly contained within the sky as an egg in its shell. Flat as the steppes from which his people had come, in this perfect world, the sun always stood at its zenith and there could be no winter, illness, or evil. Zarathustra then told how the wicked Angra Mainyu (*destructive mind*) approached Ahura Mazda with a demand for dominion over the whole world. When rejected, he launched an assault on this whole beautiful creation. In his destructive fury, he even broke the shell of heaven, causing the rancid upper waters to mix with the sweet lower waters, changing fertile land into desert and bringing drought and famine.

Legend does not record whether Zoroaster crossed mountain ranges while migrating from the steppe or whether he was born in east Persia and travelled westward over broken country. Either way, three millennia would pass before scientists discovered that the mountains between modern Afghanistan and Turkey sit on a confusion of fault lines, where five tectonic plates are in collision.[10] Eruptions and earthquakes, thought to be caused by Ahura Mazda's and Angra Mainyu's subterranean battles, were bound to linger long in folk memory. Since Zarathustra's Aryan (Iranian) people were not yet in contact with literate civilizations, his teachings were passed down verbally in the native Aryan language, which would become known as Avestan. In recent years, the world's few Avestan scholars have managed to isolate the hymns and myths that provide insight into Zarathustra's earliest vision of history. In the *Gathas*, the prophet looks both backward to "eternity past" and forward into "eternity to come." Under his integrated scheme, the act of Creation mirrors a Last Judgment when rewards and punishments will be administered to all.[11] In the meantime, the cosmic battle between Ahura Mazda and Angra Mainyu would continue.

In the final days, when good has finally prevailed, the prophet expected to lead his followers across the Bridge of Separators into a world where the perfection of Creation has once again been restored. It appears, however, that Zarathustra finally came to realize that this great event would not happen in his own lifetime. Although he had three natural sons who would die in their turn, the myth told how the prophet deposited his semen at the bottom a lake, where it would keep on shining like a lamp. At some time in the future, a virgin would enter the lake and absorb this life-giving force into her body to bear the Messianic son, Saoshyant, who would save the world.

As the prophet's followers moved into western Persia, they are thought to have converted the Magi priests and passed on the Avestan language as a living medium of communication, and these Magi then imported new elements into the faith that they had received.[12] Then, in around the late fifth century BCE, Zoroastrianism developed a 12,000-year millenarian structure, by which all history was divided into four periods of 3,000 years.[13] Instead of taking just six days, the Zoroastrian process of Creation consumed the whole of the initial

3,000 years, after which there followed two intermediate periods, each of which was subdivided into three separate millennia. Since each era would have its own savior, Zarathustra needed to deposit three packages of semen in lakes, where each would await the start of his assigned 3000 years. The first two Messiahs would battle inconclusively with the forces of Angra Mainyu for the first 6000 years; then, at the beginning of the fourth and final era, Saoshyant would rise from the lake to engage in the confrontation that would shape the destiny of all souls. Every human—without regard for wealth, rank, or sex—needed to be clear on which side they stood, for, at physical death, all would be judged according to their thoughts and deeds.

Still, the battle is not finished. All normal values become perverted as Angra Mainyu and his demons gain control of the earth.

Families will split in hatred. The son will strike the father and brother will fight against brother.... Men from the lower orders will marry the daughters of the nobles and the priests. Slaves will walk in the paths of nobles.... Religious duties will be neglected; apostasy will abound; the rituals will hardly be performed; and the sacred fires will no longer be upheld.[14]

When this reign of evil finally draws to its end, a great year marks the start of Ahura Mazda's eternal time. Then the sun will stand still in the heavens for 30 days and nights, while all plants become green and illness and death disappear from the land. As the earth gives up its dead, all humans pass through hot metal that pours out of the hills. "For him who is righteous it will seem like warm milk and for him who is wicked it will seem as if he is walking in the flesh through molten metal."[15] According to Persian mythology, the three-headed dragon of chaos would then be chained within Mount Damavand until the world finally reaches its end. At the universal resurrection, when humans are reunited with their earthly bodies, all mountains and hills are leveled to restore the primal simplicity of the Aryan steppes. The final separation would then be made between humans who were destined for the place of bliss and those less fortunate who would plunge into the depths of hell. As they cross the Bridge of Separators, they see before them the ancient yet ever-youthful figure of Mithra, who had been present at Creation and is now the most senior of all created beings. On his left is shining savior Saoshyant, while Rashu holds the scales of justice on his right. "In the weighing Rashu the just, who holds the balance of souls, neither makes it dip, neither for the just nor for the wicked, neither for the lord man nor for the ruler of the land."[16] A beautiful maiden then escorts the just into the bliss of paradise, while a horrid hag throws the lost into a pit of misery and darkness.

The demon Visarsh will seize the wicked person's soul and will beat it and torment it scornfully and wrathfully and the wicked person's soul will cry out in loud lamentation and will weep and utter many pleas, entreatingly and make many struggles in vain.[17]

Still Ahura Mazda is merciful, and some may spend only a short period in torment before being admitted to paradise.

In the sixth century BCE, devout Zoroastrian Cyrus the Great set about governing his vast empire according to the prophet's teaching. Instead of persecuting those of other faiths, he tried to show justice and tolerance to all who lived within his huge empire. Being a mobile and nonliterate people, early Zoroastrians might have left little for archaeologists to dig up, and (astonishingly) the bulk of their oral tradition was not committed to paper the ninth and tenth centuries CE. Still, their apocalyptic faith remained influential across wide areas of the Middle East long into the Christian era.

Some would argue that Zoroastrianism was the world's first monotheistic religion, others that that it brought dualism to both Judaism and Christianity. For theological purists, the issue lies in whether he presents Ahura Mazda and Angra Mainyu as co-existent and equal divinities or whether the destructive spirit stands alongside Mithra, one level down. But Zarathustra and his priests did not think like twenty-first century scholars and that issue must remain unclarified. Whatever the theoretical position, religious believers who came under Zoroastrian influence in later centuries increasingly portrayed evil as an independent force in a cosmos of polar opposites—children of light against agents of darkness, angels of good in conflict with demons of evil, the fallen temporal world set against otherworldly divine spheres. Within Christian popular culture, in particular, God and Satan—like Ahura Mazda and Angra Mainyu—would remain locked in the battle until the end of time.

— 2 —

David's Righteous Branch: The Jewish End-Time

Somewhere around 1200 BCE—near the time Zoroaster was preaching on the Persian plain and Mycenaean cities were at war with Troy—a people who were already known as Israelites were building their first settlements in the land of Canaan. Although archaeologists have found no evidence that any had spent time in Egypt, the Bible presents them as newcomers who were very separate from other Canaanite people. In reality, they not only all spoke versions of the same Semitic family of languages but also shared many of the same regional myths and legends.

"Most high" god El (Elohim) stood alone as head of the Canaanite pantheon. This white-haired and elderly gentleman, who lived in the heavens, embodied every known virtue. But venerable features belied sexual vigor, for, with consort Asherah, El had fathered a whole council of "sons of god," who, at the most expansive, could be likened to the stars in the sky. Translators and commentators have long resisted evidence of some biblical passages that place the roots of Jewish religion not with Abraham or Moses but squarely within the context of Middle Eastern myth. This is most clearly illustrated in a passage that tells how Yahweh became Israel's special god. "When the Most High gave to the nations their inheritance, when he separated humankind, he fixed the bounds of the people according to the number of the gods. The Lord's portion is his people, Jacob his allotted share."[1] The passage distinguishes two gods: El is translated as "the Most High" and Yahweh as "the Lord" and, in common with El's other sons, he is given responsibility for just this one people. Following Caananite tradition the Israelites would then transfer El's honors, titles, and even physical description onto their own Yahweh, until he became the supreme—and later indeed the only—God.

Still, for many centuries, relationships between El's offspring could be turbulent. Fertility god Ba'al and his sister/lover Anat fought endless battles with Yamm, god of the chaos and the ocean, and his ally Mot, lord of death and the underworld. This Canaanite re-enactment of the primal struggle was fought out with no quarter expected or given on either side. With his pointed beard and horned helmet, Ba'al could command respect as a warrior, but his consort Anat was the more fearsome opponent—only happy when wading across the battlefield, satiated on human flesh and knee deep in blood, with the heads of fallen enemies slung round her waist and their hands tied in her sash. In his role as fertility god, Ba'al rode the storms, commanding the thunder and lightning to bring the rain that kept livestock in good health and delivered prosperous harvests. With so much at stake, it is no surprise that many Israelites chose the precautionary route of worshipping both Yahweh and Ba'al. Even at this early stage, it is thought that Jews were divided between an urban elite, which was inclined toward the Canaanite model, and Yahwistic tribal society. Biblical writers looked back to a short-lived golden age in around 1000 BCE, when King David was reported to have drawn the Jews together into a single kingdom with a united devotion to Yahweh. Then his son Solomon took a cosmopolitan collection of wives and concubines and set about introducing the whole panoply of Canaanite worship and kingship. This "disobedience" brought civil war and a division of the kingdom into the larger Israel, based on Samaria in the north and Judah in the south, which had its capital in Jerusalem. From this time, prophets—"men with garments of hair"—took it on themselves to remind fellow Jews that any compromise with Canaanite religion would bring disaster on the whole people. Ninth-century preacher Elijah recorded that, by his time, just 7,000 Israelites remained true to the pure worship of Yahweh. Famously, he set about demonstrating his god's power by bringing fire onto Ba'al's altar and slaughtering 450 of his prophets.

Sexuality is the most powerful symbol of fecundity known to humans, and Ba'al's followers believed that sacred prostitution could encourage fertility across the whole environment. In response, Hebrew prophets used sexual images to highlight continued breaches of the covenant between Yahweh and his people. Whether speaking literally or figuratively, Hosea told how God instructed him to marry a prostitute. Her later unfaithfulness provided a metaphor for Israel's adulterous relationship with local gods. Jeremiah then told how Yahweh forbade him to marry so that—like his God,—he would never know the security of a faithful and loving relationship. To the distress of feminist believers, Ezekiel used a long, even pornographic, story of two whores to illustrate Judah's continuing fall from grace.[2]

Besides being a jealous and warlike God Yahweh was also defender of the poor and weak. This message, first passionately argued by the prophet Amos, would become a running theme through the centuries. "Ah, you who make iniquitous decrees," announced Isaiah, "who write oppressive statutes, to turn aside the needy from justice and to rob the poor of my people of their right, that widows may be your spoil, and that you may make the orphans your prey!"³ Failure to deliver social justice was seen as yet another damning proof that the Israelites had deserted their own god.

Ba'al worship still flourished in the eighth century BCE at a time when the Assyrians started to threaten both Jewish kingdoms. Powerless against this most brutal enemy, by all precedents, the Jews should have deserted their inadequate war god Yahweh and delivered allegiance to the manifestly more powerful Ashur. Assyrian king Sennacherib delivered his advice to the people of Jerusalem with the warning:

> Do not let Hezekiah mislead you by saying, The Lord (Yahweh) will surely deliver us. Has any of the gods of the nations saved their land out of the hand of the king of Assyria? Where are the gods of Hamath and Arpad? Where are the gods of Sepharvaim? Have they delivered Samaria out of my hand? Who among all the gods of these countries have saved their countries out of my hand, that the Lord should save Jerusalem out of my hand?⁴

Prophets Hosea, Amos, and Isaiah responded by preaching that Yahweh was, in reality, so powerful that even Assyrian monarchs followed his command by bringing vengeance on his faithless people. While Mithra Saoshyant and Rashu distribute bliss or damnation according to each individual's deserts, the Hebrew prophets could only anticipate that communal punishment would be imposed on the whole community.

*

Some scholars identify the reign of Josiah in the late seventh century BCE as a time when editors (or one editor) set about strengthening the prophetic message. Within the documents that were then being gathered into the collection that would later become the Hebrew Bible, there seemed to be some lack of clarity on the nature of the covenant between Yahweh and his people. It needed to be made clear that their God had only agreed to deliver the promised land in return for a commitment that his people would worship him alone.⁵ In order to provide Israel with a compelling ancient history that would predate any contact with Canaan, scribes added miraculous elements to tales of the captivity in and exodus from Egypt as well as later wandering in the desert. In the *Book of Joshua*, they recount how Yahweh then kept his side of the bargain by delivering the promised land of Canaan to his own people. According to this narrative, Yahweh personally orchestrated the brutal process of ethnic cleansing. First, he hardened the inhabitants' hearts "so that they would come against Israel in battle, in order that they might be utterly destroyed, and might receive no mercy, but be exterminated." Then he applied sanctions on any Israelite leader who failed to pursue the slaughter down to the last living creature.⁶ In the most dramatic—and indeed inconceivable—of all nature miracles, Yahweh even halted the sun in its tracks so that Joshua would have enough time to complete the task of wiping out the Amorites.

> "Sun, stand still at Gibeon,
> and Moon, in the valley of Aijalon."
> And the sun stood still, and the moon stopped,
> until the nation took vengeance on their enemies ...[7]

If this interpretation of the biblical narrative is correct—as many scholars believe—then it follows that that these later editors were more concerned with threatening their idolatrous contemporaries than with constructing an accurate historical record. Later scribes place the key message for their own times in the dying Joshua's mouth:

And now I am about to go the way of all the earth, and you know in your hearts and souls, all of you, that not one thing has failed of all the good things that the Lord your God promised concerning you.... But just as all the good things ... have been fulfilled for you, so the Lord will bring upon you all the bad things, until he has destroyed you from this good land that the Lord your God has given you. If you transgress the covenant of the Lord your God, which he enjoined on you, and go and serve other gods and bow down to them, then the anger of the Lord will be kindled against you, and you shall perish quickly from the good land that he has given to you.[8]

Those concerned with the Canaanites' fate can take comfort from the fact that many of those same enemy people, who had supposedly been exterminated, would reappear later in the bible narrative. Like storytellers of old, these editors told of mythic past and future battles that demonstrably never happened in real history.

Therefore, as I live, says the Lord of hosts, the God of Israel, Moab shall become like Sodom and the Ammonites like Gomorrah, a land possessed by nettles and salt-pits, and a waste for ever. The remnant of my people shall plunder them, and the survivors of my nation shall possess them.[9]

Read together, tales of past and future conflict between Israel and its neighbors provide a fitting prelude to generations of blood-curdling apocalyptic literature.

After eighth-century prophets Hosea and Amos forecast that the northern kingdom of Israel would fall to the king of Assyria, the younger "First" Isaiah lived to see the disaster, which obliterated the 10 northern tribes. Late-seventh-century prophet Jeremiah then predicted that Yahweh would punish the smaller southern state of Judah and in 596 BCE his successor Ezekiel may well have watched as Jerusalem fell and Solomon's Temple was destroyed by the armies of Babylonian ruler Nebuchadnezzar.

Israel's earlier prophets are today mined for visions of the Apocalypse. Biblical literalists argue that, if Isaiah can know the name of Persian Emperor Cyrus II, who was born some hundred years after his own death, and sixth-century Daniel can foretell events in the third-century Hellenistic empire, then their writings must also carry messages for the contemporary world. Scholars, in contrast, find it impossible to accept that biblical prophets (alone of all the world's population) could have access to detailed information about the distant future. When these early prophets did look forward, scholars argue, their forecasts were earthly, immediate, and readily enough foreseen by any close observer of contemporary events. Apparent pre-knowledge of rulers and empires therefore provides liberal scholars with unambiguous evidence that the passage in question is a later addition.

The Babylonian exile would prove to be a watershed in Jewish belief. After living with no concept of personal judgment, the afterlife, and the end of time, exiled Jews now found themselves exposed to Zoroastrian speculation on just these issues.

*

As a priest (who, in the view of some commentators, showed symptoms of schizophrenia), Ezekiel was a member of the more privileged class that was taken into exile. These unwilling visitors to Babylon were encouraged to settle in national groups and follow their distinctive ways of life and worship, but still they found separation from Jerusalem and temple worship intolerable. "By the rivers waters of Babylon," wrote the psalmist, "there we sat down and there we wept, when we remembered Zion . . . How could we sing the Lord's song in a foreign land?"[10]

Ezekiel described how the heavens opened as he stood beside the river Chebar, and he received a vision of strange beasts—part human, part animal, part bird— of living coals, "wheels within wheels," and a firmament that shone like crystal.

And there came a voice from above the dome over their heads . . . And above the dome over their heads there was something like a throne, in appearance like sapphire; and seated above the likeness of a throne was something that seemed like a human form.[11]

The prophet may even have seen the dead bodies of Judah's soldiers as they lay on the plains of Jericho after King Zedekiah's final defeat in 587 BCE. He now told how he heard a sound of rattling as dry bones came together "bone to its bone." Drawing from this image, he delivers what can be interpreted as the Bible's first promise of personal resurrection.[12] Judah, he declared, will know that Yahweh is lord "when I open your graves and bring you up from your graves, O my people, and I will put my spirit within you and you shall live."[13] He looked forward to a time when widely scattered Jews would return Jerusalem. With the temple rebuilt, a new Davidic monarchy in place, and covenant restored, then at last Yahweh could say "I will be their God and they shall be my people."

Gazing even deeper into a mythical future, Ezekiel foretold how Gog, king of a northern land of Magog, would invade Judah with a huge army. Returning to his role as warrior god, Yahweh would then intervene to defeat the invading hordes. The people of Judah would take no part until the slaughter was over, when they would be given the task of burying the mass of bodies and ritually cleansing the land. Yahweh then commands his people to gather all the birds and wild beasts to join in a banquet, at which—in language reminiscent of the gruesome Anat myth—humans and animals join together to "eat the flesh of the mighty, and drink the blood of the princes of the earth... You shall eat fat until you are filled, and drink blood until you are drunk, at the sacrificial feast that I am preparing for you."[14]

*

The gap in time that passes between the end of Chapter 39 and the beginning of Chapter 40 in the *Book of Isaiah* has been the subject of much controversy. Set around 690 BCE, Chapter 39 deals with King Hezekiah of Judah's reception of Babylonian ambassadors and the prophet's warning against showing them too much of his wealth. Then, by the next verse, some 150 years have passed, Babylon has fallen to the Persians, and the writer knows Emperor Cyrus II by name. Literalist believers may assert as a matter of faith that both passages were written by the same hand; for the historian, it is beyond dispute that they were not.

In words of the King James Version that would be memorably set to music by George Frederick Handel, a new anonymous prophet announces that the conflict between Yahweh and his people is finally over.

Comfort ye, comfort ye, my people saith your God.
Speak ye comfortably to Jerusalem,
and cry unto her that her warfare is accomplished, that her iniquity is pardoned.
For she has received from the Lord's hand double for all her sins.
The voice of one that crieth in the wilderness, "prepare ye the way of the Lord.
Make straight in the desert a highway for our God."

This "Second Isaiah" is well familiar with Zoroastrian teaching and imagery. Like the Aryan prophet before him, he proclaims that "every valley shall be exalted and every mountain and hill made low" when the earth will regain the evenness of creation to greet the arrival of the true God. The new triumphal route across the Syrian Desert (which on the ground is already remarkably flat) is to be prepared for Yahweh's triumphant return to the holy city and even the ocean is subdued to provide "a path in the mighty waters."[15] In those first triumphant chapters, there is no bridge of separators, no angel holding scales, and no fiery pit for the wicked. As communal punishment had been imposed for idolatry, so communal salvation is now bestowed on Judah. For this prophet, the whole Jewish nation has become transformed into Yahweh's faithful servant, destined to bring unity to all creation. His universal monotheistic message more closely follows Zoroastrian than Jewish precedent.

I will say to the North, Give up, and to the South, do not withhold; bring my sons from afar and my daughters from the end of the earth, Every one who is called by my name, whom I created for my glory, whom I formed and made. Bring forth the people who are blind, yet have eyes, who are deaf, yet have ears! Let all the nations gather together, and let the people assemble.[16]

Past alien rulers may have served Yahweh's purpose by punishing his unfaithful people; now this unnamed prophet presents Cyrus as his shepherd and Messiah.[17] This is altogether too much for one commentator, who concludes that such verses must be a later addition to the original text. "Who," he asks, "can take seriously a prophet who in God's name proclaims the impending *salvation* of humanity through the agency of a pagan conqueror?"[18] In this prophet's eyes, however, the pious Zoroastrian emperor was no pagan, but a fellow searcher after truth. Babylonian exile might have been less painful than the Assyrian version, but both aimed to extinguish a conquered people's national identity by removing the leaders and crafts-folk and impoverishing those who remained. To the prophet's delight, Cyrus was now drawing up plans to send the exiles home, where they would work on the task of restoring local prosperity and pride in partnership with Persian officials.

Commentators have debated whether the latter part of Isaiah, from Chapter 40 to the end, is the work of just one or perhaps two or even more unnamed writers. Some argue that the language and key message remain consistent, while others point out that much of the old optimism is lost. That is, perhaps, no surprise. The exiles finally returned under the leadership of traditionalist priests, who cared only about rebuilding the temple and restoring the old order of society. On arrival, they were taken aback to discover that many of those left behind had abandoned the ritual laws and even "married out" of Judaism. On the other side, followers of "the second Isaiah" were equally shocked that these same people were barely surviving in the deepest poverty. Postexile society was now deeply split between those who remained determined to concentrate all resources on the immediate task of rebuilding the temple and their opponents, who argued that any available funds should be directed to the relief of poverty. As temple work was brought to a halt, even prophecy became divided. "Minor prophets" Zechariah and Haggai aligned themselves with the priestly cause. Taking Ezekiel as their model, they argued that no salvation could be achieved until the building work was complete. Haggai announced that the people themselves had to take the blame for economic disaster—"because my house lies in ruins while all of you hurry off to your own houses. Therefore the heavens above you have withheld the dew and the earth has withheld its produce."[19]

Either the second Isaiah himself or one of his followers argued the opposing case. "Is not this the fast that I choose: to loose the bonds on injustice, to undo the thongs of the yoke to let the oppressed go free, and to break every yoke? Is it not to share your bread with the hungry, and bring the homeless poor into your house: when you see the naked, to cover them and not to hide yourself from your own kin?"[20] Evidence of this division between governing and radical factions resurfaces through the succeeding centuries and, in varying contexts, it will remain a running theme through the whole narrative of End-Time belief.

The returning exiles may have believed that Jerusalem stood at the center of the cosmos. In the worldly perspective, however, they had returned to a depopulated and impoverished satrapy, barely 25 miles long, that stood on the fringe of the huge Persian Empire. Unable to defend their land by military force, the returned Jews no longer had any significant voice in regional politics. Yet, for all its worldly misfortunes, Jerusalem remained the focus of expectation.

Rejoice with Jerusalem and exult in her, all you who love her; share her joy with all your heart, all you who mourn over her. Then may you suck and be fed from the breasts that give comfort, delighting in the plentiful milk. For thus says the Lord: I will send peace flowing over her like a river, and the wealth of nations like a stream in flood; it shall suckle you and you shall be carried in their arms and dandled on their knees. As a mother comforts her son, so will I myself comfort you, and you shall find comfort in Jerusalem.[21]

As earthly hope faded, so compensatory visions of the future became detached from the real world and lodged in a miraculous parallel universe. Ezekiel had presented the destruction of Gog as Yahweh's single-handed triumph; now Zechariah reassured his country people that "many peoples and strong nations shall come to seek the Lord of hosts in Jerusalem." With mounting expectation, he graphically described Yahweh's future triumph over Hadrach, Tyre, Sidon, Damascus, Aram, Ashkelon, Gaza, Ekron, Ashtod, and Philistia. "Tyre has built itself a rampart," he declared, "and heaped up silver like dust, and gold like the dirt of the streets and it shall be devoured by fire. But now, the Lord will strip it of its possessions and hurl its wealth into the sea." With these improbable victories accomplished, the daughters of Jerusalem would rejoice and greet the arrival of their king with a great shout.[22]

*

Zoroastrians look back on Alexander of Macedon's victory at the 333 BCE battle of Issus as the darkest day in history. As the Persian Empire collapsed after what, at least by the standards of the day, had been two centuries of enlightened rule, it seemed as though the evil Angra Mainyu had at last been let loose. Every worst fear seemed justified when, at the fall of Tyre, the young Greek king crucified every male of military age and sold other survivors into slavery. When Alexander died in 323 at the age of 32, his great empire was divided between three of his generals. As communities from different nationalities lived cheek by jowl during this period of Hellenistic domination, the eastern Mediterranean lands seethed with interacting ideas that were drawn from across the range of cultures.

Although ancient Mesopotamian and Canaanite tablets were now long buried, the image of an ocean that represented chaos and an underworld where ancient gods and monsters fought endless battles still survived within popular culture. During the coming centuries, tales of cosmic conflict would reappear in both the canon of both the Hebrew Bible and Christian New Testament.

After breaking the Persian Empire, Alexander of Macedon gathered 10,000 of his soldiers and, in a famous ceremony, joined them with Persian wives. By this dramatic gesture, he delivered the message that, from his time, east and west would be one.

While the Greeks are most readily associated with the classical tradition of philosophy associated with Socrates, they also brought a more magical and mystical tradition, centered around the sayings of oracles and sibyls. As the classical era passed, mysterious beliefs, which can be traced back to sixth-century mathematician and mystic Pythagoras, rapidly gained popularity. Although little is known of his life, this sage left a "Pythagorean" community, which only admitted enquirers after complex initiation procedures. Members were divided between an inner circle of "learners," who were privileged to explore an intuitive knowledge of spiritual truths, and an outer circle of "listeners." Within this tradition, the concept of "wisdom" is divorced from logical thought processes to become a transcendental insight, not far distant from the Eastern concept of "enlightenment." Even Socrates' pupil Plato taught that the world had become divided between the ideal and the material—"form" and "substance." Followers concluded from this that every eternal human soul is imprisoned within a mortal body. While these ideas would take many forms as they spread into different cultures and across huge areas, this core belief that knowledge exists on two levels continued to provide a binding thread of a way of thought that would become known as *Gnosticism*. On the surface of any text was an open meaning that was accessible to all; beneath lay a deeper message that would remain hidden until it could be mystically revealed by some woman or man who was worthy to penetrate the depths of knowledge (*gnosis*).

Syncretism is defined as the attempt to reconcile diverse and even opposite religious views within a single belief system. While all religious faith is, at root, syncretistic, this fusion of religious rose to an extraordinary level in the Hellenistic world. In one scholar's words:

The Gnostic systems compounded everything—oriental mythologies, astrological doctrines, Iranian theology, elements of Jewish tradition, whether Biblical rabbinical or occult, Christian salvation-eschatology, Platonic terms and concepts. Syncretism... pervaded the whole thought of the age and showed itself in all provinces of literary expression.[23]

The word Gnostic also describes specific sects—many of which originated in the southern part of modern Iraq—that flourished in the centuries before and after the birth of Jesus of Nazareth. These groups developed a common esoteric theology in which God is perceived as a transcendent being, hidden from his creatures by layers of "realms," which are each ruled by a hostile archon. In time, Gnosticism penetrated other faiths—first Judaism and then Christianity and Islam. Throughout, it will hold an ambiguous position in the End-Time narrative. While, on one level, concentration on inner wisdom and unity with the divine can be appear to contradict outward visions of heaven and the Apocalypse, on another level, such speculation can also provide fruitful stimulus for messianic speculation.

*

During this Hellenistic age, Judaism was an actively proselytizing faith. The New Testament *Book of Acts* gives a vivid description of the crowd that gathered in the streets of Jerusalem in the early first century CE. Here were both natural-born Jews and converts, who all spoke the languages native to areas where they had settled.

> Parthians, Medes, Elamites, and residents of Mesopotamia, Judea and Cappadocia, Pontus and Asia, Phrygia and Pamphylia, Egypt and the parts of Libya belonging to Cyrene, and visitors from Rome, both Jews and proselytes, Cretans and Arabs—in our own languages we hear them speaking about God's deeds of power.[24]

Scattered Jewish communities, which had not yet been consigned to impermeable ghettos, found themselves in the front line of syncretistic pressure. Still, while the many Jewish apocalyptic writings of the following centuries did betray influences from both East and West, they never lost contact with their own distinctive Hebrew inheritance.

The five sections that make up a compilation known as 1 Enoch are thought to have been produced over a period of some 50 years, from about 200 BCE. In order to lend weight to any narrative, it was then both a widespread and respectable practice to write under the pen name of some past worthy. According to Genesis, Enoch lived near the beginning of time, grandfather to Noah and just seven (admittedly very long) generations from Adam. Notably wise and virtuous, he was spared death and taken bodily up to heaven. His recorded accomplishments were indeed formidable. "He was the first among men who learned writing and wisdom and wrote down the signs of heaven according to the order of their months in a book, that men might know the seasons of the years to the order of their separate months."[25] Enoch had also been identified with two characters in Sumerian legend, who were reputed to have close contact with heavenly powers and a unique knowledge of the cosmos and insight into the future.[26] As the only characters in the Hebrew Bible to be taken up into heaven without experiencing death, Enoch and the prophet Elijah would later be identified as the two witnesses of the Apocalypse.[27] The patriarch now tells how an angel takes him into the presence of that white-haired old man, who is readily identified as high god El of Canaanite myth. Zoroastrian portents of the Apocalypse are again evident. "And the high mountains shall be shaken, and the high hills shall be made low, and shall melt like wax before the flame."[28] The oldest section, named the *Book of Watchers*, takes its theme from an unsettlingly polytheistic verse in Genesis.

When people began to multiply on the face of the ground, and daughters were born to them, the sons of God saw that they were fair; and they took wives for themselves of all that they chose.[29]

According to the better-known creation narrative, evil was brought into the world through the disobedience of Adam and Eve. In 1 Enoch, humans become the victims of a cosmic fall of divine beings (later identified as angels) who existed in heaven before humans were ever created. Both—theoretically irreconcilable—myths would develop parallel lives through later apocalyptic writing and the poems of John Milton. This angelic fall brought a disastrous loss of human innocence.[30]

And Azâzêl taught men to make swords, and knives, and shields, and breastplates, and made known to them the metals of the earth and the art of working them, and bracelets, and ornaments, and the use of antimony, and the beautifying of the eyelids, and all kinds of costly stones, and all coloring tinctures. And there arose much godlessness, and they committed fornication, and they were led astray, and became corrupt in all their ways. Semjâzâ taught enchantments, and root-cuttings, 'Armârôs the resolving of enchantments, Barâqîjâl (taught) astrology, Kôkabêl the constellations, Êzêqêêl the knowledge of the clouds, Araqiêl the signs of the earth, Shamsiêl the signs of the sun, and Sariêl the course of the moon. And as men perished, they cried, and their cry went up to heaven.[31]

In earlier writings—notably in the *Book of Job*—Satan (or Belial) appears not as a wicked force but as God's prosecuting counsel; here in Enoch, rebellious angels take their place as cosmic agents of evil. Although Semjâzâ is named as leader of the fallen angels, it is Azâzêl's image that would become imprinted on posterity. Traditionally associated with the animal sin-offering, driven into the wilderness at Yom Kippur, it is he who carries the goat's horns which will identify the devil in Christian art. The fate that Zoroaster predicted for Angra Mainyu is now pronounced on Azâzêl.

The Lord said to Raphael: "Bind Azâzêl hand and foot, and cast him into the darkness: and make an opening in the desert . . . and cast him therein. And place upon him rough and jagged rocks, and cover him with darkness, and let him abide there for ever, and cover his face that he may not see light. And on the day of the great judgment he shall be cast into the fire."[32]

In later chapters, 1 Enoch describes how nature itself will become out of joint to herald the end of time. As the fruits of the earth fail and the stars transgress their order and rivers run with blood, all the nations will become stirred up, Then parents will cast away their own babes and "a man shall not withhold his hand from slaying his sons and his sons." In that Day of Judgment, sinners will perish with their possessions and splendor in shame, slaughter, and destitution.[33]

The *Book of Jubilees* continued themes developed in the earlier *Book of Watchers*. Here the devil Mastema (hostility) lets pass no opportunity to bring evil to the whole of creation. Having charge of vast legions of demons, he sends out spirits "to do all manner of wrong and sin, and all manner of transgression, to corrupt and destroy, and to shed blood upon the earth."[34]

Still, if there is evil, so there must be good, and angels, who had previously been anonymous messengers of God, are now named as warriors for virtue. The archangel Michael (he who is like God) appears in 1 Enoch as leader of the heavenly host and (like Mithra) the celestial being who is closest to his god. In attendance are archangels such as Gabriel (God is my strength), Raphael (God heals), and Uriel (fire of God), alongside a growing array of heavenly beings. From now on, the battle between good and evil will be fought out in celestial time and space between massed ranks of opposing armies.

After being rejected for inclusion in the Hebrew Bible, Enoch school writings still had wide influence in Jewish communities until leading rabbis determined to suppress all apocalyptic speculation after the second temple was destroyed in 70 CE. They were only rediscovered when early nineteenth-century European explorers found that 1 the work remained an integral part of the Ethiopian Bible. The visions of one other pseudonymous author, in contrast, have always been readily accessible to both Jews and Christians.

*

The *Book of Daniel* remains a puzzling work; written half in Aramaic and half in Hebrew, it starts by telling such stories from the Babylonian exile as how Daniel successfully interpreted Nebuchadnezzar's dream and Shadrach, Meshach, and Abednego survived the burning fiery furnace. Then in Chapter 7—still in Aramaic—it plunges four centuries forward to deliver a coded account of the varying fortunes of Babylonian, Medean, Persian, and Greek empires. From Chapter 8 to the end, it then moves into Hebrew to describe a visit to heaven, comment on the contemporary political narrative, and conclude with a glimpse of the End-Time. While debate continues on whether this later section was the work of one or more hands, no serious Jewish or Christian scholar can entertain the literalist position that it was all written by a man called Daniel in Babylon at the time of the exile.

Throughout the early chapters, the narrative is told in the third person, with characters observed from the outside. In its linguistic origin, the word *apocalypse* means unveiling or revealing, and here the writer tells of a dream. "I, Daniel, saw in my vision by night the four winds of heaven stirring up the great sea. And four great beasts came up out of the sea, different from one another."[35] With inspiration still grounded in the ancient Babylonian combat myth, the first three beasts are identified as the eastern empires that have lost their power—Babylonian by a lion with wings of an eagle, Medean by a bear, and Persian by a leopard with four wings of a bird. Then, out of the ocean of chaos, there emerges Alexander's more threatening Hellenistic empire.

After this I saw in the visions by night a fourth beast, terrifying and dreadful and exceedingly strong. It had great iron teeth and was devouring, breaking in pieces, and stamping what was left with its feet. It was different from all the beasts that preceded it, and it had ten horns. I was considering the horns, when another horn appeared, a little one coming up among them... There were eyes like human eyes in this horn, and a mouth speaking arrogantly.[36]

Within any herd, power was thought to lie with the animal that has the largest horn, and each horn represented one in a series of Hellenistic rulers, the first and largest representing Alexander himself and the little one, which grew as "Daniel" watched, the current ruler Antiochus IV, officially known as Epiphanes "manifest god" (corrupted by opponents to Epimanes "the mad"). In order to decipher these apocalyptic chapters, the reader does need some background knowledge of Antiochus' reign. Judea was then torn by a conflict, verging on civil war, between traditionalist Jews and Hellenizers, who had embraced the Greek culture. Antiochus reacted violently when the traditionalists staged an abortive rebellion against his rule

When news of what had happened reached the king, he took it to mean that Judea was in revolt. So, raging inwardly, he left Egypt and took the city by storm. He commanded his soldiers to cut down relentlessly everyone they met and to kill those who went into their houses. Then there was massacre of young and old, destruction of boys, women, and children, and slaughter of young girls and infants. Within the total of three days eighty thousand were destroyed, forty thousand in hand-to-hand fighting, and as many were sold into slavery as were killed.[37]

The king then forced his way into the temple precinct, outlawed key Jewish practices such as circumcision, and replaced temple worship with his own ritual. After priests and scribes who resisted were brutally killed, the Maccabee family led a popular revolt.

The latter part of Daniel should therefore be read as an allegory on history and current affairs, written in a secret code that is comprehensible only to the initiate. This contemporary political narrative is both introduced and concluded by visions of the Apocalypse. The writer tells how he was brought into the presence of the familiar El figure—named here the Ancient One—"His clothing was white as snow, and the hair of his head like pure wool... A thousand thousand served him, and ten thousand times ten thousand stood attending him. The court sat in judgment, and the books were opened."[38] Then, out of the clouds of heaven, appears "one like the Son of Man."[39] Perhaps no phrase in literature has been subjected to more scholarly analysis. Literally meaning no more than "someone like a human being," and used earlier as the form of address used by God when addressing the prophet Ezekiel, it now develops messianic overtones. In a later section of 1 Enoch, a divine being in human form, who had been present at creation, appears alongside God.

From the beginning the Son of Man was hidden, and the Most High preserved him in the presence of His might, and revealed him to the elect and the congregation of the elect and holy shall be sown, and all the elect shall stand before him on that day. And all the kings and the mighty and the exalted and those who rule the earth shall fall down before him on their faces and worship and set their hope upon that Son of Man, and petition him and supplicate for mercy at his hands.[40]

This figure stands in judgment, hurling kings into realms of darkness from which they can never hope to be raised.

Although Son of Man imagery would later become central to Christianity, it was first used when addressing Jewish readers. In order to erase later overtones, some Jewish scholars have interpreted it as a collective term to represent the Jewish people. While this can me made to fit into the Daniel narrative, it take no account of its wider use in Enoch. An alternative explanation, that the character is an angel, must therefore be preferred. Here, then, is the Mithra-like figure of the archangel Michael, whose name means "the one who is like God."

In the heat of Antiochus' persecution, the prophet still needed to know the date when the temple sanctuary would be cleansed of Antiochus' profanity so that the End-Time could finally arrive. After first setting dates that were not realized, Daniel asked the question that would be repeated so often in later years; "my lord, what shall be the outcome of these things?" "Go your way, Daniel," replied the angel, "for the words are to remain secret and sealed until the time of the end." After being accepted into both the Hebrew and the Christian canons, Daniel's symbolism would acquire great significance for all later apocalyptic speculation. In intervening centuries, End-Time believers have made huge investments of time and energy, trying to unravel what was then "secret and sealed" and to fix on a date for the "outcome of these things." "Happy are those" concluded the angel, "who persevere and attain the thousand three hundred and thirty-five days. But you, go your way, and rest; you shall rise for your reward at the end of the days."[41]

The beast with iron teeth that had now arrived from the west was "different from all the beasts that preceded it" because Hellenistic rulers—in common with the Romans who followed—imposed a cultural imperialism on conquered people that was alien to earlier conquerors from the East. Some Jews did compromise with their new masters, but, for those who stood firm, the language of apocalypse was a convenient vehicle for coded communication between like-minded people. The message of heavenly intervention and future reward for the martyred dead could also, once again, provide consolation to those who found themselves deprived of meaningful earthly power.

*

The mid-twentieth-century discovery of the Dead Sea Scrolls aroused high excitement in scholarly circles, and these ancient documents have been combed for evidence of apocalyptic belief. It was long accepted that the scrolls were the work of a devout inward-looking community—forerunner of many later millennial sects—that were based at Qumran, beside the Dead Sea. In recent years, though, archaeologists have reported that the this site more closely resembles a trading post than a religious community, and it has even been suggested that the documents could be the contents of the temple library that was hidden away when Roman soldiers started to overrun the country.[42] Whichever hypothesis turns out to be correct, it is clear that Jewish people around the time of Jesus of Nazareth were much taken up with apocalyptic speculation. Most of the scrolls are copies of both biblical and noncanonical books. Alongside Daniel, Psalms, Deuteronomy, Genesis, and Isaiah, both 1 Enoch and Jubilees feature high amongst those most frequently copied.

Images of the battle between good and evil reappear in the writings that were generated within the Qumran communitiy. God "created man to govern the world," declares the *Instruction of the Two Spirits*, "and has appointed for him two spirits in which to walk until the time of his visitation: the spirits of truth and wickedness."[43] The *Rule of the War of the Sons of Light and the Sons of Darkness* describes the preparation for conflict, when the forces of Michael and Belial meet on equal terms in a last great battle. As pagan rulers exercised power in the real world, so Belial would enjoy his time of victory before the divine Michael finally triumphs at the end of time. Those who had been martyred for their faith would then be resurrected into their heavenly reward.

*

It is not easy to unravel the ways in which ancient Jews came to anticipate the arrival of a final deliverer.[44] The word Messiah (or Christ from the Greek) literally means "the anointed one," and the idea of a future savior has its roots in the real or mythical anointing of King David in about 1000 BCE. "I will establish your posterity for ever," declared the psalmist. "I will make your throne endure for all generations." The hope for a royal Messiah of David's line persisted even after many of David's real descendants had perished in the civil war that followed Solomon's death. Centuries later Jeremiah could summon a royal Messiah to save Judah from Babylonian armies:

The days are surely coming, says the Lord, when I will raise up for David a righteous Branch, and he shall reign as king and deal wisely, and shall execute justice and righteousness in the land. In his days Judah will be saved and Israel will live in safety.[45]

Since the high priest was also anointed with oil, it was even suggested that the Jews could expect the arrival of two Messiahs: one, descended from David, would operate in the political arena, while the other, descended from Aaron, would realize religious aspirations. A Dead Sea scroll writer charged the faithful to abide by established precepts "until there shall come the prophet and the Messiahs of Aaron and Israel."[46] After Antiochus' death, hopes focused on the Maccabee family, and for a period of some 20 years, John Hyrcanus held both anointed roles of king and high priest, as well as that of prophet. But the coming of a Messiah could signal a time of terror as well as hope. "Let him come," said the Jewish teacher, "but let me not see him."[47]

Anticipation for the End-Time ran particularly high some 60 years later, when the prophet John started to baptize for the forgiveness of sins in the river Jordan. Clad in a camel-hair coat and living on locusts and wild honey, he warned that the one who came after him would carry his winnowing-fork is in his hand, "and he will clear his threshing-floor and will gather his wheat into the granary; but the chaff he will burn with unquenchable fire."[48]

Though names and imagery would change, the key ingredients for later apocalyptic speculation were now in place. From ancient Middle Eastern civilizations came the conflict myth, the oceans of chaos, beasts of destruction, heroic gods of salvation, and individual demon possession. Zoroastrianism then added the three core End-Time concepts of divine visions (apocalypticism), the coming of one or more saviors (messainism), and the division of time into eras (millenarianism). From this source came also the concept of an eternal struggle between good and evil, which heralds a specific time of tribulation, as well as a Last Judgment, with all due punishment and reward. In the earlier Jewish tradition, we encounter the concept of sin through human choice, Yahweh's implacable vengeance against apostasy, and the expectation of a Messiah from the line of David. During the exile, Ezekiel explored the hope of human resurrection and described God's gory struggle with the evil empire of Magog in a final climactic battle (*Armageddon*). Later prophets and noncanonical writers would introduce demonic fall as an alternative cause of sin and clarify the role of a personalized devil. Most tellingly, they elevated the Apocalypse from the temporal world to a magical universe where human beings were helpless to influence events. Jewish and Christian visionaries then became skilled in wrapping the real events of history and current affairs within allegory and apocalyptic language. When brought together in Jewish, Christian, and Muslim writings, these elements would combine to form an explosive cocktail that still threatens to detonate many centuries later.

3

The Secret of the Kingdom: The Christian End-Time

During the last two decades of the nineteenth century CE, the pastor's son at Kaiserberg Alsace was already proving to be something of a *wunderkind*. Brought up in a family that prized both music and theology, Albert Schweitzer first played the organ in public at the age of nine and, by his early 20s, he had won recognition as Europe's premier exponent of Johann Sebastian Bach's organ works. Also shining as an academic student, he would soon become one of Germany's leading theologians. For almost a hundred years, biblical students from universities such as Halle and Tübingen had approached the Bible on the assumption that this of all books deserved to be analyzed with the greatest possible intellectual rigor. Albert had not yet turned 30 when he submitted the volume that, for good or bad, would make his name as a scholar. In *The Quest of the Historical Jesus*,[1] he scrutinized how each German writer had answered three key questions on the life of Jesus of Nazareth: Did he really exist? What was his message? How had this original message been modified by later New Testament writers? Question one posed little problem; there seemed no doubt that Jesus was indeed a historical figure. The next two aroused more controversy.

As a teacher, Schweitzer had responsibility for introducing his students to the study of *eschatology*, which covered all End-Time speculation, whether immediate or distant, gradual or apocalyptic. As the young lecturer read through more than 200 books, he became increasingly convinced that writers from the liberal tradition (within which he had himself been raised) had lost touch with the living figure that emerged from the Bible narrative. In place of the disturbing preacher, exorcist, and healer who declared himself as the Son of Man, and—more secretively—the Messiah or Christ, these interpreters presented him as little more than a wise teacher. Schweitzer angrily dismissed writers who could explain away, for instance, the feeding of the 5,000 by suggesting that one boy's generosity had shamed others in the crowd to open their own lunchboxes. "That Jesus expected the final consummation to be realized supernaturally, whereas we can only understand it in terms of moral effort, is merely the result of the change in fundamental thought forms."[2] Christians had to make a choice between believing in an eschatological or a noneschatological Jesus, he concluded. They could not have both.

Schweitzer discovered that the whole life and teaching of Jesus of Nazareth fell coherently into place when the gospels were consistently examined from an end-time perspective. After his baptism by John the Baptist, Jesus delivered just one message: that the kingdom of God was immanent. Even the Sermon on the Mount fits into the picture. Speaking to crowds drawn from of his own overtaxed and impoverished peasant class, he aligned his message with that taught by those in the Second Isaiah school of prophesy, who had predicted that God's kingdom would introduce a topsy-turvy world in which the poor would be rich, the hungry full, the merciful blessed, and the meek would inherit the earth. "Those who are at the top here are at the bottom there," agreed the Talmud, "and those who are at the bottom here are at the top there."[3] Jesus also taught his followers to repeat a prayer in which they asked God to make conditions on earth mirror those in the heavenly kingdom and to protect the faithful from the coming Tribulation and attacks by "the evil one."[4] In parable after parable he delivered apocalyptic images of weeds growing up among good crops, wise and foolish virgins waiting for a bridegroom's arrival and how the good seed and the bad, the watchful and the careless would be only be separated at the final judgment. As guests spurned their invitation to a wedding feast, talents were distributed, and the prodigal son returned home, apparently irrational verdicts lay wholly at the discretion of an all-powerful deity. When puzzled disciples asked him to explain his parables' meaning, Jesus replied that he needed to wrap his message up in stories in case all became clear to people who had not been predestined for salvation.

And he said to them, "To you has been given the secret of the kingdom of God, but for those outside, everything comes in parables; in order that 'they may indeed look, but not perceive, and may indeed listen, but not understand; so that they may not turn again and be forgiven.'"[5]

Since both physical and mental illness were then believed to be caused by demon possession, acts of exorcism and healing delivered the message that Satan's armies were in retreat. Tales of "nature miracles," like raising the dead and walking on water, also heightened belief that the supernatural realm was breaking through into everyday life. The apocalyptic dimension became explicit at the twin events of Temptation and Transfiguration. A millennium earlier, Zoroaster told how Angra Mainyu had enticed Ahura Mazda by offering him dominion over all kingdoms of the world; the three first gospels now tell how Satan offered the same to Jesus. Then, at the Transfiguration, the disciples were given a glimpse of the heavenly kingdom as Moses and Elijah talked with Jesus, who stood in dazzling white clothes, "such as no one earth could bleach them."[6]

Liberal Christians prefer to reject the authenticity of the "Little Apocalypse," as first recounted in Chapter 13 of Mark's Gospel. Here Jesus describes a coming time of Tribulation, that will be brought on the world by the twin events of the destruction of Jerusalem's temple and the unfolding of the Last Judgment. Predictions of war and social disruption mirror older traditions of apocalyptic writing.

> Brother will betray brother to death, and a father his child, and children will rise against parents and have them put to death; and you will be hated by all because of my name. But the one who endures to the end will be saved... And if anyone says to you at that time, "Look! Here is the Messiah!" or "Look! There he is!"—do not believe it. False messiahs and false prophets will appear and produce signs and omens, to lead astray, if possible, the elect.[7]

Still Jesus' saying in Mark 9:1 could not be lightly dismissed. "Truly I say to you, there are some standing here who will not taste death before they see the kingdom of God come with power." Since no gospel writer would invent unfulfilled prophesy, the words had to be authentic.

Since Mark's was the first gospel committed to writing, German scholars had focused their critical attention on that one book, but, by Schweitzer's time, it was well established that earlier End-Time material, drawn from a common source, also lay embedded in the narratives of Matthew and Luke.[8] Placing the three side by side, Schweitzer decided that Jesus' whole ministry could be fitted into less than a year and a great crisis took place about halfway through these few short months. When Jesus became convinced that the kingdom was about to break, he took his disciples aside and issued them instructions. They were to prepare for a short, one-way, journey and preach only to the Jewish community.

> Take no gold, or silver, or copper in your belts, no bag for your journey, or two tunics, or sandals, or a staff; for laborers deserve their food... If anyone will not welcome you or listen to your words, shake off the dust from your feet as you leave that house or town. Truly I tell you, it will be more tolerable for the land of Sodom and Gomorrah on the day of judgment than for that town.... When they persecute you in one town, flee to the next; for truly I tell you, you will not have gone through all the towns of Israel before the Son of Man comes.[9]

But they did return. In Schweitzer's words, "there followed neither the sufferings, nor the outpourings of the spirit, nor the *parousia* (coming) of the Son of Man. The disciples returned safe and sound and full of proud satisfaction."[10]

At that point Jesus shed the crowds in order to prepare for a final trial that was now destined to happen when all Jews came together in Jerusalem to celebrate the Passover. It was at this time that he clarified his own position within the coming apocalyptic events. To the question "who do men say that the Son of Man is?," the disciples replied that followers speculated whether he was John the Baptist, Elijah, Jeremiah, or one of the prophets. Then, challenged to say who they thought he was, Simon Peter answered "You are the Messiah, the Son of the living God." After praising him for remaining open to this message form God, "he sternly ordered the disciples not to tell anyone that he was the Messiah."[11] He now concluded that, instead of inflicting general Tribulation on all humans, God now intended to concentrate all the End-Time suffering on himself—Jesus of Nazareth—the Christ/Messiah. Only the initiate would understand the full significance when this royal messiah entered Jerusalem on a donkey. "Lo, your king comes to you" forecast Zechariah, "triumphant and victorious is he, humble and riding on a donkey."[12] During the next week Jesus did everything possible force confrontation: arguing with the Jewish authorities, purging the temple of money changers and even forecasting that the sacred building would be utterly destroyed. Finally, he immersed himself in the train of apocalyptic events that would usher in the end of time. Schweitzer concluded his *Quest of the Historical Jesus* with cryptic words, which were purged from later editions of his book and have only recently been restored to their place in the text.

In the knowledge that he is the coming son of man, Jesus lays hold of the wheel of the world to set it moving on that last revolution that is to bring all ordinary history to a close. It refuses to turn and he throws himself upon it. When it does turn it crushes him, instead of bringing the eschatological condition, that is, the condition of perfect faithfulness and the absence of guilt, he has destroyed these conditions.[13]

*

In his determination to interpret the biblical narrative faithfully, Albert Schweitzer had sawn off the theological branch on which he sat. Although, for the rest of his 90-year life, he retained a dedication to the person of Jesus, he could never intellectually reconcile this devotion with the fact that this prophet from Nazareth had been so profoundly mistaken. When he offered himself for medical work in Africa, officials at the Paris Evangelical Missionary Society made him promise that he would never preach to Africans or disturb simpler-minded colleagues by airing his alarming conclusions. Since Albert Schweitzer had nothing left to say in public, these conditions posed no problem. Still, flanked by David Livingstone and Mother Teresa, this Gabon River doctor holds his place as one of just three modern missionary celebrity icons.[14]

The even more radical German theologian Rudolf Bultmann would later ask whether his predecessor had undermined the whole basis of faith. "If Jesus' expectation of the near end of the world turned out to be an illusion—the question arises whether his idea of God was not also illusory."[15] Bultmann made the point that the constant intrusion of the long-discredited three-story universe into all apocalyptic writing made nonsense of creedal statements like "he ascended into heaven" and "he descended into hell." "No one" he declared, "can appropriate a world picture by sheer resolve since it is already given by one's particular situation and all our thinking is irrevocably formed by science."[16] If the Christian proclamation was to retain any validity, he concluded, the message itself had to be demythologized. In order to achieve this, every preacher needed to leave members of the congregation in no doubt about what they were and were not expected to believe. But this was easier to proclaim from an academic study than to put in practice from a work-a-day pulpit. Most clergy had now become acclimatized to the fact that many problems discussed in theological college were best not shared with pious members of their congregation. Then, as large numbers drifted away from the church in the latter half of the twentieth century, fundamentalist belief rapidly gained ground among those who remained. Increasingly, stories that the Christian community had long treated as instructive myth became reclassified as literal history and, far from demythologizing their own faith, many preachers took up the task of mythologizing long-established areas of natural science.

Up to the mid-twentieth century, liberal Christians, and particularly liberal Protestants, could be identified by their theological beliefs rather than their position on issues of discipline, such as gay rights and women's ordination. Between them, Schweitzer and Bultmann (with no little help from the carnage of World War I) had fatally undermined this older liberal tradition, and it did not help when, from his station on the Gabon River, the older man pronounced that a contemporary ethic could be built on his new axiom "reverence for life." While this would provide a useful slogan for the growing environmental movement, it brought no resolution to the debate over biblical authority. Caught between unacceptable skepticism on the one side and rigid dogmatism on the other, Cambridge theologian Charles Dodd re-examined Schweitzer's theory, with particular focus on the core text in Mark 9:1: "Truly I say to you, there are some standing here who will not taste death before they see the kingdom of God come with power." As a chair of the committee that produced the *New English Bible*, he managed to get the concluding phrase changed from "the kingdom of God *come* with power" to "*having come* with power." Under his new interpretation—known in theological jargon as "realized eschatology"—Jesus' teaching had never been wrong because the kingdom had indeed arrived with his own first coming. Under his interpretation, all the parables and miracles could be reinterpreted as confirming a situation that already existed. "You no longer look for the reign of God through a telescope," declared Dodd; "you open your eyes to see."[17] In the controversy that followed, linguists queried his right to change the tense of the verb "come," while others showed ways in which realized eschatology undermined Jesus' unambiguous message. Most tellingly, it was pointed out that the early church clearly interpreted this verse in a literal, apocalyptic manner.

For some half-century after Schweitzer published his *Quest of the Historical Jesus*, it appeared as though a "wall of resistance" had been built around any serious debate over the apocalyptic content of Jesus' ministry. On the one side, Dodd's interpretation had been rejected as unsatisfactory, while on the other, Schweitzer's ruthless examination of the evidence had caused his own belief systems to hit the buffers. When reviewing the state of play, New Testament scholar Tom Wright could conclude on the one side that "Schweitzer has hardly had a single follower who has adopted his position in every detail" and, on the other, that "his basic position . . . survives intact." He identifies a new group of theologians who continue to follow the old master's eschatological approach, "while refining it so that the very serious weaknesses can be eliminated."[18] While Wright converses with other scholars through learned works, in his other role as Bishop Tom of Durham, he must also communicate with an uncomprehending laity. When the time comes to explain Mark 9:1 in his popular *Mark for Everyone*, he makes do with the single comment—which Schweitzer would surely have savaged—that "the coming of God's kingdom with power has a lot more to do with the radical defeat of a deep-rooted evil than with the destruction of the good world that God has made."[19] Today, those "refinements," that would make Schweitzer's eschatological interpretation acceptable to liberally-minded believers, have still failed to materialize.

North American scholars remain bitterly divided on the basic issue of whether Jesus was a social reformer, healer and deliverer of wise sayings or an End Time prophet. At one extreme, "fundamentally anti-fundamentalist" liberal theologians reject the whole apocalyptic thrust of Jesus' teaching. Founded in 1985 by theologians Robert Funk and John Dominic Crossan the Jesus Seminar of like-minded theologians and lay people meets regularly to consider authenticity of various aspects of Jesus' teaching. After discussion, participants vote on the likelihood that individual sayings are likely to reflect Jesus' teaching by allocating colors, ranging from the extremes of red (authentic) to black (inauthentic). Sayings under debate are drawn from the four canonical gospels of Matthew, Mark, Luke, and John as well as the non-canonical "Gospel of Thomas. While most scholars place Thomas as a second century document, which shows strong Gnostic influence, a minority of scholars insist that it is one of the earliest Christain sources, written, at about the same time as Mark in about 50 CE. More a collection of sayings than a narrative, Thomas presents Jesus as a preacher of "realized eschatology."

His disciples said to him, "When will the kingdom come?"

Jesus said, It will not come by waiting for it. It will not be a matter of saying "Here it is or there it is." Rather the kingdom of the father is spread out upon the earth, and men do not see it.[20]

Drawing analogies from early myth, some interpreters argue that apocalyptic language was something approaching a secret code, which the speaker delivered and the listener heard with the mutual understanding that neither would interpret the words literally. This did not overcome the fact that the early church clearly anticipated the coming of a very real Kingdom.

In contrast, mainstream theologians protest that, in their obsession with fighting fundamentalism, Seminar members consistently ignore key Bible messages. Positioning half as a member of the "Schweitzer camp," Dale Allison continues to insist that Jesus was an "eschatological prophet."

One can only amputate so much before the patient is killed. If we really decide that our earliest sources ... are so misleading on this one topic. Then maybe they cannot lead us to Jesus at all ... As in the fairy tale, if the birds have eaten too many of the crumbs, the trail cannot be found. Indeed one might go so far as to urge that, if the sayings of the earliest Jesus tradition, taken in their entirely, are not congruent with the sort of things that Jesus tended to say, then our task is hopeless.[21]

*

There is no agreement on when Luke wrote his second work, the *Acts of the Apostles*, with estimates ranging from between 30 and 70 years after the events that he described. Although this may seem a long time, many ancient religious texts had been passed down verbally for very much longer and, while Luke may have made modifications to reflect changed times, there is no reason to doubt that the work provides a broadly faithful record of early church tradition and history. During the 40 days during which the risen Jesus was reported to have appeared to and talked with his disciples, they pressed him to answer the old question, "Lord, is this the time when you will restore the kingdom to Israel?" But, like Daniel's angel, the risen Jesus can only reply that "It is not for you to know the times or periods that the Father has set by his own authority."[22]

When the disciples met to celebrate the Jewish feast of Pentecost after Jesus' Ascension, Luke narrative described how "tongues of fire" descended on their heads. Seized with apocalyptic excitement, they ran into the street and started talking in a form of mantric babbling (recorded elsewhere in the ancient world) that appeared comprehensible to people of all races. In the first Christian sermon, Peter announced that all present were witnesses to the end of time. First he quotes a passage from the Hebrew prophet Joel, just replacing the neutral opening phrase "then afterwards" with the apocalyptic "in the last days."

In the last days it will be that I will pour out my Spirit upon all flesh, and your sons and your daughters shall prophesy, and your young men shall see visions, and your old men shall dream dreams. Even upon my slaves, both men and women, in those days I will pour out my Spirit; and they shall prophesy.

And I will show portents in the heaven above and signs on the earth below, blood, and fire, and smoky mist. The sun shall be turned to darkness and the moon to blood, before the coming of the Lord's great and glorious day. Then everyone who calls on the name of the Lord shall be saved.

Peter goes on to explain that Jesus had been handed over to be crucified and killed "according to the definite plan and foreknowledge of God," "but God raised him up, having freed him from death, because it was impossible for him to be held in its power." He then quotes the psalm which declares that "God has made him both Lord and Messiah."[23]

The Acts of the Apostles then describes how members of the Jerusalem church sold their possessions and pooled the proceeds in a common fund. Emotion ran so high that husband and wife Ananias and Sapphira were struck dead when they held back part of the money they had promised to the community.[24] After this early experiment in communism had plunged the Jerusalem community into poverty—from which it had to be bailed out by contributions from other congregations—church leaders introduced the more cautious policy of continuing to proclaim an early end of the world while behaving as though this would take some time to happen.

During those early years after Jesus' death, apocalyptic expectations still ran high within mainstream Judaism, and scholars find it hard to detect whether writings originated within mainstream Judaism or "the Jesus sect." Jewish historian Josephus gives an account of an enterprise of about 45 CE that provides a chilling overture to so many later messianic follies,

Theudas, persuaded a great part of the people to take their effects with them, and follow him to the river Jordan; for he told them he was a prophet, and that he would by his own command, divide the river, and afford them an easy passage over it. Many were deluded by his words. However, (the Roman procurator) Fadus.... sent a troop of horsemen out against them. After falling upon them unexpectedly, they slew many of them, and took many of them alive. They also took Theudas alive, cut off his head, and carried it to Jerusalem.[25]

While Jesus proclaimed the arrival of a divine kingdom, he never forecast his own second coming. Paul of Tarsus' First Epistle to the Thessalonians is thought to be the earliest surviving Christian document. Written some 30 years after Jesus' death, it addresses concerns over how people who had already died and those who remained alive could be treated equally at the second coming of Christ. The apostle assured his readers that they had no cause for concern.

For the Lord himself, with a cry of command, with the archangel's call and with the sound of God's trumpet, will descend from heaven, and the dead in Christ will rise first. Then we who are alive, who are left, will be caught up in the clouds together with them to meet the Lord in the air; and so we will be with the Lord for ever.[26]

He reminded the Thessalonians that the day would come "like a thief in the night. When they say, "There is peace and security," then sudden destruction will come upon them, as labor pains come upon a pregnant woman, and there will be no escape! But you, beloved, are not in darkness, for that day to surprise you like a thief." Paul's suggestion that the faithful will be removed from earth before the Tribulation sharply contradicts Mark's Little Apocalypse, in which believers are expected to suffer alongside those other men, women and children who have the misfortune to be alive at the time.

During his time as a Pharisee, Paul would have become familiar with Jewish apocalyptic writings, in which, the temporal world is portrayed as wholly evil and the eternal as wholly good. Following Zoroastrian precedent, he teaches that the earthly and divine realms will be separated at the time of judgment. But, while Rashu the just weighs the fate of individuals by the balance of the good and evil acts which they had performed in their lifetime, Paul now divides them according to whether they had believed in the risen Christ.[27] This concept of justification by faith was first challenged in his own time when James first bishop of Jerusalem (and probably Jesus' natural brother) defended the alternative doctrine of justification by works, "What good is it, my brothers and sisters, if you say you have faith but do not have works? Can faith save you?"[28]

Although differences of interpretation could remain, the single thread runs through epistles by different authors: be on your guard; the End-Time is coming. "You also must be patient," wrote James. "Strengthen your hearts, for the coming of the Lord is near." "For yet in a very little while," says the anonymous author of Hebrews, "the one who is coming will come and will not delay." Peter's name joins the chorus. "For the time has come for judgment to begin with the household of God; if it begins with us, what will be the end for those who do not obey the gospel of God?"[29] Although many biblical writers talk of a deceiver, the word *Antichrist* only appears in letters ascribed to John. "Children," he declares, "this is the last hour. As you have heard that the Antichrist is coming, so now many Antichrists have come. From this we know that it is the last hour."[30]

*

In 66 CE, the Jews rebelled against Roman emperor Nero in protest against harsh taxation and perceived insults to the faith. After early Jewish victories, the tide of war turned when Vespasian brought some 60,000 legionaries to crush the uprising. After breaking opposition in the north, the Roman general mounted a long siege of Jerusalem before returning home to challenge for the position of emperor. Vespasian's son Titus inherited his task of finishing the war in Judea and, by 70 CE, both city and temple lay in ruins.

It was so thoroughly laid even with the ground by those that dug it up to the foundation, that there was left nothing to make those that came thither believe it had ever been inhabited. This was the end which Jerusalem came to ... a city otherwise of great magnificence, and of mighty fame among all mankind.[31]

Titus then moved on the mountain fortress of Masada, which turned out to be occupied by the bodies of 967 defenders, who had preferred suicide to capture. Jewish historian Josephus estimated that this First Jewish War his people incurred more than a million dead and almost as many sold into slavery, alongside an untold number who left their ruined homeland to settle in different parts of the empire. Although the reported scale of population displacement has been questioned, this new wave of fugitives certainly strengthened existing Jewish populations; among these were many Jews who professed allegiance to the emerging "Jesus sect." It appears that these Christian Jews built their own synagogues/churches in opposition to those mainstream Jewish places of worship, known to the Christians as "synagogues of Satan."[32]

Roman rulers were prepared to tolerate local faiths on the one condition that all shared in the imperial rites that held the whole structure together. Those eccentric Jews who called themselves Christians appeared to have a special calling to proselytize across the gentile world. Some decades earlier, Paul and James had come to an agreement that the Jewish law, which forbade the consumption of "food sacrificed to idols," should be extended to gentile Christians.[33] This ruling not only prevented converts from taking part in imperial rites, but—since every meal was seen as a religious gathering—even prevented them from sharing food at the family table. Nero's decision to persecute these troublemakers, therefore, won wide support across the empire.

The fact that the *Book of Revelation* was then thought to have been written by the disciple John "who Jesus loved" explains why, out of several similar writings that can be dated to the late first century CE, it alone would find a place the Christian Bible. But John was a common name, and this writer makes no claim to apostolic pedigree. "I, John, your brother who share with you in Jesus the persecution and the kingdom and the patient endurance that are ours in Jesus, was on the island of Patmos because of the word of God and the testimony of Jesus."[34] Probably written during the Emperor Domitian's last years, in about 95 CE, John of Patmos could even have been constructing his apocalypse at the same time that another author, who also called himself John, was working on a non-millennial meditation on Christian love which would be accepted as the Fourth Gospel. The two works could hardly be more different. Leaving aside passages specific to the Jesus Sect, the *Book of Revelation* compares more closely in style and content to Jewish apocalyptic writings that were then in circulation than it does to other Christian writings that found acceptance in the New Testament.[35]

Books were then both rare and valued possessions, and silent reading remained a seldom-acquired skill. With its dramatic style and heightened images of angels and monsters, the *Book of Revelation* (like the later Anglo-Saxon tale of *Beowulf*) was intended for declamation in crowded gatherings, rather than private study. The author opens with messages to six churches in Asia Minor and one in Macedonia, which he had probably visited as a roaming prophet. These scattered Christians were powerless to influence events in the wider Roman Empire, and the sense of abject helplessness fuelled desire for heavenly intervention. The *Book of Revelation* must, therefore, be read as an impassioned assault on Rome and a plea that God should lay this evil empire low.

Through the text, the reader keeps meeting the number 7. First only Jesus, the Lamb, is adjudged worthy of breaking the seven seals on the scroll of life. As these open one by one, they release four horsemen of The Apocalypse, who bring war, famine, and disease. Then earthquakes darken the sun, the moon turns to blood, and the whole sky rolls back like a scroll. At this point, 144,000 believers (12,000 each from the 12 tribes of Israel) receive identifying marks on their foreheads and right hands to separate them from the disasters that will follow.[36]

God sends two witnesses—widely interpreted to be Elijah and Enoch—with power to prophesy for 3½ years (1,260 days). As seven angels blow trumpets and seven more pour out bowls (vials), the devil unleashes all kinds of fearsome creatures and cosmic woes on those who do not carry the mark of salvation. Descriptions summon memories of Ezekiel, father of the Jewish apocalypse.

> In appearance the locusts were like horses equipped for battle. On their heads were what looked like crowns of gold; their faces were like human faces, their hair like women's hair, and their teeth like lions' teeth; they had scales like iron breastplates, and the noise of their wings was like the noise of many chariots with horses rushing into battle. They have tails like scorpions, with stings, and in their tails is their power to harm people for five months.[37]

As the seventh angel empties the last bowl, the forces of Satan gather for the final battle of Armageddon, which would be fought at the historic battlefield of—har-Megiddo, the hill of Megiddo.

In a dramatic evocation of ancient myth, John now summons up a pregnant queen of heaven, who, looking backward, brings together goddesses Artemis of Ephesus, Isis of Egypt, and Asherah of Canaan and, looking forward, provides a model for the Christian cult of the Virgin Mary. Clothed in a garment of light, with stars round her head and the moon at her feet, she and her messianic child join in battle with the evil serpent, which sweeps stars from the sky with its tail.

Daniel had described how four beasts of chaos rose from the ocean; John now calls up just two—one from the sea and a second from the land. The first, which has ten horns and seven heads, is ridden by the whore of Babylon. In Daniel's vision, horns had represented rulers, but the issue is complicated here by which, if any, of the three short-lived emperors who followed Nero in 69 BCE are included to make up the correct number. More certainly, "whore of Babylon" was a common metaphor for the city of Rome and the seven heads for the city's seven hills. The second subordinate beast, which comes from the land, has been identified as the Roman imperial priesthood.

Scholars now link the mysterious assertion that one of the heads "seemed to have received a death-blow, but its mortal wound had been healed" with legends about Nero's death. With his empire falling apart in rebellion and enemies at the door, he was said to have committed suicide by driving a dagger into his own throat. Rumors then circulated that Nero had returned to life with his wound miraculously healed and taken refuge with the Parthian rulers of Persia.

Real-life pretenders, who claimed to be the resurrected emperor, rose in rebellion against the Roman state in 69, 80, and finally 88 CE—the last just a few years before John is thought to have written his Revelation. As a semidivine being brought back to life by Satan, murderer of his own mother and allegedly also his wife, first persecutor of Christians and initiator of the Jewish War, Nero made the perfect Antichrist to stand against the true royal Messiah, Jesus of Nazareth. To seal this identification, John revealed the secret number 666. Scholars have discovered that, in the first century, every letter had an equivalent numerical value. Spelt out in Greek, *Neron Caesar* added up to 666 and, when other scribes trascribed *Nero Caesar* from Latin text they adjusted, the total to the Latin equivalent of 610. The confirmation that *Babylon* means Rome and that the Antichrist was a historical figure significantly alters the reading of John's apocalypse. With Antiochus Epiphanes and Nero now established as the twin pillars of evil, large portions of Revelation, like Daniel before it, takes on the character of historical allegory rather than forecasts of the future.

The seventh angel then empties the seventh bowl to bring about the utter destruction of Rome and all its satellites.

> And the kings of the earth, who committed fornication and lived in luxury with her, will weep and wail over her when they see the smoke of her burning; they will stand far off, in fear of her torment, and say, "Alas, alas, the great city, Babylon, the mighty city! For in one hour your judgment has come."[38]

Ezekiel's birds of the air now gather for God's great supper of human flesh. As those who carry the sign of the beast or have worshipped its image are thrown into the lake of fire, "the rest were killed by the sword of the rider on the horse, the sword (teaching) that came from his mouth."[39]

Those who have studied the text in forensic detail claim to identify some 300 references to passages from Isaiah, Ezekiel, Daniel, and other books of the Old Testament, but Zoroaster's shadow still falls as John reports that "no mountains were to be found" at this Apocalypse.[40] Then, "as the messiah appears out of the sun, in bloodstained clothes and riding a white horse," the writer calls up ancient imagery to describe how holy fire then consumes the devil and all his minions.

> Then I saw an angel coming down from heaven, holding in his hand the key to the bottomless pit and a great chain. He seized the dragon, that ancient serpent, who is the Devil and Satan, and bound him for a thousand years, and threw him into the pit, and locked and sealed it over him, so that he would deceive the nations no more, until the thousand years were ended. After that he must be let out for a little while.... And the devil who had deceived them was thrown into the lake of fire and sulphur, where the beast and the false prophet were, and they will be tormented day and night for ever and ever.[41]

In the time of rejoicing that follows, John sees a new and exactly measured Jerusalem descend from heaven "prepared as a bride adorned for her husband." The work then concludes with End-Time assurance, "The one who testifies to these things says, 'Surely I am coming soon.' Amen. Come, Lord Jesus!"[42]

*

While John of Patmos did possess a talent for dramatic rhetoric, his writing could also descend to a level of incomprehensibility that would later trigger interminable debate.

> This calls for a mind that has wisdom: the seven heads are seven mountains on which the woman is seated; also, they are seven kings, of whom five have fallen, one is living, and the other has not yet come; and when he comes, he must remain for only a little while. As for the beast that was and is not, it is an eighth but it belongs to the seven, and it goes to destruction.[43]

When John of Patmos called for "a mind that has wisdom," capable of penetrating hidden mysteries, he was clearly using the language of Greek Gnosticism. Later church fathers would make such a thorough job of rooting this heresy out of Christian teaching that most information on the later Gnostic sects has to be gleaned from the works of those who thundered against them. Teachers were accused of diluting the true faith with alien Greek, Jewish, and Eastern beliefs and practices, of replacing orthodox expectation of resurrection with concepts of reincarnation, of introducing dualistic concepts of good and evil and speaking in riddles that were impenetrable to all but the initiate. Even more seriously, Gnostic believers threatened to replace the historical figure of Jesus with their own less clearly defined savior, who could be experienced only in the spiritual dimension. Recently discovered Gnostic documents do also carry apocalyptic visions, which elaborate on celestial warfare, worldly catastrophe, satanic forces, and the fiery abyss, from which the faithful will finally emerge into an eternity of divine light.[44] Starting from the assumption that the physical world is no more than an accidental byproduct of the great cosmic struggle, it was a short step to conclude that those destined for salvation were free from earthly government. Thus released, like-minded groups of enthusiasts could choose between adopting extreme regimes of asceticism on the one side and libertine excess—under which they became free to abandon constraints governing sexual behavior, the use of food and drink, and even violence—on the other.

While early Christian father Irenaeus of Lyons led the assault, he continued to insist that belief in a coming Apocalypse, as described in Revelation, lay at the core of Christian orthodoxy. Then, in the mid-third century, as the white heat of expectation began to decline, Egyptian theologian Origen of Alexandria took issue with the idea of a literal Apocalypse. Physical interpretations of resurrection, he announced, might be "preached in the churches. . . . for the simple-minded, and for the ears of the common crowd who are led to lead better lives for their belief," but the more sophisticated would take such tales as allegorical descriptions of the spiritual body that would one day receive immortal life.[45] Origen would lay the foundation of an enduring Eastern tradition that holiness can only be achieved through poverty and devotion, within which a spiritualized version of End-Time vocabulary can be absorbed into the communal liturgy.

> He [Christ] anointed us as we went into combat, but he fettered the devil; he anointed us with the oil of gladness, but he bound the devil with fetters that cannot be broken to keep him shackled hand and foot for the combat. But if I happen to slip, He stretches out his hand, lifts me from my fall, and sets me on my feet again.[46]

More than a century after Origen's death, church leaders joined in conference to condense belief into the Nicene Creed, which would act as a touchstone of orthodoxy across different branches of the Christian community. While these dignitaries accepted unambiguous biblical teaching that Christ would come again "to judge both the living and the dead," they added that Jesus' "kingdom shall have no end." This small addition branded all those who held the millenarian position that a period of satanic rule would follow the second coming as heretics.

This long drawn-out dilution of End-Time expectation could only arouse powerful reaction. In about 170 CE, holy man Montanus started to deliver a "new prophesy" in the remoter parts of Asia Minor. After Roman noblewomen Priscilla and Maximilla abandoned their husbands to join him on the road, the three started to deliver ecstatic prophesies—best compared with those found in modern Pentecostal churches—that were claimed to be direct outpourings of the Holy Spirit. From the beginning, women took a prominent position in the Montanist movement, contributing as prophets, priests, and even bishops. One even carried her feminine insights into heavenly spheres.

> Having taken the form of a woman, Christ came to me in radiant garment and placed in me wisdom and revealed to me this: this place is holy and in this place Jerusalem will come down from heaven.[47]

The holy place to which she referred was a stretch of land between two insignificant local settlements of Pepuza and Tymion, which Montanus had measured as an exact fit for John of Patmos' New Jerusalem. Since the second coming would be speeded by the blood of saints, the prize of martyrdom must be actively sought. Legend describes how prophetess Perpetua's executioner held back from carrying out her sentence, until "she took the hand of the trembling gladiator and guided it to her throat."[48]

As Montanism spread out rapidly across Palestine and into North Africa, church authorities struggled to decide whether this "new prophesy" was really the Holy Spirit's work. First, Irenaeus negotiated with the Pope in Rome to keep the movement within Christian boundaries; then the narrow and irascible

Tertullian pronounced it a genuine revelation, putting to shame the mainstream church, that had become "little more than a conclave of bishops."

*

Late in the fourth century, young North African Aurelius Augustine rebelled against his Christian mother, took himself a concubine, and accepted the Manichaean faith, which had enthusiastically embraced ancient Zoroastrian vision of endless competition between twin and opposing powers. "I teach that there are two primary elements, God and Matter," announced a sage. "To Matter we ascribe all maleficent, to God all beneficent potency, as is proper."[49] After being reconciled with the orthodox church and ordained as a priest in later life, Augusitine confronted his old dualist beliefs with all of a convert's enthusiasm.

In this signification of the word existence there is implied a nature which is self-contained, and which continues immutably. Such things can be said only of God, to whom there is nothing contrary . . . For the contrary of existence is non-existence. There is therefore no nature contrary to God.[50]

As Augustine rose in the church hierarchy, he faced an even more pressing challenge nearer home. Almost a century earlier, the emperor Diocletian had unleashed the last and most severe of all Christian persecutions. Although this finished in 313 CE, when Constantine declared Christianity an official religion within the Roman Empire, the experience divided the North African church from top to bottom. Following the teaching of the priest Donatus, purists rejected all clergy who had compromised with the state—and this extended not only to the culprits but also to all whom they had ordained or even baptized.

Although, once again, dependant on opponents' writings, violence certainly ran deep through the Donatist movement. Extremists known as Circumcellions "burned houses and churches, beat people, cut off a bishop's hands and tongue, and blinded others with a mixture of lime and acid."[51] Increasingly obsessed with martyrdom, they could even turn violence on themselves. "It was their daily sport" reported Augustine, "to kill themselves by throwing themselves over precipice, or into water or into fire." By the end of the fourth century, it is estimated that an alternative Donatist church with some 400 bishops was in full rebellion against the North African orthodox hierarchy and, by extension, with Rome.

Persecution, which had hitherto been inflicted by pagans on Christians, was now directed at these heretical Christians. "As the lions were turned on them," reported Augustine, "so the laws by which they hoped to crush an innocent victim were turned against the Donatists."[52] Since the empire was ruled by a Christian monarch, disputes between Christians were now fought out in the public arena. In the course of a bitter row over succession to the see of Carthage, the Donatists appealed to Constantine, in effect asking him to declare that their sect was the catholic (universal) Church of Christ. After this petition was rejected by both emperor and pope, Augustine laid out the counter-position. Since Donatists did not deny the true nature of Christ, every effort should be made to bring them back into the Catholic fold by peaceful means. However, if this did not produce a response, the state could resort to force on Jesus' own authority.

> Whence the Lord himself bids the guests in the first instance to be invited to his great supper, and afterwards compelled, ... he said to them "Go out into the highways and hedges, and compel them to come in." In those therefore who were first brought in through gentleness, the former obedience is fulfilled; but in those who are compelled, the disobedience is avenged.[53]

Augustine used this passage to justify the secular state's role in helping to enforce religious conformity and, for centuries to come, Jesus' words, "compel them to come in," would serve as a convenient euphemism for torture and death at the stake.

*

The imperial city was sacked by the Visigoths in 410 CE, just 5 years after Emperor Honorius declared that Donatism was a heresy. With internal church struggles still raging and mindful that John of Patmos had gleefully predicted just such a catastrophe, it came as no surprise that outsiders laid the blame on Christians. "It was for this reason," recorded Augustine, "that I, kindled by zeal for the house of God, undertook to write the books on the City of God against their blasphemies and errors."[54] Augustine confessed that, in his younger days, he had accepted a literal interpretation of Revelation with as much enthusiasm as anybody else. Seeds of doubt may have formed when he attacked Mani for promoting the equal and equivalent power of good and evil. He now asked whether the author of Revelation could not be charged with presenting a similar dualism between God and Satan? Those who wished to communicate with non-Christians had to distance themselves from crude apocalyptic speculation.

Augustine constructed his theology on the principle that all men had been born in sin and the saved had been selected before the act of creation. According to his analysis, there were two "comings" of Jesus—one past, the coming in mercy, and one future, the coming in judgement. In the first, God had given humans a chance of salvation when the church—which he identified as the New Jerusalem—descended from heaven in spiritual form and the devil was bound for all eternity. Then, at some unknown time in the future, the second coming in judgement would signal the resurrection of all humanity. Following Origen's lead, he concludes that this will be "a resurrection of souls, not of bodies." But, when he faced up to the End-Time choice, this apologist for predestination still allowed some measure of human free will to return through the back door. "Consequently," he declared, "let any man who does not want to be damned in the second resurrection take good care to rise in the first."[55]

While Augustine could not dismiss Revelation as a canonical part of the Bible, he did turn his face against any attempt to interpret it as a blueprint for future events.

Admittedly, The Apocalypse contains many obscure texts that exercise the reader's intelligence and only a few so clear that one may rely on these in laboriously studying out the remainder. This is due chiefly to the fact that he is repeating the same themes—so various that, wherever John seems to be saying constantly new things, you find out that he is repeating the same themes, now this way, now that.[56]

In conformity with the new Nicene orthodoxy, he asks whether John's words "after that he (the devil) must be let loose a little while" could possibly mean that the Catholic Church would one day be defeated—for however short a period. "God forbid! Never shall he lead astray that Church."[57] Since Augustine still accepted that Revelation had been written by Jesus' beloved disciple, his comprehensive rejection of the work was bound to cause controversy, but, in just 12 short sections within the much larger *City of God*, he did change the direction of official Catholic End-Time doctrine.

*

During the millennium and a half that had passed between the death of King David and the accession of Constantine, Judeo-Christian religious and secular power had never for any significant period been securely united in a single authority figure. Since religion and state were separate, apocalyptic visions could provide cover for protest against secular authority. Now, as clergy filled influential roles in secular affairs under Christian rulers, religious enthusiasts could not be allowed to describe secular power as the creation of Satan. But neither Augustine's logic nor the threat of persecution could eradicate all millennial speculation. As long as most of the population remained illiterate, clerical authorities could exclude "the simple-minded" from recondite theological debate, But educational standards would improve and, as disaffected priests and monks shared their own heterodox views with the masses, laypeople began to chafe at their exclusion from religious debates that crucially impinged on their own salvation.

In the shorter term, however, across the Mediterranean basin, Jews, Catholic and Christians—both orthodox and heretical—would find themselves caught up in an irresistible and wholly unforeseen tsunami of Islamic conquest.

4

The Book Shall Be Laid Down: The Islamic End-Time

The child Muhammad was born into the Hashemite clan in the Arabian city of Mecca in around the year 570 CE. Through the century, members of the parent Quraysh tribe had been growing wealthy on profits from the carrying trade. During the (relatively) cool season, their camel caravans would travel south to buy spices and silks from the Orient and fragrant bark of incense trees from Yemen and Ethiopia at the Indian Ocean seaport today known as Aden. Then in the (very) hot season, other teams would carry this high-value cargo north for sale in the markets of Egypt, Syria, and Byzantium. For all this commercial success, Arabia remained a turbulent society, where tribes fought endlessly for control of trade routes and water sources. Just once a year, all came together at the Ka'bah shrine in Mecca, which, according to legend, had been built by the first man, Adam, and restored by patriarch Abraham, along with his son Ishmael, who was revered as father to all Arab people. Inside the building was a holy stone that was believed to be a remnant of Adam's original structure and, set into one corner of the outside wall, lay the Black Stone, which had reputedly been sent from heaven. Also stored within the Ka'bah were some 360 idols that were venerated by different Arab communities.

As the Meccans struggled to survive in a harsh environment, they clung to a belief that everybody's fate had been fixed by a multitude of supernatural powers that were beyond human knowledge or control. But other faiths were now challenging traditional polytheism. Arabs had long been in touch with Persian Zoroastrians who lived just a boat's ride distant from the peninsula's southern and eastern shores. Nomadic Jewish tribes also occupied desert territory in the Medina area, and Jewish traders were also settling in Yemen. Some 1,500 miles away, at the caravan trail's northern extremity, Meccan traders also encountered the bitterly divided Christian world.

After being orphaned in early life, the young Muhammad was brought up in the house of his uncle Abi Talib. Reflecting the Christian story of how Jesus visited the temple in Jerusalem, a Muslim tradition (*hadith*) tells how this lad accompanied his uncle on a journey from Mecca to Syria, where a holy man identified him as a future prophet. However historically questionable that tale may be, Muhammad was certainly exposed to an unusually wide range of religious influence during the years when—first as employee, then as husband—he managed the widow-merchant Khadija's caravans.

At the age of 40, the Prophet began to deliver messages described as having come from the angel Gabriel, that would later form the text of the Qur'an. At their core lay an affirmation of the existence of one indivisible God. "Say: He, Allah, is One. Allah is He on Whom all depend. He begets not, nor is He begotten and none is like Him."[1] Human destiny, once subject to the whim of many gods, now lay in the hands of a single just and merciful deity who controls each human life from birth to death and into the afterlife, just as he also controls the whole universe, from creation to the end of time. From the beginning, the Prophet insists that the Hour of Judgment is close. "O people! guard against (the punishment from) your Lord; surely the violence of the hour is a grievous thing." "The hour is coming, there is no doubt about it; and because Allah shall raise up those who are in the graves."[2] That terrible hour will be marked by cosmic events—"when the earth shall be shaken with a (severe) shaking, and the mountains shall be made to crumble with (an awful) crumbling" and "when the heaven becomes cleft asunder, and when the stars become dispersed, and when the seas are made to flow forth, and when the graves are laid open."[3]

The hadith reinforces this sense of urgency. "Behold, God sent me with a sword just before the Hour and placed my daily sustenance beneath the shadow of my spear."[4]

For all its uncompromising monotheism, Muhammad's message finds room for Zoroastrian visions of fire and crumbling mountains. From the ancient combat myth comes a beast that emerges from the earth; from Ezekiel, the figures of Gog and Magog (Yajuj and Majuj); from John of Patmos' Revelation, the sound of God's trumpet announcing the arrival of a new creation.

> And the trumpet shall be blown, so all those that are in the heavens and all those that are in the earth shall swoon, except such as Allah please; then it shall be blown again, then lo! they shall stand up awaiting. And the earth shall beam with the light of its Lord, and the Book shall be laid down, and the prophets and the witnesses shall be brought up, and judgment shall be given between them with justice, and they shall not be dealt with unjustly. And every soul shall be paid back fully what it has done, and He knows best what they do.[5]

In the apocalyptic second coming, Jesus—the prophet Isa, son of Marium—descends to earth in judgment.[6] No longer son of God and subject to death like any other mortal, he takes his place in the End-Time narrative as the penultimate prophet, before Muhammad's arrival.

In his five key tenets of Islam, Muhammad ranked belief in the apocalypse only behind acceptance of the one undivided God. These are:

Belief in God/Allah
Belief in the last days
Belief in angels
Belief in the scripture
Belief in the prophets

The End will be near when imbeciles rule over the wise, dishonesty and hypocrisy are rated as virtues, the sexes cross roles, with men obeying their wives and each wearing the other's clothing and, finally, the sun rises in the west. Even the closest family relations will disintegrate.

The fathers together with their sons shall be smitten and brothers one with another shall fall in death till the streams flow with their blood, for a man shall not withhold his had from slaying his sons and his sons' sons.[7]

Thirty deceivers (*dajjals*) will precede the arrival of the final one-eyed impostor, the Masih al-*Dajjal*. The tradition describes how Isa then emerges from heaven to kill this evil figure: "his cheeks will be flat and his hair straight. When he lowers his head it will seem as if water is flowing from his hair, when he raises his head, it will appear as though his hair is beaded with silvery pearls."[8] Although the Islamic messiah (*mahdi*) does not appear in the Qur'an, early tradition describes how he now comes to rid the world of error, injustice, and tyranny. As the final drama unfolds, Zoroastrian, Christian, and Jewish images jostle with others unique to Islam. As humans cross the bridge that separates the old world from that which is to come, their deeds are weighed in a vast pair of scales. Beneath lies a yawning pit, where a stone will fall for 70 years before it hits the bottom. Here Azrael, angel of death—"immense and fearful to behold"—writes the names of the dead on a scroll. While, to faithful eyes, his wings appear to be spread in comfort, to unbelievers they look like pincers. According to the Judeo Christian tradition, evil beings like Azrael and Satan can act in hostility to God as independent agents of evil, but Islamic monotheism can tolerate no such division of power; this angel of death acts under the command of the one all-powerful Allah. Like Augustine of Hippo before him. Muhammad faced the problem of balancing the omnipotence of God on the one side with his mercy on the other. While the all-knowing deity had surely recorded all outcomes that had been set firm from the time of creation, justice still demanded that individuals must be held responsible for those actions that propel them to paradise or hell.

The truth is from your Lord, so let him who please believe, and let him who please disbelieve; surely We have prepared for the iniquitous a fire, the curtains of which shall encompass them about; and if they cry for water, they shall be given water like molten brass which will scald their faces; evil the drink and ill the resting-place.

Any number of good deeds could be outweighed by a single grave sin that had not been repented at the time of death. But in the cause of mercy "we will set up a just balance on the day of resurrection, so no soul shall be dealt with unjustly in the least; and though there be the weight of a grain of mustard seed, (yet) will We bring it, and sufficient are We to take account."[9] In common with contemporary Christians, Muslims, stretch the imagination to describe ever more awful ways in which the damned are tortured by demons and evil creatures.

The least tormented of Hell's denizens shall, on the day of arising, wear sandals of fire, the heat of which will cause the brains to boil. And should you ever doubt the intensity of Hell's torment, then bring your finger near a flame and draw a comparison from that.... Were Hell's inhabitants to come across a fire such as ours they would plunge into it submissively in order to flee from their condition.[10]

Christian artists and writers have struggled to present the joys of heaven with the same sense of drama as they do the sufferings of hell. An eternity of "waiting around," dressed in white,[11] within an environment of harps, wings, and haloes, can appear a pallid reward for virtue. If the Muslim hell was to be presented as a place of physical torture, then paradise must offer a beguiling vision of sensory bliss. In this flowery and well-watered garden, the saved would enjoy 10 times the riches of any king and drink delicious nectar from the most beautiful precious vessels. All around would be glades of trees where multitudes of flutes hang from every branch to produce the most exquisite sounds when stirred by gentle breezes. In this perfect world, every possible object of desire would be consummated before it could even be imagined. While Christians might anticipate a sexless afterlife, Muslims, most emphatically, did not. In this very male environment, every man would be endowed with two beautiful wives and 70 "dark-eyed houris," whose virginity is restored after every sexual encounter. Much discussion has centered on who these women might be. It has been suggested that the wives could be the individual's own partners, restored to youth and beauty, and the houris are the wives of those who have been consigned to hell. Alternatively, female companions could—like the trees, flowers, and flutes—be supernatural blessings of paradise. Neither answers the problem of why very few women appear to enter paradise in their own right. According to one tradition, the Prophet told male companions how he had looked down into hell.

I saw the fire and I have not seen to this day a more terrible sight. Most of the inhabitants were women. They (his companions) said, O messenger of God, why? He then said, Because of their ingratitude. They said "Are they ungrateful to God?" He said, "No, but they are ungrateful to the companion [husband] and ungrateful for the charity. Even if you continue to do good things for them, and a woman sees one (bad) thing from you, she will say I never saw anything at all good from you."[12]

For the better part of a thousand years after the Babylonian captivity, Judeo-Christian writers delighted in constructing apocalyptic dreams and revelations of heaven. The mainstream Islamic tradition of the Qur'an and early hadith, in contrast, centers on just one. The Qur'an, Sura 17—*The Night Journey*—opens with the verse, "Glory be to Him Who made His servant to go on a night from the Sacred Mosque to the remote mosque of which We have blessed the precincts, so that We may show to him some of Our signs; surely He is the Hearing, the Seeing." The Prophet's earliest biographer tells how Gabriel took Muhammad to Jerusalem on a white animal named Buraq, "half mule, half donkey with wings on its side with which it propelled its feet." He gives details of a meeting with Abraham, Moses, and Jesus. "I have never seen a man more like myself than Abraham. Moses was a ruddy faced man, tall, curly haired with a hooked nose ... Jesus son of Mary was a reddish man with lank hair with many freckles on his face as though he had just come from a bath."

Many of Muhammad's followers found the whole narrative incredible. "By God," declared one, "this is a plain absurdity! A caravan takes a month to go to Syria and a month to return and can the Prophet do the return journey in one night?" His young wife Aisha is even recorded as telling how "the Prophet's body remained where it was but God removed his spirit by night."[13] Still the tale was elaborated in later centuries.

After the completion of my work in Jerusalem a ladder was brought to me finer than any I have ever seen. ... My companion mounted it with me until we came to one of the gates of heaven which is called the Gate of the Watchers. An angel called Isma'il was in charge of it, and under his command were twelve thousand angels each of them having twelve thousand angels under his command.

The prophet then asked for a vision of hell and, when the covering was removed, the flames blazed high in the air until he feared that everything would be consumed. In the pit below, he saw women who had fathered bastards on their husbands hanging by their breasts along with "those who had sinfully devoured the wealth of orphans ... in whose hands were pieces of fire like stones which they used to thrust into their mouths and they would come out of their posteriors."[14] This story of Muhammad's Night Journey would prove a fertile base for Gnostic speculation. By one account, Muhammad passed through 70 curtains until he was brought into the presence of God, where he was given the heavenly book and inducted into the hidden knowledge. "And God hereby caused me to know the knowledge of the earlier and the later ones, and the light of my heart. And the light of his throne covered my sight so that I could not look, but began to see with my heart and could not see with my eye."[15]

If the Qur'an carries only hints of this apocalyptic journey, the sacred book provides a clear, if brief, narrative of millennial events on the eastern frontier of the known world. Three centuries before the time of Muhammad, some Egyptian scribe had gathered ever more extravagant stories about Alexander the Great into one document, which became known as the *Alexander Legend*. One passage told how the emperor had built barriers against the terrible tribes of Gog and Magog, which inhabited the Asian steppes beyond the Caucasus Mountains. Images of Alexander show him wearing a two-horned helmet, and the Qur'an took up the story of Zulqarnain (the two-horned one), who travelled to the land of the rising sun.

He followed a course until when he reached [a place] between the two mountains, he found on that side of them a people who could hardly understand a word. They said: O Zulqarnain! Surely Gog and Magog make mischief in the land ... He said: ... I will make a fortified barrier between you and them; bring me blocks of iron; until when he had filled up the space between the two mountain sides. ... He said bring me molten brass which I may pour over it. So they were not able to scale it nor could they make a hole in it.[16]

While the historical Alexander had pursued enemies to the Caspian Sea, he never stopped to carry out building work, and archaeologists date all fortifications in the region to later centuries. But these destructive tribes would not be constrained forever. "Even when Gog and Magog are let loose and they shall break forth from every elevated place. And the true promise shall draw nigh, then lo! the eyes of those who disbelieved shall be fixedly open: O woe to us! Surely we were in a state of heedlessness as to this; nay, we were unjust."[17] Bringing the two passages together, commentators would describe how, as the last days approached, the tribes of Gog and Magog would break down Alexander's Wall and carry destruction into the civilized world. At the same time, the forces of Islam would become involved in one climactic struggle with Byzantium, which would mark the end of time and the Last Judgment of all mankind.

*

The Islamic calendar measures history from the year 622 CE, when the Prophet led his followers out of the hostile city of Mecca to make their home some 200 miles to the north in the settlement that would become known as Madinat un-Nabi—the City of the Prophet—or, more simply, Medina. Two years later, he led the new forces of Islam against the main Quraish army at the battle of Bedr. The Qur'an ascribed victory to divine assistance. "Does it not suffice you that your Lord should assist you with three thousand of the angels sent down?"[18] During the last 10 years of his life, Muhammad dispatched raiding parties against local tribes and further afield across the Arabian Peninsula and into Syria. Setting a long-term precedent, in 629 CE, he defeated a Jewish tribe that occupied the oasis of Khaybar and permitted them to stay in their homes on payment of an annual poll tax (*jizya*). By the time Muhammad died in 632, he had won a wide reputation across the region as a successful soldier. From early times, Muslims believed that he had been the last in a line of prophets that stretched from Adam through Old Testament figures, such as Noah (Nuh), Abraham (Ibrahim) Moses (Musa) and David (Daud), to John the Baptist (Yahya) and Jesus (Isa). While followers might debate interpretation, the faith that final prophet Muhammad bequeathed was complete and could not be modified by later divine revelation. Warnings against future deceivers are collected in the hadith.

> There will be Dajjals and liars among my Community. They will tell you something new, which neither you nor your forefathers have heard. Be on your guard against them and do not let them lead you astray.[19]

The Qur'an does not foretell the expansion that would follow so quickly after Muhammad's death in 632 CE. Just five years later, Caliph Umar entered Jerusalem in triumph to pray on the ruined Temple Mount. Another 20 years on, Islamic armies had conquered all of Arabia and Egypt, destroyed the ancient Persian empire, and overrun great swaths of Byzantine territory. After just a century, they had conquered the Sudan, Afghanistan, and the Caucasus as well as North Africa, much of southern Italy, and most of Spain. They had even carried the message into North India and were turning their eyes toward China. The Muslims brought some level of stability and—apart from Italy and Spain—Islam remains the first religion in all these conquered countries. The newcomers fought under rules of war that prohibited the killing of women and children and (at least theoretically) the looting of possessions. Although conquest will always be a brutal process, unlike earlier Huns and later Moguls, they left no lasting trail of devastation. Indeed, these Muslims were often welcomed by subject people, who could emerge from the process of conquest with lower tax demands and greater freedom of worship than they had enjoyed under old masters. Except on the Byzantine frontier, where conflict could be fierce and bloody, set-piece battles were comparatively rare.

Conditions for conquest were unusually favorable. Sassanid rule in Persia was already so weakened that the dynasty could be "knocked out after a punch or two."[20] The eastern Roman Empire had seen great days in the previous century when Justinian I set about reconquering the whole Mediterranean basin and poured vast resources into building his magnificent Church of the Holy Wisdom (Hagia Sophia). But Justinian's ambitions had cost his empire dearly and, before he died, it was also struck by plague, which continued to return year on year. According to some estimates, this illness had wiped out half the population of Constantinople and some 100 million people across the whole empire, leaving Byzantium impoverished and depopulated before this new threat. Beyond the two ancient empires, political units tended to be small, fragile, and all too frequently occupied with fighting one another. Yet it remains one of history's mysteries how a handful of tribes people, who never before or since posed a significant military threat to their neighbors, could have constructed such a large and stable empire within so short a time. Although, despite prohibitions, Muslim warriors did fight for booty, their particular strength came from their single-minded commitment to the apocalyptic struggle in which they were engaged.

When leading his followers out of Mecca (*hijra*), Muhammad set believers a model of constant motion. "Islamic history started with a great departure," writes one commentator. "To convert was to leave one's home in order to fight for the cause; salvation lay in going forth for heroic ventures and a new world ahead, not in patiently staying by one's fields or camels."[21] The twin concepts of *hijra* and *jihad* were, therefore, closely related from the beginning. The Companions of the Prophet formed an élite that had thrown off worldly ties and separated themselves from the mass of earth-bound humanity. The Arabic root *jhd* provides a family of words that relate to military struggle and moral striving, and both find a place within the Qur'an.

The holders back from among the believers, not having any injury, and those who strive hard in Allah's way with their property and their persons are not equal; Allah has made the strivers with their property and their persons to excel the holders back a [high] degree, and to each [class] Allah has promised good; and Allah shall grant to the strivers above the holders back a mighty reward.

And

Surely those who believed and fled [their homes] and struggled hard in Allah's way with their property and their souls, and those who gave shelter and helped—these are guardians of each other.[22]

Believing that they lived in the last times, which must follow closely on the Prophet's death, Islamic warriors cared little for family and possessions and left few permanent monuments. They fought on the frontier, either expanding Islam's territories or protecting the faith from its enemies. All was part of the divine purpose: "Conquer what seems good to you," declared the hadith. "... You have never conquered any city, nor will you conquer any city until the Day of Resurrection, except that to which God gave Muhammad its keys beforehand."[23] In common with Christian warriors, with whom they would later engage in apocalyptic conflict, they expected to receive their reward in heaven.

When a fighter goes out in the path of God, his sins are placed on the doorpost of his house, and when he leaves it behind, he leaves all of his sins; not even so much as the wing of a mosquito stays on him.[24]

While the idea of the warrior jihad provided the armies of Islam with the motivation to carry frontiers ever forward, the concept of an inner and "greater" moral jihad would resurface in later, more peaceful times.

*

As soon as Caliph Umar took command of Jerusalem, he built an unpretentious mosque on the ruined temple site where, by Muslim belief, Abraham had offered Ishmael as a sacrifice to God, and Muhammad had risen to heaven on his Night Journey. Some half century later, Caliph Abd al-Malik started work on the much grander Dome of the Rock. In the act of raising a structure that would stand comparison with the Hagia Sophia, al-Malik proclaim the arrival of a powerful empire that was founded on pure monotheist belief. In contrast, Christian fathers had long struggled to construct formulas that would allow the faithful to worship Jesus Christ and the Holy Spirit as divine beings without attracting the charge of polytheism. Trinitarian wordings, which appear abstruse to modern believers, then assumed huge significance. Did the Holy Spirit "proceed" from the both the Father and the Son, or just the Father? Most crucially, did Christ have two natures—human and divine—and, if so, which was the more important and how was one related to the other? These issues were still being debated as those Middle Eastern lands were being overrun by Muslim armies. Here, the lower orders of society were inclined to embrace the Arian family of heresies, which stressed Jesus' human over his divine nature, while their rulers followed orthodox doctrines, which emphasized the divine over the human.

The second commandment did also deliver an unambiguous prohibition; "You shall not make for yourself an idol, whether it is in the form of anything that is in heaven above, or that is on the earth beneath, or that is in the water under the earth. You shall not bow down to them or worship them." While, to Muslim eyes, all Christians were tainted by polytheism, the sin took its most blatant form in Byzantium, where the Virgin Mary was worshipped as Queen of Heaven and believers lavished devotion on so many images of saints.

While Muslim fighters certainly dreamt of the incalculable quantities of loot that would be found behind the walls of Constantinople, they also believed that the Final Hour could not arrive until this great bastion of polytheism had been destroyed. When the first Umayyad caliph Muawiyah launched a land and sea assault in 674, his forces were finally repulsed after three years of bitter fighting—reportedly leaving 30,000 dead in front of the formidable fortifications. Although those walls would hold for another 776 years, Muslim armies set about dismembering the rest of the Byzantine Empire piece by piece—first the Middle East and then Greece and the Balkans—until Constantine's capital city was reduced to a small Christian enclave within an ocean of Islam.

Facing disaster on such a scale, devout Syrian Christians concluded that the Muslim victories could only signal a punishment from God. In the mid-seventh century, documents circulated that purported to tell how fourth-century bishop Methodius of Olympus had predicted the Muslim conquest. In reality, the document had been written pseudonymously some three centuries later, after the Muslims had already arrived. Drawing from a Syriac Christian source, the unknown author makes God move mountains so that Alexander's wall can be converted into massive gates.

Alexander prayed to God without interruption and he heard his prayer. The Lord God gave a command to the two mountains which are called the "Breasts of the North" and they came together to within twelve cubits. Alexander built bronze gates and covered them with bitumen, so that if anyone wished to force them open by steel or open them with fire, he would be able to do neither.[25]

Coming forward to his own time, the writer then told how, "in the seventh millennium," the seed of Ishmael would break out from the "deserts of Ethribus" with a mandate to inflict God's punishment on all those Christians who had sunk into deep depravity.

The like of it was not perpetrated in any of the preceding generations that men arrayed themselves in the licentious clothes of harlots... and ran riot in drunkenness and had intercourse with one another... And brothers and fathers and sons all polluted themselves with the same woman.[26]

After recounting the bloodshed brought by Muslim armies, this *Pseudo-Methodius* made much of hardship caused by the poll tax and also bewailed widespread Christian apostasy to Islam.

While John of Patmos could portray pagan Roman emperors as Antichrists and beasts of destruction, *Pseudo-Methodius* now greets their Byzantine successors as agents of salvation. As the narrative changes from supposed history to messianic vision, he looks to the arrival of a last emperor who will utterly destroy the Muslim armies, abolish taxation, and bring a time of peace. This emperor-savior would then travel to Golgotha, take off his crown, and hang it on the cross before yielding his spirit to God. This act of submission then acts as a sign for Alexander's gates to burst, allowing the final Antichrist to lead the hordes of Gog and Magog into the great battle in Jerusalem, when Jesus and Michael would descend from heaven to win the final apocalyptic victory. Although prophesies for an imperial victory over the forces of Antichrist would remain unfulfilled in the east, Latin translations of *Pseudo Methodius* would make expectation for a savior emperor a key ingredient in western apocalyptic expectation

*

By Arab tradition, leaders were chosen in meetings of prominent men, who selected the person best qualified to hold the community together. As a close friend of Muhammad and early convert to Islam, first caliph Abu Bakr would become revered as Al Siddiq (the upright), but his tenure was brief and, as he approached death after just two years, he recommended Umar al-Khattab, who had been another of the Prophet's companions. After 11 years supervising a huge increase in territory, he, in turn, charged a small group of leading men to select a successor from among themselves. Of the two serious candidates, the Prophet's cousin Ali ibn Abi Talib considered himself uniquely qualified for the position; after his own father and Muhammad's childhood protector Abi Talib died, he had himself grown up in the Prophet's household and married Muhammad's daughter Fatima. Proud of his status as one of the *Alh al beit* (the people of the house), it appears that he had accepted the first two caliphs' appointment with some reluctance. In the event, however, the choice went to the other candidate, the prophet's companion Uthman ibn Affan. Disaffection grew as Uthman took every opportunity of enriching family members and filling positions of authority with his own supporters. In 655, Medina descended into anarchy as Uthman was first held under house arrest and then murdered. With different factions jostling for power, the succession did finally fall on Ali.

That year, 655, marks the outbreak of a five-year conflict that has become known as the First Fitna. Taking account of apocalyptic overtones in both languages, the word *fitna* is best translated into English as "tribulation." After Ali's enemies had retreated, first to Mecca and then to Basra, a period of inter-Muslim warfare and bloodshed followed, which was widely interpreted as a time of trial before the appointed Hour. This confusing conflict became reduced to a confrontation between Ali and Muawiyah governor of Syria. On the practical side, Muawiyah's prosperous base assured superiority in men and money, but, on the debit side, he was descended from the Quraysh tribe's Umayyad clan, which had fought against the Prophet at Bedr before accepting Islam with apparent reluctance. Even after Muawiyah had secured the caliphate, Ali's partisans stubbornly rejected the Umayyad family's right to rule, and they now proclaimed that true religion and law (*sharia*) could only be transmitted through divinely inspired, sinless, and infallible imams who were directly descended from the Prophet—in preference, from Fatima's line.

After Ali's death, followers expected Fatima's son Hasan to continue his father's bid for the caliphate, but, to the fury of supporters, it soon became clear that he had no stomach for fratricidal warfare, and he withdrew to Medina, where he was said to have been poisoned by one of his own wives, who was in Muawiyah's pay. When Caliph Muawiyah died in 680, Alids in the Iraqi city of Kufa invited younger son Husayn to lead them in rebellion against the Umayyad successor Yazid. According to the narrative, Muhammad ibn al-Hanafiyya, who was Ali's son by a different wife, begged his brother to take shelter in Yemen, but Husayn instead chose the path of martyrdom. While on the road to Kufa with just 128 family members and other followers, he met the Umayyad governor with what was reportedly a 70,000-strong army. Facing such huge odds, Husayn stepped forward with his baby son in his arms, and both were killed alongside 72 supporters, while surviving women and children were taken off to Yazid's palace. The Battle of Karbala still provides devotees with defining archetypes for the conflict between good and evil and the acceptance of holy martyrdom. As members of the minority community within the Islamic world, the Shi'a (*Shiat Ali*—the partisans of Ali) identify with Husayn and await the miraculous return of a Mahdi who will bring salvation to a suffering people. The fault line that divides the majority Sunni (*Ahl as-Sunnah wa'l-Jamā'ah*—people of the tradition and the community) from the minority Shi'a can be illustrated from contrasting perspectives on the Mahdi's role. Accepting that the true and unchangeable Islamic faith was handed on intact through generations of Umayyad and Abbasid caliphs, Sunnis expect that any future Mahdi will restore the conditions that existed in the caliphate's golden age and bring a sense of renewal to the faithful community. To Shi'a, eyes, in contrast, as rebels against the Prophet's true heirs, those same Umayyad and Abbasid caliphs had perverted true Islamic faith. A future Shi'a Mahdi would therefore sweep away all past corruption, to introduce a new order of faith, law and human justice.

However, while this historical narrative does reach back into the roots of Islamic history, much would happen before those early partisans of Ali became "Shi'ites" in any modern usage of the term. During that time, partisans of Ali would divide and sub-divide into a bewildering variety of millennial sects.

*

As Persians and Iraqis flocked to convert to Islam, many aligned themselves with Ali's cause. The First Fitna became plunged into confusion when Muawiyah and Ali agreed to submit their cases to arbitration. Outraged by Ali's concession on an issue of principle, some followers, widely known as Kharijites (those who went out) formed a dissident force of enthusiasts who claimed to have traded their mortal existence for a life of total obedience to Allah. Disaffection focused on the area of southern Iraq, between the towns of Kufa and Basra, which had long been a meeting place of competing faiths. While some Kharijites expressed excessive devotion to the Alid line of imams, others professed "proto-communist" convictions that all men held equality before God and any suitably pious and talented individual—whether free or slave—could aspire to the position of imam or even caliph. On this basis, they claimed the right to kill any ruler who did not live up to the standards set by to the first two caliphs. In 658, Ali led his army in a merciless massacre of Kharijite forces, and three years later, an enemy took revenge by striking him down with a poisoned sword while he was at prayer.

As Muawiyah grew increasingly alarmed at this huge influx of new Muslims (known as *mawali*), he introduced a system of discrimination between believers on the basis of racial origins. Instructions to one governor were very clear.

> Be watchful of Persian Muslims and never treat them as equals of Arabs. Arabs have a right to take in marriage their women, but they have no right to marry Arab women. Arabs are entitled to inherit their legacy, but they cannot inherit from an Arab. As far as possible they are to be given lesser pensions and lowly jobs.[27]

Most importantly, taxes were now raised on non-Arab Muslims at much the same level as they had paid before conversion. Just five years after the Battle of Karbala, 62-year-old Medina Arab Mukhtar ibn Abu 'Ubayd raised the disaffected mawali of Kufa in rebellion against Umayyad Caliph Yazid. At face value, this was another conflict over the succession, but Mukhtar presented Ali's younger son, Muhammad ibn al-Hanafiyya, as a new brand of revolutionary Mahdi who would return to take vengeance on the usurpers. Mukhtar's revolutionary message continued to spread even after he had been killed and the uprising put down, and a radical sects known as Kaysanites gained strength so rapidly that they soon outnumbered more moderate Alids. Then, when Mukhtar's chosen Mahdi Muhammad ibn al-Hanafiyya also died, the story spread that he had gone into hiding within Mount Radwa near Medina, where he was, guarded by lions and tigers and fed by mountain goats. In God's time, he would return "to fill the world with justice and equity as it was full of injustice and oppression."[28]

This idea of *occultism* is alien to classic Islam, where even Muhammad must die like all other men. "Surly you shall die," said the Qur'an, "and they [too] shall surely die. Then surely on the Day of Resurrection you will contend with one another before the End."[29] Precedent can only be found in Zoroastrian myth, where the prophet's sons lie hidden at the bottom of lakes and the three-headed dragon is chained inside Mount Damavand until the world reaches its end. As local mawali chiefs delivered loyalty to various leaders, Mukhtar's Kaysanites subdivided into many sects, united only in acknowledging that the true line of imams must descend through the hidden Mahdi Muhammad ibn al-Hanafiyya. Sunni writers would later name no less than 72 "damned and heretical" sects,[30] some of which were suspected of indulging in libertarian practices, that threatened to undermine good order within society. Even more moderate members of the Shi'a were accused of importing Gnostic, Zoroastrian, Jewish, Manichean, and heretical Christian ideas that contradicted orthodox Islamic teachings. Widely respected Sixth Imam Jafar al Sadiq[31] demonstrated Shi'a syncretism by stressing the importance of both the "red vessel" of the Prophet Muhammad's legacy and the "white vessel," of the Judeo-Christian and specifically Shi'ite traditions.

The red case is a vessel in which are the weapons of the Apostle of God . . . It will never leave us until the one among us, members of the House (the Alid Mahdi), arises. The white case is a vessel in which are the Torah of Moses, the Gospels of Jesus, the Psalms of David and the Books of God. The scroll of Fatima . . . has in it every event which will take place and the names of all the rulers until the hour comes. Al-Jami'a is a scroll seventy yards long which the Apostle of God . . . dictated from his own mouth and Ali ibn. Abi Talib . . . wrote in his own handwriting. By God, in it is everything which people need until the end of time.[32]

In the mid-eighth century, many radical sects transferred their allegiance to the Abbasid family to assist in toppling the corrupt and pleasure-loving Umayyads, Then, once in power, new caliph Abul Abbas—"Shedder of Blood"—turned on his old supporters, demanding that all subjects should show their loyalty by accepting Sunni teachings. All Shi'ites became potential targets of persecution as Abbasid assassins spread across the empire, searching out imams and surviving descendants of the Prophet. Under this pressure, smaller sects disappeared and the partisans of Ali divided into two dominant sects. The distinction between "Sevener" Ismaili and "Twelver" Shi'a, rests on the number of imams that would follow Husayn before the last of each line was occulted, to become the hidden Mahdi. Division was again dressed in a complex dispute over legitimacy. Some years before his death in 765, Imam Jafar had named his eldest son Ismail as successor. Then, when the son died before the father, the majority adopted younger son Musa as their seventh imam, while more radical dissidents remained loyal to the deceased Ismail's young son Muhammad. After being smuggled away, beyond the reach of Abbasid assassins, this child succeeded in surviving into the ninth century. Refusing to accept news of his death, followers then announced that their seventh Ismaili imam Muhammad ibn Ismael had gone into occultation, from which condition he would one day return to purge the world of sin.

According to Twelver history, every imam after Husayn had been poisoned by assassins working under the instructions of Unayyad and Abbasid caliphs. When eleventh in line Hasan al Askari was murdered in 874 CE, adherents smuggled his infant son, twelth Shi'a imam Muhammad ibn Hasan into hiding, from where he kept in touch with followers through intermediaries. News then spread that he too had gone into occultation and would not communicate again until he would return as Mahdi and savior in God's good time. The major Shi'a division between radical Ismaili Severners and moderate Shi'a Twelvers was now laid down. While Twelver belief would later become mainstream Shi'a, for the coming centuries, it was the Ismaili Severners who would bring both disaster and triumph to the Islamic world.

*

According to Ismaili cosmology, world history, from creation to the end-time, was divided into five circular prophetic eras. Each was marked by the arrival of a notable "speaker" (*natiq*), followed by a "representative" (*wasi*) who was responsible for transmitting the speaker's message. Each Speaker was followed by six imams, with the seventh and last doubling as speaker of the next era. In order, these were:

The Speaker	**The Representative**	**Seventh Imam**
Adam	Seth	Noah
Noah	Shem	Abraham
Abraham	Ishmael	Moses
Moses	Aaron	Jesus
Jesus	Simon Peter	Muhammad
Muhammad	Ali ibn Abi Talib	Muhammad ibn Ismail (the Mahdi)

As years passed, expectation increasingly focused on 899 CE (by the Islamic calendar, 286 years after the *hejira*) as the date when the seventh Ismaili imam and mahdi, Muhammad ibn Ismail, would return to bring retribution on the faithless. Always at risk from Abbasid assassins, carefully trained and highly motivated missionaries (who could also turn their hands to military combat) established outposts across the Muslim world.

Abu Sa'id al Hassan first visited the prosperous island of Bahrain as a missionary, but then returned in the apocalyptic year of 899 with an armed band of followers. After establishing his headquarters on the island and conquering substantial territory on the Arabian mainland, he set about building a messianic state on professed principles of reason and equality. After passing through seven stages of initiation, followers—known as Qurmatians—received equal portions of land, while also enjoying freedom from taxation, and access to interest-free loans. Later travelers described a flourishing trading and farming community, whose prosperity was based on the labor of many thousand Ethiopian slaves.

If the Qurmatians did look after their own, they could be spectacularly violent to outsiders. After Abu Said was killed in battle, his fanatical son Abu Tahir launched a merciless jihad against usurping Abbasids and all Sunni Muslims. After narrowly failing to capture Baghdad, he then launched an attack on the Holy City of Mecca at pilgrimage time. During 17 dreadful days of slaughter in 930 CE, his forces massacred many residents and—at least by report—some 20,000 pilgrims. At the Ka'bah, he filled the holy Zamzam Well with bodies and carried off the Black Stone, which was held to ransom for 20 years until an Abbasid caliph bought the precious object back at very high cost. Angry Ismailis asked how Abu Tahir could have brought their movement into such disrepute.

This is a sacred place where a murder was unlawful even in the age of ignorance; and the defamation of the people living in Mecca is considered inhuman. You have violated that tradition, and even rooted out the Black Stone, and brought it to your land. . . . God curse you and be again accursed and execrable.[33]

Meanwhile, the author of this rebuke, Abdullah Al-Mahdi, had been busy establishing his own Ismaili caliphate. After narrowly escaping from Syria, he established a power base in Tunisia in 920 and set about the larger conquest of North Africa. After announcing that Muhammad ibn Ismail had not, after all, been the last imam and coming up with three "hidden imams" to link himself back to Fatima and the Prophet, he announced that the positions of first Fatimid caliph eleventh Ismaili imam were combined in his person. By now, the Baghdad Abbasids had also lost control of the eastern Islamic lands to powerful Ismaili families, but, once in positions of authority, these new rulers chose to put extremism behind them to rule in manner designed conciliate both Sunni and Shi'a subjects.

*

Even as rulers and imams were constructing elaborate patterns of inheritance, two major cultural movements were carrying Islamic civilization to ever-higher levels of sophistication. On the one side, Sufism was putting down the foundation for later mystical thought, while, on the other, a revival of Aristotelian philosophy was laying the basis for analytical scholasticism and enlightened learning. Analysing Sufism has been likened to describing an elephant in a totally dark room; as inquirers feel their own part of the beast, all give different descriptions. Having once rejected the intellectual path, the enquirer can select from a wide variety of routes to understanding—stories, poetry, sacred readings, art, calligraphy, rituals, physical exercises, dance, and prayer. Many of the greatest Sufi teachers were content to earn their living in the simplest of jobs while seeking to become men and women "who prefer God to everything so that God prefers them to everything."[34] Rejecting doctrinal religion, the Sufis pursued that ancient Gnostic search for the hidden meaning that was thought to lie behind all faith and knowledge. Although rooted in the Shi'a, Sufi wisdom and practices would cross into the Sunni and find followers within both Judaism and Christianity.

After Socrates died in ancient Athens, he passed the philosophic tradition on to his two most brilliant pupils. Until this time, Greek culture and learning been mainly filtered through the intuitive tradition of the visionary Plato, but the time for a re-evaluation of the more scientifically oriented Aristotle had now arrived. Abbasid caliph al-Ma'mun set this process in motion in the early ninth century when he established a House of Wisdom as a center of all knowledge in his capital city of Baghdad. Here, scholars labored over translations of works on mathematics, astronomy, medicine, chemistry, zoology, and geography from Greek, Indian, and Persian original manuscripts. The Caliph also built an observatory and imported the Indian system of mathematical notation, which, for the first time, included a symbol for zero. Angry traditionalists protested against this ruler "who squandered the public treasury of the Muslims in translating the books of atheistic, Greek, materialistic philosophers, an act which resulted in the denial of Muhammad's prophethood and of the resurrection after death."[35] After a slow start, centers of learning spread across the Arab world from Isfahan, Aleppo, and Cairo in the east to Fez in Morocco and Cordoba in Spain. Scholars from across the Islamic world converged on Cairo when the Fatimid caliph established Al-Azhar mosque in 972 as a university for the study of both religious and secular subjects.

Restless Persian scholar Ibn Sina (known to the world as Avicenna) produced some 450 treatises that ranged across all areas of knowledge, with a particular focus on interpreting the rationalist philosophy of Aristotle to his own generation. This task did pose serious problems. Since Aristotle had built his philosophy on the assumption that nothing beyond the logical web of cause and effect could be accepted as true, tales of miracles and heaven and hell must either be quietly ignored or interpreted as allegories. While Avicenna would remain a pious Muslim, his blind contemporary al Ma'ari travelled into dangerous territory. His sayings still find a place in humanist collections. "They all err—Moslems, Christians, Jews and Magians (Zoroastrians)... One man intelligent without religion and one religious without intellect."

O fools, awake! The rites ye sacred hold
Are but a cheat contrived by men of old
Who lusted after wealth and gained their lust
And died in baseness—and their law is dust.[36]

Controversy could be a drawn-out process. Islamic orthodoxy's most powerful defender, Abu Hamid, was born 21 years after Avicenna died. After being orphaned young, he was raised as a Sufi and adopted the name of Al-Ghazali, the Spinner, which was code for a gazelle, or lover of God. As a Sufi, Al-Ghazali was bitterly opposed to the Aristotelian method of penetrating truth by "accumulating facts and making deductions" rather than "developing a fine line of communication with ultimate knowledge"[37]; as a Muslim, he became convinced that Aristotle only offered a route to unbelief. He, therefore, withdrew into the desert, to return after 12 years as the ultimate "Authority of Islam."

Al-Ghazali laid down that scholars could work in the natural sciences on condition that their conclusions never contradicted revealed teachings. By this rule, Avicenna had clearly left the House of Faith. Al-Ghazali's major work, *The Incoherence of the Philosophers*, targeted all Aristotelians.

Anyone who changes the apparent meaning without a decisive and (clearly demonstrated) proof must be taxed with unbelief. Such is one who denies the corporeal resurrection of the body and sensible punishments in the hereafter on the basis of conjectures, fancies and claims of improbabilities without clear proof.... There is no (clearly demonstrated) proof of the impossibility of the bodily resurrection of souls. Mentioning such a notion would severely harm the religion.[38]

To reinforce the point, Al-Ghazali published his own most graphic descriptions of the bliss of paradise and punishments of hell.

According to Aristotle's cosmology, the world, with all its attributes and species, had existed eternally in the past and would continue to exist forever. Unsurprisingly, Al-Ghazali found that this was a direct contradiction of the Islamic universe, which was finitely constrained between Creation and the Hour. As the center of scholarship moved to Muslim Spain, Cordovan scholar Ibn Rushd (Averroes) mustered scholarly arguments to prove that "first existent acts," which never began and will never cease, can exist within a created world.[39] "If it is eternal in the sense that it is an eternal process of origination and that its origination has no beginning nor end, then certainly that which conveys the meaning of eternal organization has a greater right to be called 'creation' than that which conveys the meaning of a limited creation."[40] Still, like Origen before him, Averröes did recognize that the mass of people had to be offered a simpler faith if religion was to fulfill its function as guardian of morality and social order.

In short the philosophers believe that religious laws are necessary political arts, the principles of which are taken from natural reason and inspiration, especially in what is common to all religions, although religions differ here more or less. The philosophers further hold that one must not object through a positive or through a negative statement to any of the general religious principles, for instance whether it is obligatory to serve God or not, and still more whether God does or does not exist, and they affirm this also concerning other religious principles, for instance bliss in the beyond or eternal punishment.[41]

Both Avicenna and the younger Averröes were leading physicians, who deserve to be rated among the fathers of modern medicine and pharmacology. Avicenna justified the Aristotelian theories of causation from observation in day-to-day practice. If it can be repeatedly shown that the same medicine cures a particular illness in a variety of patients, then this relationship of cause and effect has been clearly established. Al-Ghazali, in contrast, argued that there can be no natural causal links in a world that has been created by God. By his own illustration, when cotton comes into contact with a fire, it is still God, not the fire, that burns the cotton. It follows from this that, if God is the immanent cause of everything, there can be little reason to study natural phenomena. After Al-Ghazali's orthodox beliefs had recaptured the intellectual field, Islamic scholars made little further contribution to scientific advancement.

Backward Western Europe had been far removed from centers of scholarship. Then, as Islamic culture took hold in accessible Spain, large numbers of Christians from Bologna, Paris, Oxford, and other emerging centers of learning arrived to explore the huge body of knowledge that was stored in such places as Cordova. They returned carrying translations of Aristotle, new medicines, and such treasures as the abacus and astrolabe. This transmission of Arab learning across the Pyrannees would trigger a powerful burgeoning of European scholarship.

As Christian monarchs launched into the long process of Spanish reconquest, a Muslim poet could only bewail the passing of this glittering Islamic civilization.

> Where is Cordoba, the seat of great learning,
> And how many scholars of high repute remain there?
> And where is Seville, the home of mirthful gatherings
> On its great river, cooling and brimful with water? ...
> Despoiled of Islam, now peopled by infidels!
> Those mosques have now been changed into churches,
> Where the bells are ringing and crosses are standing.[42]

5

The Day of Antichrist Approaches: Europe before 1346

By 1000 CE, few Europeans had acquired the habit of measuring history by dates and that millennial watershed apparently passed with little concern. Still doom paintings that were designed to strike the fear of imminent judgment into the hearts of illiterate people were already appearing on church walls and society was awash with end-time imagery, belief, and terror. In particular, virtually every medieval man and woman, from pope and emperor to the lowest serf, carried some vision of that "ancient enemy"—the Antichrist—who would usher in the last things. While a few sophisticated scholars might prefer to allegorize Antichrist as a generalized force of evil, most interpreted him as a physical figure of destruction. Multitalented abbess Hildegard of Bingen summoned gruesome imagery to describe how a supernatural demonic creature would emerge from Mother Church's womb.

> From the navel to the groin she (the church) had various scaly spots. In her vagina there appeared a monstrous and totally black head with fiery eyes, ears like the ears of a donkey, nostrils and mouth like those of a lion, gnashing with vast open mouth and sharpening its horrible iron teeth in a horrid manner.[1]

According to one stubborn tradition, the faithful needed to watch for a Jew of the tribe of Dan, who would have been conceived by Satan on the Whore of Babylon. As the pseudo-Metdothius fable became more widely known, it was even claimed that those dreadful creatures locked behind Alexander's eastern gates were none other than the 10 lost tribes of Israel who ate "only the meat both of humans and of brute animals as well as that of aborted foetuses." When the Antichrist appeared in the last times, these Jewish destroyers would emerge "from the four corners of the earth, and will surround the entire camp of the saints and the great city of Rome . . . No wonder for their number is like that of the sand which is on the shores of the sea; it is certain that no people, no kingdom will be able to resist them."[2] For all the competition from false Christians and destructive Jews, those who seriously searched for the Antichrist could never overlook the threat from Islam. Since Muhammad himself was long dead, suspicion could fall on Saladin or the whole body of those who professed the Prophet's faith.

In 1073, monk-pope Gregory VII, known as Hildebrand, decided that he would never achieve the much-needed church reform without first destroying the influence that secular rulers' wielded over clerical appointments. In particular, he aimed to break the widespread practices of *nepotism*—the promotion of family members—and *simony*—the sale of religious positions and favors—which were together threatening to draw national churches into the hereditary feudal system. Hildebrand took the papacy into an apocalyptic struggle.

I have labored with all my powers that the Holy Church . . . might remain free, pure and Catholic. But because this is not pleasing to our ancient enemy, he stirred up his members against us to bring it to nought . . . and no wonder! For the nearer the day the Antichrist approaches, the harder he fights to crush out the Christian faith.

Lines of division between church and state would always be confused in a society where bishops and religious houses ranked among the largest landowners and members of the clergy filled key positions of state. Throughout the medieval period, popes remained locked in conflict with a succession of Holy Roman Emperors, whose power centered on the German-speaking lands, as they later did also with kings of France. Bitter protagonists faced each other across the centuries—Pope Alexander III and Holy Roman Emperor Frederick I (Barbarossa): Gregory VII and Henry IV: Gregory IX and Frederick II; Boniface VIII and Philip IV of France: John XXII and Emperor Louis IV. While emperors commanded the larger battalions, popes could call up the words of Jesus.

And I tell you, you are Peter, and on this rock I will build my church, and the gates of Hades will not prevail against it. I will give you the keys of the kingdom of heaven, and whatever you bind on earth will be bound in heaven, and whatever you loose on earth will be loosed in heaven.[3]

By virtue of this "power to bind and loose," any pope, however corrupt or unworthy, had sole right to define the boundaries of orthodox belief and excommunicate any ruler, along with all his subjects. As the struggle progressed, popes even claimed that, as God's representative on earth, they possessed "fullness of power" over all rulers in secular as well as religious affairs. This startling assertion was supported by a highly prized document known as the *Donation of Constantine*. This eighth-century forgery purported to prove that the first Christian emperor had transferred supreme authority over the Western Roman Empire to Pope Sylvester I and his successors in St. Peter's chair. Believing that the story was true, poet Dante Alighieri would blame Constantine for all the church's ills.

Well then, tell me what was the amount of the treasure
Our Lord required of Peter before
He handed over the keys into his keeping? . . .
Ah Constantine, how much ill you produced
Not by your conversion but by that endowment
Which the first rich father accepted from you.[4]

Pseudo Methodius could now be quoted as counter to high papal pretentions. While John of Patmos had identified Roman Emperor Nero as the Beast Antichrist, this unknown author brought a savior emperor into the apocalyptic narrative. In this medieval clash of ideologies, either pope or emperor could be reviled as Antichrist or blessed as redeemer Messiah.

*

In 1095, Pope Urban II summoned a church council in the French city of Clermont. When routine business was finished, he mounted an open-air platform to address the large crowd that had gathered to hear a very special message. Since five different chroniclers left broadly similar accounts, Urban's words can be reconstructed with some accuracy. First, he described how Byzantine emperor Alexios I had asked for Western help in defending his Christian lands against Seljuk Turks, who had broken out of the Asian steppes and now blocked the pilgrim route to Jerusalem.

O what a disgrace if a race so despised as the Turks, so base and full of demons, should overcome a people so faithful to the All-Powerful God . . . Let those who delight in making private wars against the faithful turn their wrath against infidels, who should have been driven back before now. . . . Let robbers become soldiers of Christ. Let those dejected in mind and body offer themselves to the glory of heaven. And if any who go should lose his life, by land or sea or in fighting the pagans, his sins will be remitted. This I will grant by the power invested in me by God.[5]

Rewards and punishment were clear-cut. Those who took the cross and continued to the end could be assured of salvation; those who made a promise that they did not fulfill or who turned back would be excommunicated. Even as he spoke, Urban was interrupted by shouts of *"deus le volt"*—"God wills it" and listeners stepped forward to take the cross. Among the first was Aldemar, Bishop of Le Puy. In a bid to keep the venture under direct church control, Urban made this prelate overall leader of the First Crusade.

Of the many images in Revelation, it was that of New Jerusalem that resonated most powerfully at the start of this second Christian millennium. Men and women who had recently survived all-too-real famine and hunger thrilled to the Pope's vision of a golden city and land that flowed with milk and honey.

Jerusalem is the navel of the world; the land is fruitful above all others, like another paradise of delights. The Redeemer of the human race has made it illustrious by His advent, has beautified it by His presence, has consecrated it by His suffering, has redeemed it by His death, has gloried it by His burial.[6]

The more Urban spoke of the New Jerusalem, the more certain it seemed that Jesus could not come again until his holy city was once more in Christian hands. How far Urban himself interpreted his crusade in apocalyptic terms can remain a matter of debate; certainly a huge wave of End-Time fervor swept across Europe. The image of the Antichrist loomed large as "popular epics portrayed Moslems as monsters with two sets of horns (front and back) and called them devils with no right to live."[7] As Urban preached his crusade across southern France, others carried it into Normandy and Flanders. Most notably, small and elderly Peter the Hermit drew huge crowds as he rode his donkey across the German-speaking world. Among those who responded were impoverished journeymen and laborers from new manufacturing cities of Flanders and the Rhineland, who owed fealty to no lord. As Peter's People's Crusade moved slowly toward the Danube, it continued to attract a motley band of masterless men—many accompanied by their women and children—who were fired by this unique chance to find a better life while achieving the eternal salvation that had seemed so unattainable within their brutal everyday surroundings.

*

Substantial Jewish communities had become established in the Rhineland as businesspeople moved out of southern Europe to take advantage of increased trading opportunities on that river. Since these newcomers brought much-needed capital and skill, Jew and Christian had previously lived together in acceptable—if not always uninterrupted—harmony in cities such as Cologne, Speyer, Worms, and Mainz. Tension increased as undisciplined gangs of crusaders now scavenged their way along the riverbanks. If these zealots saw Muslims as demons, at least they were remote demons; here in the Rhineland, agents of the Antichrist were living very visibly within the Christian community. A chronicler constructed the thoughts that must pass through crusaders' heads:

Among them [Rhineland citizens] is a people which does not acknowledge deity. What is more, their ancestors crucified God. Why should we let them live? Why should they dwell among us? Let our swords begin with their heads. After that we shall go on the way of our pilgrimage.[8]

Tension heightened as tales of how the Jews were poisoning wells and sacrificing Christian children began to circulate among crusader groups. The greatest danger centered on a single band of religious fanatics that had formed around minor nobleman Emicho, Count of Leningen. Chroniclers recorded that this man saw himself as a latter-day Saul, chosen by God to smite the Philistines, and that he had received an apocalyptic revelation that promised a coronation in heaven.[9] However motivated, Emicho "had no mercy on the elderly, on young men and young women, on infants and sucklings, on the ill. He made the people of the Lord like dust to be trampled under foot."[10] During that summer of 1096, Emicho's crusaders systematically wiped out whole Jewish communities that could number several thousand people. Some Christian rulers did try to stop the slaughter. From his base in southern Italy, the Emperor Henry IV issued instructions that Jews in his empire must be left in peace, but his voice could carry no weight from such a distance. The Bishop of Speyer saved lives more effectively by evacuating his city's Jews to fortified villages. The archbishop of Mainz's offer of shelter within his palace walls failed when his soldiers discovered that burghers had opened the city gates to Emicho's men. When young Jewish men men tried to fend off the invaders, they were quickly brushed aside. When offered the option of conversion or death, Rabbi Isaac ben R. Moses "stretched out his neck and they cut off his head immediately."[11] Reports described how others in the Mainz community chose to die.

> The Jews, seeing that their Christian enemies were attacking them and their children, and were sparing no age, fell upon one another—brothers, children, wives, mothers and sisters—and slaughtered one another. Horrible to say, mothers cut the throats of nursing children with knives and stabbed others, preferring to perish thus at their own hands rather than be killed by the weapons of the uncircumcised.[12]

Emicho's personal crusade would reach a humiliating end when his followers were cut to pieces by Christian Hungarian knights.

*

Peter the Hermit left Germany at the head of a varied collection of some 20,000 crusaders. Having sold their possessions and severed home roots, these poor people experienced great hardship as they crossed territory that could produce barely enough food to support the local population. Many died of hunger or were picked off by marauding bands; others died in battle with Christian lords and kings. Hostility increased as news went ahead that unruly pilgrims had flattened and plundered the city of Belgrade—thankfully after its citizens had made for the hills.

Having expected to receive help from professional soldiers serving under their feudal lords, EmperorAlexios I was appalled to see Peter's rag-tag survivors arrive at his city's gates. He did try to greet them courteously, even allowing parties into Constantinople on controlled sightseeing tours, but, when these pilgrims started stealing anything they could find, even to the lead off church roofs, he decided that they must move on without delay. As Peter's pilgrims advanced into Seljuk territory—indiscriminately massacring Muslims and Greek Christians as they passed—Peter recognized that his rabble was unfit to confront the full Turkish army. He had returned to Constantinople when they were cut to pieces at Civetot. "The People's Crusade was over," concluded one historian. "It had cost many thousands of lives; it had tried the patience of the Emperor and his subjects; and it had taught that faith alone, without wisdom and discipline, would not open the road to Jerusalem."[13]

A greatly reduced band of ragged and barefooted survivors did manage to coalesce into a tightly knit band, which became known as the Tarfurs. Historians have not established the name's derivation or the identity of that King of the Tarfurs—possibly a Norman or Flemish knight—who took a prominent part in planning the later campaign. Sheltered behind huge shields constructed from any detritus that lay to hand, these Tarfurs did fight fiercely, but, as they travelled through Syria tales of rape and murder followed close behind. Muslim chroniclers recorded how defenders of Antioch watched them dig up and eat Muslim bodies with apparent relish. Such tales might be dismissed as black propaganda were they not also confirmed in the Christian record.

Some of our men did not find there what they needed due to both the length of the stop and also the difficulty of finding food. . . . After a time some cut open dead bodies, to find gold coins which had been hidden inside their bellies, while others sliced the flesh into pieces to cook and eat it.[14]

Urban's First Crusade ended in an orgy of violence when Jerusalem fell on November 16, 1099. In this moment of triumph, crusaders rushed through the streets, killing every Muslim—man woman and child—who fell into their hands. When the Jews took shelter in their synagogue, the building was burned down over their heads. Then, after the destruction was over, blood-drenched crusaders offered thanks to God in the Church of the Holy Sepulcher.

Writing in 1951, crusade historian Steven Runciman summarized the atrocity's long-term effects.

No one can say how many victims it involved, but it emptied Jerusalem of both its Muslim and Jewish inhabitants. Many even of the Christians were horrified by what they had done; and amongst the Moslems . . . there was henceforward a clear determination that the Franks must be driven out. It was this bloodthirsty proof of Christian fanaticism that re-created the fanaticism of Islam. When, later, wiser Latins in the West sought to find some basis on which Christian and Moslems could work together, the memory of the massacre stood always in their way.[15]

*

According to Robert Grosseteste, Bishop of Lincoln, heresy is "an opinion chosen by human perception, contrary to Holy Scripture, publicly avowed and obstinately defended."[16] When properly interpreted, the Bible could be used to justify even the most brutal act. "If a man does not abide in me," says the fourth gospel, "he is cast forth as a branch and withers; and the branches are thrown into the fire and burnt."[17] While Byzantine emperors were already burning heretics at the stake in the sixth century CE, it appears that the punishment was used only randomly in the West until the late twelfth century. Innocent III's Third Lateran Council of 1215 then laid down that burning should be the standard penalty for recalcitrant heretics. Innocent's nephew Clement IX founded the Roman Inquisition in 1233 and Innocent IV approved the use of torture for extracting confessions some two decades later. Inquisitors were instructed to hunt for heretics with all diligence and those convicted had no right of appeal against a guilty verdict. The use of fire deprived the victim of a physical body for the day of resurrection while also providing onlookers with a dramatic enactment of those flames of hell that would engulf sinners on the Last Day of Judgment.

Orthodox believers could claim grounds for concern. In 1018, a group of preachers had appeared in southern France who were reported to have "denied baptism, the cross and all sound doctrine. They did not eat meat, as though they were monks and pretended to be celibate, but amongst themselves they denied all sound doctrine. They were messengers of Antichrist and caused many to wander from the faith."[18] Just four years later, 10 apparently pious clergymen were identified as heretics in the city of Orléans and burned to death by an angry mob. As strange teachings spread across southern France and northern Italy, concerned lay-people petitioned the authorities to "stand forth against the new heretics who everywhere and in almost all churches boil up from the pit of hell as though their prince were about to be loosed and the day of the lord was at hand."[19]

It has been suggested that these religious ideas, which appear to carry both Zoroastrian and Gnostic influence, may have been brought along the Danube by wandering preachers, who were following the trade routes from Persia.[20] While scattered groups of Cathars ("the pure ones") appeared across Europe in the course of the eleventh century, the main concentration was in southern France—where they also became known as Albigensians, after their center in the Languedoc city of Albi. Rejecting the Catholic hierarchy, Cathars appointed their own bishops and clergy. Behind them was a larger mixed-sex class of *perfecti*, who were believed to have access to the scriptures' hidden meaning. These dedicated people lived modestly within the community, following their own trades, as they ministered to those common folk who were known as "good people." Cathar faith was grounded in the dualist belief in an eternal conflict between good and evil, and, because the temporal world belonged to Satan, the faithful could expect nothing better than a life of suffering. As part of this fallen world, the church's whole priestly hierarchy was redundant and its sacraments worthless. Secular rulers also had no right to inflict their laws on true believers. Baffled how a devout lifestyle could coexist with clearly heretical belief, inquisitors insisted that apparent moral rectitude must serve as cover for secret orgies and wickedness, but such accusations were never substantiated by evidence.

Innocent III—arguably the most powerful of all popes—was elected in 1198, just 11 years after Saladin's Muslim army retook Jerusalem on October 2, 1187. Facing a disaster of such magnitude, he asked whether God would ever permit Christian armies to succeed in the Holy Land as long as heretics were still allowed to flourish so near to home. In 1204, he sent Cistercian monk Arnauld-Amalric to preach the orthodox gospel in Cathar country. Then, when sermonizing bore no fruit, the same man returned at the head of a notoriously brutal crusade. Innocent appears to have read his legate's report on the destruction of Béziers without concern.

While discussions were still going on with the barons about the release of those in the city who were deemed to be Catholics, the servants and other persons of low rank ... attacked the city without waiting for orders from their leaders. To our amazement, crying "to arms, to arms!," within the space of two or three hours they crossed the ditches and the walls and Béziers was taken. Our men spared no one, irrespective of rank, sex or age, and put to the sword almost 20,000 people. After this great slaughter the whole city was despoiled and burnt.[21]

Arnauld-Amalric may have been more personally implicated than his account suggested. As observers protested that Catholics and Cathars were dying together, he is reported to have replied, "kill them all, God will know his own."[22]

Violence increased after Simon de Montfort the Elder assumed leadership of the Albigensian Crusade. This French nobleman appears to have seen no contradiction in combining devout religious orthodoxy with extreme brutality and a burning desire to take over the lands of all southern noblemen who showed Cathar sympathies. In the first of many mass executions, he supervised the burning of some 140 perfecti at Carcasson on a single pyre. As his soldiers approached Toulouse, they set upon peasants who were at work in their fields before killing some 10,000 more within the city.

The Count de Montfort sent his brutal sergeants into Toulouse to begin their exactions, their filthy affronts and atrocities. All through the town they went, threatening and clubbing their victims, seizing whatever they wanted in every quarter. In every street you would have seen unhappy men and women weeping and in pain. Bitter tears they shed, bitterly their hearts mourned, as de Montford's men took and the townspeople gave.[23]

With a death toll variably estimated at between 200,000 and one million, the Albigensian Crusade has been rated (alongside the 30 Years War and twentieth-century genocides) among Europe's great humanitarian disasters. After the crusading impetus flagged, Clement XI's Roman Inquisition took up the unrelenting task of hunting surviving Cathars out of their secret places.

Having learnt his trade as an inquisitor in Languedoc, fanatical monk Conrad of Marburg returned to his native Germany. After showing unusual dedication to the task of burning Cathars across Thuringia and Hesse, Gregory extended

The Day of Antichrist Approaches: Europe before 1346   69

his authority across all the German states. News of Conrad's arrival at the head of a band of angry followers could strike fear into any community. In the chronicler's words,

> Throughout various cities the Preaching Friars cooperated with him and with his aforementioned lieutenants; so great was the zeal of all that from no one, even though merely under suspicion, would any excuse or counterplea be accepted, no exception or testimony be admitted, no opportunity for defense be afforded, not even a recess for deliberation be allowed. Forthwith he must confess himself guilty and have his head shaved as a sign of penance, or deny his crime and be burned. Furthermore one who has had his head shaved must make known his associates; otherwise he again risks the penalty of death by burning. Whence it is thought that many innocents have been burned for many ... brought charges of which they were ignorant against those to whom they wished ill.[24]

After five years of terror, Conrad and his lieutenants were waylaid and murdered by the roadside. The chronicler recorded that few mourned their passing.

*

As soon as the kings of England and France heard that Jerusalem had fallen to Saladin, they set about putting together the Third "Crusade of the Princes." Richard I of England was awaiting good sailing weather in Sicily when he heard that the abbot of a Calabrian monastery "had the spirit of prophesy and used to predict what was to come to the people." Joachim of Fiore had indeed foreseen Saladin's conquest, and Richard was anxious to know how his own expedition would fare with the task of winning Jerusalem back. Summoned from his monastery in the toe of Italy, this unassuming churchman stood before a charismatic monarch and his Anglo-Norman courtiers.

While Judgment Day and the End-Time had always retained a prominent position in church teaching, Joachim was the first serious theologian in 700 years to examine those concepts through the prism of John of Patmos' *Book of Revelation*. Rejecting uncanonical Greek concepts such as as Carpathian gates and savior-emperors, his brain overflowed with an apocalyptic world of magical numbers, beasts and dragons, angels and trumpets. Before answering Richard's question, he had to convince his listeners that the world was indeed nearing its end and, to achieve this, he needed to identify two beasts—one from the sea and the other from the land—that would mark the arrival of the Apocalypse. He therefore argued that the Muslims (the beast from the sea) and heretical Christians (the beast from the land), would shortly come together to make war on true Christians. Then he put names to all seven heads of John's apocalyptic dragon. The first five—Herod, Nero, Constantius, Muhammad, and Melsemothus—were figures from history (though a variety of more credible candidates would later challenge obscure North African chief Melsemothus' right to the fifth head). The sixth belonged to Saladin—who was still alive—and the seventh—the Antichrist—had probably already reached the age of about 15. According to

Joachim's visual representation, a swirling figure half way down the dragon's body represented the future Tribulation, while Gog and a further "ultimate Antichrist" were lodged in the dragon's tail. Bringing all these signs together, he assured Richard that his crusade would recapture Jerusalem.

> Then the King of England asked him "When will this be?" Joachim answered him, "When seven years have passed since the day of Jerusalem's capture" [i.e., on October 2, 1194]. The King of England said to him, "Why therefore have we come thus far so quickly?" Joachim answered, "Your coming was most necessary. Because the Lord will give you victory over your enemies and will exalt your name over all the princes of the earth."[25]

Back in the real world, Richard's army retreated from the holy land—mission unfulfilled—two years before Joachim's promised date. Undeterred, the Calabrian abbot continued his quest to understand the end-time mysteries. "For God," he declared, "who in times past endowed the prophets with the spirit of prophesy has given me the *spiritus intelligentae* so that I can clearly understand all the mysteries of the Scriptures."[26] Comprehensively rejecting all Aristotelian disciplines of logical thought that were permeating northward out of Islamic Spain, Joachim embarked on a search for the deeper spiritual meanings that could be only be revealed through intuition.

Like John of Patmos, Joachim played with magic numbers that could help him order historical events in cosmic patters. While the Ismaili Muslims had organized history, from Creation to the Hour, into six separate eras, Joachim preferred seven. He then placed these eras (aetates), within three larger ages (*status*), which he named after the persons of the Trinity. The First Age of the Father, from Adam to Jesus, covered the time when humans lived under fear of the Old Testament law. The Second Age of the Son—from the birth of Jesus to some point in the very near future—was the time of the church, when humans had become reconciled to God. The world now stood at the end of the fifth era of the second age, when "the fifth angel poured his bowl on the throne of the beast, and its kingdom was plunged into darkness; people gnawed their tongues in agony, and cursed the God of heaven because of their pains and sores, and they did not repent of their deeds."[27] Joachim forecast that two groups of "spiritual men" would emerge to help secure victory over the Antichrist and the Third Age of the Holy Spirit would finally arrive some time before the year 1260 CE. Then "a new leader will arise out of Babylon. Namely a universal pope of the new Jerusalem, that is, of the holy Mother Church."[28] At that glorious time, the Eastern and Western churches would be reconciled, the Jews converted to Christ, and all forms of punishment would become redundant. The fourth angel from Revelation would then appear, carrying "the eternal gospel to proclaim to those who live on the earth—to every nation, tribe, language and people."[29] At this great culmination, humans would be loosed from the rigors of both secular and religious law.

Always a devoted son of the church, Joachim of Fiore kept succeeding popes up to date with progress, and they, in turn, encouraged him to continue this esoteric quest to unravel the secrets of Creation and Judgment and, shortly before he died in 1202, Joachim did manage to submit final manuscripts to Innocent III. While his interpretation was clearly out of line with the Augustinian tradition, Revelation remained a canonical book of the Bible, and it was not at all clear that the abbot's millennial interpretation could be called heretical. To papal eyes, it could only be preferable to pseudo-Methodius' alternative apocalypse, which assigned all credit for salvation to a divine emperor. While Innocent's Fourth Lateran Council did register some concern over the Calabrian abbot's interpretation of the Trinity, half a century would pass before his whole millennial structure would be placed under examination for heresy.

*

When Francis of Assisi approached Innocent III, seeking permission to found the order of mendicant (begging) friars, members of the curia advised that approving such a radically new rule could only provoke conflict within the church. According to legend, Innocent was inclined to turn down the request until he had a dream in which he saw Francis holding up his own tottering palace. At about the same time, Spanish canon Dominic de Guzmán was returning from a preaching tour in Cathar country when he met up with papal legates returning home after their preaching mission had failed. Dominic dismissed their whole approach to the task.

It is not by the display of power and pomp, cavalcades of retainers, and richly-housed palfreys, or by gorgeous apparel, that the heretics win proselytes; it is by zealous preaching, by apostolic humility, by austerity, by seeming, it is true, but by seeming holiness. Zeal must be met by zeal, humility by humility, false sanctity by real sanctity, preaching falsehood by preaching truth.[30]

Joachim was vindicated when Dominic, in turn, received papal approval to establish his own order of preaching friars. With Francis' Friars Minor and Dominic's Order of Preachers, his two groups of "spiritual men" were now in place and ready to usher in the Third Age. To add to the general wonder, forged Joachite works provided details on political events that the abbot could not have known by any natural means.

Before his election as Gregory IX, Innocent III's nephew Ugolino had acted as Cardinal Protector of the Franciscan order, and he had often worn the habit and walked barefoot with the founder and his disciples. As long as this elderly pontiff remained in good health, the Franciscans could be confident that they had an ally in Peter's chair. In return, they supported the pope loyally through his protracted struggle with Holy Roman Emperor Frederick II. While Clement continued to claim supremacy over all the crowned heads of Christendom, the emperor was equally determined to stop the pope meddling in temporal affairs. To reinforce the point, Frederick set about the brutal conquest of the Papal States and much of Italy. As the struggle intensified, many Franciscans became convinced that they could see the master's prophesies unfolding before their eyes. By their interpretation, Francis of Assisi had been the fifth angel of Revelation, who loosed a time of tribulation on the world. Frederick also fitted the Antichrist's profile surprisingly well; a man of biting wit and skeptical instincts, rumor spread that he mocked Christian beliefs and sacraments and denounced Moses, Jesus, and Muhammad as frauds and deceivers. Franciscans put it about that this new Nero would be sucked into the crater of Mount Etna, which was widely believed to be hell's mouth. Even after Frederick met an unremarkable death from dysentery in 1250, it was still whispered that he remained hidden in a German mountain, from where he would break out in the Last Days and carry destruction through the world.

As forecast by Innocent III's advisers, relations between the Franciscans and members of the parish and diocesan (secular) clergy had indeed been deteriorating. In 1254, young Paris University friar Gerard of Borgo san Donninio revisited the Calabrian abbot's predictions that the Third Age of the Holy Spirit would begin by 1260 CE—which was then just six years off. In that apocalyptic year, when Joachim's third angel carried his eternal gospel through the heavens to bring in the Third Age, the writings of Joachim of Fiore would replace both Old and New Testaments as holy writ and there would be no room left on earth for bishops, priests, and monks. In the following year, the Franciscan and Dominican ministers general added to general concern by bringing out a joint statement, which announced that their two orders did indeed have a special mission to save the world in the Last Days.[31] Members of the secular clergy responded by attacking the whole mendicant principle; deducing from the Bible narrative that Jesus must have carried a purse, they argued that, while he did allow his disciples to accept gifts, he had never sanctioned begging. After waiting in Paris until the dispute died down, Franciscan Bonaventure and Dominican Thomas Aquinas took their degrees together. While both would become canonized theologians, Bonaventure came from the mystical tradition, which traced its roots to Plato, while Aquinas built his Christian theology on the teachings of Aristotle, as mediated through Avicenna. Gerard of Borgo's intervention had proved that Joachim's apocalyptic theories were still revered in the wilder reaches of Bonaventura's Franciscan order. Aquinas determined to strike at the old master's whole apocalyptic structure.

Since it was from the Abbot Joachim that the aforementioned heretics... received the stimulant of that poisonous error, our Doctor (Aquinas) sought out Joachim's book in a certain monastery, and when it was presented read the whole thing through. Whenever he found anything erroneous or suspect, he condemned it with underlining. He forbade that the book should be read or believed and nullified its teachings with his own hand.[32]

*

During the last years of his life, Francis of Assisi had become increasingly concerned that his own Franciscans were being drawn into the prevailing culture of clerical excess. He therefore produced a *Last Testament* that laid down rules of behavior in the clearest possible manner. "Those who came to receive life," he declared, "gave all that they had to the poor and were content with one tunic patched inside and out, with a cord and trousers. And we did not wish to have more." The document commanded, "by the obedience they owe me" that Franciscans "should not accept any churches, poor dwellings, or anything else constructed for them unless these buildings reflect the holy poverty promised by us in the rule." He then insisted that his friars should not seek any protection from Rome, but "wherever they are not received, they should flee into another land and do penance with God's blessing."[33] By this time, however, his Franciscans already owned friaries, churches, schools, and clinics. While all agreed that his ideal of holy poverty must be preserved, the order divided over how this ideal should be interpreted. At issue was the fundamental principal of whether they were simply forbidden to own goods and property as individuals or, as the Testament now decreed, that they could neither own nor use anything beyond the strict necessities for life. That raised a further problem of whether any line could, in practice, be drawn between subsistence and excess. While the majority welcomed Gregory's ruling that the Final Testament was not binding on those who had taken the Franciscan vow of poverty, a hard core of rigorists—"spiritual Franciscans"—rejected any compromise. In their eyes, Francis' final Testament approached the sanctity of holy writ, and any pope or minister general of the order who tried to modify it would himself be guilty of heresy. Most crucially, it soon became clear that these rigorists placed their vow of poverty above that of obedience—whether that was due to an immediate superior or to the pope himself.

We believe that we really would be apostates before God and fugitives from the eremetical state if of our own will we were to abandon the way of life to which we have been called by the inspiration of God and the confirmation of the Supreme Pontiff. This would make us perjurers before Christ and worthy of damnation.[34]

In Bonaventure's eyes, such disobedience could only be classed as heresy. After becoming minister general in 1257, he clamped down on dissidents and steered the order away from Joachite speculation over end-time events. Since the Roman Inquisition recruited investigators from both orders of friars, conformist Franciscans now sat in judgment over their own spiritual brethren.

As Gerard of Borgo san Donninio languished in prison chains, rigorist theologian Peter John Olivi toured Franciscan houses delivering his commentary on the Calabrian abbot's vision of a Third Age. Facing persecution from the both the Vatican and the General Chapter of their own order, spiritual Franciscans now looked for the arrival of Joachim's "angel pope," who would bring the church back to the path of holiness. When Nicholas IV died in 1292, cardinals spent the next two years quarrelling over the choice of a successor. As a desperate compromise, they finally elected the unlikely Pietro Angelerio, who was not only some 85 years old but also a member of the strict Order of the Poor Hermits. Now, at last, the spirituals could rejoice that they had found their angel pope and, as his only decisive act, he did give them permission to form their own rigorist order. But, as soon as he had been installed as Celestine V, this elderly pope started to prepare an act of abdication, which he implemented after just five months in office. To Spiritual eyes, the election of lawyer-cleric Boniface VIII could only mean that the papacy had once again fallen into the clutches of the Antichrist. Not only described by enemies as a "horrible sodomite,"[35] Boniface also made his own End-Time position clear by asking "why so many fools were awaiting the end of the world."[36] After capturing, imprisoning, and reputedly murdering Celestine, Boniface overturned his predecessor's permission for the formation of the new rigorist order. Rumors now circulated that angel-pope Celestine V remained in a state of occultation, from which he would one day return to reclaim his rightful position and save the faithful poor.

Florentine poet Dante Alighieri, who had his own reasons for hating Boniface, placed this pope's condemnation in the mouth of Simon Peter.

The man who now usurps my place
—my place, my place, where there is now a vacancy
At any rate in the sight of God—
Has made my burial place a sewer for blood and filth.[37]

Dante consigned corrupt popes to the eighth circle of hell. In the *Inferno*, he and his companion Virgil found the notoriously corrupt Nicholas III in the form of an "unhappy spirit who, upside down, *was* stuck in like a stake." Mistaking Dante for Boniface (who was still alive), Nicholas called out:

Are you standing there already,
Boniface are you standing there?
My information was out by several years.
Are you so soon sated with your wealth,
For the sake of which you shamefully and deceitfully
Took the beautiful lady (the church) and made havoc of her?

Once the mistaken identity had been corrected, Nicholas explained that, when Boniface did arrive to take his place in hell, he would be sucked into a narrow fissure in the rock, "where others have been dragged down, who were my predecessors in simony."[38]

While touring Paradise, Dante found Joachim of Fiore and Thomas Aquinas (apparently happily) coexisting within a group of learned clerics.[39] But, even as Dante was recording the Calabrian abbot's bliss in heaven, his books were being publicly burned in the outside world. Just a year after Peter John Olivi died in his bed in 1298, the Franciscan General Chapter formally condemned all Olivi's and

Joachim's books as heretical. This would mark the start of a persecution within the order that would bring spiritual Franciscans and many of their sympathizers to the stake. However successfully the flames of the auto da fé could destroy human bodies, they still signally failed to obliterate Joachim of Fiore's ideas and they would continue to influence End-Time thinking within the Western church for another two centuries and beyond.

*

The high male death rate in European wars and distant crusades, and increasingly rigorous imposition of clerical celibacy, combined to create a surplus population of marriageable women across the whole of Europe. As a growing terror of female sexuality gripped this male-dominated society, women were increasingly perceived as fickle creatures whose lustful nature made them unsuited for serious responsibility. Shut out from religious and secular employment, women from the upper and middle orders of Flemish society sought companionship and spiritual support in religious communities that were dedicated to prayer, good works, and pursuit of apostolic poverty. Their piety centered on the Eucharist, which they interpreted as an enactment of the mystical union that existed between Christ and the female Christian soul.

These pious women belonged to a larger lay organization, known in full as the Poor Brethren of Penance of the Third Order of St. Francis. In this growing persecution male *beghards* and female *beguines* were interrogated about their links with spiritual Franciscans. Chief Inquisitor Bernard Gui produced a training manual which advised on the most effective method of examining these errant laypeople He instructed interrogators to ask whether suspects supported the order's heretical practice of reading "the Gospels and Epistles in the vernacular, interpreting and expounding them in their own favor and against the existing establishments of the Roman Church." As laypeople, who took their faith into the streets, bewildered beghards and beguines would then be accused of ignoring the fact that "articles of faith must be preached and expounded publicly ... not by simple laymen, but by doctors and preachers of the word of God" and were questioned on their right to wear the customary habit and live in communities that were not officially sanctioned by church authorities. Suspects were questioned over obedience to the pope, belief in purgatory and the merits of indulgences as well as on attitudes to obedience and poverty and whether spiritual Franciscans who had been burned at the stake should be regarded as holy martyrs. Finally, they were interrogated over whether they viewed the heretic Brother Peter John Olivi as "a lamp and light sent by God" and believed in Joachim's eras, ages and angels of the apocalypse.[40] Gui finally advised interrogators to watch out for any evidence that superficial piety was just a front for nameless sins—in particular, the sexual "joining of hic with hic ... when nature joins hic with haec."[41] While stubborn heretics could be burnt at the stake, those who recanted were more often consigned to dreadful prisons from which they might one day be released into a life of penance and pilgrimage, when they would wear a yellow cross on their tunics and carry rods, with which any onlooker could beat them as they saw fit.

*

While Augustinian theologians were obliged to follow the master's austere teaching on predestination, Peter John Olivi always championed the cause of human free will. "This is something," he declared, "that every human being senses with complete certainty within himself."[42] But, as determinism can bring emotions of helplessness, so freedom can open the door to libertarianism. The origins of that amorphous movement known as the Free Spirit can be traced to 1210, when a group of unusually pious clerics at the University of Paris (*Amaurians*) became aware of Joachim's doctrine of Three Ages. Basing their teaching in the Gnostic tradition, these reformers asserted that that, since "all things are one, because whatever is, is God," every believer should search for a mystical union with the divine. Under investigation, a ringleader insisted that "he could neither be consumed by fire nor tormented by torture, for he said that, insofar as he was, he was God."[43] An inquisitor recorded other Amaurian deviations.

They denied the resurrection of bodies and said that there was no paradise or hell; one who possessed the knowledge of God, as they did, had paradise within himself, but one who was in mortal sin had hell within himself, like a decayed tooth in his mouth ... If anyone was "in the spirit," they said, even if he were to commit fornication or to be fouled by any other filthiness, there would be no sin in him, because that spirit, who is God, being entirely distinct from the body, cannot sin.[44]

All but a very few who recanted their errors were burned at the stake on a charge of promoting pantheism.

Early in the next century, Paris was plunged into ferment over the trial, torture, and execution of the Grand Master and other leading members of the Order of Knights Templar. Two years later, Flemish mystic Margaret Porete faced the same inquisitor who had sent Templars to the flames. Under examination was her French-language book, *Mirror of Simple Souls*, which many would later rate as a classic of mystical devotion. In its pages, she constructs a dialogue in which Love and Reason debate that complete union with God that cannot be achieved until human logic gives way before divine inspiration. Porete wrote in sexually charged language, which echoes both the biblical *Song of Solomon* and contemporary poems of courtly love.

He is fullness,
And by this I am impregnated,
This is the divine seed and Loyal Love.[45]

Some years earlier, Margaret's home bishop had condemned the *Mirror of Simple Souls* as heretical. Since then, she had changed the text, and the revised version had been approved by three theologians, but, despite every effort, she now stood trial for her life as a lapsed heretic. Convinced that no trained scholar could have the humility to understand what she had written, she refused to speak in her own defense and was burnt at the stake in the Place de la Grève in Paris on June 1, 1310. It was said that onlookers were "moved to tears of compassion at the sight of her nobility."

It can be difficult to assign labels to different medieval "heretics." Some scholars describe Margaret Porete as a free spirit and others as a beguine, but boundaries were never clear and she surely never thought to classify herself.

Since the pope had assumed the power to define what was and was not heretical under the power to bind and loose, pious folk who chose to express their faith in unconventional terms did so at risk of their lives. While (sometimes borderline) orthodox mystics who flourished during this period would not have described themselves as Free Spirits, they did draw from the same sources of inspiration. Inquisitors who examined mystical texts phrase by phrase had little difficulty in identifying passages with apparently Gnostic and even pantheist overtones. When brought before a panel of Franciscan inquisitors, Dominican mystic Meister Eckhart marshaled his defense with quotations from both classical and Christian authors before rounding it off a scriptural text from the fourth gospel "You, the father, are in me, and I am in you that they also may be one in us."[46] Nevertheless, 17 of his propositions were pronounced "clearly heretical" and 11 more "ill-sounding, rash, and suspected of heresy." It is thought that Meister Eckhart died shortly after making a profession of faith and act of submission to the pope.

From their own viewpoint, Catholic inquisitors did have cause for concern. Through the coming centuries, distinctively dressed female and male "adepts" of the Free Spirit would roam the highways of Europe, while loosely organized sects also appeared across widely dispersed centers of population. While some would preach poverty and strict sexual chastity, others would claim freedom from all the old constraints of moral behavior. Libertarian behavior could even be justified from scripture. "To the pure all things are pure, but to the corrupt and unbelieving nothing is pure; their very minds and consciences are corrupted."[47] While it remains difficult to distinguish fact from inquisitors' propaganda, it does appear that much-persecuted "Adamites" embraced nudity and free love in both social and religious settings. Within just years of Eckhart's death, one Cologne mystic could describe this new moral anarchy through his own imagined conversation with an incorporeal image.

"Whence have you come?" The image answers "I come from nowhere."—"Tell me, what are you?"—"I am not." "What do you wish?."—"I do not wish."—"This is a miracle. Tell me, what is your name?"—"I am called Nameless Wildness." "Where does your insight lead to?"—"Into untrammeled freedom."—"Tell me, what do you call untrammeled freedom?"—"When a man lives according to his caprices without distinguishing between God and himself, and without looking before or after."[48]

While, on one level, the intense focus on inward union with God "without looking before or after" can be the very antithesis of apocalyptic belief, adepts of the Free Spirit remained heavily dependent on Joachim of Fiore's millennial vision of a Third Age of the Holy Spirit, when believers would be released from both religious and secular law. In North Italy, "poor, demented visionary" Gherardo Segarelli gathered enthusiasts—described by opponents as "debauchees, cowherds, swineherds, loafers who roamed the streets eyeing the women, and good-for-nothings for knew neither work nor prayer"—into his Apostolic Brethren.[49] After he and four followers were burned in 1300, his radical sect continued to expand under successor Dolcino of Novara, who was rumored to be the bastard son of a priest. It is recorded that common folk sold their houses, gardens, fields, and vineyards to help spread the message in marketplaces across the north Italian planes. Inquisitor Bernard Gui described their beliefs.

They have that state of perfection in which the first apostles of Christ lived. And they declared themselves not bound to obey any man, the supreme pontiff or any other, inasmuch as their rule, which they claim came directly from Christ, is one of freedom and a more perfect life.... Also, that no man can be saved or enter into the kingdom of heaven unless he is of their condition or order. Also that no Pope of the Roman Church can absolve anyone unless he be ... living in complete poverty, without property of his own, and in humility, not engaging in wars or molesting anyone, but permitting everyone to live as he likes.[50]

The old Franciscan Frederick II myth now became turned on its head. Instead of being the Antichrist, this long-dead emperor was transformed into the Messiah who would return to rescue the poor and excluded from persecution by both church and state. Identifying Boniface VIII as both Antichrist and Whore of Babylon, Dolcino predicted that Frederick would put him to the sword, along with all his cardinals, bishops, priests, and monks. Only his own Apostolic Brethren (variously estimated at between 1,500 and 6,000 men women and children) would then be considered fit to inherit the joys of the final millennial age.

After receiving papal blessing, the Bishop of Vercelli announced a crusade—complete with full remission of all past sins—to destroy the Apostolic Brethren. As Dolcino and his "sister in spirit," beautiful Margaret of Trent, led their followers into the Southern Alps, they planned to set up a model Third Age community, in which all goods would be held in common and distinctions of rank and sex abolished. Marriage, that was then seen as a form of property, would be abolished in favor of "unions according to the heart" in which couples would hold each other naked until they reached a condition in which they could perform a sexual act that was purged of all sin.

In order to survive in a barren environment, the Brethren conducted daring guerilla raids into the neighboring valleys and countryside. As starvation took hold, they captured villagers and punished relatives when unreasonable demands for ransom were not paid. "They hung many of the faithful servants of Christ upon the gallows, amongst others a child of about 10 years old; that they mutilated other persons, cut off nose, lips, hands and feet of some women."[51] More than 1,000 Brethren were "killed, drowned and burnt" by the bishop's crusaders in the final battle of Carnacco of 1307. When Margaret and Dolcino were found alive, their punishment was intended to serve as an example to all After watching as his lover was burned, Dolcino had his nose, lips and "other parts" cut off before he too was burnt at the stake. Still the movement lived on in northern Italy for some decades. Whether their beliefs could have had any direct influence on future generations of radical millenarians must remain a matter of conjecture.

*

The fourteenth century has been described as the most terrible in human history. In the eyes of many, disaster began when Clement V left Rome to enjoy first the protection of the King of France and then the luxuries of Avignon's Palais du Papes. Second Avignon pontif John XXII even succeeded in supplanting Boniface VIII as the ultimate papal Antichrist when he launched into a bitter trial of strength with Holy Roman Emperor Louis IV. After excommunicating every diocese and region that he considered disloyal, he gloated over the prospect that "corpses would lie unburied in piles for so long that their stink would infect the healthy; the innocents would have to go without sacraments for so long that irreverence would grow, heresy would thrive and so would distress of the soul."[52] This inflexible man also set about crushing the spiritual Franciscans and rooting out every view that could be interpreted as heretical. In straight contradiction to the revered Francis, he even condemned the suggestion that Christ and his disciples had ever lived in a state of apostolic poverty without possessions. Anticlericalism spiraled out of control as rich, corrupt and usually immoral members of the curia appeared to find satisfaction in burning pious—if sometimes simple—poor folk, who, by general consent, could expect to fare better than their accusers on the Day of Judgment. Under examination, one Spiritual Franciscan praised those "faithful Catholics and glorious martyrs" who had died before him.

He believed that once the carnal church was destroyed—which it would be in a short time—the spiritual church to reign after its destruction would recognize that those Friars Minor and beguines had been condemned unjustly by the carnal church, consider them glorious martyrs, and accord them a feast day just as there is now a feast of the martyrs of Christ.[53]

Still, if the Avignon papacy—and, in particular, the pontificate of John XXII—had got the fourteenth century off to an unpromising start, nobody could have foreseen the sufferings that were yet to come.

6

Do Not Let Your Sword Cool: Plague and Reformation

The bubonic plague had already killed millions across Asia by the time Genoese galleys docked in the Sicilian port of Messina in October 1347. After the illness that would become known as the Black Death came ashore and started to ravage the sea port, townsfolk sent a message to the archbishop of neighboring Catania, pleading that the ancient bones of saint and martyr Agatha should be dispatched on loan without delay. As these relics were being prepared for the journey, terrified Catanian townsfolk tore the reliquary keys from the sacristan's hand and announced that "they would rather die than allow the relics to be taken to Messina." According to legend, a mere sight of Agatha's veil had been enough to save her own city from an eruption of Mount Etna, so the archbishop bathed her bones and carried the sanctified water to Messina. The record of his procession through that city's stricken streets illustrates how well-founded terror can so easily spill over into apocalyptic fantasy.

At the wish of the Archbishop, they determined to march devoutly around the city reciting litanies. While the whole population was thus proceeding around the streets, a black dog, bearing a drawn sword in his paws, appeared among them, gnashing with his teeth and rushing among them, and breaking the silver vessels and lamps and candlesticks on the altars, and casting them hither and thither.[1]

Within just a few months, the plague had found a ready home in huddled and insanitary Italian cities. Siena appears to have fared particularly badly with 65 percent of the population reported dead, while just half Florence's 90,000 citizens are thought to have survived. Through 1348, the Black Death raged through

North Africa, Spain, France, and Germany and along the Adriatic Sea. In 1349, it crossed the channel to devastate England before moving on to Scandinavia and Russia. By best, albeit uncertain, estimates, somewhere between a third and half of the whole human population of Europe perished in this worst of all natural disasters. Still, this was not the end; for another three centuries, the plague would return with devastating intensity to ravage different regions and communities.

Those who had been raised on images of doom could only conclude that the righteous God was wreaking vengeance on a corrupt and disobedient people. "My mind is stupefied," wrote a citizen of Florence, "as it approaches the task of recording the sentence that divine providence mercifully delivered upon men, who deserve, because they have been corrupted by sin, a last judgment."[2] Surrounded by suffering and death, people who doubted whether their own paltry prayers could sway such an implacable deity looked for ways of finding shelter under the Virgin's sky-blue cloak or enlisting the supplications of the region's most powerful saint.[3]

The idea that the practice of self-flagellation can influence the actions of an angry divinity can be traced through human history, from antiquity to the present day. As the plague reached southern France, Avignon Pope Clement VI attended ceremonies where "many of both sexes were barefooted, some were in sack cloth, some covered with ashes, wailing as they walked, tearing their hair, and lashing themselves with scourges even to the point where blood was drawn."[4] Organized groups of flagellants were soon travelling across German-speaking lands.

They moved in a long crocodile, two by two, usually in groups of two or three hundred but occasionally more than a thousand strong. Men and women were segregated, the women taking their place at the rear of the procession. At the head marched the group Master and two lieutenants carrying banners of purple velvet and cloth of gold. Except for occasional hymns the marchers were silent, their heads and faces hidden in cowls, their eyes fixed on the ground. They were dressed in somber clothes with red crosses in back, front and cap.[5]

On arrival in the town center, they would strip off their upper clothes and form a circle so the Master could beat those who confessed to failings. Then all would lash their backs with whips whose thongs were fixed with metal studs. With the End-Time so clearly approaching, they proclaimed that the movement would remain active for 33 years, after which the millennium would arrive and Christendom would be redeemed. In the meantime, they poured abuse on the clergy, disrupting church services and—like Apostolic Brethren before them—predicting that messianic Emperor Frederick II would return from the dead to heal the divisions between rich and poor and put all bishops, priests, and monks to the sword.

Once again, Christians laid blame on the Jews. As a string of massacres broke out in the south of France, people noticed that Jews collected pure running water from streams in preference to that from polluted urban wells. It seemed logical from this to conclude that the Jews had poisoned the wells. Panic spread when a German Jewish physician confessed under torture that Rabbi Jacob of Toledo had organized a conspiracy to poison all the wells in Europe. According to the confession, this physician had received a pouch full of red and black powder, concealed inside an egg, which he had used to poison the German town of Neustadt's water supply. Although Pope Clement reminded his flock that Jewish communities were suffering as much as their Christian neighbors, Jews continued to be attacked and killed. Persecution even increased when flagellant groups began to target whole communities. It has been estimated that the Black Death provoked about 350 massacres, with some 60 large and 150 smaller Jewish communities being exterminated in this largest genocide before the twentieth century.[6] Reeling from such losses, many European (*Ashkenazi*) Jews left the Rhineland and other flourishing trading centers to join a mass migration into the flat lands that lay between the German and Russian borders, from modern Lithuania in the north, through Poland to Ukraine in the south. Here, they brought skills in crafts and trade that enriched communities that had previously been starkly divided between a rich aristocracy and their oppressed landless peasants.

*

The Black Death had left the Christian church stripped of manpower. With perhaps 35 percent of the higher (clergy) and an even a higher proportion of lower clerical orders now dead, popes and bishops filled the gaps by recruiting men who knew no Latin and were often barely literate. As late medieval society began to recover from this unique trauma, the Western Catholic Church was ill-equipped to recover the trust of a disillusioned people.

By the early 1370s, Avignon Pope Gregory XI was growing particularly worried about the security of English church property and personnel. According to report, Oxford theologian John Wyclif (Wycliffe) was teaching that kings had the right to confiscate any church property that exceeded the requirements of holy poverty and to punish clerics who were adjudged to be in a state of sin. Repudiating the core papal doctrine of *plenitudo potestatis*, Wyclif also denied that the bishop of Rome had the right to interfere in secular affairs or discipline either clerics or laypeople beyond the boundaries of his own diocese.

In 1373, the King of England, the Archbishop of Canterbury, the Bishop of London, and the Chancellor of Oxford University received a papal letter demanding that Wyclif should be placed under formal investigation for heresy. All were coolly received. Arriving at a time when English King Edward III was in his final illness and son and heir Edward the Black Prince was also near death, power lay with the next son, John of Gaunt, and feisty Joan, "Fair Maid of Kent," mother to the child who would succeed as Richard II. Although formally condemned in the archbishop's court, Wyclif found powerful supporters. Fancying his suggestion that they might have legitimate grounds for laying hands on the church's wealth, both regents let it be known that they would protect the offending scholar. At the same time, most Oxford academics believed that the university should resist papal interference. When the university chancellor tried to carry out the pope's instructions, he was himself briefly imprisoned by his own academic colleagues.

With investigation stalled, Wyclif travelled far down the route where Protestant reformers would follow more than a century later. Since the church could have no other head but Christ, all papal claims to supremacy were clearly blasphemous. Wyclif also rejected the orthodox position that the church was made up of all who had been baptized, redefining it as a community of those whom God had predestined to salvation. From this position, he concluded, "neither the pope, nor the Lord Jesus Christ, can grant dispensations, or give indulgences to any man, except as the deity has determined by his just counsel."[7] Wyclif finally rejected church teaching on transubstantiation, concluding that the bread at the Eucharist is "by its own nature, veritable bread, and sacramentally Christ's body."[8] Although it remains unclear whether Wyclif personally translated Bible passages, he did strongly defend the right of individual believers' to read and interpret the vernacular text.

For Christian men are certain of belief by the gracious gift of Jesus Christ, that the truth taught by Christ and the apostles is the Gospel, though all the clerks of Antichrist say never so fast the contrary, and require men to believe the contrary, on pain of cursing, poisoning and burning.[9]

Again, Gregory XI did have grounds for concern. Besides training the coming generation of clergymen, Wyclif now sent out lay preachers, known as Lollards (*mumblers*), who were charged with the task of establishing informal groups of true believers. "The material churches," he instructed, "should not be decked with gold, silver and precious stones sumptuously; but the followers of Jesus Christ ought to worship their Lord humbly, in mean and simple houses."[10]

After Gregory died in 1378, the Catholic Church was plunged into 40 years of schism. France, with allies Scotland, Naples, and Castile, recognized Avignon Pope Clement VII, while the German-speaking lands, England, and a variety of smaller nations acknowledged Roman Pope Urban VI. Only wealthy Flanders was divided, with the Dutch-speaking merchant towns supporting Rome and Francophone nobles rallied behind Avignon. In one of his first actions, Urban prevailed on English churchmen to preach, fund, and deliver a crusade to drive the French—and by extension, his rival Clement—out of this wealthy area. After the campaign, led by the pugnacious Bishop of Norwich, turned out to be an incompetent and bloody failure, the disgusted Wyclif declared that the papacy had been finally revealed as divided, corrupt, and worldly. The rot lay not with any one pope but with the institution itself.

For the Pope may obviously be the Antichrist and yet not that sole single individual, who beyond any one else promulgates laws antithetical to the laws of Christ, but, rather, the multitude of popes holding that position since the Donation of Constantine, along with the cardinals and bishops of the church, plus their accomplices.[11]

As the elderly Wyclif retired to his parish, his writings became ever more apocalyptic and violent in tone. With the whole ecclesiastical structure now at the Antichrist's mercy, he was convinced that the Tribulation could not be far distant.

In his later years, Wyclif and his Lollards also became increasingly identified with the movement for social reform that had erupted into the Peasants' Revolt of 1381. Radical priest John Ball had used an old proverb for his text.

When Adam delved and Eve span
Who was then the gentleman?

Now near death, Wyclif developed a belief in the common ownership of goods that would reappear in millenarian communities through the coming centuries.

Every man ought to be in a state of grace; if he is a state of grace he is lord of the world and all that it contains; therefore every man ought to be lord of the whole world. But because of the multitude of men, this will not happen unless they hold all things in common.[12]

When John Wyclif died peacefully on the last day of 1384, English heretics were still hanged, drawn, and quartered as traitors rather than burned at the stake for religious deviance. With his conscience troubled by the crime of murdering his cousin Richard and usurping the English throne, next king Henry IV (known as Bolingbroke) demonstrated loyalty to Rome by bringing England into line with the rest of Europe. His ultra-orthodox son Henry V personally supervised the persecution of Lollards, even to lending a hand in the business of burning. Still, those Lollards continued to spread ever more radical versions of Wyclif's message. "Behold now we see so great a dissemination of the Gospel," declared one, "that simple men and women, and those accounted ignorant laymen in the reputation of men, write and learn the Gospel, and, as far as they know how, teach and scatter the word of God."[13] Although Catholic churchmen made every effort to ensure that Wyclif's followers suffered the ultimate penalty which he had avoided, secret Lollard cells continued to survive until well into the sixteenth century.

*

Even as the English authorities were pursuing Lollards, crowds were flocking to hear university lecturer Jan Hus (Huss) preach in Bethlehem Chapel, Prague. The English link was very clear; Wyclif's books were already circulating widely among scholars, and some of Hus' followers were in correspondence with English Lollards.[14] Schism plumbed new depths in 1409, when a third pope was installed in Pisa, while the sitting tenants in Avignon and Rome were still refusing to yield. A church council was called in Constance six years later, with the twin purposes of bringing this shameful division to an end and rooting out the "English heresy" once for all. Summoned before the Council on what proved to be an empty imperial safe-passage, Hus faced detailed questions that were designed to prove, item by item, how closely his teaching depended on Wyclif. Witnesses reported his stand on holy poverty, the true nature of the church, the denial of transubstantiation, the inefficacy of indulgences, the identity of the Pope as Antichrist, and the right of secular rulers to sequester church property. The final document of condemnation was directed, over Hus' head, at the dead Englishman.

Because by the witness of truth a bad tree customarily bears bad fruit, for that reason the man of damned memory, John Wyclif, like a poisoned root, by means of his death-bearing doctrine bore many pestiferous sons... Against them this Council of Constance... purposed to rise and to uproot their errors as noxious brambles from the Lord's field by the most watchful care and the knife of ecclesiastical authority, lest the cancer spread to the destruction of others.[15]

Once exposed as Wyclif's "pestiferous son," Jan Hus was delivered to the secular arm and burnt on July 7, 1415.

As soon as news of the execution reached Prague, the mob rose in fury. Beyond being a religious reformer, Jan Hus was now raised to be the symbol of a nascent Bohemian national identity. First orthodox priests were driven from their churches and some even killed, while Hussite clergy were installed in their place. Then, in the memorable 1419 Defenestration of Prague, 13 City Councilors were thrown from the Town Hall's upper windows and either died in the fall of were dispatched as they lay injured on the ground. Bitter and bloody conflict between the kingdom of Bohemia and the wider Holy Roman Empire could no longer be avoided. Key demands for religious liberty were identified in the Four Articles of Prague; the laity were henceforth to receive Communion in both bread and wine: there would be no restriction on free preaching, the church was to be divested of its wealth, and punishment would be meted out on all who committed mortal sins.

Divisions soon opened up within the reform movement. While the ubiquitous Hussite badge of a chalice served notice that laypeople's right to receive Communion in both kinds was nonnegotiable, affluent members of the Prague party (*Ultraquists*) were open to compromise on other parts of the package; but the word *compromise* did not fall within the vocabulary of those radical preachers who set themselves up to speak for the poor.

In the year 1419 evangelical priests, who were followers of Master John Hus... began to frequent certain mountains near Bechyne Castle, with the sacrament of the Eucharist, along with men and women from various regions and towns of the kingdom of Bohemia.[16]

Naming their mountain Tabor, after that biblical height where the disciples were supposed to have witnessed the Transfiguration extremist leaders established a community that (whether consciously or not) closely followed the model set by Dolcino's Apostolic Brethren. While English Lollards might be content to withdraw into secret house churches, Taborites preferred to interpret Jesus' warning that "he who is not with me is against me" in the most literal possible manner. Every outsider was a legitimate target of violence.

Only God's elect were to remain on earth—those who had fled to the mountains. And they said that the elect of God would rule on the earth for a thousand years with Christ, visibly and tangibly. And they preached that the elect of God who fled to the mountains would themselves possess all the goods of the destroyed evil ones and rule freely over all their estates and villages.[17]

Blind but brilliant general Jan Zizka led the Taborite army to a series of startling victories against the vastly superior crusading forces that gathered to suppress them. After Zizka died in 1424, raiding parties began to range into German-speaking lands. While the regular Taborite army fought under general Prokop the Great, smaller bands, known as orphans, mounted guerilla attacks under his namesake Prokop the Little. Martin Luther would recall these invasions a century later. "The Bohemians laid waste to Germany far and wide. Nuremberg had to pay tribute to them and they got as far as Zeitz. Several times the Germans had to take to their heels."[18] The struggle was waged with matching savagery on both sides. While Taborite clergy urged their soldiers to exterminate all enemies of the Truth, opposing crusaders were throwing some 1,600 Hussites down the deep silver mine shaft at Kutna Hora—"some alive, some first decapitated ... the executioners often being exhausted by the fatigue of slaughter."[19] Tables turned on May 30, 1434 when Catholics and Ultraquist Hussites joined forces to destroy this millenarian army at the brutal battle of Lipany. With some 13,000 radical Hussites—including both Prokop generals—dead. survivors took to the mountains, while those Ultraquists, who had helped to destroy them, were allowed to follow their more moderate reformed ways for another two centuries.

*

The people of Florence did not immediately warm to Dominical friar Girolamo Savonarola's overblown preaching style when he first arrived in the city to take up the position of Prior of St. Marco. Several years would pass before crowds gathered to hear his sermons on the *Book of Revelation*. Drawing on images from Joachim of Fiore and other apocalyptic texts, he denounced citizens for frittering away their lives at just the time when God was preparing a terrible judgment. The friar's prophesy appeared to be fulfilled when French king Charles VIII led an army across the Alps in 1494. Using a cover story that he was leading a crusade against the Turks, in truth, Charles planned to absorb the Kingdom of Naples into his empire. As French and Swiss mercenaries brought death, famine, and all kinds of disease—most notably the first-ever European manifestation of syphilis—Savonarola revealed that this French king was the agent of God's punishment on the sinful people of Italy.

> I saw Italy at war with famine everywhere
> God let loose the plague,
> And his judgment falls upon us;
> These are the fruits of your way of life,
> Blind and helpless from your little faith...
> In your folly you seek delights of song and music;
> But, sunk in vice, you have no virtue in you.
> Alas. Alas, Alas! All fear of God is lost.[20]

As Borgia Pope Alexander VI struggled to put together a coalition that could hold back the French and the ruling Medici family fled Florence, the Prior of St. Marco led the city's delegation to welcome the French king to their city.

With good order descending into chaos, Savonarola grasped this chance of placing Florence under God's direct rule. In speeches and writings, he thundered against the frivolity that permeated all aspects of Florentine life. Most notoriously, he attacked the humanist philosophy and fascination with pagan antiquity that drove those artistic currents that would later become known as the Italian Renaissance. Agents toured the streets searching out luxurious and immoral items—such as pictures of beautiful women (especially when naked), playing cards, jewellery, ornaments, and works by pagan and immoral poets—for public burning. Caught up in the great emotion, legend tells how artist Botticelli was spotted throwing his own work onto Savonarola's great Bonfire of the Vanities. Even more significantly, all those in Savonarola's divine republic were expected to repudiate those trade and banking activities that had brought Florence great prosperity in the past and would surely do so again when better times returned.

While Catholic historians have rehabilitated the Borgia pope's political and administrative reputation, they can do little to justify his private life, which, even by contemporary popes' relaxed standards, would always stand as a public scandal. Apart from time-honored sins of simony and nepotism (the latter, in his case, being a euphemism for promoting his own disreputable brood of children), Alexander stood accused of both murder and incest. Savonarola lamented this descent into unabashed sin. "The earth is so oppressed by every vice that never by itself it will unfold, and Rome, its head, is crawling on the ground."[21] When he allied Florence with a group of cardinals who were plotting Alexander's dethronement, the two men became set on a collision course, and the rebellious friar was excommunicated in the autumn of 1497. At home in Florence, jealous Franciscans were now able to exploit the fact that apocalyptic enthusiasm was waning as fast as it had arisen, and many were impatient to revive the city's worldly prosperity. In May 1498, the rebellious friar was burnt at the stake alongside two of his closest associates in Florence's Piazza della Signoria. Just two years later, disciple and artist Sandro Botticelli kept the friar's message alive in his own fashion by placing a cryptic Greek inscription on his painting *The Mystic Nativity*, which hangs today in London's National Gallery.

I Sandro painted this picture at the end of the year 1500 in the troubles of Italy in the half time after the time according to the eleventh chapter of St. John in the second woe of the Apocalypse in the loosing of the devil for three and a half years. Then he will be chained in the 12th chapter and we shall see him trodden down as in this picture.

With the fiery prophet safely dispatched, opponents had reason to hope that his challenge to papal authority had died with him. The new printing technology ensured that this did not happen After being the fifteenth century's most widely published author during his lifetime, Savonarola's sermons continued to sell in Italy, Germany and France after his death and Martin Luther would rate this Dominican friar among the most influential precursors of Protestantism.[22]

*

By instinct, Martin Luther was a more conservative theologian than either Wyclif or Hus. As an Augustinian Friar, his whole training had centered on the Bishop of Hippo's writings, and he would later recount how at first he "devoured, not merely read, Augustine." Then, when he refined his central doctrine of justification by faith out of the Pauline epistles, "it was all over with Augustine." Still, his end-time thinking never strayed far from the Augustinian mainstream.

When Erasmus published his Greek New Testament in 1516, he asked whether the *Book of Revelation* deserved its place within the biblical canon. This had only been secured in the first place on the grounds that it was the Apostle John's work and Erasmus now mounted a formidable case that this could not be true. Moreover, leading fathers had never placed the book at the center of their teaching. "Ancient theologians quote passages from this book rather for illustration and ornament than for support of serious propositions."[23]

After announcing that Revelation was not a book of the Bible, Zurich reformer Ulrich Zwingli proceeded to ignore it completely. While John Calvin of neighboring Geneva was less dogmatic, this was the only book of the Bible for which he wrote no commentary. Luther's position would remain ambiguous. While he was initially inclined to side with Erasmus, he later refused to dismiss the book outright. With so much of his theological structure based on the authority of scripture, he could not easily take it in himself to determine what should or should not be included within the canon. If he could exclude any book, he would have given priority to the Epistle of James, which explicitly contradicted his own central doctrine of justification by faith. In common with other mainstream reformers, Luther remained convinced that the Holy Spirit chose to enter the human soul in response to hard study of scripture rather than through apocalyptic dreams. Still he brooded obsessively on the Last Judgment, Satan and all his devils Gog and Magog and the Antichrist. Like Wyclif and Hus before him, Luther identified the Antichrist communally as "the multitude of popes ... along with the cardinals and bishops of the church."[24] The armies of Gog were those Muslim Turks who had overrun much of Eastern Europe and were now threatening Vienna and South Germany. Beyond that, Satan and his multitude of devils inhabited every crevice of the created world. An early hymn reflects Luther's own tortured fear of judgment.

> Forlorn and lost in death I lay,
> A captive to the devil.
> My sin lay heavy night and day
> For I was born in evil.
> I felt but deeper for my strife
> There was no good in all my life
> For sin had all possessed me.

Since humans could only be saved through faith, it had to be sacrilegious for Pope Leo X to offer Christians the opportunity of gaining entry into heaven for themselves and their loved ones by the purchase of indulgences. With the crusading age long past, these instruments now raised money for a variety of expeditions against heretics and the pope's political opponents, as well as for the grandiose rebuilding of St. Peter's Rome. Rapturous Dominican preacher Johannes Tetzel ignored theological niceties as he toured the countryside to promote this lucrative short cut to salvation.

Remember that you are in such stormy peril on the raging sea of this world that you do not know if you can reach the harbor of salvation . . . You should know: whoever is contrite and puts alms into the box, as his confessor counsels him, will have all his sins forgiven. Do you not hear the voices of your dead parents and other people, screaming and saying "Have pity on me, have pity on me . . . We are suffering severe pain, from which you could rescue us if only you would." Open your ears because the father is calling to the son and the mother to the daughter.[25]

At just this time, when Satan and his papal Antichrist had reached the very summit of their powers, it could only be that the end of the world was very close.

After Luther made his famous gesture of nailing 95 theses for debate to the door of Wittenberg Cathedral in 1517, it came as a surprise that his own prince stepped up to protect him from the burning that was surely in store. Elector Frederick III—"the Wise"—was an unlikely midwife at the birth of Protestantism. His great passion for collecting had endowed the Wittenberg castle church with a rumored 17,443 holy relics, which ranged from a branch of the burning bush to a quantity of the Virgin Mary's milk. As founder and protector of Wittenberg University, he took the position that Luther's arguments deserved more serious debate than the church authorities would allow. Also, in the real world of politics, he was determined to exploit the dispute to establish Saxon independence from both pope and emperor. As other north German princes rallied to the cause, their secular ambitions became increasingly entwined with Luther's religious reforms. Wholly reliant on those who had saved his life, Martin Luther now determined that his reformed church would never interfere in secular affairs. According to the Lutheran doctrine of the Two Kingdoms, the clergy's responsibility was restricted to the definition of doctrine, the preaching of the word, and the administration of sacraments. Beyond that, kings, princes, and magistrates enforced laws that were—at least in principle—supposed to protect the poor and weak. Basing his political philosophy on Paul's warning that "he who resists the authorities resists what God has appointed, and those who resist will incur jugdment."[26] Luther effectively bestowed divine right on rulers and magistrates, alongside the duty of absolute obedience on subjects. From that, it could only follow that rulers had the right to determine the religion followed within their own territory and punish any who chose a different path (*cuius regio, eius religio*—whose realm, his/her religion).

While Luther's doctrine may have provided some fragile structure across two centuries of bloody religious strife, it could not satisfy those enthusiasts who believed that they had a higher duty to create a godly community—a New Jerusalem—where Jesus of Nazareth and his saints would rule at the second coming. Like Savonorola before them, these dissidents believed that such a state of perfection could only be achieved within a theocratic state, where the elect of God would set laws and policy—and even, on occasion, determine who would live or die.

*

Just four years after Luther nailed his theses to the church door, follower Thomas Müntzer left Wittenberg for the south Saxon silver mining city of Zwickau. Situated near the Bohemian border, reformed religion was here already dividing along lines of wealth and social class. Müntzer's first duty was to provide vacation cover for Erasmus' friend John Egranus, who preached learned sermons to the prosperous congregation of St. Mary's Church. When Egranus returned, Müntzer moved on to neighboring St. Catherine's, where laymen Nicholas Storch, Thomas Dreschel, and Mark Thomas Stübner were already conducting courses of Bible study along more radical lines. There may be no evidence that connects these three "Zwickau Prophets" with those Taborites who still survived in mountains across the Bohemian border, but their messages were very similar. With the millennium fast approaching, they announced, neither the Catholic sacraments nor the Protestant Bible could bring salvation. In the coming apocalyptic age, all people would be equal and goods held in common. In the meantime, the faithful needed to separate themselves from all existing institutions of government to concentrate wholly on the apocalyptic events that were to come.[27] Although Müntzer would always deny that his life's message was borrowed from the Zwickau Prophets, it does appear that his thinking did clarify during those months at St. Catherine's. The three prophets then left to spread their radical form of Protestantism in Luther's own University of Wittenberg. They were already making significant inroads when the great man hurried back from the castle, where he had been living under princely protection, to confront them face to face. The Zwickau Prophets then dropped out of the historical record.

When Müntzer urged the Zwikau Council to drive all priests, monks, and friars from the city, its members preferred to expel him instead and he travelled on southwards across the Bohemian border. Once in Prague, Müntzer was given freedom to preach from the pulpit of Hus' own Bethlehem Chapel and in other Hussite churches. At a time when printed copies of both authentic and pseudo-Joachite books were coming into circulation, Müntzer announced that the Third Age of the Holy Spirit would soon arrive in Bohemia and from there spread out across the world.

Luther's and Müntzer's reformations were now clearly parting company. On the one side, belief in the absolute authority of scripture was fundamental to the mainstream Protestantism that was being developed by Luther, Zwingli, and Calvin. It followed that mainstream reformers' first priorities were that the Bible should be translated into the vernacular and that all people should acquire the literacy skills necessary for reading its contents. But here in Prague, Müntzer was preaching that the Bible consisted of dead words, which could never, of themselves, create faith. Giving his brand of radical Protestantism a Gnostic twist, he went on to argue that, since the Bible had been written by spirit-filled authors, it could only be interpreted by those whose hearts had already been filled by the Holy Spirit. According to this new radical brand of Protestantism, salvation lay only within that community of the Holy Spirit, which was the hidden church of the elect. Imitating Luther's iconic action, Thomas Müntzer pinned a long document on the door of Prague's main church. While much of the text was incoherent, one key sentence lay at its core: "For anyone who does not feel the spirit of Christ within him, or is not quite sure of having it, is not a member of Christ but of the devil."[28]

As Müntzer considered the process of separating wheat from tares in the Last Judgment, he pondered over Jesus' instruction to "collect the weeds first and bind them in bundles to be burned, but gather the wheat into my barn." The unresolved issue seemed to lie in whether this End-Time separation would happen on earth or in God's final heavenly kingdom. Müntzer reached a clear and violent answer. "The ungodly have no right to live unless the elect permit it."[29] Since the same criteria must apply both to rulers and the ruled, he concluded that true believers had God's authority to kill tyrants.

As soon as conservative Hussites understood the violent implications of Müntzer's teaching, they lost no time in expelling him from their country and he set off once again to search for his New Jerusalem. After some wanderings—and more ejections—he was offered a post in the Saxon town of Allstedt, which lay just miles down the road from the mining town of Mansfeld, where Martin Luther had spent much of his childhood. In streams of letters and pamphlets, each man accused the other of being both Satan and Antichrist. Although both anticipated a very early Judgment Day, Luther urged his followers to wait in a spirit of quiet devotion while leaving the larger unreformed community to its own devices. Müntzer, in contrast, planned to spend what little time was left actively working to achieve a more just and equal society—if necessary, by violence. The tone of debate can be gauged from Müntzer's assault on the way that Luther had abandoned holy poverty to enjoy the comforts of princely hospitality.

If one did not see through your villainy, one would swear by all the saints that you are a pious Martin. Sleep softly dear flesh! I would rather smell you through God's wrath roasting in your obstinacy in the oven or in the pot on the fire than have you cooked in your own juices. May the devil devour you.[30]

Between penning such missives, Müntzer was organizing his followers into a paramilitary league, which would use Allstedt as a base for violent attacks on the surrounding ungodly. When the Catholic Count of Mansfeld tried to prevent his local miners from attending church in Allstedt, Müntzer urged his followers to "wash their hands in the blood of tyrants" and set off for the neighboring Saxon city of Mühlhausen.

Long-standing tensions between landowners and tenants then erupted into the bloody Peasants' War of 1524 to 1525. According to Luther's doctrine of Two Kingdoms, the key issues in dispute—serfdom, taxes, feudal duties, personal liberty, and general oppression—lay outside the church's area of responsibility. To Müntzer, in contrast, all injustice would have to be overcome if the New Jerusalem was to be in place in time for Jesus' Second Coming. Along with his new companion, itinerant bookseller Hans Hut, he travelled widely across the affected area, announcing that the End-Time battle had arrived. While Müntzer did not start the Peasants' War, some historians hold him personally responsible for bringing Saxon peasants into the conflict. His inflammatory language certainly stoked class hatred.

Get going while the fire is hot! Do not let your sword cool, do not lay it down. Use your hammers on the anvil of Nimrod and destroy their tower ... At them! At them while you still have the day, God marches ahead of you. Follow, follow![31]

Meanwhile, from his Wittenberg study, Luther was urging landowners to kill their rebellious subjects, assuring them that any who died "with conscience" to protect the rule of law would become true martyrs in the sight of God. He insisted that full responsibility for slaughter must lie on his old enemy's head. "This is particularly the work of that archdevil who rules in Mühlhausen and does nothing except stir up robbery, murder and bloodshed."[32]

On May 15, 1525, Thomas Müntzer led a band of untrained peasants, armed mainly with scythes and flails, to confront the well-equipped mercenaries of Hesse and Saxony on the millennial battlefield of Frankenhausen. The outcome was simple massacre. Estimates of peasant deaths vary between 3,000 and 10,000, against just four killed in the princely army. After being captured on the field, Thomas Müntzer was put to the torture and executed in his own city of Mühlhausen. Bookseller Hans Hut was one of the few who escaped. The total number of peasant dead in the war is estimated at around 100,000.

*

Even before the outbreak of fighting, that same sense of millennial expectation that had inspired the Zwickau Prophets had been stirring across the German-speaking lands. While mainstream reformers Martin Luther and Ulrich Zwingli might raise hopes with the rhetoric of freedom, they held back from adding substance to aspiration. In the summer of 1521, a band of enthusiasts, shouting "Woe, Woe," invaded the Swiss town of Zurich. After announcing that Zwingli was the demonic dragon of Revelation, they gave his followers just 40 days to repent before the city would be destroyed. Similar events were recorded elsewhere. The roots of Baptist belief can be traced to the day, four months before Frankenhausen, when the Zurich City Council called a meeting to debate the validity of infant baptism. On the traditionalist side, Zwingli defended this ancient practice on the grounds that it provided the structure for a universal church, which embraced all those bound together by the sacrament. Against him, young Zurich citizen Conrad Grebel argued that infant baptisms were invalid because the rite lacked any foundation in scripture. After the City Council ruled in Zwingli's favor, dissidents withdrew to hold clandestine ceremonies of adult baptism in neighboring villages. This was a momentous act of separation. According to medieval belief, since church and society were one, everybody lived under obligation to accept those orthodox beliefs and regulations that were enforced by secular governments. Now *Anabaptists* (those baptized again) were insisting that the true church was a voluntary association of the faithful that existed and operated beyond any government control. Since both Catholics and mainstream Protestants adjudged this to be seditious talk, the Zurich City Council decreed that all those who had been baptized for a second time should be condemned to death by drowning. Still, the movement gathered impetus.

Because God wished to have his own people, separated from all peoples, he willed for this purpose to bring in the right true morning star of his truth to shine in the fullness of the final age of this world, especially in the German nations and lands... In order that his holy work might be made known and revealed before everyman, there developed first in Switzerland an extraordinary awakening.[33]

Anabaptism was never a homogeneous movement. As the Peasants' War approached its bloody climax, radical religious groups began to appear across widely dispersed areas. In this time of cosmic climax, when the End could be no more than a few years distant, preachers declared that only rebaptism could provide that mark of salvation that would ensure believers a place among the 144,000 of the saved. After bookseller Hans Hut had managed to escape alive from the Frankenhausen battlefield, he preached that the Kingdom of God would arrive within the next three years and launched into a campaign of mass re-baptism. While Hut urged subjects to murder their rulers and take control of their own destinies, other peace-loving Anabaptist prophets were proclaiming that persecution could only be countered by the renunciation of violence. Furrier Melchior Hoffman left his home in southern Germany to wander barefoot through Scandinavia and the Netherlands. Alongside trading furs, he preached and baptized converts, always leaving behind self-sufficient Anabaptist cells. His work was unusually successful in the province of Holland, where Anabaptism took a particularly firm hold.

In January 1528, Emperor Charles V's Imperial Diet of Spier followed the lead set in Zurich by decreeing that "every Anabaptist and rebaptized person of the age of reason" should be killed without trial.

(They) shall be condemned and brought from natural life into death by fire, sword and the like, according to the person, without proceeding by the inquisition of the spiritual judges and let the same (punishment be inflicted on the) pseudo-preachers, instigators, vagabonds and tumultuous inciters of the said vice of anabaptism.[34]

Parents who failed to present their children for baptism "within a reasonable period" were also condemned to death.

While numbers remain uncertain, thousands of Anabaptists are known to have died during the years between 1527 and 1533 when persecution was at its height. People told how mounted soldiers roamed the countryside, killing without trial or sentence. Since no believer would endanger her or his immortal soul by denying the mark of salvation, the answers to very simple questions were enough to determine guilt. Those sent to prison also stood little chance of survival.

On one occasion more than twenty men, widows, pregnant women and girls were thrown into horrible, dark dungeons, to spend the rest of their lives without seeing either the sun or the moon and to end their days on bread and water. They were condemned to remain in those dark dungeons, to die, to stink and to decay, the dead and the living together, until none of them remained.[35]

The emperor could issue edicts; implementation remained a matter of discretion for the different estates within his loose realm. While some Protestant administrations did persecute Anabaptists, many more died in Catholic lands. In 1533, Jacob Hutter and and other Austrian refugees found safe haven in the eastern part of the modern Czech Republic, known as Moravia. Even after Hutter himself returned home, to be captured, tortured, and burned alive, his Hutterite followers continued to share common ownership of goods in peaceful communities. Meanwhile, Melchior Hoffman and some Dutch followers had found shelter in neutral Strasbourg. After announcing that this was the New Jerusalem, he too spread word that the world would end within three years. It was said that he deliberately provoked his own arrest on another prophet's assurance that, after half a year in prison, he "would leave Strasbourg with 144,000 true preachers, apostles and emissaries of God, accompanied by signs and miracles, and so fortified by the Spirit that no one would be able to resist them."[36] However, the city authorities had now decided that this flood of Anabaptist refugees constituted a threat to good order. Instead of being released after six months, Hoffman remained caged in a tower until he died 10 years later. During this time passersby could hear a harmless lunatic chanting psalms and calling down divine woe on all the godless scribes of Strasbourg.

*

With Hoffman behind bars, and so many of the first-generation prophets dead, Anabaptist leadership passed to the middle-aged Dutch baker Jan Matthijs. Although a huge man of intimidating presence, he was reported to be barely literate and to hold some very simple beliefs—which most definitely did not include quiet acquiescence in the face of persecution. With Strasbourg now closed to his people, Matthijs needed to find another city where the saints could gather in readiness for Judgment Day. More than 100 miles to the north but conveniently close to the Dutch border, the German city of Münster was owned by an absentee lord, who, even though not an ordained clergyman, claimed the title of prince-bishop. Mobilizing the support of disaffected citizens, Matthijs managed to seize control and start work on the task of converting Münster into New Jerusalem. Here again, all resources would be held in common.

Everything which has served the purposes of self-seeking and private property, such as buying and selling, working for money, taking interest and practicing usury—even at the expense of unbelievers—or eating and drinking the sweat of the poor (that is making ones own fellow creatures work so that one can grow fat) and indeed everything that offends against love—all such things are abolished amongst us by the power of love and community.[37]

As Dutch Anabaptists arrived in increasing numbers, Münster came under desultory siege from the Bishop's mercenaries. Matthijs was furious when Catholic and Lutheran residents joined to protest at their city's transformation. "Everywhere," he declared, "we are surrounded by dogs and sorcerers and whores and killers and godless and all who love lies and commit them."[38] After initially announcing that all those who refused rebaptism would die, he reluctantly conceeded that such a large-scale massacre of Protestants and Catholics would provoke instant retribution from surrounding princes. As a compromise, he decreed that ofenders must abandon every possession and leave the city. Preferring to face a bleak future life of beggary alone, many Catholic and Lutheran merchants agreed to leave, while their wives and families kept their city homes and accepted mass rebaptism.

After marrying a strikingly beautiful ex-nun named Divara, Jan Matthijs presided over a time of excess, when churches were plundered of their treasures and every book other than the Bible searched out and burned. The boundary to physical violence was finally crossed when—according to the most credible account—a local blacksmith accused Matthijs of being no better than "a crazy, lying shit-prophet who was not worth a baker's fart." The record leaves some confusion over whether it was Matthijs or young Dutch successor Jan Bockelson who struck the blacksmith down on the spot.[39] If Bockelson was making a bid for power, he did not have to long to wait. In the ultimate futile gesture Matthijs and a handful of followers left the walls to engage the whole bishop's army in single-handed combat—and were immediately cut to pieces. With his only rival dead, Bockelson threw off all his clothes and ran through the streets naked, before collapsing in silent ecstasy for three days. He then stood before the crowd and announced that he would introduce a new dispensation based on principles had God had delivered directly to him. Although as small a man as Matthijs was large, this 25-year-old tailor's apprentice was already an accomplished actor who could grasp and manipulate the emotions of any crowd. "Listen to me you Israelites," he announced. "You who inhabit the holy city of Jerusalem should fear your heavenly Father and repent your earlier lives! The trumpet of the Lord will soon issue its frightful sound and send thousands of angels down to us."[40] Assuming power under the more dignified name of Jan of Leiden, he appointed a council of 12 Elders, who held absolute power of life and death. With all religious, moral, and political misdemeanors—down to "idle conversation," disputes, anger, envy, women's disobedience to husbands, and children's to parents—now punishable by death, everybody's life was, in principle, forfeit. As terror gripped the city, numbers of both men and women were indeed executed.

With the Lutheran and Catholic men gone, only about a third of the city's 10,000 remaining population was male and, of these, just 1,500 were of military age. In July 1534, citizens were shocked to learn that the Council had introduced compulsory polygamy. All existing marriages would be considered void until they were reconfirmed by pastors, childless marriages were to be broken up, and all unmarried women (including those whose husbands had been expelled) assigned to new husbands. Each individual decision would be taken by the Council of Elders without right of appeal and had to be obeyed on pain of death. To set the example, Jan of Leiden married the widowed Divara and set her over a harem of 15 other very young wives. When leading citizens rose in protest, it did, for a time, appear that introducing polygamy may have been a step too far, but order was soon restored. First 25 malcontents were summarily shot. Then, "to make sure that the enemy did not suspect from the frequent gunshots that the townsmen were experiencing dissention among themselves and to avoid wasting so much gunpowder," 60 more were executed by the sword—some by the prophet himself, for his own "amusement and practice." Then, if this hostile witness can be believed, "raging with unbridled wantonness, everyone was now carried away with obscene lechery, and they were set ablaze with such promiscuous lustfulness that no restraint was kept on their prodigious sexuality."[41]

Through all crises and orgies, Jan of Leiden did marshal the city's slender defense with some skill, and one major attack was heavily defeated. As the

Anabaptists rejoiced in victory, an obsequious prophet proclaimed that Jan of Leiden had inherited the scepter of King David and become Messiah and King over the whole world. He accepted the title of King of New Jerusalem as no more than his due.

> Now I am given power over all the nations of the earth, and the right to use the sword to the confusion of the wicked and in defense of the righteous. So let none in this town stain himself with crime or resist the will of God, or else he shall without delay be put to death with the sword.[42]

Concerned that other Münsters might materialize within their own territories, princes and cities were now providing the bishop with financial and material support; then, as he started building an impenetrable barricade, poverty and hunger took hold inside the city walls. Still, even in this state of siege, the court of King Jan grew ever more lavish.

> When about to go forth in public he sometimes put on a gleaming scarlet and purple garment, sometimes a shaggy one made entirely of silk, sometimes a black one of damask decked out with animal skins of different color, sometimes a wavy one decorated with raindrops of different shapes, sometimes a muslin one with interwoven threads of gold or silver, sometimes a silken one with slit sleeves that were tied back with golden pins underneath.[43]

As discontent grew, two citizens stole out at night to report where the walls were weakest. Jan of Leiden's messianic kingdom of Münster fell to the forces of reaction on June 22, 1535. Ignoring his own promise of safe conduct, the bishop employed three executioners, who worked for days on the task of punishing rebels.

While in prison awaiting inevitable torture and execution, Jan of Leiden received a letter from a fellow Anabaptist leader.

> We have heard unbelievable and terrible things about your kingdom. If what we hear is true—and regrettably it seems to be—we find it impossible to understand how you could have done such things in the name of Holy Scripture.[44]

Dutch and German believers now rallied behind ex-Catholic priest Menno Simons, who taught that retaliation and violence could never be an acceptable response to state oppression. Later Anabaptists would remain deeply embarrassed by events of those 20 months that separated Jan Matthijs' arrival in Münster and the city's final fall to the bishop's army. Taking their lead from Hutterites in the east and Mennonites in the west, communities of Anabaptist descent would adopt the strict pacifist ideology that still characterizes their worldwide communities.

7

Everything That Is Hidden Is Found: Mystics and Explorers

On December 10, 1198, 33-year-old Ibn Arabi attended the funeral of his father's close friend Ibn Rushd, who was known as Averroes. Although the younger man still held the great philosopher in reverence, their paths had increasingly diverged. Under the influence of his elderly "spiritual mother" Fatima of Cordova (who, in her day, could reportedly be mistaken for a girl of 14), Arabi had abandoned rationalism to pursue the Sufi mystic path. Following the Gnostic tradition, he looked beyond the realm of being to search for the unknowable and unpredictable "God who is not." Throughout his life, Arabi could only feel contempt for all the "blind *ummas*," who sought to constrain faith within legalistic rules. Although a devout Muslim, he respected Christian teaching and maintained a deep devotion to the person of Jesus. "Let thy soul be as matter for all forms of belief," he advised.[1] Splitting away from the Aristotelian tradition of Muslim philosophy, Arabi insisted that truth could not be found through rational deduction but by opening oneself to divine emanations. Since God and the universe were one, it could be argued that God was everything and everything was God. "When God is called the Apparent, the corporeal aspect of the universe is meant and when he is called the Hidden, the incorporeal aspect of the Universe is meant."[2] Soon after laying Averroes to rest, Arabi left Spain for the eastern Mediterranean, where he wandered huge distances as he contemplated the oneness of all things. Although Arabi won the friendship of princes, he also respected the rights and beliefs of common folk; winning wide respect, he became known as the "Greatest of the Sheiks."

As Arabi travelled across Palestine and Syria, he found himself surrounded by signs of Western invasion. Although the kingdom of Jerusalem had fallen to Saladin some 12 years earlier, the city of Acre remained in crusading hands. Here Richard the Lionheart's 1191 massacre of Muslims—when 2,700 vanquished Turkish hostages were led out of the city and decapitated—remained unforgotten and unforgiven. By the time he died in 1240, Ibn Arabi would also have heard that the fast-expanding Mongol empire had reached the fabled site of Alexander's wall by the Caspian Sea and Caucasus Mountains. Living in the shadow of invasion from both west and east, he contemplated whether the final apocalyptic conflict might be close. Taking his lead from eighth-century tradition, Arabi forecast that the Mahdi would appear in Mecca to lead an army of 66,000 Muslims (all of whom were direct descendants of the Prophet Isaac) against Constantinople. As they called out "Allah Akbar," the first line of walls would fall—then the second—then the third and the city would capitulate without any use of the sword. At just this time, the Antichrist would appear in the Persian province of Khorassan. As this destroyer moved west toward Syria, he would be joined in Isfahan by great armies of Turks and Jews. Just 18 days after the fall of Constantinople, the armies of the Antichrist and the Mahdi would join in battle on the plain of Acre.[3] At this millennial moment, the shining figure of Jesus would appear on a white minaret on the walls of Damascus and the forces of the Antichrist would be put to the sword along with all those "blind ummas" who had perverted true Islam.

Just 20 years after al-Arabi died in 1240, it appeared as though his apocalyptic forecast would soon be realized. When Genghis Khan's grandson Möngke succeeded to the position of Great Khan in 1251, he determined to complete the patriarch's ambition of creating a world empire. Providing his brother Hulagu with a great army, Möngke instructed him to extend Mongol rule westward into Iraq, Syria, Egypt, and beyond. Traditional tactics were brutal but effective. Any city that resisted would be destroyed and the inhabitants slaughtered; those that capitulated would be spared to live under Mongo rule. Terrible stories filtered west. Baghdad, ancient capital of the Abbasid caliphate, and the Syrian city of Aleppo had both been utterly destroyed and the ancient city of Damascus was overrun. Cairo was next in line.

Just a few years earlier, Egypt had come under the control of a new Sultan Qutuz and an aristocracy drawn from elite soldiers known as Mamlukes. With their name meaning "one who is owned," these men had started life as slave boys who had been selected for intensive military training. Combining innate intelligence with ruthless ambition, these slaves had made themselves masters of Egypt. In early 1260, Sultan Qutuz received Hulagu's envoys, who carried a letter demanding that Cairo must surrender.

You should think of what happened to other countries . . . We have conquered vast areas, massacring all the people. You cannot escape from the terror of our armies. Where can you flee? What road will you use to escape us? Our horses are swift, our arrows sharp, our swords like thunderbolts, our hearts as hard as the mountains, our soldiers as numerous as the sand. Fortresses will not detain us, nor arms stop us. Your prayers to God will not avail against us. We are not moved by tears nor touched by lamentations. Only those who beg our protection will be safe.[4]

Facing massive odds, Sultan Qutuz still determined that he would not surrender his newly won lands without a fight. After executing Hulagu's envoys, his Mamlukes put together an army of some 20,000 men. However, in the meantime, news of the Great Khan Möngke's death had arrived and, following custom, Hulagu returned for the election of a successor, leaving what he deemed to be adequate forces to finish the job in Egypt. The apocalyptic struggle at Ain Jalut can be seen as a "hinge of history"; had Cairo fallen, there would have been little to prevent Mongol advance across North Africa and into Spain. In the event, the Egyptian Mamlukes inflicted the Mongol army's first-ever defeat in open battle, and the myth of invincibility was broken.

Still, as Hulagu's retreating army left a trail of devastation in its wake, the sense of impending doom lingered on.

While fourteenth-century Sunni teacher Ibn Kathir dismissed Ibn Arabi's mystic ideas as heretical, he still constructed a similar picture of the Last Things. Looking for the old signs that ignorance had replaced knowledge and morals were collapsing in adultery and drunkenness, he anticipated that, as the end drew close, more females would be born than males, until a single man would be challenged to provide for the needs of 50 women. As the end drew near, the Mahdi would appear in Mecca and march on Byzantium. Breaking his treaty obligations, the Christian emperor would then raise 80 banners, each with 12,000 soldiers, but the Mahdi's Muslims would sweep across this great human wall to destroy the city of Constantinople. As the Antichrist then appeared out of the East to break down Alexander's wall, he would again be joined by Jews and Turks to engage in the last great battle. When Jesus finally struck the Antichrist with his holy lance, the evil one would begin to dissolve like salt in water. At this point, "just leader" Jesus gathers all surviving Christians to the true faith to usher in a time of universal victory for Islam. "He breaks the Cross and kills the pigs. Peace reigns everywhere and swords are used as sickles."[5]

Before he died at the age of 73, Ibn Kathir may have heard of the rise to power of another great destroyer of Mongol heritage. With his capital on the Silk Road in Samarkand, Timur the Lame (Tamburlaine) entertained no ambition to build a unified empire; in 35 years of relentless warfare, from India to Russia and Central Asia to the Mediterranean Sea, he single-mindedly pursued personal wealth at the expense of defenseless populations. Leaving little legacy but burned cities, huge piles of skulls, and a country stripped bare of skilled artisans (who had all been transported to Samarkand) this all-too-corporeal Antichrist finally brought the great age of Islamic culture to its most bloody end.

*

Even as medieval Christians were killing unbelievers in Jesus' name, great Islamic cities of Cordova and Cairo had continued to function as multicultural centers of culture, where Muslims, Jews, and Christians generally managed to exchange religious and philosophical ideas in a spirit of harmony. Moses ben Maimon (Maimonides) was born in Cordova in 1135—just nine years after Muslim philosopher Averroes was also born in the same city. While both were still young, their peaceful homeland was overrun by more fanatical Muslims from North Africa, and Maimonides' family had to choose between conversion and exile. After years of wandering, they settled in tolerant Fatimid Cairo, where Maimonides became the leading rabbi (teacher) as well as physician to ruler Saladin.

When the two Cordovan philosophers set about reconciling their separate faiths with classical Greek learning, Averroes could call up a long tradition of rationalist Islam. With no such background in Judaism, Maimonides had to address the task from basic principles. After gaining an unrivaled knowledge of the Hebrew scriptures and Torah, the Jewish scholar addressed those elements of End-Time faith that seemed most at odds with classical Greek philosophy. His controversial *A Guide to the Perplexed* aimed to help those thoughtful people who found it hard to reconcile the laws and traditions of revealed religion with ancient Greek discovey of scientific cause and effect. Maimonides identified three key stumbling blocks: resurrection—the coming of the Messiah—final rewards and punishments.

The concept of resurrection only entered Jewish consciousness after the Babylonian exile and, as late as the first century BCE, the Sadducees had still argued that this belief had no place within Jewish belief. Scriptural authority appeared to rest on just two verses from the last chapter of the late and dubiously canonical *Book of Daniel*.

And many of those who sleep in the dust of the earth shall awake, some to everlasting life and some to shame and everlasting contempt. But go your way till the end; and you shall rest, and shall stand in your allotted place at the end of days.[6]

Although end-time and messianic traditions had developed later, these had never been codified into clearly defined doctrinal certainties. In order to discredit the idea of physical resurrection, Maimonides needed to dispose of the popular belief that God himself was some kind of bodily being. He argued that, just as humans can see the world without understanding why it exists, so they can recognize God through his actions without comprehending the abstract nature of his existence. Since God has no physical existence, he had to be approached through the human being's only nonbodily dimension, which was the intellect. It followed that the whole purpose of life was to achieve a mystical union between the human intellect and the one incorporeal God; and, as every Gnostic knew, only a select few could achieve that exalted end. Even then, once that intellectual resurrection was achieved, the remaining physical body would have to pass through the normal process of death. Critics did not miss the fact that Maimonides had reconciled End-Time belief with Aristotelian logic at the expense of denying bodily resurrection and placing spiritual rebirth beyond the reach of most human beings.

By long tradition, Jewish rabbis based their messianic expectation on an enigmatic verse from the *Book of Genesis*. As Jacob blessed his sons, one by one, he delivered a special promise to the fourth: "the sceptre shall not depart from Judah, nor a lawgiver from between his feet, until Shiloh come; and unto him shall the gathering of the people be."[7] However fragile the link, the words, "until Shiloh come" had become the defining text for the promise that a divinely inspired Messiah would lead the Jews back to Palestine and establish a time of peace and obedience to God's will. Again, Maimonides needed to remove any magical element from this promise.

> Let no one think that in the days of the Messiah any of the laws of nature will be set aside or any innovation introduced into creation ... Do not think that the King Messiah will have to perform signs or wonders or bring anything new into being.[8]

According to his interpretation, the first messiah would be a human being of David's line who would establish an era of peace and justice before dying naturally. He, in turn, would then be succeeded by a dynasty of natural sons—not unlike Shi'a imams. At this point, Maimonides could go no further; on the one side, concepts of heaven and hell clearly lay beyond reconciliation with a rationally constructed universe; on the other, dispensing with these sanctions would prove a step too far for the faithful. He therefore offered no commentary on the final article of rewards and punishment.

After Rabbi Meir Abdulafia read Maimonides's *Guide for the Perplexed*, he sent letters to all European rabbinic academies urging that all Maimonides' works should be declared heretical. But the great scholar still commanded high respect across the Jewish world, and reaction was initially slow. When it was suggested that this one book should be strongly condemned while other works were accepted as orthodox, the idea was roundly dismissed by both sides. Critics insisted that any attempt to reconcile revealed religion with immutable laws of nature could only undermine the foundations of faith.

> Fools who know not and discern not wisdom say that the universe operates through mere chance without divine guidance ... May they perish! They are indeed beasts. They are fools. They lack faith. Woe unto them, woe unto their souls! Twere better had they never come into the world.[9]

As the "Maimonidean controversy" repeatedly blew up over coming centuries, a division between those who supported and those who opposed a rationalist approach to religious interpretation became ever more deeply entrenched. It gained a social dimension as rich and better-educated Maimonideans were accused of constructing a form of Judaism that would improve their standing within Muslim or Christian societies.

The sons ... have defiled themselves with the food of gentiles and the wine of their feasts. They have mixed with them and become used to their deeds ... courtiers have been permitted to study Greek wisdom, to become acquainted with medicine, to learn mathematics and geometry, other knowledge and tricks, so that they make a living in royal courts and palaces.[10]

*

As the thirteenth century advanced, mystical ideas that were themselves arguably heretical began to gain firm hold among the anti-Maimonideans. Even those who devote a lifetime to understanding the Jewish *kabbalah* (the receiving—that which has been handed down) admit that this can be a daunting task. Though often presented under the pseudonymous name of ancient martyrs and holy men, scholars agree that most kabbalistic writings were the work of Jewish mystics who lived in twelfth and thirteenth century Spain and southern France. As wandering holy men explored the secrets of Creation, they drew inspiration from Sufi, Chinese, Hindu, and particularly Gnostic sources, which they mixed in with their own Hebrew Bible. The search for truth spread wide: "everything that is hidden and not revealed, it is found."[11] Some believed, like Gnostics of old, that inner mysteries had to be concealed from the uninitiated behind layers of metaphor and riddle; others insisted that new insights must be explained clearly so that all could understand. After the "broadcasters" won the debate, one of the most obscure and intricate belief systems in human history came to dominate Jewish devotion.

The first kabbalistic reference to a Messiah is hidden deep within an obscure twelfth-century text.

What is the meaning of "all the souls in the Body"? We say that this refers to all the souls in man's body. New ones will be worthy of emerging. The Son of David (Messiah) will then come. He will be able to be born, since his soul will emerge among the other new souls.[12]

At a time when Christians were waiting for the world to end on Joachim of Fiore's predicted date of 1260 CE, Jewish kabbalists had also reached a very similar conclusion. Basing calculation on the six days of creation and the psalmist's "a thousand years in thy sight are but as yesterday," it seemed that the world was destined to last for just 6,000 years. Of these, the first 2,000 belonged to the Age of Chaos and the second to the Age of the Torah. The third age of the Messiah would was therefore destined to start in the Jewish year 4,000—which translated in the Christian calendar to 1240 CE. Even after this date had passed with the prophecy unfulfilled, the expectation that a divine Messiah would soon return to his holy temple in Jerusalem remained implanted in Jewish End-Time expectation.

When the congregation in the Land of Israel increases and they will pray at the holy mountain and their cry for help shall rise up to heaven, the King Messiah will reveal himself among them and gather in the remaining exiles ... And the warriors of Israel will be gathered unto him from the four corners of the Earth, and he will assemble a great army and smite the princes of Ishmael (Islam) and Edom (Christianity) that are in Jerusalem and evict the gentiles therefrom.[13]

In 1260, 20-year-old Abraham Abulafia set out on a pilgrimage to the Holy Land to seek the 10 lost tribes of Israel, but he arrived just as victorious Mongol hordes were sweeping across Syria and hurriedly returned to Europe. After gathering students around him, Abulafia announced that he was the Messiah and launched into the life of a wandering teacher. He alone understood all secrets of the universe.

By my loosening of the bonds of the seals, the Lord of All appeared to me and revealed to me his secret and informed me about the end of the exile and about the time of the beginning of redemption. He compelled me to prophesy.[14]

Announcing that the messianic redemption would now take place in the year 1290 CE, Abulafia set off to teach the Kabbalah in Christian Rome. On receiving news that a strange Jewish mystic was approaching his city, Pope Nicholas III ordered that a stake for his burning should be set up beside the gate through which he would enter. In the event, Nicholas succumbed to a stroke before this Jewish Messiah arrived and Abulafia spent just six months in a Franciscan jail. Working through "prophetic books" and face-to-face discussion with devoted disciples, he now taught that believers could only reach true understanding by meditating on the many names of God and penetrating the secret meanings that lay behind the 22 letters of the Hebrew alphabet.

Creation took place by means of sayings. At each stage in the creation of the universe, the Bible introduces the account by stating, "and God said." Creation therefore took place through words. These words, however, consisted of letters. Therefore, the letters of the Hebrew alphabet are the most basic building blocks of creation. Subsequently, if an individual knows how to correctly manipulate the letters of the alphabet, he is able to make use of the same spiritual forces that originally brought the universe into being.[15]

Although Abulafia finally died in exile on a tiny island off Malta, his prophetic interpretation of the Kabbalah would continue to carry influence across eastern Mediterranean lands.

The weighty *Zohar* was supposedly constructed in the head of second-century CE Rabbi Shimon ben Yohai during the 12 long years that he remained hidden in a pitch-dark cave, without books or writing materials, as Roman soldiers searched for him in the outside world. Modern scholars follow internal evidence to identify it as a collection of thirteenth-century writings from Spain and Southern France. The *Zohar* replaces the single undivided deity with a God, described by one scholar as "a composite of forces and dynamic processes which are in a constant state of fluctuation and activity."[16] Instead of being helpless creatures in the hands of a higher fate, humans have the power to influence God's actions and even to affect his very nature. Appearing in the last years of the century—just as Margaret of Porete was composing her *Mirror of Simple Souls*—this Jewish work also presented unashamedly sexual images of human union with God. "By arousal below, there is similarly arousal above ... male and female, desire prevails, worlds are blessed, and above and below are enjoyed."[17] The *Zohar* maps out different areas of the divine body in an anthropomorphic diagram, where male and female elements combine to form a single whole. In stark contrast with Maimonides' monochrome intellectualism, the afterlife is portrayed in full Oriental color. Here can be found reincarnation, the repayment of past actions for good or ill (*karma*), and even the possibility of rebirth into the bodies of animals and plants. In this pantheist work, something of God could be found in every sentient and nonsentient object in the universe. Hope for the future was fixed on the one place on earth where the divine and human presences come into contact.

The *Shekinah* has never departed from the Western Wall of the Temple, as it says, Look! This one is standing past our wall and is the head of faith of the whole world ... From the place that Torah goes out to the world. And why (has the *shekinah* never departed)?. To protect Israel from the lion's den, from the mountains of leopards, the pagan peoples.[18]

In the *Zohar*'s fleeting world, the Messiah can take the form of a young deer who pursues the seeker after truth. "Look, this verse chases after you and looks out from behind your wall like a hind of the field skipping after you with thirteen leaps, leaping after you and cleaving to you."[19] Devotees treated the *Zohar* as Holy Writ, above the Torah and below only the Hebrew Bible itself. Families would read sections at evening prayers and word even passed that knowledge of its secrets could heal illness and keep demons and evil forces at bay.[20] Throughout ran the comforting assurance that Israel would grow strong and destroy the gentiles who had persecuted her for so long.

When the divine light shall fall upon Israel without let of hindrance, all things will return to their proper order—to the state of perfection which prevailed in the Garden of Eden before Adam sinned. The worlds will all be joined to one another and nothing will separate Creator from creature. All will rise upward by ascents of the spirit, and creatures will be purified until they behold the Shekinah "eye to eye."[21]

With hidden meaning concealed behind a mist of Gnosticism, the *Zohar* could be quoted in support of almost any position. In a Jewish scholar's words, "it was not the Kabbalah, but the popular conception of it, that made it possible for pseudo-Messiahs, often themselves misled, to mislead people."[22]

*

Until the fateful spring of 1391, Christians, Muslims, and Jews generally coexisted peacefully in the city of Seville and other towns and cities across central and southern Spain. Then fanatical priest Ferran Martinez began to spread the "blood libel" that Jews crucified Christian boys and drank their blood. After months of abuse and pillage, armed Christians sealed both gates into Seville's Jewish quarter and roamed through the streets, killing men, women, and children. Some 4,000 are thought to have died in the massacre. As matching violence flared across the country, Catholic priests held their pectoral crosses before Jewish eyes, offering a choice between conversion and death. By the time the violence subsided, a new and distinct group had emerged within Spanish society. Alongside Christians, Muslims, and Jews were converted Jews (*conversos*—or, more abusively, *morranos*), who were scorned as gentiles by their own people and dismissed by Christians as thinly veiled Jews.

Almost a century later, Queen Isabella of Castile arranged the appointment of her confessor Tomás de Torquemada as Grand Inquisitor of Spain. Since his inquisition had no jurisdiction over non-Christians, this fearsome fanatic set himself the task of preventing conversos from returning to their old ways, "like dogs to their vomit." He charged the faithful to report any conversos who ate unleavened bread, wore clean and fancy clothes on Saturday, or cleaned their house on Friday. Many had confessions extracted under torture. As fires lit across the kingdom of Castile, some 500 supposed heretics were burned at the stake in Seville alone within a space of just three years.[23]

With all Spain now in Christian hands, Isabella and her husband Ferdinand of Aragon dreamed of a day when a Christian ruler would rule over a pure Christian state. If the task of purging the country of real and closet Muslims could not be achieved in their lifetime, they could, at least, start by expelling the Jews. In 1492, Jewish families gathered the few belongings they were permitted to carry and left to find new homes. Many crossed the short land border into Portugal—only to face the option of conversion or another expulsion. Others took the short sea journey to the North African Barbary Coast, where some starved to death, others were consigned to Moroccan galleys, and a fortunate few established their own businesses. But Jews were still respected for hard work and enterprise, and some European rulers were anxious to recruit those talents that the Catholic monarchs of Spain had so lightly discarded. Nursing ambitions to raise his seaport of Livorno to a level where it could compete with Venice and Genoa, the Duke of Tuscany offered Jews incentives to settle on his land. Among other initiatives, a number of Livorno Jews went into partnership with their Barbary coreligionists to purchase those West African slaves who had survived the dreadful Sahara crossing and distribute them across European markets.

While some Spanish (*Sephardic*) Jews were settling in Europe and Africa, the majority travelled further east into the Ottoman lands to establish Jewish communities across countries of the eastern Mediterranean. Living on the brink of survival, many carried the sacred writings to their new homes and looked to God to bring the salvation that could not be delivered by human agency. As immediate problems eased, some of the more dedicated began to migrate to the Galilean town of Safed, which was reputedly close by the cave where Rabbi Shimon ben Yohai had composed the *Zohar*. Within a few short decades, Safed expanded from a small town of some 1,500 mixed race inhabitants to become a home and study center for some 18,000 students of the Kabbalah.

*

In order to be understood by untutored people, the *Zohar*'s varied layers of symbolism and magic needed to be interpreted by learned rabbis As indicated by his name, Moses Cordovero's ancestors had emigrated from Maimonides' home city. In Safed, he set about the task of reconciling mainstream rabbinic monotheism, which placed God far beyond human understanding, with the kabbalist assurance that the same God could be found close to humans and within all Creation. Most importantly, this teacher supplied the *Zohar* with an ethical base.

Of the man who resembles the Form in body alone it is said: "A handsome form whose deeds are ugly." For what value can there be in man's resemblance to the Supernal Form in bodily limbs if his deeds have no resemblance to those of his Creator?[24]

According to tradition, Ashkenazi Jew Isaac Luria arrived in Safed on the same day the Sephardic Moses Cordovero died. Joining the funeral procession, he heard a message that he had been selected to take the old master's place. Centering his teaching on tragedy and death, this newcomer liked to roam the cemeteries, feeling the emanations that came from the dead and wondering how their lives impacted the living. Just two years later, he too was dead—in punishment (so it was whispered) for having revealed too much about the coming messianic era. Although Luria only left a few poems to supplement books already written in Cairo, diligent students reproduced his message in great detail. They told how the divine universe had suffered a catastrophe and—like glass receiving boiling oil—it shattered when exposed to full divine light. Still, every time a Jew performed one of God's commandments, a shard of light would be returned to its source, until all Creation would one day be whole again.[25] Today, scholars respectively identify Cordovero's and Luria's versions of the Kabbalah as products of Judaism's scholastic and mystical traditions. As the sixteenth century turned to the seventeenth, it was Luria's version that would come to dominate messianic expectation across the whole Jewish diaspora.[26] In time, the mass of devout Jews, who were too preoccupied by worldly concerns to penetrate his convoluted writings on their own account, would come to interpret Lurianic kabbalism as both a call for personal devotion and a nationalistic challenge that they must return to the Holy Land. Messianic hope sharpened anger at past and present sufferings and renewed desire to separate from non-Jews, who could never share the same expectation.

Have they not accused us: "You poisoned our wells"? Have they not slaughtered our brethren by the thousands? Have they not cried: "You use the blood of our children as sacrifice on the Passover—you use it for your pregnant women"? Have they not robbed us of our possessions? Are we not condemned to wander as outcasts, so that many of us are without shelter as Cain who slew his brother? Have they not broken us on the wheel and delivered us into the hands of executioners like diseased cattle? Have they not burned our children, violated our women, and, when the plague came, did they not rage more terribly among us than the pestilence itself? Yet, with all this, the Lord has not turned his wrath away from us.[27]

Israel had suffered enough, and the arrival of its savior Messiah was surely long overdue.

*

Although the 1500 CE only marked half a millennium, the approach of this turning-point did arouse widespread End-Time excitement across the Iberian peninsula. Christianity appeared to have triumphed when the last vestiges of Muslim rule were rooted out in 1492 CE and all Jews had left Spain by July 31 of the same year. Spanish millennial fervor therefore reached its height in the dying years of the fifteenth and early sixteenth centuries—at just the time when the Inquisition was at its most powerful.

Three ships left the Andalusian port of Palos de la Fronteran on the evening of the August 3, 1492 A resilient myth represents the little fleet's commander, Christopher Columbus, as a modern explorer who sailed westward to find a route to the Orient in the face of dire predictions that his ships would fall off the world's rim. In reality, Arab scientists had known that the world was a sphere for some 500 years, and this fact had been accepted in Europe for more than a century. Outstanding doubt lay not in the earth's shape but in its size. While Arab scientists had calculated the earth's circumference correctly, Columbus preferred to accept a wildly mistaken European estimate that the Cathay coast lay just 2,500 miles west of the Canary Islands.

Christopher Columbus had long poured over millennial writings, which suggested that the age of the Antichrist would follow quickly on the collapse of Muslim rule in the Iberian peninsula.[28] He found one passage on the destruction of Alexander's gates of particular interest.

Have not the Tartars who were within those gates gone forth from them? For those gates have been broken. . . . I know that, if the church would be willing to unroll the sacred text and the holy prophesies of the Sybilline oracle and of Merlin, of Aquile and Joachim and many others . . . it would discover what it needs to know, that is, some greater certainty regarding the time of Antichrist.[29]

Working from an ancient Christian calculation that the world, from Creation to Judgment, would survive for 7,000 years, he concluded that "there are lacking about one hundred and fifty-five years for the completion of the seven thousand at which time the world will come to an end."[30] Signing his name as Christoferens—Christ-Bearer—Columbus saw his expedition as just a part of a final crusade that would destroy the Muslim empire and usher in the Day of Judgment. By sailing west, he planned to open China and the Orient to Catholic missionaries, who would seal off the Muslim empire of Gog from its rear. "God made me the messenger of the new heaven and the new earth of which he spoke in the Apocalypse of St. John," he declared, "... and he showed me the spot where to find it."[31] Until the day he died in May 1506, Columbus continued to believe that he had explored the eastern coast of Asia and, in spite of all evidence to the contrary, the myth that Native Americans were descended from the 10 lost tribes of Israel would continue to resurface until it became enshrined in the *Book of Mormon* more than three centuries later. Christopher Columbus had always enjoyed the company of friars, and in his later years, he adopted the Franciscan habit. Now interpreting his life in messianic terms, he reminded Ferdinand and Isabella of the old prediction that "he who will rebuild the House upon Mount Zion will come from Spain" and urged them to commit the gold that now flowed from the New World to the reconquest of Jerusalem.[32]

When 12 Franciscan "Apostles of Mexico" set out to convert the Aztecs, they interpreted their own mission as "the beginning of the last preaching of the Gospel on the eve of the end of the world."[33] Even as they travelled alongside lay compatriots who stole everything of value they could lay hands on, these Franciscans still tried to live by the founder's model of apostolic poverty.

> It was very desirable that bishops should be, as in the Primitive Church, poor and humble ... It was much better that the Indians should not see luxurious bishops, dressed in delicate shirts sleeping with sheets and mattresses and wearing soft garments, for those who have the care of souls should imitate Christ in humility and poverty, bear his cross on their shoulder and wish to die for it.[34]

The friars were surprised to discover that native Americans were a "humble people" who lacked the inbuilt European acquisitive instinct. Some were reported to be "of such simplicity and purity of soul that they did not know how to sin. Confessors ... search for some shred of sin by which they can grant them the benefits of absolution."[35] Then European diseases spread across the land and indigenous populations proved ill adapted to plantation work. The old Calabrian Abbott's vision of a glorious new age of the Holy Spirit vanished without trace when both secular church and religious orders chose to become deeply implicated in the Atlantic slave trade.

8

Before the End of the World Come: A Messianic Century

As soon as news of Queen Mary Tudor's death reached European Calvinist cities, English refugees began to pack their possessions and prepare to return home. Raised within the royal court's reforming faction, new Queen Elizabeth planned to build an unequivocally Protestant church that would still retain continuity with past tradition and practice. In order to dress the new order in some ancient history, scholars unearthed a thirteenth-century myth that told how Joseph of Arimathea had visited England in 83 CE and a fictitious British king named Lucius had then adopted Christianity as a national faith. While devoid of historical substance, these tales could justify the claim that the first Latin missionary, St. Augustine, had only imported Roman corruption.

Elizabeth offered her subjects a deal; as long as they were prepared to observe the outward forms of unity, she would refrain from "opening windows" into their souls. While many Catholics could accept this compromise, others refused to make any outward show of conformity with a church that had cut its ties with Rome. At the opposite end of the great divide, a few extreme Protestants (whether or not they also rejected infant baptism) were now committed to the Anabaptist definition of the true church as a self-governing and voluntary association of the elect. While these separatists might be described as *puritans*, the word also embraced those who were prepared to conform while still working from within to establish a more uncompromisingly Protestant form of church government and worship.

As the Marian refugees settled into English bishoprics, deaneries, and parishes, they imported those Calvinist assumptions to which they had become acclimatized. Through the years of exile, many had worked diligently on an English version of the Calvinist Geneva Bible. While they had drawn on William Tyndale's

New Testament and Miles Coverdale's Complete Bible, everything still needed to be checked against the best available Hebrew and Greek sources. The New Testament was already in print by the time Mary died, and the Old Testament would follow just two years later. With the official Bishops' Bible chained to every church lectern, this Geneva version was more commonly found in private homes. Produced in cheap editions, with prefaces to every book and explanatory notes around each margin, this version would underpin Protestant piety through the coming century.

Just one section of the Geneva Bible did pose a problem. Quite apart from John Calvin's well-known antipathy towards the *Book of Revelation* the Geneva Bible's standard format left no space for detailed exposition. Readers could be advised that that the New Jerusalem consisted of "the holy company of the elect," that "the great harlot who is seated on many waters" was the Church of Rome— even that the first Christian millennium lasted from the birth of Jesus to the papacy of Sylvester II (which lasted just four years from 999 to 1003 CE), but such marginal comments provided no insight into deeper messages that had to be hidden within such a complex text.

Interest in this last neglected book could only increase. Zwingli's successor in Zurich, Heinrich Bullinger, preached sermons on the Apocalypse, and millennialist John Knox would later inspire pupil James VI of Scotland to put royal pen to paper and write *A Fruitfull Meditation on Revelation 20.7*. In England, John Foxe's hugely popular *Acts and Monuments (Book of Martyrs)* provided a detailed account of martyrs' suffering from apostolic times to the Marian persecution. The author blamed popes, monks and friars for stirring up all kinds of wars and civil disturbances.

Waves of apocalyptic fervor swept England, first at news of the St. Bartholomew's Day massacre in 1572 and then, 16 years later, with the approach of Philip II's Spanish Armada. In response to growing demand, the Geneva Bible's 1599 edition carried an expanded commentary on Revelation written by French Huguenot François du Jon. Anxious to identify the influential Gregory VII as the millennial Antichrist in place of the unremarkable Sylvester, du Jon descended to to manipulating dates. Having postponed the opening of the first Christian millennium to the time of Christ's death instead of his birth, he then ignored the awkward fact that Gregory VII had ascended the papal throne in the 1070s rather than the 1030s. With these obfuscations, he could declare that "the thousandth year falleth precisely upon the time that the wicked Hildebrand . . . , a most damnable necromancer and sorcerer, who Satan used as an instrument when he was let out of bonds, thenceforth to annoy the Saints of God with cruel persecution, and the whole world with dissentions and most bloody wars."[1] With the Geneva Bible now securely placed within the apocalyptic camp, Calvinist scholars could hunt for clues on how many seals had already been broken, how many bowls poured out, and how many trumpets sounded within the passage of historical events. After that it would be possible to settle on a date when the sixth angel would announce the arrival of a great Tribulation and the slaughter of one third of all humankind. As neighboring

Europe became gripped by the savage 30 Years War, few would dare to deny that the world's end was drawing very close.

Meanwhile, the Catholic Church had been passing through a state of counter-reformation. In 1540, Basque knight Ignatius Loyola and a handful of followers received permission from Pope Pius III to form the order of Jesuits, who would provide the shock troops for an intellectual assault on Protestant beliefs. While the Roman curia maintained its traditional Augustinian reticence on things apocalyptic, it occurred to the Jesuits that the reformers were surprisingly vulnerable in this very area. If they could show that Luther. Zwingli and Calvin had ignored the Apocalypse, they could cut the ground from under Protestant feet and present themselves as the true defenders of scripture. Their immediate task was to break the connection between Antichrist and the papacy.

In around 1580, Spanish Jesuit Francisco Ribera began work on a commentary on Revelation, which challenged the "historical" Protestant analysis of biblical prophecy. Abandoning the literal thousand year millennium, he focused on Daniel's "a time, two times, and half a time," if "a time" represented a year, he concluded, then the period added up to three and a half years—or 1260 days.[2] Uncoupling Daniel from Revelation, he argued that only John's letters to the churches in the first three chapters referred to events that had happened in the past. All the rest—seals, bowls, and trumpets—lay in the future and would be accomplished within the coming three and a half years of Tribulation. Since the papacy was timeless, it followed that the Antichrist had to be a single, identifiable human being, who had yet to arrive. Citing Western and Eastern church fathers, Ribera argued that this destroyer would be a Jew who would appear in Jerusalem, rebuild Solomon's Temple, accept the worship of the Jewish people, before ruling for that terrible period of three and a half years. This Antichrist would finally claim divine power and conquer the world while locusts in the form of barbarian armies wreaked havoc on the human race. As the church fled into the wilderness, six heavenly trumpets would blow, with the last sounding the end of Tribulation after the Antichrist's death. Although Protestants reacted with alarm, Ribera's apocalyptic vision found no immediate favor in the Vatican. While he had taken care to describe the papacy of his own time as the "mother of piety, pillar of the Catholic faith and witness of sanctity," he did admit that, it had in the past been the Whore of Babylon and he predicted that it would apostatize again at the end of time.[3] Still respected Jesuit Cardinal Bellarmine set about importing Ribera's key concepts of the individual Jewish Antichrist and the three-and-a-half-year tribulation into mainstream Catholic theology. Positioning the Roman church as the defender of scripture, he publicized the reformers' doubts on whether the two apocalyptic books of Daniel and Revelation had any place in the Bible and even suggested ways in which the name Luther could be converted to the beast's symbol, 666. As Protestants clung to "historical" methods of prophetic analysis, Cardinal Belamine steered Catholic apocalyptic towards events that were to be fulfilled in the future. Although both Catholic and Protestant versions were founded only on speculative interpretations of inscrutable ancient texts, each had its own inner logic when presented to believers who looked forward to a world that would be free of religious hatred and violence.

Academically inclined clergy in the two major Protestant countries of Germany and England felt obliged to rebut this unwelcome Catholic assault. After completing his Cambridge degrees and settling into a Bedfordshire parish, Thomas Brightman established the habit of reading the Greek New Testament from end to end every two weeks. He took up his pen to refute Ribera by proving from scriptural and historical authority that the papacy was indeed a corporate Antichrist, as well as the beasts of both Daniel and Revelation. He added that the threatening Ottoman Turks were the empire of Gog. Having identified Satan's allies, he warned of the judgment that was yet to come.

Hearken, therefore, diligently awhile and receive out of this Prophesy not some obscure signs but the most evident arguments that thy husband [Christ] is about to arise even now for the avenging of thy grief, and that he may give over this whore [the papacy] into thy hands to pour out upon her the whole rage of thy jealousy. And that thou mayest more fully rejoice, receive withal tidings of the final destruction of the Turks presently, after the destruction of Rome. For she must first be defeated ... after that the Christian world shall be purged from the wicked abominations of Rome by the last and universal slaughter thereof.[4]

Now dating the beginning of Christian history to the conversion of Constantine in the early fourth century, Brightman identified the millennium as that period of unopposed papal power that ended when Wyclif poured out the first bowl of the wrath of God. After Luther and Calvin had emptied two more bowls, four still remained for release in final apocalyptic years that were fast approaching. Brightman measured the performance of Protestant churches against John of Patmos' judgments on the seven churches of Asia. By his assessment, the Calvinist churches of Geneva and Scotland met the same standard as the church in Philadelphia, which kept God's word "with patient endurance" and therefore deserved to be protected from the coming trial. In sharp contrast, he likened the Church of England to the lukewarm congregation in Laodicea, which was so "wretched, pitiable, poor, blind and naked" that it would be spewed out of God's mouth in the last days.[5] While Brightman would probably have been spared hanging in punishment for such an attack on the established church, he could still be flogged and have his tongue pierced by a hot iron. He therefore shielded his conclusions from uneducated eyes by writing in Latin and publishing in the Netherlands. His work did not become available in English until after he died in 1607. His whole output would then be reprinted in 1644 by order of the rebellious English parliament.

If any conflict could be reasonably mistaken for Armageddon, it was surely the 30 Years War and from his university in Hesse, Johann Alsted could recognize signs of the End-Time everywhere he looked. In origin yet another war of religion between Catholic and Protestant, this conflict had dragged wide areas of

Germany and the French borderland into a state of anarchy, leaving up to half the prewar population dead from starvation, violence, or the plague. Before taking shelter in more peaceful Transylvania, Alsted developed his own interpretation of the seals, bowls, and trumpets of Revelation. Using astrological evidence, he succeeded in demonstrating that the end of the age was indeed very close.

Alsted's English contemporary Joseph Mede did not readily fit any stereotype of a blinkered End-Time believer. Later described as a caricature Cambridge don, he was skilled in both Greek and Hebrew and was a good enough biblical scholar to suggest that the Book of Zechariah could be the work of more than one author. Beyond his own subject, he took an interest in both the natural world and the history of ancient Egypt and was also among the first to suggest that the condition then known as demon possession might be a symptom of mental disturbance. Still, he spent long hours searching his Bible and other texts, trying to build up a "Prophetical-Chronology" of times from creation to the end of history, when "all the kingdoms of the world should become kingdoms of our Lord and his Christ."[6] Again, Joseph Mede's English *Key of the Revelation Searched and Demonstrated* was first published in Latin and appeared posthumously in English after the English Civil War had opened the floodgates of millennial speculation. Mede used an unsophisticated formula to calculate the expected end of time. Accepting Ribera's argument that "a time, two times and a time, and a half," represented 1,260 days, he insisted that these were *apocalyptic* days which should properly be converted to years,[7] Looking backwards into antiquity, he concluded that the millennium of papal power would last for 1,260 years from the time when the popes first gained secular power. The variant depended on which event in antiquity any commentator preferred to select as the significant moment to set the clock ticking. By suggesting two—the sack of Rome by Vandal king Genseric in 455 CE and the deposition of last Roman Emperor Romulus Augustus 21 years later—Mede allowed some latitude within the early decades of the eighteenth century. The Second Coming of Christ would then be followed by the Tribulation, the battle of Armageddon, and a thousand-year rule of saints.

While works by Brightman and Alsted continued to command attention, Mede's *Key of the Revelation Searched and Demonstrated* remained the standard apocalyptic reference work on both sides of the Atlantic Ocean into the nineteenth century. Mede was on the academic staff of Christ's College at the same time that John Milton was a student at the same college and scholars debate whether the poet drew from Mede's work when writing *Paradise Lost* and *Paradise Regained*. More certainly Mede's book had a place in Isaac Newton's library at nearby Trinity College later in the century. After suffering some kind of mental breakdown at the age of 39, this great physicist abandoned experimental science and regressed into the "alternative" realms of alchemy and apocalypticism. After marshalling mathematical evidence, Newton settled on Charlemagne's supposed grant of secular power to Pope Leo III in 800 CE for the beginning of those 1,260 millennial years—by which surprising selection he managed to defer the End until well into the twenty-first century. Religious skeptic Voltaire would dryly remark, "A proof of the sincerity of his faith is his writing a commentary on Revelation. Here he finds it clear, to a demonstration, that the pope is Antichrist, and explains the rest of the book exactly as the other commentators have done. Possibly he meant, by this commentary, to console the rest of the human race for the great superiority he had over them."[8]

*

In November 1642, thousands of apprentices and "masterless men" lined up behind makeshift weapons on the battlefield of Turnham Green. While all were determined to halt King Charles I's advance on London, many were also convinced that they must stand firm against this royal Antichrist. Millennial religion and radical politics would flourish side by side within the ranks of Parliament's New Model Army. In this emotionally charged setting, common soldiers felt free to challenge the unequal social order that the Norman conquerors had chosen to impose on an egalitarian Anglo-Saxon nation. "What are the lords of England but William the Conqueror's colonels? Or our barons but his majors? Or our knights but his captains?"[9] Before the outbreak of war, "Freeborn" John Lilburne had experienced the pain and indignity of being pilloried and flogged at the cart-tail for distributing puritan literature and refusing to take the oath in court. As an officer in the New Model Army, he now led the pressure group known as Levellers. After arranging that two elected "agitators" should represent the concerns of each regiment, he campaigned for the settlement of long arrears of pay and to ensure that the men who had risked their lives on the battlefield would be allowed to influence those political and social structures that would emerge at the war's end. "I am confident," declared a supporter, "that it must be the poor, the simple and mean things of this earth that must confound the mighty and strong."[10]

Charles I's surrender in May 1646 not only undermined the belief that monarchs held their power direct from God by divine right but also created an awkward vacuum in legal authority. While the Long Parliament (already shorn of royalist supporters) still sat in Westminster, real power lay with generals who had gained power by force of arms. Anxious to cover military rule with some measure of legitimacy, in October 1647 commander-in-chief Oliver Cromwell summoned representatives of both officers and men to debate the merits of alternative systems of government. As they took their places in to Putney Church, beside the River Thames, popular Colonel Rainsborough represented the common soldiers, while Cromwell's son-in-law General Henry Ireton spoke for the high command. After circling the issues and adjourning for prayer, Rainsborough finally voiced the Leveller view that (at least for the male half of the population) legitimate government must be grounded in some kind of social contract between the ruler and the ruled.

For really I think that the poorest he that is in England hath a life to live, as hath the greatest he; and therefore truly, sir, I think it's clear, that every man that is to live under a government ought first by his own consent to put himself under that government; and

> I do think that the poorest man in England is not at all bound in a strict sense to that government that he has not had a voice to put himself under.

While Rainsborough stopped short of advocating the common ownership of goods and property, Ireton concluded that any settlement that left the landless majority with effective control of the political process could lead nowhere else.

> Man may justly have by birthright, by their very being born in England, that we should not refuse them air and place and ground, and the freedom of the highways and other things, to live among us ... But that by a man's being born here he shall have a share in that power that shall dispose of the lands here, and of all things here, I do not think it is a sufficient ground.[11]

In any case, Cromwell and Ireton understood the stark fact that, in the current political climate, any parliamentary election held under universal male suffrage would deliver a royalist majority. After the meeting broke up, Cromwell convinced parliament to settle arrears of pay and suppressed the Levellers by force of arms.

Ireton's worst fears must have appeared vindicated when, just months later, visionary "true Leveller" Gerrard Winstanley led followers to dig up common land on St. George's Hill in Cobham, Surrey that had been under threat of enclosure by private landlords. Soon "Digger" camps were appearing across the southern English counties. Ignoring the messianic currents of his time, Winstanley focused on real living conditions for "plain folk" rather than their future bliss or misery. Nursing deep loathing for all who made a living out of preaching, Winstanley announced that priests and clergy were in league with rulers and landowners, who sought to avert attention from present misery to uncertain rewards in a life to come. "And so [they] tell us of a heaven and hell after death, which neither they nor we know what will be."[12] He looked forward to the establishment of a "true commonwealth government" that would banish all greed and force, foster a spirit of cooperation, and treat the earth as a resource for all humankind.

> And thus you Powers of England, and of the whole World, we have declared our reasons why we have begun to dig upon George Hill in Surrey ... Break in pieces quickly the band of particular property, disown this oppressing murder, oppression and thievery of buying and selling of land, owning of landlords and paying of rents and give thy free consent to make the earth a common treasury without grumbling.... And hereby thou wilt honour thy father and thy mother: Thy father, which is the spirit of community, that made all and that dwells in all. Thy mother, which is the earth, that brought us all forth: That as a true mother, loves all her children. Therefore do not hinder the Mother Earth from giving all her children suck. Property and single interest divides the people of a land and the whole world into parties and is the cause of all wars and bloodshed and contention everywhere.[13]

For all his vision, Winstanley's Diggers proved to be just one more ephemeral movement, to be thrown up and discarded in these turbulent times. Cromwell's crisis of legitimacy became yet more acute after he sanctioned the expulsion of those moderate—mostly Presbyterian—members of parliament who might not support the millennial act of executing the King Charles I and then finally closed the door on the Long Parliament's sad Rump.

Through more than a century of radical reformation, enthusiasts like Thomas Müntzer and John of Leiden had focused attention on one passage from Daniel 7. After the prophet had described how he had seen four beasts emerge from the sea, an angel explained the meaning of his vision. "These four great beasts are the four kings who shall arise out of the earth. But the saints of the Most High shall receive the kingdom for ever, for ever and ever."[14] Revolutionary reformers found the meaning very clear; after four earthly monarchies had come and gone, a fifth monarchy of true believers (saints) would emerge to usher in the Last Days. Now, as all worldly authority fell away, a band of veteran soldiers and other radicals, who called themselves Fifth Monarchy Men, gathered around Cromwell's own second-in-command, Major General Thomas Harrison. While Cromwell never formally identified with them, he does appear to have shared many of their beliefs and expectations, and he now determined to establish his own millennial parliament of saints. Since faithless electors would never choose godly representatives, he determined that members should be nominated by independent puritan churches across England and Wales. In 1653 CE, 140 "holy and godly men" (of whom just 15 were committed Fifth Monarchists) gathered in Westminster to receive their general's charge. Observers noted that Cromwell seemed uncharacteristically nervous, sometimes pausing to correct himself or failing to complete sentences. According to one report, he finished the address by announcing that they had met together on the very day when God would manifest himself in the power of Jesus Christ—which, to millennial ears, could only mean that the Last Things would unfold on that very day. Fifth Monarchy "Man" Anna Trapnel was moved to deliver an extended hymn of praise "uttered in prayers and spiritual songs, by an inspiration extraordinary, and full of wonder."

> When Babylon within, the great and tall,
> With tumults shall come down,
> Then that which is without shall fall,
> And be laid flat on ground.
> Oh King Jesus thou art longed for,
> Oh take thy power and reign,
> And let thy children see thy face,
> Which with them shall remain.[15]

Foisted with the nickname Barebone's Parliament (after Fifth Monarchy member Praise-God Barbone, whose name headed the alphabetic list of members), this assembly was derided across the nation as a collection of "pettifoggers, innkeepers, millwrights and stocking-mongers."[16] For all that they embarked on far-seeing projects for the advancement of trade and learning, reform of the law and prisons and even the reconstruction of poor relief, proceedings were constantly disrupted by disagreement between extremist and more moderate delegates. Five months later, members reached impasse over Harrison's proposal to abolish the tithes that provided clergy families with their only income. After 40 radicals had walked out to confront Cromwell, those left behind passed a motion "that the sitting of this Parliament any longer as now constituted, will not be for the good of the Commonwealth." Ever the pragmatist, Oliver Cromwell accepted the semiroyal title of Lord Protector of England just two weeks later, and the Fifth Monarchy Men would seek to undermine his ungodly rule until the day he died.

Still, millennial intensity grew as ever more enthusiasts claimed to have received their own special inspiration from God. "It is no new work of Satan to sow heresies and breed heretics," bewailed one pamphleteer, "but they never came up so thick as in these latter times. They were wont to peep up one by one, but now they sprout out by huddles and clusters (like locusts out of the bottomless pit). They now come thronging up in swarms, as the caterpillars of Egypt."[17]

Most alarming were the Ranters. While medieval inquisitors' more lurid tales about adepts of the Free Spirit might be discounted for lack of confirmation, the Ranters of Commonwealth England bequeathed ample evidence of moral deviancy in their own records. The Epistle of Titus still provided that key justification that "to the pure all things are pure, but to the corrupt and unbelieving nothing is pure." At the very mention of sin, even in broad daylight, Ranters would light a candle and search in every corner of the room before announcing that they could find none. Ex-soldier-turned-minister Joseph Salmon summoned mystical language to describe his own spiritual progress into licentious ways.

To descend from the oneness of eternity, into the multiplicity, is to lose oneself in an endless labyrinth. To ascend from variety into uniformity, is to contract our scattered spirits into their original center and to find ourselves where we were, before we were ... 'Twas given to me that I might drink, I drank, that I might stumble, I stumbled, that I might fall; I fell, and though my fall was made happy ... I was ark'd up in the eternal bosom, while the flesh was tumbling in the foaming surges of its own vanity.

Lawrence Clarkson of Preston employed more earth-bound language in addressing a meeting of like-minded folk:

I affirmed that there was no sin, but as man esteemed it sin, and therefore none can be free from sin, till in purity it be acted as no sin ... Therefore till you can lie with all women as one woman and not judge it sin, you can do nothing but sin ... Sarah Kellin then present did then invite me to make trial of what I had expressed ... Now I being, as they said, Captain of the Rant, I had most of the principal women come to my lodging for knowledge.[18]

With alarming habits of shaking ecstatically while at prayer, disrupting conventional church services, and removing their clothes at small provocation, the earliest Quakers could be confused with hard-line Ranters. Searching for the "inner light" that was the spark of God within every human being, they called one another "my one flesh" and "fellow creature"—or, more simply, just "friend." Roundly condemned by more conventional Christians, Quakers held together in small groups, acknowledging no sacraments or clergy, looking forward only to the Second Coming, which could be no more than a year or two distant. More staid modern Quakers acknowledge that the movement acted as a magnet for both men and women who suffered from a variety of mental disabilities. In October 1656, ex-soldier and leading Quaker James Naylor created great scandal by riding into the city of Bristol, followed by supporters, who threw their clothes on the ground and chanted "Holy, holy, holy." Hauled to London to face charges of impersonating the Messiah, he protested that, while he never claimed divine gifts, everything he did sprang from that presence of God that was within him. Narrowly escaping execution, James Naylor was tortured and flogged across both cities.

When Charles II was recalled to the throne after Cromwell's death, England experienced no blood-bath on the scale of that which marked the fall of Münster. Still, as Harrison and nine others who had signed the old king's warrant of execution were being hauled to their death, a small group of Fifth Monarchy Men did stage an abortive rebellion. Millennial believers had not forgotten that the last three figures of the looming year 1666 CE spelled out the mark of the Beast. As plague hit the city in the year before, deranged Quaker holy man Solomon Eagle walked naked through the stricken streets with a charcoal brazier on his head, calling down destruction on the evil city. Prophesy appeared to be fulfilled in the year itself when fire swept through London, destroying St. Paul's Cathedral and 84 churches, along with countless businesses and private homes. But, as royal favorite Christopher Wren set about building a new cathedral and yet more beautiful churches, life returned to normal once again. Now at last, egalitarian firebrand Gerrard Winstanley could pass his latter years in comfort as master of Ham Manor, Cobham, Chief Constable of Elmbridge, and a successful Quaker businessman. But, to the dismay of Stuart monarchs Charles II and James II, the concept of the divine right of kings would never again find secure footing on British soil.

*

As soon as the brutal Duke of Alba became governor of the Spanish Netherlands in 1567, Dutch Protestants started to cross the channel to find refuge in London and other urban centers across the east of England. By 1571, Norwich was providing shelter for some 4,000 refugees and, 16 more years on, it was said that some half the city's population was of foreign origin. Radical puritan belief was already entrenched in the University of Cambridge and gaining ground across East Anglia and the Eastern Midlands and the tide of migration then began to flow in the opposite direction after the newly liberated Dutch United Provinces introduced toleration for all Protestants and Jews. The pace of emigration increased after the authorities decided to make an example and hanged separatist leaders Henry Barrow and John Greenwood side by side at Tyburn in April 1593.

In 1618, pastor John Robinson and his ruling elder William Brewster led members of a separatist congregation from the Lincolnshire village of Scrooby to seek freedom of worship in the Dutch city of Leiden. Ten years later, these exiles decided that Brewster should take a party of some hundred younger members to the new lands of North America. Before they left, their pastor Robinson explained that the whole Protestant world faced a crisis of faith.

> He took occasion also miserably to bewail the state and condition of the Reformed Churches, who were come to a period in religion, and would go no further than the instruments of their Reformation. As, for example, the Lutherans, they could not be drawn to go beyond what Luther saw ... And ... the Calvinists, they stick where he left them; a misery much to be lamented; for though they were precious shining lights in their times, yet God had not revealed his whole will to them ... It is not possible the Christian world should come so lately out of such thick antichristian darkness, and that full perfection of knowledge should break forth at once.[19]

Once settled in their new American homes, lay preacher Robert Cushman took up the same message, confronting these Pilgrims with the End-Time events that lay ahead.

> And if it should please God to punish his people in the Christian countries of Europe (for their coldness, carnality, wanton abuse of the Gospel, contention &) either by Turkish slavery or by Popish tyranny ... when Satan shall be set loose, to cast out his floods against them, here is a way open for such as have wings to fly into his wilderness.[20]

The image of wilderness—or desert—carried powerful associations in the ears of people whose lives were steeped in Bible stories. From Genesis, they would remember how Abraham's wanderings took him to the Negev Desert before he could settle in the land that was promised to him. The *Book of Exodus* told of 40 years' wandering in the wilderness, when the children of Israel "ate the manna, till they came to the border of the land of Canaan." and from the Hebrew prophets they had learned that those year of wandering were a time of purification where the faithful could worship Yahweh without being tempted to follow false gods. From the *Book of Revelation*, they recalled the vision of a woman "clothed in the sun" who gave birth to the Messiah and "fled into the wilderness, where she had a place prepared by God" and found nourishment for the messianic period of 1,260 days.[21] Drawing on all these biblical sources, the Scrooby pilgrims believed that they had opened a route through the wilderness, along which all who had "wings to fly" could follow and escape the coming judgment.

While it is estimated that some 21,200 emigrants took the journey to North America during those first two decades before the English Civil War, scholars still debate the "push" and "pull" factors that influenced so many to embark on such a perilous enterprise. Church historians have tended to stress the millennial motive, viewing the pioneers as "an organized task force of Christians, executing a flank attack on the corruption of Christendom" with the objective of providing the saints in England and Europe with a "working model" for complete reformation.[22] Economic historians, in contrast, offer evidence that landless people were first attracted by promises of property and a better quality of life in New England. While the "working model" image overstates the case, a significant number of enthusiasts certainly did board ship to build a society that would be fit to greet their returning Lord. The division between millennialists and secularists only became apparent after they had settled in the New World.

Listening to rousing sermons formed an essential rite of passage in all preparations for travel to the New World. As members of the Virginia Company prepared to dispatch the very first settlers in 1622, poet and Dean of St. Paul's John Donne emphasized the gravity of the task that lay ahead.

Before the end of the world come ... before all things shall be subsumed to Christ, his kingdom persisted and the last enemy death destroyed, the gospel must be preached to those men whom ye send ... One less stop here, Ye shall have made this land, which is but as the suburbs of the old world, a bridge, a gallery to the new; to join all to that world that shall never grow old, the kingdom of heaven. You shall add persons to this kingdom.[23]

Just eight years later, puritan clergyman John Cotton travelled from his Lincolnshire parish to the port of Southampton to send Governor Winthrop's party on its way to New England. Although both Donne and Cotton dressed their message in apocalyptic language, their content was very different. Donne urged the Virginians to take English religion and culture and win new worlds for Christ; Cotton pronounced that the Anglican order had irretrievably fallen from grace and they must act as a faithful remnant to preserve any portion of true religion that remained. Speaking from the text "Moreover I will appoint a place for my people Israel, and I will plant them, that they may dwell in a place of their own, and move no more," he advised them to "neglect not walls, and bulwarks, and fortifications, for your own defense; but ever let the name of your Lord be your strong tower; and the word of promise the rock of your refuge."[24]

Back in his parish in Boston, Lincolnshire, Cotton was already involved in a radical experiment in church government through which he aimed to preserve the unity of the parish system while at the same time giving practical expression to the Anabaptist doctrine that the true church was a communion of the elect. To achieve these twin—and apparently irreconcilable—objectives, he organized his congregation into two parts. On the inside, those who could make an acceptable profession of conversion took communion and held all positions of authority; on the outside were sinners, who were expected to hear sermons and repent their faults, but were given no responsibility. As soon as new Archbishop William Laud set about imposing uniformity of practice on all clergy in 1633, Cotton knew that his holy experiment would never survive inspection. Charismatic puritan preacher and teacher Thomas Hooker had now also lost his living as lecturer at Chelmsford, and both families boarded ships that were bound for the New World. Sympathizers saw the departure of two such eminent puritans as a defining moment in the End-Time narrative. "I saw the Lord departing from England," declared one, "when Mr. Hooker and Mr. Cotton were gone."[25] From their new homes, these two men kept in touch with Lancashire preacher and teacher Richard Mather. Seeing nothing at home but "fearful desolation," he, his wife, and four children also embarked at Bristol in 1635. Now clear of the Anglican hierarchy, these three clergymen presided over congregations in Boston, Massachusetts, that were organized along the lines that John Cotton had piloted in Boston, Lincolnshire.

From his prestigious pulpit, Cotton announced that the angel of Revelation had now poured out the fourth vial of desolation and the sinful world was hastening toward its end. But Hooker and Cotton differed on how they could best build a society that was fit to meet its maker. Hooker looked for a parliament of saints in which all those within the inner circle of the elect would have a say in colonial government. When he realized that Governor Winthrop would never delegate power, he led out his flock out of the colony to found the independent settlement of Connecticut. For his part, Cotton looked to establish a theocracy within which the secular council and church elders would exercise authority within their own spheres. "If the people be governors," he asked, "who shall be governed?" English puritans expressed increasing alarm as ministers who refused to implement the two-tier congregational system were frozen out of the Bay Colony. After John Cotton died, Richard Mather married his widow to establish a dynasty of clerics that would keep the millennial lamp alight into the next century. Both his son Increase Mather—president of the young Harvard University—and grandson Cotton Mather wrote voluminous tracts on the coming End. By the time he reached his early 20s, third-generation Cotton Mather had become convinced that New England was a special battleground between God and Satan and all were threatened by eternal damnation. His introduction to a children's book was enough strike terror into any young person of a hysterical disposition.

They which lie, must go to their father, the devil, into everlasting burning; they which never pray, God will pour out his wrath upon them; and when they bed and pray in hell fire, God will not forgive them, but there must lie forever. Are you willing to go to hell and burn with the devil and his angels?[26]

Cotton Mather lived to regret his involvement—or at least failure to intervene—in the death of 13 women and 6 men who were executed (along with others who died in prison) during the Salem witchcraft trials of the 1680s. Some saw it as an act of God's judgment that he was survived by just two of his own 15 children.

Ten years before these dreadful events, clergyman Michael Wigglesworth was already speaking of disappointment. His epic poem *Day of Doom* would become a New World publishing phenomenon, with copies treasured and diligently read in puritan households. As God surveyed the scene below "with awful voice, th' Almighty thundering spake."

> Are these the men that erst at my command
> Forsook their ancient seats and native soils,
> To follow me into a desert land,
> Contemning all the travel and the toil...
> Is this the people blessed with bounteous store,
> By land and sea full richly clad and fed...
> For whose dear sake an howling wilderness
> I lately turned into a fruitfull paradeis?[27]

God's judgment was clear; the first generations of settlers had lamentably failed to fulfil the great task that had been committed to them.

*

Zionist Jews do not agree on how the earliest gentile advocates of Jewish return to Palestine should be incorporated into Israel's national story. Some treat English puritans as prototype heroes and martyrs in the national cause; others argue that the very concept of Christian Zionism is a contradiction in terms. Certainly the idea that the Jews were an elect people who would play a key role in the End-Time drama lay deep within the evangelical consciousness.

During the reign of Edward VI, Norfolk men Robert and William Kett had suffered lingering deaths in punishment for rebellion. When their nephew Francis was granted a Cambridge fellowship, it seemed likely that he would settle peacefully into mainstream clerical life. But Francis held unorthodox millenarian beliefs; in his human nature, declared Kett, Jesus was "gathering a church in earth in Judea" and that "divers Jews shall be sent to divers countries to publish a new covenant." He advised followers that "Christ with his apostles are now personally in Judea gathering of his church and the faithful must go to Jerusalem there to be fed with angels food."[28]

Although Henry IV's statute *de heretico comburendo* remained in force throughout Elizabeth's reign, the punishment of burning at the stake was, in practice, reserved for those few Protestants who denied either the divinity or the human nature of Christ. It therefore seems likely that the authorities took issue with Kett's Christology rather than his "Judaizing" opinions Either way, he was burned at the stake in the moat of Norwich Castle in 1588, beneath the same walls where uncle Robert had met his death.

> When he went to the fire he was clothed in sackcloth, he went leaping and dancing: being in the fire above twenty times together clapping his hands, he cried nothing but blessed be God... and so continued until the fire had consumed all his nether parts, and until he was stifled with the smoke.[29]

The full title of Thomas Brightman's largest work proclaimed his apocalyptic concern for Jewish restoration: *A Most Comfortable Exposition of the last and most difficult part of the Book of Daniel wherein the restoring of the Jews and their calling to the faith of Christ, after the overthrow of their three last enemies is set forth in lively colours*. According to Brightman's analysis, it was the Jewish people, not the Christian church, that deserved the title "bride of Christ." Now, at last, those who "had been banished from the marriage bed for so many years and generations, shall at length return.... Then finally shall the voice ring out Hallelujah, for the marriage of the Lamb and his wife."[30] He then announced that Jews would be restored to Palestine when the Last Things began to unfold in 1650 CE.

Christian Zionism reached national attention when prominent lawyer Sir Henry Finch produced a pseudonymous treatise on the return of the Jews, which was heavily dependent on Brightman's work. In *The Calling of the Jews. A Present to Judah and the Children of Israel*, Finch looked forward to a mass migration of Jews to the Holy Land. With God's help, they would then win a great battle beside the Sea of Galilee and destroy the Turkish empire. "The same judgment is to be made," he declared, "of their returning to their lands and ancient seats, the conquest of their foes, the fruitfulness of their soil, and the glorious Church they shall erect in the land itself of Judah."[31] As a self-proclaimed expert on the apocalypse, King James I felt personally insulted by the work, and Fitch was imprisoned, then released after fulsome apology.

It has been suggested that this interest in a Jewish return to the Holy Land may have been inspired through contact with Lurianic Kabbalism. Although Jews had been excluded from England since Edward I expelled the whole community in 1290, puritan traders were in regular contact with Jewish partners in Amsterdam and a *marrano* community was also well established in London. By 1632, Joseph Mede could justify his interpretation of the millennium not only from the Bible but also from the opinions of learned Hebrews concerning the great Day of Judgment.

Those Bible-centered Christians who dominated the nation after the execution of Charles I could quote chapter and verse on how God had given the land of Canaan to the children of Israel.[32] Enthusiasts extracted both Old and New Testaments passages from their context to construct a narrative for Jewish return to the Holy Land. One key passage in Isaiah linked this event with a restoration of Israel's 10 lost tribes from all those places where they had been scattered.

On that day, the Lord will extend his hand yet a second time to recover the remnant that is left of his people, from Assyria, from Egypt, from Pathros, from Ethiopia, from Elam, from Shinar, from Hamath, and from the coastlands of the sea.[33]

Turning forward to Revelation, enthusiasts also pondered the connection between the salvation of 144,000 faithful Jews and the arrival of New Jerusalem from heaven. At the same time, special attention also focused on an ambiguous passage in St. Paul's *Epistle to the Romans*.

And so all Israel will be saved; as it is written, "Out of Zion will come the Deliverer; he will banish ungodliness from Jacob." "And this my covenant with them when I take away their sins." As regards the gospel they are enemies of God for your sake; but as regard election they are beloved for the sake of their ancestors.[34]

By puritan interpretation, this last phrase confirmed that the Jews must play their part in the great End-Time drama. The key elements of biblical prophesy were now in place: Christ would not return until the 10 lost tribes of Israel had been identified, the Jews had become Christian and returned to the Promised Land. It only remained unclear in what order these events would happen. While some English puritans argued that the Jews must receive their enlightenment in Palestine, others contended that the initial conversion would be best achieved in godly England. Whether that transformation would be accomplished by slow persuasion or sudden apocalyptic act of God remained yet another issue for debate.

Even as millennial excitement increased within the restricted world of English puritanism, so a sense of expectation was nearing bursting point across the Jewish diaspora. The first stirrings of messianic fervor have been traced to followers of the Rabbi Judah Loew of Prague in around 1599. Using their own esoteric mathematics, kabbalistic scholars now identified 1648—just two years earlier than Brightman's forecast—as the year when the world would end. Although the designated time came and went with no sign of the Messiah, terrible massacres of Jews across Eastern Europe only helped intensify apocalyptic hunger. According to some interpretations, the Messiah was delaying his appearance until Jewish people were scattered across the whole world. Since the name "Angle-terre" was translated out of Hebrew as "the end of the earth," the opening of England to Jewish immigration acquired ever-increasing significance.[35] While Oliver Cromwell kept in touch with London's marrano community, he was also coming under increasing pressure from domestic Zionists. One Suffolk preacher declared himself "persuaded that the Jews shall receive their Christ's Nativity day from England. . . . rather than from any other church in Christendom," while Fifth Monarchist Mary Cary pronounced herself convinced that, after admission to England, "the Jews should suddenly be converted in a single day and gathered together as a distinct nation and returned to the Holy Land."[36]

Amsterdam rabbi Menasseh ben Israel always discounted stories that Native Americans were Israel's 10 lost tribes as no better than Jesuit fabrications. His mind changed when fellow Jew Antonio de Montezinos claimed to have met a circumcised people in Ecuador who were descended from the tribe of Ruben, observed Jewish customs, and even recited the Shema—"Hear Oh Israel, the Lord our God is one God." Converted overnight to the millenarian cause, ben Israel secured an invitation to present the case for Jewish readmission before Cromwell and the English people. After announcing that the British parliament had "done great things valiantly," he predicted that "the opinions of many Christians and mine do concur herein, that we both believe that the restoring time of our Nation into their native country is very near at hand." He found Cromwell sympathetic. Aside from his own millenarian sympathies, the Lord Protector believed that moving wealthy Jewish trading houses from Amsterdam to London could help secure English control over vital North Atlantic slave trade routes. In the event, the rabbi's well-publicized visit aroused bitter opposition to any idea of reintroducing the Jews. As anti-Semitic pamphlets flooded the streets, Cromwell introduced a policy of limited and controlled Jewish immigration, which remained in place after the Restoration. Still, within a couple of decades, London traders had secured a lion's share of the North Atlantic slaving routes without Jewish assistance.

*

When 22-year-old Smyrna trader's son Sabbattai Sevi first proclaimed himself Messiah in the apocalyptic year of 1648, very few took his message seriously. Hearing voices in his head and suffering from huge swings in mood (today recognized as symptoms of bipolar disorder), he traveled widely around the Ottoman Empire. Meanwhile, the younger Nathan of Gaza described how he too was being drawn into Lurianic kabbalism.

When I had attained the age of twenty, I began to study the book Zohar and some of the Lurianic writings... In that same year, my force having been stimulated by the visions of the angels and the blessed souls, I was undergoing a prolonged fast in the week before the feast of Purim. Having locked myself in a separate room in holiness and purity... the spirit came over me, my hair stood on end and my knees shook and I beheld the throne-chariot of God [merkabah], and I saw visions of God all day long and all night.[37]

When the two men came together in Palestine, Nathan announced that Sevi was the one for whom the Jews had been waiting. Launching into their prophetic mission in 1665, with Sevi presenting himself as Messiah and Nathan as Elijah, they preached the imminent discovery of the 10 lost tribes, the return of the Jews to Jerusalem, the coming destruction of evil, and the final redemption of the messianic age. Letters that described how the lost tribes had risen to destroy the Muslim empire and the new Messiah was raising the dead and walking through prison doors circulated widely among Jewish communities.[38] Soon both Sephardic and Ashkenazi Jews started to converge on the Holy Land.

In a time when constant reports from sundry places and lands gave out to the world that the Israelites were on a journey towards Jerusalem, from sundry parts in great multitudes and they were carried with great signs and wonders by a high and mighty hand of extraordinary providence.[39]

In distant Boston, Increase Mather followed the twin phenomena of the Jewish Messiah and the fire of London with mounting excitement. Coming together in the apocalyptic year of 1666, he could only conclude that the End-Time had indeed arrived.

We find the sixth angel pouring out his vial over the River Euphrates whereby the water thereof is dried up that the way of the Kings of the East may be prepared.... Now I humbly conceive that the Jews be the fairest for the claim of his title of the Kings of the East.... For then will their eyes be open to see the true Messiah.[40]

To his acute disappointment, another ship then brought news of Sevi's apostasy and the great Jewish disappointment. According to the narrative that reached Boston, he turned Muslim in preference to having his body used for target practice by the Sultan's crack archers. After son Cotton Mather sorrowfully renounced his father's "Judaizing" tendencies, it appeared that the Zionist cause had exhausted its Christian advocates.

Still across the Jewish world, significant pockets of believers clung to the messianic expectation. By some accounts, the real Sabbattai Sevi had gone into occultation while another took his place in the Sultan's service; yet more claimed that the Messiah's real body had been assumed to heaven and a mere shadow accepted conversion; others announced that Sevi had bravely fulfilled the Messiah's destiny by descending into the evil underworld of Islam. While most Jews tried to forget the whole sorry episode, a growing number of Sabbatian communities would keep on watching for their Messiah's return.[41]

*

As in Western Europe, the year 1666 was anticipated with dread across the whole of Christian Russia. Just a decade before this momentous date, newly appointed Patriarch Nikon brought apocalyptic chaos by submitting the service books in use across the country to detailed scrutiny with a view to bringing the Russian liturgy and worship into line with practice in Constantinople. By normal judgments, no major issues of doctrine were at stake. Three instead of two fingers would be used to deliver the blessing and make the sign of the cross; processions would move round the church in a counterclockwise rather than a clockwise direction; five holy loaves (*prosphora*) were to be used during the Eucharist instead of the customary seven and three instead of two alleluias would be sung in the Gloria. Apparently minor changes would also be made in the wording and spellings within the ancient service books. Certain types of icons were also anathemized, and church buildings, like Moscow's St. Basil's, that were built on the "tent" design were to be replaced. Instead of introducing change with consultation, Nikon chose to enforce his reforms with ruthless ferocity. Dissident bishop Paul of Kolomna was first banished to a monastery in the frozen north and then burned at the stake. The Patriarch's agents then toured the country conducting church-to-church and even house-to-house searches, gouging the eyes out of prohibited icons and then parading the defaced objects through the streets.

With passions running high on both sides, opponents searched for hidden threats to basic doctrine; the traditional two fingers had stood for the two natures of Christ, while three now represented the persons of the Trinity; perhaps "begotten not made" carried different connotations from "begotten *but* not made." But surface meaning was not all. From antiquity, conservatively minded worshippers of many faiths had held that religious ritual would only bring benefit if it was performed exactly as it had been handed down. The form of an act of worship, therefore, could therefore count for as much as its content. Scholars now believe that the Russian rite was, in reality, older than that used in Constantinople and it could be argued that God had abandoned that city—the second Rome—just because its priests had modified the ancient rituals; Perhaps Russia—the third Rome—would now also fall.

Like some mediaeval pope, Nikon believed that the spiritual took precedence over the temporal power, and he persuaded inadequate Tsar Alexis II to give the imperial seal of approval to every move. Apart from being heresy, resistance to the Nikon reforms also became treason to the state and, on both counts, the only possible punishment was death. Nikon's changes had, at least in part, been driven by secular considerations. As the Russian state looked to expand into the Balkans, standardization with Byzantine practice would strengthen any future attempt to intervene on behalf of those Orthodox Christians who now lived under Ottoman rules. But the patriarech had overreached himself, and he was unseated in 1660 after Alexis finally withdrew his support. Still, the same synod that deposed its patriarch reconfirmed the changes that he had introduced, and persecution continued unabated.

With both tsar and patriarch—state and church—revealed as Antichrist, defenders of the old rites, who would be known as Old Believers, now knew that the world's end was very near. As long-standing social resentments fed religious anger, civil disobedience spilled into open rebellion. Alexis died in 1675, to be succeeded by his liberal-minded but severely disabled eldest son Feodor. When he in turn died just seven years later, the country descended into vicious civil war, which was led on either side by the families of Alexis' two wives. This was resolved in 1684, when one boy from each family was nominated joint tsar (with the future Peter the Great junior of the two). After sister by the first marriage Princess Sophia grasped real power, persecution of Old Believers rose to new levels of intensity. All who were conspicuously absent from the church or could even be identified by gossip were to be arrested and forced, under torture, to name others. Those identified as Old Believers were then obliged to make a full act of submission to the church and all its rituals, after which all their actions would be monitored to ensure that they did not relapse. In this time of apocalyptic tribulation, Old Believers were being offered a choice between suffering a martyr's death or being consigned to the flames of hell for all eternity. With the end of time clearly upon them, Old Believers embraced a cult of mass suicide on a scale probably unique in human history. According to their own records, some 20,000 burned themselves to death—usually in large groups—during that half-century before 1700 CE.[42] One example must serve for many. Since the time of Ivan the Terrible, a century earlier, Russian tsars recruited the help of loyal orthodox monasteries to control the remote northwestern lands around Finland and the White Sea. In return, the monks were given exclusive rights to exploit some of the region's most productive farmland, fisheries, and forests. Squeezed of their livelihoods, peasants appealed to the Kremlin in vain.

Merciful Lord Tsar... have mercy on us poor and helpless orphans... [Many of us] have lost all our belongings and we have fled in all directions... and many orphaned peasants with their women and children are crying loudly and seeking food in monasteries and boyar estates.[43]

As Old Believing clergy fled into this remote area, disaffected people flocked to their support, and then turned on the offending monasteries. In January 1687, wandering monk Father Ignatii led some 2,000 peasants across frozen Lake Onega to take possession of the island-based Rozhdestvenskii Monastery, which had supported Nikon's reforms from the beginning. After expelling the monks, the invaders could do no more than settle down to await Sophia's inevitable retaliation. When the imperial force arrived, they did defend the island as best they could, but when the cause was clearly hopeless, Ignatii gathered the defenders into the main church. After piling tinder around the walls, he led a unison prayer of martyrdom:

It is sweet for me to die for the laws of your church, Oh Christ, since they are more powerful than my physical strength. Lord, accept my death as a favorable sacrifice for my many sufferings, which I am yearning to overcome. Grant me forgiveness for my sins and reckon me among the assembly of your saints in the Kingdom of Heaven.

With the imperial army watching in horror, these Old Believers set the tinder alight, and some 2,000 were reported to have burned to death without a word of protest or cry of pain. Stories of a heavenly vision would later circulate.

Father Ignatii appeared with a cross in great glory and brightness. He rose up and ascended high; behind him were other monks and a countless multitude of people. All dressed in white robes, also in great brightness and glory. They marched in rows behind Father Ignantii, climbing to heaven and crossing through the heavenly doors.[44]

More would follow. After the Rozhdestvenskii brothers returned, a monk known as German led more peasants across the water. On this occasion, they imprisoned and tortured the monks and mounted raiding parties to scavenge for food and even abduct women from the mainland. When the imperial forces arrived, the whole ghastly process of self-immolation was repeated—only on this occasion, the monks were forced to die along with their captors.

Tsar Peter made a successful bid for power after Sophie had ruled for seven years, and the persecutor ended her days in monastic solitary confinement with the bodies of dead supporters hanging outside her window. Although persecution did ease, the Old Believers still could not reconcile themselves to their new tsar's style of secular "enlightened" government, and they continued to describe Peter as the Antichrist. The movement split into two parts, each of which would then subdivide within itself. On the traditionalist wing were the Popovtsky, who rebuilt a structure of priests and sacraments; more radical were the Bespopovsky, who rejected priests and all sacraments except baptism. Clinging to the belief that the world would soon end, inward-looking groups of Bespopovsky often held goods in common and avoided contact with the outside world of the Antichrist. After being scattered across the world by further periods of persecution, it is thought that, some one million Old Believers still follow the pre-Nikon rites of Orthodox worship.

9

In the Hands of an Angry God: End-Timers in Conflict

With religious wars consigned to the past and sectarian passions cooled, seventeenth-century tortured faith was supplanted by eighteenth-century Enlightenment. Across Europe, many clergy began to present God as an unmoved mover; once he had wound up the clock of life, he could stand back and allow his creatures to work out their own destiny for better or worse. Thoughts of End-Time fire and torture were far from the mind of English man of letters Joseph Addison as he wrote a hymn of praise to this remote deity:

> The spacious firmament on high
> With all the blue ethereal sky,
> And spangled heavens a shining frame
> Their great original proclaim.

At least across Protestant northern Europe, scholars could now challenge whether even God had the power to disrupt the immutable laws of physics or intervene in historical processes. French philosopher Voltaire and Scot David Hume even challenged God's very existence. At this academic watershed, scholars agreed that issues under debate should be settled by experimental observation of cause and effect rather than obedience to holy writ and ancient precedent.

Still, in the New England colonies, Protestant clergy had managed to retain their grip on intellectual and social life. In 1729, at the age of 26, Jonathan Edwards succeeded his maternal grandfather as minister of a flourishing Congregationalist church in Northampton, Massachusetts. As this young man delivered his message of guilt and redemption, religious emotions that erupted within his own congregation were carried across the wider region by English evangelist

George Whitefield and a small army of itinerant preachers. Within five years of Edwards' arrival, evangelical sympathizers across America and in the British Isles were keeping in touch with this Great Awakening that was moving across the New England colonies.

While Whitefield could employ all the tricks in an actor's book, Edwards delivered his message in a soft-spoken voice with few gestures. First, he might ask those below why God had allowed them to wake again into the world when they had so richly deserved to be sent to hell during the night. In his iconic sermon, *Sinners in the Hands of an Angry God*, he described how humans were suspended over the flames of hell with the support of just a single spider's thread or had to pick their way across hell's rotten covering, which could give way under their feet at any time. Listeners could be reduced to gibbering wrecks and elders called a halt after one respected citizen cut his own throat in terror. Two decades of work in Northampton ended when members of the congregation rebelled over their minister's plan to tighten qualifications for church membership. Turning down offers from Scotland and Virginia, Jonathan Edwards accepted a position as missionary to a Native American community.

While theoreticians like Mede and Alsted could contemplate the end of time from the detachment of an academic study, Edwards needed to integrate theories of the millennium with his day-to-day evangelical work. At its core lay the Great Commission, which the risen Jesus had left with his disciples.

Go therefore and make disciples of all nations, baptizing them in the name of the Father, the Son and the Holy Spirit, teaching them to observe all that I have commanded you. And lo, I am with you always to the close of the age.[1]

Some 1,700 years on, this New England preacher was obsessed by the amount of work that still remained to be done. If Christians were to have any hope of fulfilling Jesus' commandment in the real world, they would need a great deal more time than millennial writers generally allowed. Just as the Great Awakening was reaching its height, Jonathan Edwards came on the recently published *Notes on the Revelation of St. John* by English dissenting clergyman Moses Lowman. This author, at least, had scant patience for writers and preachers who laced prophecy with phrases like "the time is at hand" and "which must shortly come to pass." Following Protestant tradition, Lowman allocated first the seals, then the trumpets, and finally the bowls of Revelation to consecutive periods of Christian history. By his reckoning, the fifth bowl had been poured at the Reformation and the emptying of the sixth would not now be far off. Believing, like any secular Enlightenment thinker, that the world was steadily becoming a better place, Lowman delayed the final ruin of papal power and the pouring of the final bowl until some time after the year 2000 CE. Then, at last, Jesus would rule with his saints for a millennium of bliss. Only when that time was complete would Satan be loosed to bring Tribulation to the world, Judgment Day would finally arrive, and the coming of a New Heaven and New Earth would mark the end of earth-bound time.

Things foretold in this prophesy will soon begin; but I think they can determine nothing at all concerning the time when it will end... The period is much longer and reaches from the Time of the Vision to the Day of Judgment.[2]

Jonathan Edwards expanded on Moses Lowman's theme in a series of sermons, later published as *A History of the Work of Redemption*.

All will not be accomplished at once, as by some great miracle... His is a work that will be accomplished... by the preaching of the gospel, and by use of the ordinary means of grace, and so shall be gradually brought to pass. Some shall be converted and be the means of others' conversion... And doubtless one nation shall be enlightened and converted after another, one false religion and false way of worship exploded after another....

Then shall the joyful sound be heard among them, and the sun of righteousness shall arise, with glorious light shining on those many dark regions of the earth that have been covered with heathenish darkness for many thousands of years.[3]

That time of Tribulation, when Satan was loosed on the world, would indeed come, but with the date now set more than a millennium into the future, it would be of little direct concern to those who were alive in the mid-eighteenth century. Such a far-off consumation could indeed be presented as allegory for the ultimate triumph of both the church and liberal civilization.

Waves of revival continued to sweep over New England and those areas of upstate New York that had become known as burnt-over country after Jonathan Edwards died in 1758. With excitement all around, preachers told how God was still pouring out his spirit over all flesh in the latter days.[4] Early in the new century, Charles Grandeson Finney employed "ordinary means of grace" to fire the Second Great Awakening. As penitent benches filled at the end of a meeting, crowds would gather round, waving arms and singing hymns of joy. Finney dismissed those who argued that the End would only come through magical act of God. If the world "should now be swept out of the universe," he asked, "could we suppose that it was created with a benevolent design?"[5] Apocalyptic prophecy, which had strengthened sufferers in times of ancient persecution, seemed to have little place in the new and vibrant United States of America, which was ready to play a key role in the salvation of humanity. In one speaker's words:

In America, the state of society is without parallel in universal history. With all our mixtures, there is a leaven of heaven; there is goodness there; there is excellent principle there. I really believe that God has got America within anchorage, and that, upon that arena, He intends to display his prodigies for the Millennium.[6]

*

As Wesleyans and Anglicans preached religious revival across the British homeland, pious laypeople and clergy became increasingly involved in projects for social reform, including—most urgently—the abolition of the slave trade and then of the whole institution of slavery. As these new evangelicals, preached repentance to sinful people and worked to reform statute law, it seemed possible that injustice and equality would be eliminated and the world would draw closer to the state of New Jerusalem. This philosophy underpinned the flowering of overseas missions through the years leading up to and following the turn of the eighteenth and nineteenth centuries. Teenage Reginald Heber, later to be Bishop of Calcutta, took barely 20 minutes to write words for the hymn that would speed pioneers to remote postings across the world.[7]

> From Greenland's icy mountains, from India's coral strand;
> Where Afric's sunny fountains roll down their golden sand:
> From many an ancient river, from many a palmy plain,
> They call us to deliver their land from error's chain . . .
> Waft, waft, ye winds, His story, and you, ye waters, roll,
> Till, like a sea of glory, it spreads from pole to pole:
> Till for His ransomed people, the Lamb for sinners slain,
> Redeemer, King, Creator, in bliss returns to reign.

*

During those same years, however, another radically opposed stream of apocalyptic conjecture was also gathering strength. In 1787, American revivalist Elhaman Winchester arrived in London and set up a pulpit in Clarkenwell. Launching into a "course of lectures on the prophecies that remain to be fulfilled," he asked whether all the people in the world could possibly be converted within 1,000 years, let alone just 300, as Edwards had suggested—"especially when we consider that man's life will be so long, that he that dieth a hundred years old shall die a boy."[8] Rejecting Edwards' long-term millennial vision as unscriptural, Winchester argued that prophecy must start from a belief that "all the books of the Bible are genuine and authentic and that all the scriptures, especially the prophecies, were given by inspiration, and have been or must be hereafter fulfilled." Provided people read the scriptures in a "plain and obvious sense . . ." he insisted, "they will rarely, if ever, differ in their interpretation."[9] Winchester was back in America when the French Revolution broke over Europe just five years later. To many it seemed that, far from being set far in the future, the promised Tribulation had now arrived.

In 1798, Fellow of the Royal Society Edward King followed closely as French General Berthier marched his troops toward Rome. Counting back by Daniel's apocalyptic 1,260 years, he deduced that the papacy had first won temporal power when Byzantine General Belisarius' army destroyed the Italian kingdom of the Goths.

Is not the Papal power, at Rome, which was once so terrible and so domineering at an end? But let us pause a little.—Was not this the End, in other parts of the holy Prophesies, foretold to be, at the end of 1260 years?.... And now let us see;—hear;—and understand. THIS IS THE YEAR 1798.—And just 1260 years ago, in the very beginning of the year 538, Belisarius put an end to the empire and dominion of the Goths at Rome ... leaving thenceforward from A.D. 538—no power in Rome, that could be said to rule over the earth excepting the ECCLESIASTICAL PONTIFICAL POWER.[10]

Joseph Mede's historical approach to prophecy was vindicated as millennialists settled on a single date when the End-Time clock started ticking. Eccentric army officer James Hatley Frere (whose duties in the pay office never took him near a battlefield) welcomed the fall of Rome as "an event wonderfully adapted to mark the expiration of the long period of 1260 years, during which it has pleased God, with much forbearance and long suffering, to permit the triumph of his enemies of truth."[11] Now that the age-old riddle was conclusively broken, every prophecy seemed to fall into place. As apocalyptic violence spread across Europe, the Emperor Napoleon emerged to fill the role of Antichrist.

But by long millennial tradition, not one but two empires of Antichrist needed to collapse before Jesus could come again, and the Islamic empire of Gog still needed to fall. As recently as 1683, the Ottoman sultan appeared to have Eastern Europe at his mercy when his armies threatened the gates of Vienna. As this Islamic power stood on the brink of collapse more than a century later, European powers eyed Ottoman land—from the Balkans in the north to Egypt in the south and including the Holy Land itself—as territory fit for expansion. In that same year of 1798, Napoleon's French army landed in Egypt, only to find itself cut off from home when British Admiral Horatio Nelson destroyed his fleet at the Battle of the Nile. As British influence spread across the region, it appeared that the Antichrist's Muslim empire of Gog was also about to fall.

As enthusiasts combed political events for apocalyptic meaning, it became very evident that Winchester had been over hasty in predicting that people who read the scriptures in a "plain and obvious sense" could not "differ in their interpretation." While James Hatley Frere and his supporters insisted that Old Testament prophesies about the Jews had now been inherited by the British, others insisted that prophetic promises delivered to ancient Jews still applied to their modern descendants.

A recent commentator has boldly declared that the Revelation of St. John has nothing to do with the Jew, but that it relates to the Christian Israel and hence, in concert with Mr. Frere, has chosen to decorate the Protestant British nation with the names, titles and privileges of the ten tribes of Israel.

By this argument, the Jewish people remained the true olive tree and other branches of Christendom had been grafted onto this main trunk. Far from being agents of renewal, the existing British churches were in such a state of corruption that they had become agents of the Antichrist, and would be utterly destroyed in the final judgment.[12] Now that the sixth bowl of Revelation had surely been poured out, the emptying of the seventh bowl would soon usher in the Second Coming of Christ in judgment. As enthusiasts debated how this would happen, Frere's vision of redemption through British Israel rapidly gave way before his critics' insistence that the End-Time had to wait until Jews from all the 12 tribes of Israel had accepted Jesus as their Messiah and returned to live within the geographical boundaries of the Promised Land. These new redeemed Jews would then emerge as God's most powerful agents for converting all people on earth. Had these enthusiasts any day-to day contact with real-live Jews, they would have quickly discovered that this vision was far removed from any kind of reality. But reality mattered little. Those who followed Jonathan Edwards might plan to transform society "by use of the ordinary means of grace"; these new apocalypticists expected that all would be achieved by the miraculous application of divine power, working within the hearts and minds of contemporary Jews.

From Montanists and Donatists of antiquity through Apostolic Brethren, Taborites, and Lollards to Anabaptists and Fifth Monarchy Men, millenarian religion flourished side by side with radical politics; now, under the French Revolution's influence, apocalyptic belief became increasingly identified with political reaction. Since the divine plan left no room for human endeavor and the future Tribulation offered only early destruction for most of humankind, right-wing believers concluded that initiatives for economic, political, and social reform were Satan's work. The "rise of the Christian Right" can therefore be discerned in Britain more than a century before it happened in North America.

*

When the dissenting London Missionary Society (LMS) looked around for a popular preacher to deliver a keynote sermon at its 1823 annual meeting, it seemed appropriate to invite a man who was then making his name in fashionable London society. Two years earlier, Church of Scotland minister Edward Irving had travelled south to take charge of the struggling Caledonian Chapel in what was then the run-down area of Hatton Gardens. Addressing his congregation with wide gestures and deliberately employing archaic language, Irving would have cut a strange figure in any modern pulpit; at the time, however, members of his congregation likened him to John the Baptist, come again to proclaim a new religious dispensation. According to legend, his popularity soared when Foreign Secretary and Leader of the House of Commons George Canning looked in to inspect this phenomenon and then praised Irving's oratory from the House of Commons dispatch box. Soon fashionable carriages blocked every road around Hatton Gardens at service time and Irving could even count literary giants Samuel Taylor Coleridge and Robert Carlyle among his personal friends.

Nobody warned the LMS directors that Edward Irving had now embraced the new millennial cause. In the short period since travelling south, Irving had come under the influence of two very different men. After James Hatley Frere discovered that nobody of importance took his earth-shaking discoveries about the approaching apocalypse seriously, he managed to convert Irving and convinced him to argue the cause in public. If the Tribulation had either already come or was on the brink of arriving, the whole leisurely paraphernalia of missionary societies had surely become irrelevant. Irving had also been drawn into the orbit of ultra-Tory banker. member of parliament and leading member of his own congregation Henry Drummond. Infuriated by the fact that both Anglican and dissenting divines were supporting the cause of Catholic emancipation, Drummond believed that English Protestants had apostatized from the true faith and joined forces with the Antichrist. He looked for a time when the land would come under "one absolute autocrat; with a Priest on the throne; where there shall be no toleration, no republicanism, no liberalism; and where those who say that the people are the only source of legislative power shall be held accursed."[13] Drummond also concluded that missionary work was futile until the scattered Jews had all been restored to the Promised Land. As he recorded in note form:

Paul, when converted, the most zealous of all the apostles/the Jews, when once converted, the most zealous of all the nations, Till Paul was converted, the Gospel made small progress among the Gentiles, but by him it prospered wonderfully. Till the calling of the Jews, the general conversion of the gentiles not to be expected, but by their restitution, the whole world shall turn to Christ.[14]

LMS directors, who expected Henry Irving to contribute the normal heartwarming sermon, faced major disappointment. Once the congregation was trapped in the pews, Irving launched into a three-hour diatribe, which was first obliquely and then directly targeted at his host Society. He opened with sarcasm.

Men must have a livelihood before they could live or act; they must have protection to cover them from the tyranny of power, a law to save them from the riots of people: they must be well paid if you want them to work well.[15]

Like some spiritual Franciscan of old, he then contrasted this worldly image with the apostolic model. Jesus had instructed his missionaries to go into the world "without a purse, without a scrip, without a change of raiment, without a staff... without a hope or desire of worldly goods, without the apprehension of worldly loss, without the care of life, without fear of death."[16] By the time that members of the congregation were either collapsing from fatigue and discomfort or dissolving in anger, the preacher concluded by placing the blame for the "comparative failure" of overseas missions squarely on his hosts. Instead of controlling operations from the center, the LMS and other societies needed to allow workers in the field to act as the spirit guided them. The unrepentant preacher then added insult to injury by publishing his 100-page sermon as a blueprint for any future missionary initiative.

At about this time, Irving came on a Spanish book that helped to clarify his millennial thinking. After settling down to learn the language, he appears to have recruited native Spanish speakers to help translate the work into English. While Jesuits had taken the lead in the original counterattack against Protestantism, two centuries on, Catholic rulers were now becoming alarmed that the order was gathering too much power. When King Charles III expelled all Jesuits from both the homeland and Spanish colonies in 1767, Chilean priest Manuel Lacunza found himself shipped to Italy and then stripped of holy orders on the pope's orders. After withdrawing to live as a hermit, this defrocked priest focused his mind on biblical promises for the Second Coming. Whether or not Lacunza was familiar with Ribera's long forgotten work his own *The Coming of the Messiah in Glory and Majesty* repeated the earlier Jesuit's core thesis; Daniel's "a time, two times and a time and a half" represented a future the 1,260 *day*—3½ year time of Tribulation. The Antichrist would then arrive in Jerusalem as a single Jewish individual, before Jesus finally returned to gather the faithful to himself. Since the unfrocked Jesuit concluded by forecasting that the Church of Rome would align itself with the forces of evil in the last great conflict, his work was quickly consigned to the Vatican's *Index of Forbidden Books*; but even as the original Spanish text was being consigned to oblivion in Catholic Europe, Irving's best selling English translation made Lacunza's message ever more widely available across the Protestant world.

In a 200-page introduction, Irving agreed that Daniel's "a time, two times and a time and a half" represented 1,260 days—not years—and that this short but devastating time of Tribulation would come very soon.

> There is a universal belief in the church, that an age, a long age of blessedness, of at least a thousand years, is to run before the end of this world, and consequently before the coming of Christ ... You must either give up the certainty of the millennium or the uncertainty of the Lord's coming. And because both are revealed in scripture, they (the missionary societies) cleave to the former as being more pleasant to the infidel mind.[17]

As all fashionable society—excepting only Henry Drummond—now deserted Irving's chapel, reports emerged that women in the congregation had received the apostolic gift of tongues. At the same time, Edward Irving became embroiled in bitter dispute over Christ's human nature. Centuries earlier, his argument that Jesus shared humanity's sinful nature (though without actually sinning) would surely have sent him to the stake; in his own day, it cost his position as an authorized Church of Scotland minister. Still, he collaborated with Henry Drummond in forming the new Catholic Apostolic Church, which would keep the light of true religion burning amid the surrounding ocean of apostasy until Jesus' return. Irving also helped establish an annual "prophetic conference" at Drummond's country seat at Albury, Surrey, before dying at the age of 42, apparently wasted by a mixture of disappointment, controversy, and overwork.

Although key jargon terms did not appear in print until the early 1840s, they were probably coined earlier within the hothouse atmosphere of prophetic conferences. Having coined the word *premillennarian* to describe those allies who believed that the Tribulation would occur before the millennium, these enthusiasts needed to produce the term *postmillennarian* to describe those followers of Jonathan Edwards, who reversed the order and placed the millennium before the Tribulation. The third term *amillennarian* was added later to describe anybody who did not look forward to any Tribulation or millennium. That might be because, like Origen, they allegorized the whole idea of an End-Time or, alternatively, argued that the whole process had been fulfilled in antiquity when Vespasian sacked Jerusalem in 70 CE. Halfway between *post-* and *a-*lay orthodox Augustinian Catholic belief, which adjudged that the millennium opened with the church's foundation, but—following the creeds—agreed that the Second Coming and Last Judgment still remained future events. In practice, however, these terms had limited relevance beyond the hothouse atmosphere of prophetic conferences. Although comparatively few clergy and even fewer laypeople had ever paused to conceptualize the finer points of apostolic expectation, most did understand the distinction between a literal and an allegorical interpretation of the Bible. While operating within a postmillennial environment, the great majority of missionary "foot soldiers," who left for remote parts of the world, were unquestioning literalists who believed that their actions could somehow hasten the Second Coming of Jesus—in whatever form it might take.

*

After experiencing so many waves of religious revival, American society has been described as, "drunk on the millennium."[18] In 1831, Joseph Smith led his Latter-day Saints out of New York State to search out a site for the New Jerusalem in the Missouri wilderness. In Virginia, African American Nat Turner had learned to read at an early age. After growing up with the belief that he was no ordinary mortal, he became a Baptist evangelist and developed the idea that he was some kind of messiah who would lead his own people to freedom. After seeing a solar eclipse, which he interpreted as the hand of a Black man crossing the sun, he led a band of fellow slaves in bloody revolt against the White race in August of that same year, 1831. Just two years later, 50-year-old New England farmer William Miller began to preach that the world would end in 1843. The popular movement began six years later, when Miller met Boston clergyman Joshua Himes. Starting with *Signs of the Times*, this born publicist produced Millerite newspapers as well as three charts, based on Joseph Mede's apocalyptic system, which all converged on that single year of 1843.[19]

The armies of the Sultan's rebellious vassal Mehemet Ali were just then advancing on a defenseless Istanbul. Incautiously placing reliance on a single date, Himes' papers announced that the Ottoman Empire of Gog would fall on August 11, 1840. All Europe tottered on the brink of war as France supported Mehemet Ali, England and Prussia sought to bolster the Turks, while Russia prepared to gain what advantage it could out of chaos in the Balkans. In mid-July, just weeks before the August 11 deadline, the European powers finally reached a compromise that was acceptable to both the Sultan and Mehemet Ali. Miller's predictive powers would have been fatally discredited had a sharp-eyed apologist not come to the rescue. After combing the London *Times*, he unearthed an obscure British Foreign Office note, dated August 11, which stated that "provision has been made" against any risk that Mehemet Ali might return to Istanbul. "Where was the Sultan's independence that day?" demanded the jubilant researcher; "GONE. Who had the supremacy of the Ottoman Empire in their hands? *The Great Powers*."[20] Prophecy had been fulfilled and scoffers were answered.

Untutored folk, who did not understand millennial charts, could watch the erection of a "great tent" that would accommodate apocalyptic rallies of up to 5,000 people and read the Millerite publications that now flooded New England and upstate New York. As the predicted time approached, leaders let it be known that the world could end at some time within the Jewish year following March 1843. When the year passed without incident, a follower announced that he had found an error in Miller's calculations and the great day was postponed until the Jewish Day of Atonement, October 22, 1844. With a firm date now established, believers sold their possessions and left crops to rot in the field. When October 22 then came and went, many were financially ruined as the whole countryside became gripped by the Great Disappointment. One of Himes' printing workers recalled that terrible day.

Advent papers, periodicals pamphlets, tracts, leaflets, voicing the coming glory, were scattered broadcast and everywhere like autumn leaves in the forest. ... In closing the *Advent Herald* office on the 16th October, an immense edition of that paper was issued for free distribution in all parts of the land. This was considered the last edition to be published ... But the 22nd October passed, making unspeakably sad the faithful and longing ones; but causing the unbelieving and wicked to rejoice ... Still in the cold world! No deliverance —the Lord not come![21]

Fragmented groups of believers clung on to the belief that the millennium had indeed arrived secretly in heaven and surviving Millerite groups would later coalesce into the Seventh Day Adventist Church. Outside that small circle, however, Joseph Mede's structure of historical dating had been comprehensively discredited. While Americans turned their backs on millennial speculation for a generation, back in Britain a blinkered Anglo-Irish clergyman was already hard at work on an alternative End-Time scenario.

*

Devout, beautiful, and wealthy Theodosia Wingfield, Lady Powerscourt, was already a widow by the age of 21. After hearing Irving preach during a visit to London, she decided to hold her own prophetic conferences at the family's Irish seat in County Wicklow. In October 1831, 34 evangelical clergymen, 15 laymen, and 20 ladies gathered for three days of study and prayer. Brief notes provided heads for consideration: on Day Two, participants discussed "whether 1260 days means days or years"; on Day 3, they considered the coming Tribulation—"last terrible conflict at coming of Christ; Who is power that heads it? Against whom? What signs by which this power to be known? Proof whether saints are to suffer in it."[22] Two young men took a leading role in the discussion. After immersing himself in religious affairs as an undergraduate, Plymouth-born Benjamin Wills Newton had been elected fellow of Exeter College Oxford. Co. Wicklow curate John Nelson Darby had dabbled with fashionable Anglo-Catholicism before adopting fiercely conservative evangelical view. Still bearing scars from a riding accident, he cut an improbable figure in this elegant environment.

His "bodily presence" was indeed "weak"! A fallen cheek, a bloodshot eye, crippled limbs resting on crutches, a seldom shaven beard, a shabby suit of clothes and a generally neglected person drew at first pity, with wonder to see such a person in a drawing room... For the first time I saw a man earnestly turning into reality the principles which others confessed with their lips.[23]

But this unkempt clergyman did have personal magnetism, and a budding romance with the lovely Theodosia appears to have foundered when he placed his calling as wandering preacher above the prospect of domestic happiness.

At some time between the 1831 and 1832 Powerscourt Conferences, Newton and Darby made a decision to withdraw from the Church of England to establish the separatist sect that would become known as Plymouth Brethren. When the conference reassembled in 1832, proceedings dissolved into bitter dispute between separatists and Anglican loyalists.

Like some modern mendicant, Darby toured Britain and continental Europe for the next 12 years, leaving behind scattered congregations of Brethren. Spare time was still consumed by Bible study. "The testimony of Scripture," he declared, "is the only secure resting place of man amid the darkness of this world."[24] In books, pamphlets, and commentaries, later collected into 33 volumes (alongside a further 10 volumes of letters), he employed a style of written English the Brethren's own historian describes as "often slovenly, tortuous and obscure," with "thoughts seldom systematized."[25] His overall structure would later be misleadingly labeled as *dispensationalism*. The root word *dispensation* had been long used to describe how God was believed to relate to humans through a series of Biblical covenants. From the time that Noah's sons brought down God's wrath by mocking their drunken father, the first four dispensations (of Noah, Abraham, Israel, and the Gentiles) had all ended in failure. Now the fifth dispensation of the Church was also reaching its end in wholesale apostasy and the last age of the millennium was about to begin.[26]

Resolutely turning his back on every kind of secular learning, Darby focused his attention on the task of imposing a coherent narrative onto biblical predictions about the end of time. Viewed from his literalist standpoint, it seemed logical that every verse in the Bible must be afforded equal weight. Like so many predecessors, he focused particular attention on sayings by Hebrew prophets.

After severing individual texts from their historical setting and extracting any words that might be construed as a divine commitment for the future, Darby set about identifying all the biblical promises of Jewish restoration to the Promised Land and future punishment for faithlessness that still needed to be fulfilled. If a promised bloody battle had not happened in antiquity, then it must be still stored up for the future. Turning to the New Testament, he set about reconciling classic apocalyptic passages. Internal inconsistencies made this a difficult task. There was, for instance, no consensus on whether all the world would burn in the last days. While the Apostle Peter predicts that "the elements will be dissolved with fire and the earth and the works upon it shall be burned up," John of Patmos limits the conflagration to a third of the world's trees and all its grass and Mark's "little apocalypse" foresees no burning at all.[27] Since every biblical word was infallible, all three versions needed to be accommodated within a single End-Time narrative.

Darby held back from publicizing his results until Walter Miller's Great Disappointment had brought Mede's millennial methodology into disrepute. Following Ribera and Lacunza, he chose to take the Catholic position that Daniel's "a time, two times and a time and a half" should be understood as 1,260 days. Randomly doubling the resulting 3½ years to seven, he forecast a two-part Tribulation in which the first 3½ years would bring the rise of a Jewish Antichrist, the rebuilding of the Jerusalem, and the loosing of the first six woes of Revelation.[28] The terrible second 3½ "years of Wrath" would end with the Battle of Armageddon, the return of Jesus in glory, and the binding of Satan for 1,000 years. The unimaginable scale of suffering was attested by both Hebrew prophets and Jesus himself.

Thus says the Lord of Hosts. . . . Those slain by the Lord on that day shall extend from one end of the earth to the other. They shall not be lamented, or gathered, or buried; they shall be dung on the surface of the ground.[29]

Woe to those who are pregnant and to those who are nursing infants in those days! Pray that your flight may not be in winter or on a sabbath. For at that time there will be great suffering, such as has not been from the beginning of the world until now, no, and never will be.[30]

It remained to be established whether the saints would be expected to endure such a dreadful time. Paul's promise to the Thessalonians provided some scriptural guidance. "Then we who are alive, who are left, will be caught up in the clouds with them to meet the Lord in the air."

Lacunza had reminded his readers that, if the saints were to return with Jesus in triumph, they had to be removed from earth before it was consumed by the final deluge and fire. He presented his own, somewhat confused, version of the event that would later become known as the Rapture.

Those [the dead] being arisen, shall immediately ascend through the air to receive the Lord and enjoy his bodily presence: together with them shall likewise arise, or be caught up the living saints who are upon the earth. These living saints who have not passed through death, shall in a moment die—there in the air, before arriving in the presence of the Lord . . . While they are in the air . . . there shall come down upon it [the earth] that great and universal deluge of fire which shall destroy everything that liveth.[31]

It remained for Darby to decide whether this event would happen before the terrible seven year period began, at the 3½-year "half time" or at its very end. He chose the most comfortable option, announcing that the Rapture would take place, like the arrival of a "thief in the night," before the Tribulation began.

Darby's new doctrine (impenetrably described even today as "pre-Tributational dispensationalism") plunged the Brethren community into a state of "Rapture Rupture." In Newton's eyes, the very idea that the saints would be taken up to heaven before the Tribulation started was "a principle so fatal to Truth that I cannot believe that godly thoughtful minds would ever have sanctioned it."[32] By their shared literalist criteria, Darby had broken the rules of prophesy; not only did Matthew's Little Apocalypse make it very clear that the faithful would suffer along with unbelievers, Darby had also ignored Jesus' parable of the tares, which described how good corn and weeds must grow together until the final harvest. For his part, Darby was now convinced that the whole package of dispensationalist belief had been delivered to him direct from God and compromise was impossible. With two intolerant and inflexible men entrenched behind opposing positions, the Brethren movement shattered not into two but into three parts—one Newtonite, one Darbyite, and the other somewhere in between. As leader of the Plymouth Brethren's narrowest and most exclusive faction, Darby continued to pour abuse on his one-time colleague until Newton was the first to die some half a century later. An old friend of both men lamented the tragedy:

The dissentions among many dear children of God make one long for the Lord's coming, for if those who are confessedly walking in so much grace and singleness of eye cannot walk in unity and love, and, by bearing one another's burthens, fulfill the law of Christ, who can be expected to do it?

The Brethren's historian added his own comment. "The story seems only to illustrate the odd propensity of mankind for fighting it fiercest battles over those things of which it knows least."[33]

The debate on biblical literalism aroused deeper issues than any quarrel over the Rapture's timing. Although conflict would later center on Darwinian evolution, very much more was at stake. While Darby did acknowledge that the world was a sphere, many of his writings remained grounded in the ancient idea of a three-tier universe from which stars could fall from the sky and a bodily Christ and his risen saints inhabited some definable space in a location called heaven. Having explained dispensational history in terms that were tied to a 6,000-year biblical chronology, he could only ignore the fossils that were just then being hacked out of ancient Dorset rock by pioneer paleontologist Mary Anning. Earlier generations of Christians had never interpreted the Bible with such slavish literalism that core teachings of Jesus were placed on equal terms with Old Testament texts that provided advice on keeping slaves, selling a daughter for sex, stoning one's own disobedient children, and slaughtering members of peaceful farming communities.[34] At this point, Protestant Christianity divides between biblical literalists and those "liberals" who interpret ancient texts in the light of developing scientific, historical, and moral understanding. Living in separate intellectual worlds, members of the two communities cease reading each other's books and start to teach their professionals in separate institutions. While literalists become ever more identified with the political right, liberals maintain links with those on the left of center. Still, while all dispensationalists were biblical literalists, the reverse was not necessarily true.

*

Between 1862 and the time he reached the age of 77, 15 years later, John Nelson Darby crossed the Atlantic five times and lived in North America for some five years. In discussion, he found that many of Walter Miller's past followers had never understood the prophetic assumptions on which the movement had been based. "Their grand array proved to be ignorance, and no more, and the foundations fell ... Their scraps of Greek and Hebrew I could meet and their calculations of dates for the Lord's coming only baffled them."[35]

Preaching the old message, Darby urged committed Christians to leave established denominations, which were now no better than "the ruin of Christendom." His methods attracted sharp criticism.

> The aim of the Brethren is to "gather churches out of churches"; to disintegrate all existing bodies by opening a door in each, not for the exit of the faithless and faint-hearted, but of the pious and the good; and accordingly they prowl unceasingly round all our churches, seeking to reap where they have not sown, and leaving the denominations generally the exclusive privilege of evangelizing the masses.[36]

While very few prominent clergy or laypeople deserted their own denominations, many showed interest in this new apocalyptic structure that might fill the void left after the Great Disappointment. It is not known whether Darby met Presbyterian James Brookes during a visit to St. Louis; in any case, this influential clergyman embraced Darby's whole End-Time package. He, in turn, was a friend of popular evangelist Dwight Moody and teacher to one-time reprobate Cyrus Schofield, who would later construct his influential *Scofield Reference Bible* on the basis of Darby's "pre–Tribulational dispensationalism." Brookes also took the lead in establishing the most influential of all prophetic conferences which, after a few years of migration, held yearly meetings on the Canadian side of the great falls at Niagara. Brookes either wrote or at least inspired the 14-point "creed" that would become an accepted test of premillennial orthodoxy. Darby's influence can be recognized under the first heading, on the nature of biblical authority, and the last two, on the coming judgment.

1. We believe "that all Scripture is given by inspiration of God," by which we understand the whole of the book called the Bible . . . and that His Divine inspiration is not in different degrees, but extends equally and fully to all parts of these writings, historical, poetical, doctrinal, and prophetical and to the smallest word, and inflection of a word, provided such word is found in the original manuscripts.

13. We believe that the souls of those who have trusted in the Lord Jesus Christ for salvation do at death immediately pass into His presence, and there remain in conscious bliss until the resurrection of the body at His coming, when soul and body reunited shall be associated with Him forever in the glory; but the souls of unbelievers remain after death in conscious misery until the final judgment of the great white throne at the close of the millennium, when soul and body reunited shall be cast into the lake of fire, not to be annihilated, but to be punished with everlasting destruction from the presence of the Lord, and from the glory of His power.

14. We believe that the world will not be converted during the present dispensation, but is fast ripening for judgment, while there will be a fearful apostasy in the professing Christian body; and hence that the Lord Jesus will come in person to introduce the millennial age, when Israel shall be restored to their own land, and the earth shall be full of the knowledge of the Lord; and that this personal and pre-millennial advent is the blessed hope set before us in the Gospel for which we should be constantly looking.

The fact that Darby had failed to attract prominent recruits into the Brethren only increased the multiplication factor for his theories. As Niagara participants returned to homes across North America, many carried his whole dispensational package to their churches and denominations. Regional prophetic conferences for both adults and young people then spread his interpretation ever more widely.

*

In North America, as in Britain, premillennial belief developed side by side with Christian Zionism. In 1881, lay evangelist William Blackstone toured American cities gathering signatures for a petition, demanding that President Harrison should convene an international conference to debate the future of Palestine. This, after all, was the age of high imperialism.

Why shall not the powers which under the Treaty of Berlin, in 1878, gave Bulgaria to the Bulgarians and Servia to the Servians now give Palestine back to the Jews? These provinces, as well as Roumania, Montenegro and Greece were wrested from the Turks and given to their natural owners? Does not Palestine as rightly belong to the Jews? . . .

Not for 24 Centuries, since the time of Cyrus, King of Persia has there been offered to any mortal such a privileged opportunity to further the purposes of God concerning his ancient people.[37]

In the event, the Memorial attracted no national attention and the document would "sit on the table" for a full generation. But even within Blackstone's own dispensational community, missionary-minded people were asking whether the old blinkered concentration on the return to Palestine and conversion of the Jews was, indeed, the most efficient means of encouraging the Second Coming of Jesus. When enthusiast Arthur T. Pierson spoke to a student audience at Mount Hermon in 1886, he drew a map of the world to show the vast tracts that were opening up in front of premillennial believers. He then demanded "the immediate occupation and evangelization of every destitute district of the world's population" by the turn of the century.[38] Judging by the speed at which European armies were, at just that time, bringing the world under colonial control, there seemed no good reason why Christian missionaries could not do as much. Repeating Pierson's slogan "the world for Christ in our generation," some 100 delegates left Mount Hermon with plans to gather bands of students to confront this great millennial challenge. Jonathan Edwards had looked toward the time when every woman and man would be converted; Pierson asked no more than that the gospel should be *preached* across the whole world so that even a few brands could be pulled from the burning before the Tribulation arrived. Ever since members of Irving's congregation had started to speak in tongues, some enthusiasts had begun to ask whether this task really did have to be performed in a multitude of different languages or whether—like the disciples at Pentecost—missionaries could speak in a single tongue that all would understand.

While liberals offered some expectation of mercy to those who had never had a chance of hearing the gospel, Pierson insisted that all humankind stood under judgment. Even if pagans had never heard the Christian message, they could surely have deduced the love of God from the wonders of nature and humanity that they saw around them.

Yet they perversely deified blocks of wood and stone and worshipped the created thing from the sun down to the beetle. They ran from the light to their dark holes, like bugs that burrow in the earth.[39]

In order to counter the prejudice that still persisted against all those societies that did not focus on converting Jews, Pierson presented a live premillennial missionary to the 1888 Niagara Conference. Yorkshireman James Hudson Taylor had a convincing story to tell. A generation earlier, he had set up his own pioneering China Inland Mission (CIM) on just those principles that Henry Irving had laid before the LMS Annual General Meeting. His workers would receive no fixed salary, relying only on God to meet their everyday needs and they would be free to function without interference from busybody home committees. While conventional missionaries offered a model of "civilized" living, CIM workers adopted Chinese dress and preached around the countryside, offering "infallible help for every opium smoker ... for every drunkard, for every fornicator, for every gambler."[40] Hudson Taylor had no patience with magical short-cuts to language learning, and many of his missionaries returned home when the task of mastering the basic Mandarin that was needed for communication proved to be beyond them. Repeating the catchphrase "only sell success," he suppressed all bad news and exaggerated achievement to ensure that donations needed to support the operation did, in fact, arrive.

Canadian evangelist Arthur Simpson had founded his Christian Missionary Alliance just a year before Hudson Taylor appeared at Niagara. In his New York college, Simpson taught that conventional societies would always fail because they prized learning above a Bible-loving spiritual life. Demanding an "intense aggressiveness" from all recruits, he urged them to throw themselves into the challenge without care for consequences. Launching his Four-Fold Gospel (which still underpins the Christian Missionary Alliance) he proclaimed Jesus as Savior, Sanctifier, Healer, and Coming King. Under this formula, Simpson converted the refusal of medical drugs into a cornerstone of missionary enterprise.

Oft on earth he healed the sufferer by his mighty hand
Still our sicknesses and sorrows go at his command[41]

Simpson set his workers just one objective. "We are not called to a life of protest, to denounce evil by talks of righteousness," he insisted. "We are called to teach the children of God ... the divine way of overcoming sin."[42] Still Simpson's practical attempts to mount overseas operations were uniformly disastrous. When he sent six missionaries to the Congo River, one died, one joined an established society, and the other four were swiftly repatriated at public expense with chronic malaria.[43] Simpson then decided that Jesus could never return until evangelists penetrated the vast Islamic savannah country that stretched across Africa from the Nile to the Atlantic. When an ill-equipped group of youngsters from Kansas and Nebraska set out to reach the area by way of the Guinea coast and upper Niger, all either died from malaria or were forced to return home.

At about the same time that Hudson Taylor was passing on his story to the Niagara Conference, literate converts were beginning to recognize that White missionaries had failed to share the esoteric secrets that lay hidden in the Bible's last book. As indigenous millennial religion spread across Southern and Western Africa, new ecstatic forms of religion began to thrive on a varied mixture of premillennial apocalypticism, divine healing, charismatic tongues, and indigenous witch hunting—mixed together with generous quantities of heartfelt emotion.

Jonathan Edwards' End-Time philosophy had always rested on the hope that God and humans could collaborate to create a more just and devout world. It is hard to underestimate the extent to which the years of bloodshed from 1914 to 1918 undermined this optimistic view of human nature, but in the post-war years it seemed as though both liberal politics and liberal religion had lost all intellectual foundation. While many drifted into secular humanism, others who remained within mainstream Protestantism abandoned all attempts to construct a meaningful End-Time doctrine. As the twentieth Century progressed, belief in the Second Coming in judgment became the preserve of those authoritarian literalists who had never accepted Enlightenment belief in human improvement and believed that the world could only be saved by magical divine intervention.

10

When the Master Comes: Messiah and Mahdi

By the end of the eighteenth century, some 40 percent of all the world's 12 million Jews lived in the area known as the Pale of Settlement, which ran through Poland from Lithuania in the north to Ukraine in the south. For centuries, the Ashkenazi had been migrating eastward to escape brutal persecution in Western Europe; now they were joined by Russian Jews who had been expelled from the nation's heartland by Empress Catherine I. Living together in substantial communities, Jews soon discovered that life in the Pale was neither prosperous nor secure. Faced with poverty and uncertainty, they again took refuge in the kabbalah's messianic promises. After the prophet who would live under the name of Jacob Frank announced that he was Sabbatai Sevi's direct successor, he set about the substantial task of uniting Judaism and Catholicism, with a view to bringing their combined forces into his own messianic cult. Even after he had led some 500 Jewish followers to accept Christian baptism, the church authorities remained alarmed at his heretical views, and he spent the next 12 years of his life imprisoned in a monastery. Still Frank's popularity held up and, on his release, supporters greeted him as a returning Messiah. Enriched by their gifts, Frank and daughter Eve, who was destined to succeed him, lived like high-born aristocrats, in fine apartments and surrounded by armed retainers. Pious Austrian empress Maria Theresa even welcomed Jacob Frank to court on the grounds that only he could bring her Jewish subjects into the Christian fold. However, this new prophetic religion did not long survive his death, and daughter Eva died in obscurity.

Hardly less bizarre in origin, the story of Hasidism would reach a very different conclusion. Conceived, according to myth, in purity, without sexual desire on the part of either parent, Baal Shem Tov (later known in brief as Besht) was also born in that area of the southern Pale, where the constant risk of Cossack attack made life particularly precarious. Rejecting the all-pervasive Enlightenment learning of his day, Besht dealt in all the paraphernalia of magic—amulets, telepathy, clairvoyance, and communication with the dead.[1] Claiming power to ascend into heaven, he could even recount a conversation with the Messiah.

In reply to the query, "When will the master come?" the Messiah answers, when your teachings are revealed to the world and your "wellsprings shall be dispersed abroad." ... Then the impurities will be consumed and an epoch of grace and salvation will commence. Thereupon the Besht comments that he has suffered great anguish because of the length of time until his teachings will become known.[2]

Besht's pantheist faith kept close to its Zohar model. Since there could be "no place void of God," it had to follow that the whole earth was full of his glory. Every believer had, therefore, inherited a duty to achieve the fullest mystical union with the divinity by "trapping sparks of holiness and restoring them to their divine source."[3] This outcome could not be achieved by book learning or even by studying the Torah,—only through religious ecstasy and heartfelt devotion. Like the Zohar before him, Besht employed robustly sexual metaphors to explore the concept of union with God, and he encouraged followers to enjoy all the legitimate pleasures in life. It comes, therefore, as no surprise that his life-affirming faith spread quickly. As was recorded:

[T]he new sect ... extended itself over nearly the whole of Poland, and then beyond. The heads of the sect sent everywhere emissaries, whose duty it was to preach the new doctrine and procure adherents ... Young people forsook parents, wives and children, and went en masse to visit these leaders and hear from their lips the new doctrine.[4]

While Jews from the southern Pale were happy to embrace every new movement, those who lived in northerly Lithuania persevered in more conservative ways. Even if the tale that the Vilna Gaon (sage of Vilna) had committed the whole Hebrew Bible to memory by the age of three must be consigned to myth, this learned man achieved wide renown as a Hebrew scholar. When teaching his select band of students, he remained open to the kabbalah without ever allowing it to challenge the Torah's position as prime authority for Jewish orthodoxy. The Gaon reacted violently when Hasidic pantheism and libertarian lifestyles began to surface in his home city of Vilna. His uncompromising condemnation was delivered with the support of all the city's conservative rabbis.

The leaders and officers of the principal communities ... have firmly resolved to fight for the Lord of Hosts ... to disperse those wicked bands of men and drive them far away from their confines, and to put an end to their practices which are different from, and opposed to, the religion of our holy Torah ... to subdue them and make them like dust of the earth, so as to firmly establish the true faith ... Satan is still at work among us.[5]

It may not have been expected that the single event many Jews identify as beginning the modern Zionism originated in the Pale of Settlement's conservative north rather than the more radical south. As a younger man, the Vilna Gaon considered whether the metaphysical concept of a return to Zion, which was held in common by all Jews, might one day be converted into physical reality and he set off for Palestine to test the possibility. Although he never made it beyond Germany, the Gaon returned to plant the idea of return among the Lithuanian disciples. After the master died in 1797, three of his pupils named themselves *Perushim* (the separate ones) and began to plan ways of converting theory into action. Some 500 people finally set off by foot and horse cart in 1808 and 1809. Finding the old city of Jerusalem closed to all Ashkenazi Jews, they moved on to Isaac Luria's town of Safed, which was still recovering from a major earthquake that had devastated the area some 50 years earlier.

When wealthy English Zionists Sir Moses and Lady visited Safed on a fact-finding tour some 30 years later, they discovered that those early Perushim families were living on the edge of survival. Harassed by Arab and Druze raids, devastated by plague, and with their homes flattened by yet another earthquake, they lived in hastily repaired shacks that must surely be swept away by the next earth tremor. Barely surviving on charity, they protested that they planned to earn a living by farming but lacked the resources to make a start. After helping out as best they could, the Montefiores described a land of huge potential this way:

There are groves of olive trees, I should think, more than 500 years old, vineyards, much pasture, plenty of wells and abundance of excellent water; also fig trees, walnuts almonds, and mulberries &; and rich fields of wheat, barley and lentils; in fact it is a land that will produce almost anything in abundance, with little skill and labor.[6]

The Montefiores did not address the much-debated question of how observant Jews could ever be a farming people. The Book of Leviticus had laid down that the land—like humans—must have its Sabbath time of rest.

For six years you shall sow your field, and for six years you shall prune your vineyard, and gather in their yield; but in the seventh year there shall be a sabbath of complete rest for the land.... you shall not sow your field or prune your vineyard. You shall not reap the aftergrowth of your harvest or gather the grapes of your unpruned vine: it shall be a year of complete rest for the land.[7]

Rotation of crops had now replaced the practice of leaving fields to lie fallow and the Bible did not explain how hungry settlers could remain alive without growing anything to eat every one year in every seven. Disgusted members of the Rothschild family withdrew support from the Zionist movement as debate (which continues to this day) raged over whether every biblical instruction must still be obeyed literally within such a changed environment.

*

Today, as for centuries before, Jews finish every Sabbath day by expressing the hope that the Messiah will come "speedily in our day" and end each Passover celebration with the words "next year in Jerusalem." Again, such aspirations are open to either allegorical or literal interpretation. The Messianic age was traditionally feared as a time when God would, "in the blink of an eye," unleash punishment on an unrepentant world. Now, in the Enlightenment's wake, "postmillennial" Jews could assert that the end-time would arrive as the culmination of long centuries of progress. As the nineteenth century progressed, opposing attitudes to Zionism became increasingly entrenched within Jewish communities. Basing their case on the Psalmist's words, "Except the Lord build the house, they labor in vain that build it,"[8] ultra-orthodox rabbis argued that any man-made attempt to "force the end" by returning to the Holy Land before the Messianic age arrived must end in failure. In their view, Zionism was, "the struggle of the evil urge and its assistants who wish to bring us down. Israel has no greater foe and enemy (than those Zionists) who wish to deprive them of their pure faith."[9] At the other end of the spectrum, integrated Western Europeans mistrusted any movement, which threatened to undermine the social and financial position they had achieved within the host nation. However, between these two extremes, many were opening up to the Zionist message.

Despite his name (doubtless bequeathed by some Scots trading ancestor), David Gordon was an observant Lithuanian journalist who, for more than 20 years between the 1850s to the 1880s, first contributed to and then edited the journal *Ha-Maggid*. Published in Hebrew, this Zionist periodical reached a wide Jewish audience across Europe and the Middle East. While introducing a sharpened sense of Jewish nationalism, Gordon insisted that the new Zionism must continue to emphasize the hope for messianic redemption through return to the Promised Land. He also advocated a strategy of winning territory by the relentless expansion of agricultural settlements "to purchase fields and properties for our Jewish brethren in the Holy Land and to provide work for them so that they may eat of the labor of their hands and be satiated by its goodness."[10] He finally urged that the Hebrew language should cease to be a dedicated medium of worship and become the lingua franca for worldwide Jewry.

Although there was only one Jew among the conspirators who plotted the 1881 assassination of Czar Alexander II, this bloody event was soon branded as a Jewish plot, and for the next three years, Jewish homes were attacked in an estimated 166 towns across the Pale. While loss of life may not have compared with earlier Cossack massacres, Jewish families did lose loved ones and many more were reduced to abject poverty. Rather than live herded together in urban ghettoes, where they were denied access to farmland and the professions and to all but the most basic education, many chose to board ship for North America. In comparison, comparatively few looked for new opportunities in Palestine. Even as a second and more lethal wave of pogroms were devastating Pale communities in the early twentieth century, stubborn stereotypes were becoming firmly entrenched in gentile minds, under which all Jews were either wealthy capitalists who colluded to control the world's destiny or revolutionaries who plotted the destruction of civilized society.

*

The London Society for the Promotion of Christianity among the Jews—more succinctly known as the London Jews' Society (LJS)—was originally founded as an interdenominational vehicle for bringing relief to distressed British Jews. Tension between Anglican and nonconformist supporters then became acute when the organization ran into acute financial difficulties. As a demonstration that the age of miracles had not passed, dedicated premillennarian barrister Lewis Way inherited a large fortune from a complete stranger for no better reason than that the two men shared the same family name. Having bought a large estate in Sussex, Lewis Way determined to dedicate his newfound wealth to the conversion of the Jews and their restoration to the Promised Land. He laid out his purpose in doggerel verse.

> For Zion's sake I will not rest,
> I will not hold my peace,
> Until Jerusalem be blest
> And Judah dwell at ease.
> Until her righteousness return
> As day break after night
> The lamp of her salvation burn
> With everlasting light.[11]

After buying out the dissenters, he converted the London Jews' Society into a debt-free and, indeed, generously funded Anglican organization, which planned to facilitate Jesus' Second Coming by carrying the gospel back to the Promised Land. After taking Anglican orders, he and converted Jew Benjamin Solomon set out on a fact-finding tour of Russia and Eastern Europe. He set out his purpose in a letter to one of the society's patrons:

I wish it to be understood at home . . . that our immediate object is not to convert the Jews, but to deliver the Gospel in their own tongue, and thus far at least to prepare the way for its promulgation in a wilderness which is one day to be like Eden.[12]

On returning home, he turned part of his stately home into a training college. Since few Anglican clergy were prepared to leave comfortable livings for the mission field, the society then recruited 21-year-old Norwegian John Nicolayson to work as its first missionary to the Middle East.

Anthony Ashley Cooper—later Seventh Earl of Shaftesbury—was born into the highest rank of the British aristocracy. Beaten by his father and ignored by a socialite mother ("away with her memory" cried the young man, "the idea of such fiend-warmed heart is bad for the Christian soul"), he learned his apocalyptic faith from an elderly nurse.[13] Operating on the fringes of government, he would direct his formidable energies toward a memorable range of social reforms. Every action was subordinated to the single objective of making his nation fit for the Second Coming of Christ; as he confided to his diary, "May we sigh more, pray more, labor more that our enemies may cease to have power to say 'My Lord delayeth his coming'. Hasten thy kingdom, hasten thy kingdom, hasten thy kingdom. Come Lord Jesus."[14] Still there is no reason to doubt his real concern for the exploited children and workers in industrial Britain. After having little time for Jews as a young man, Ashley Cooper's views matured in later life. These people, he declared, are "of very powerful intellect, of cultivated minds, and with habits of study that would defy the competition of the most indefatigable German."[15] At this time of enthusiasm for worldwide missions, Ashley Cooper chose to channel his energies on the London Jews' Society—first as a member of its governing committee and then as national president. From those positions, he was uniquely well placed to convert messianic aspiration into national foreign policy.

The "Eastern Question" was now rising high among the priorities of European politicians. As the Ottoman Empire again threatened to collapse, European powers measured up Middle Eastern territories as future imperial spheres of influence. Having staffed his formidable army with redundant Napoleonic officers, Albanian strong-man Muhammad Ali Pasha won control of the Arabian Peninsula with its Islamic holy sites and set about building an empire along the Upper Nile. Relying on tacit French support, in 1831, he struck north into Syria and Palestine, where both Jews and Christians welcomed him as a savior from Ottoman oppression.

Many English evangelicals shared the American Millerite expectation that the fall of the Ottoman Empire would mark the beginning of the Tribulation. At this millennial moment, German missionary in Anglican orders Samuel Gobat recorded how he and one of Muhammad Ali's most senior advisers—who happened to be an Armenian Christian—sat down with their Bibles to trace how prophesy was being fulfilled.

> We had been discussing prophesy and thought to have discovered that the Turkish Empire was soon to be destroyed. I looked at these prophesies with a theological eye—he from a political point of view; so, although we seemed to have the same idea, we did not fully understand one another.[16]

When the minister dutifully passed Gobat's forecast on to his master, Muhammad Ali was "greatly encouraged" to continue the struggle against Ottoman rule.

In London, Ashley Cooper's newly widowed mother-in-law had finally married her long-time lover, British Foreign Secretary Henry Temple, Third Viscount Palmerston. While confessing that his unbelieving father-in-law "weeps not like his Master over Jerusalem, nor prays that now, at last, he may put on her beautiful garments," Ashley Cooper did conclude that Palmerston had been "chosen by God as an instrument for the salvation of his ancient people."[17] For his part, Palmerston was determined that France should not construct an Eastern Mediterranean empire that would be closed to British trade and imperil both sea and overland links with India. He was therefore sympathetic to three of London Jews' Society's key policies, that were directed at strengthening British influence in Palestine. According to the Society's program, Britain would be the first European country with a consul in Jerusalem, there would be a new Bishop of Jerusalem with responsibility for representing Protestant interests across the Middle East and an evangelical cathedral would be built within the Holy City. In 1838, Cooper rejoiced as his own millenarian nominee William Young sailed to take up the post of British Consul.

Took leave this morning of Young, who has been appointed as His Majesty's Vice-Consul in Jerusalem! What a wonderful event it is! The ancient city of the people of God is about to take its place among the nations. And England is the first of the Gentile nations that ceases to "tread her down."[18]

Although officially appointed with a limited remit to represent a small number of British residents and a growing body of tourist/pilgrims, Young managed to spread the word that all Jews now lived under British protection.

Since France and Russia had already adopted the position, respectively, as defenders of Orthodox and Catholic holy sites, Wilhelm IV of Prussia let it be known that he wished to be associated with the London Jews' Society's other two projects. Ashley Cooper welcomed the idea that Protestant thrones, "bound by temporal interests and eternal principles," should come together "to plant under the banner of the Cross, God's people on the mountains of Jerusalem."[19] While Young supervised the search for a suitable site for the Protestanat cathedral inside the city walls, Cooper exploited his position of LSJ president to steer a Jerusalem Bishopric Act through parliament. Although this new prelate would be in Anglican orders, high churchmen were alarmed to discover that alternate appointments would lie in the Prussian king's gift and the bishop would also provide pastoral care for any German Protestant congregations as were "disposed to submit to his jurisdiction." Wilhelm's message to the Ottoman governor took the form of an ultimatum. "You will be careful that no person do in any manner whatsoever oppose the erection of the aforesaid place of worship in the manner stated, and you will not act in contravention thereof."[20]

Converted Jew Michael Solomon Alexander, reached Jerusalem in 1841 to deliver "the first episcopal blessing that had fallen from Hebrew lips for

1700 years." When this first bishop died after just three years, Wilhelm IV chose the same German national who had pondered the apocalypse with Muhammad Ali's minister. Once settled in Jerusalem, Samuel Gobat explained the obstacles that stood in the way of the eagerly anticipated mass conversion of the Jewish people.

> They must not only overcome all their prejudices, but must also tear asunder, as it were, all natural ties and wonted affections; they must also expect to see the love and friendships of their relatives and friends changed to scorn and deadly hatred.[21]

As a return for some three decades of financial and human investment, just 31 adults and 28 children had been converted out of Judaism and most of these were very poor people who continued to depend on the mission for everyday subsistence. To widespread alarm, Gobat therefore diverted mission resources into educational work for the children of Orthodox Christians. As it became clear that there would be no sudden discovery of the 10 lost tribes or mass conversion of Jews before the Second Coming, Christian Zionists recognized that the traditional narrative did need re-examination. Whether or not they would be converted in advance, the Society's president Anthony Ashley Cooper (now Seventh Earl of Shaftesbury) continued to press that European governments must help the Jewish people return to the Holy Land. As he wrote in his diary; "There is a country without a nation; and God now, in his wisdom and mercy, directs us to a nation without a country."[22]

Although the Jewish population of Palestine multiplied several times over in the course of Shaftesbury's long life, few, if any, were recruited by Christian Zionists. These new settlers were an uneasy mix of Perushim and Hasidic Eastern European Jews who had left their homes for a complex mixture of religious, economic and political motives.

*

After the ninth crusade collapsed in 1272, Muslims could develop their own civilization without significant Christian interference. The situation began to change just 500 years later as the Industrial Revolution began to transform the landscape of British cities. In this new competitive world, capitalists became caught up in a worldwide search for raw materials and markets for finished goods. At the same time, the "great powers" of Europe were beginning to push out the frontiers of empire. Persian rulers of the Qajar dynasty, in particular, found that their borders were constantly under pressure from the armies of Imperial Russia in the north and British India in the south.

Predictably, Muslim leaders ascribed defeat on the battlefield to moral collapse rather than impotence in the face of superior weapons technology. Mystic teacher Shaykh Ahmad became convinced that Shi'a Islam had become corrupted to a level where it could no longer confront the growing infidel threat.

He observed how those who professed the Faith of Islam had shattered its unity, sapped its force, perverted its purpose, and degraded its holy name. His soul was filled with anguish at the sight of the corruption and strife which characterised the Shí'ah sect of Islam. . . . Forsaking his home and kindred . . . he set out . . . to unravel the mysteries of those verses of Islamic Scriptures which foreshadowed the advent of a new Manifestation . . . There burned in his soul the conviction that no reform, however drastic, within the Faith of Islam, could achieve the regeneration of this perverse people. He knew. . . .that nothing short of a new and independent Revelation, as attested and foreshadowed by the sacred Scriptures of Islam, could revive the fortunes and restore the purity of that decadent Faith.[23]

After Shaykh Ahmad's death, his followers looked for the twelfth and hidden Imam's return with increasing impatience. The larger Babi movement started as an offshoot of Shaykh Ahmad's messianic sect.

Born in 1819, Siyyid Alí Muhammad could claim descent from the Prophet on both sides of his family. At the age of 24, he took the name of Bab (Gate), which indicated that only he could provide access to the hidden imam. Choosing 19 followers, who he named Letters of the Living, he ascribed to each the personality of a Shi'a imam or one of the twelfth imam's guardians. The remarkable Tahirih, known to the world as Qurratu' l' Ayn (solace of the eyes), who had left an unhappy marriage to preach Bab's message, was assigned the role of Muhammad's daughter Fatima. Those who had tired of the mullahs' arid lectures on doctrine now flocked to hear the Bab present a new vision of personal holiness. Wrapping his message in riddles, he attempted to open those secrets that had lain hidden within the Shi'a Gnostic tradition to the understanding of "plain folk." "By God!" he taught, "if you struggle against your self and send it to the station of nearness and remembrance and intimacy in the shade of your Beloved and adore Him above all else, even if you were cut to shreds you would not be negligent of His station because the knower is he whose heart is with God."[24]

More simply, Bab continued to construct his apocalyptic message around the narrative that told how the Ummayad caliphs had usurped the prophet's son-in-law Ali and then killed Husayn and other members of the Prophet's family at the Battle of Karbala. Like Ismaili teachers before him, he predicted that that the coming mahdi would deliver a purified form of sharia and open God's final dispensation before the end of time. The Bab only overstepped Shi'a orthodoxy when he pronounced that he was the promised mahdi and savior; he became a political threat when Babism transformed from a movement for inner religious renewal into a revolutionary challenge to both religious political establishments. Tales circulated of how Qurratu' l' Ayn tore off her veil in a meeting and forced men to look into her beautiful face. Apparently overcome with shock, it was recorded that one man cut his own throat open and left hurriedly to stem the blood. When the young master called his followers to a great meeting in Karbala, it was said that all brought hidden weapons in readiness to wage a jihad against those who refused to follow his teaching, but the Bab failed to appear and the people dispersed without recourse to weapons. Retaliatory persecution increased as Babist insurrections sprang up across the country. After being captured by government troops, the Bab was moved from castle to castle in remote Azerbaijan. When finally brought to trial in 1848, nine different observers recorded his messianic confession: "I am the person you have been awaiting for a thousand years." While mullahs demanded an immediate death penalty, civil authorities were concerned that his execution would provoke yet more civil unrest. Two years later, Siyyid Alí Muhammad—the Bab—and a young disciple who refused to leave his side faced firing squads in Tabriz. After the authorities foiled a plot to assassinate the Shah, they set about tracking down and then either killing or imprisoning all Babists who failed to escape into neighboring Iraq. Feminist martyr Qurratu' l' Ayn was strangled with her own scarf in the city of Tahiri.

Before he died, Bab forecast that "him whom God shall make manifest" would follow him. After some years of division, one of Bab's earliest followers—whose name, Bahá'u'lláh, translates as "the glory of God"—emerged as the favored candidate. In 1863, he took companions into a garden outside Baghdad and, after 12 days of meditation, confided to them that he was God's messenger. Having ample time to contemplate religious truth during long periods of imprisonment, Bahá'u'lláh emerged with an innovative faith that would become known as the Baha'i. While Bab—like premillennial Christians—had insisted that humans lay helplessly in the hands of an all-powerful deity; Bahá'u'lláh presented a "postmillennial" vision of a time when God would achieve his objectives in collaboration with people of goodwill. There would be no more competition between different nations and faiths when Baha'i believers gathered to lead all humans into the world's final dispensation.

We desire but the good of the world and happiness of the nations . . . That all nations should become one in faith and all men as brothers; that the bonds of affection and unity between the sons of men should be strengthened; that diversity of religion should cease, and differences of race be annulled . . . Yet so it shall be; these fruitless strifes, these ruinous wars shall pass away, and the "Most Great Peace" shall come.[25]

With this perfect condition still far off, Bahá'u'lláh wrote a letter, named Tablet of the Kings, to key rulers—the Ottoman Sultan, the Pope, the President of the United States, and all the major crowned heads of Europe. In this, he demanded that they promote a "lesser peace" by ending the pursuit of wealth, cutting expenditure on armaments, and ruling with justice in the interests of the poor and downtrodden.

Just two years before Bahá'u'lláh died in 1892, an English traveler described how he was shown into the presence of a "wondrous and venerable" elderly man.

The face of him on whom I gazed I can never forget, though I cannot describe it. Those piercing eyes seemed to read one's very soul; power and authority sat on that ample brow; while the deep lines on the forehead and face implied an age which the jet-black hair and beard flowing down in indistinguishable luxuriance almost to the waist seemed to belie.

No need to ask in whose presence I stood, as I bowed myself before one who is the object of a devotion and love which kings might envy and emperors sigh for in vain.[26]

For all Bahá'u'lláh's high ideals, it remained a key article of Islamic faith that Muhammad was the last prophet, and only the deceiver Dajall would try to add to his final revelation. While Shaykh Ahmad stayed within the limit, both Bab and Bahá'u'lláh were adjudged to have overstepped the boundary that separated orthodoxy from heresy.

As these messianic movements disturbed Shi'a tranquility, so another prophet was emerging in Sunni British India. Mirza Ghulam Ahmad grew into maturity in the years before the Indian Rebellion at just the time when Christian missionaries were establishing a significant presence in his home state of Punjab. According to the story, Ahmad had already reached the age of 50 when Hindu holy men asked him to provide evidence that Islam was still a living religion. Following Brahmin practice, he withdrew into seclusion for 40 days before emerging to claim that God had appointed him Mahdi and Messiah. Three years later in 1889, his first 40 followers joined hands to take the pledge of loyalty (*bay'ah*) to his new Ahmadiyya movement.

Although Mirza Ghulam Ahmad believed that contemporary Islam had apostatized against the true faith, he still viewed himself as a faithful Sunni Muslim, and he warned against the coming of a great "Christian calamity" when just this one faith would dominate the world. In order to avert this disaster, Ahmad took it on himself to engage the missionaries in rational argument. In a series of long debates (just one of which lasted a full 15 days), he proposed an alternative narrative of Jesus' death. By his account, after being taken from the cross while still alive, Jesus was secretly spirited to India, where he died normally in Kashmir at the age of 120. Ahmad dismissed the doctrine of Jesus' divinity as "a Christian invention, designed to demonstrate that the living Jesus is superior to the deceased Muhammad and that Christianity is consequently superior to Islam." Contradicting both Christian and Muslim doctrine, he insisted that Jesus would have no part in the end time drama. Responsibility for defeating the evil Satan/Dajjal would fall on himself—the Mahdi Mirza Ghulam Ahmad.[27]

Having revealed his role as religious reformer and Mahdi, Ahmad needed to defend himself against the charge that he claimed to be a prophet who came after Muhammad. By complex textual analysis, he argued that, while Muhammad was indeed the most perfect of all the prophets and the final prophet of law, the Qur'an did leave room for lesser prophets who would follow after him. The longer he continued preaching, the more his claims to messianic powers expanded, and he ended by laying claim to the gift of prophesy.[28] Some 200 Muslim scholars then joined to issue a fatwa, which condemned him to death as a heretic, but the sentence could not be carried out as long as British judges controlled the Indian courts. While Mirza Ghulam Ahmad was prepared to argue with British missionaries, he always had an ambiguous relationship with the civil Raj. Declaring that the age of violent jihad was over, he looked forward to a time when he would proclaim the Ahmaddiyya message of redemption in the imperial capital.

In my vision I saw myself standing on a pulpit in the City of London and delivering in the English language a well-reasoned discourse revealing religious truths. Then I caught many birds sitting on small trees ... From this I interpreted that although not me personally but my writings will spread among them and many sincere Englishmen will join the religion.[29]

After the founder's death in 1908, his Ahmadiyya movement split into two factions. While the larger Qudiyani sect continued to elaborate messianic and prophetic concepts, the smaller Lahori group tried to make the message more acceptable to orthodox Muslims by drawing back from more extreme claims.

When members of the independent majlis came to debate Pakistan's new constitution in 1973, they agreed to add one clause, which defines any "person who does not believe in the absolute and unqualified finality of the Prophethood of Muhammad ... the last of the Prophets, or claims to be a Prophet" as non-Muslim. Facing increasing persecution in their home nations, those members of the Baha'i and Ahmadiyya faiths who chose to flee abroad carried their heterodox interpretations of Islam into countries where they would be accorded greater freedom of expression and worship.

*

Shi'a believers will always remember how Wahabi Muslims from the Arabian peninsula attacked their holy cities of Karbala and Najaf in 1805. After massacring large numbers of inhabitants, these invaders committed the further sacrilege of destroying everything that was left standing of the tombs of early Shi'a Imams Ali and Huseyn. These destroyers belonged to an emerging sect, which took its name from puritanical scholar Muhammad ibn Abd-al-Wahhab. Rejecting every belief, custom, and tradition that had no precedent in the Qu'ran or hadiths of "rightly guided" Caliphs, they set about restoring Islam to its most primitive condition. According to Wahhabi criteria, all who failed to follow their own fundamentalist path deserved to share the fate of pantheists and unbelievers. Over coming decades, Wahhab's disciples collaborated with rulers from the House of Saud as they attempted to spread reformed Islam across the Arabian peninsular and beyond.

Born in 1844, Sudan trader's son Muhammad Ahmad showed an early aptitude for religious studies and received initiation into the Sufi path. After receiving the honorary title of sheikh and gathering his own disciples around him, he embraced those Wahabi beliefs that were spreading across Islamic Africa. In June 1881, at the age of 37, he announced that end-time events had begun and a heavenly council, summoned by the Prophet himself, had appointed him mahdi, Every living creature needed to acknowledge that this had been Muhammad Ahmad's destiny from the time of his birth. This new leader even altered the ancient profession of faith by adding the words "Muhammad al-Mahdi is the Khalifa of the Prophet of God" and replacing the hajj to Mecca with jihad as the fifth pillar of Islam.

Life on the eastern side of Africa had changed greatly during the years since the Suez Canal opened to shipping in 1869. After remaining a backwater for many centuries, the Red Sea was now transformed into a major shipping channel, which linked Europe with South and East Asia. Mahdi Muhammad Ahmad set himself the task of closing the whole Upper Nile to those corrupt Western ways that threatened the purity of traditional Islam. Most immediately, he pronounced jihad against Muhammad Ali's godless successors, who claimed the whole River Nile basin for Egypt. When the Egyptians recruited evangelical Christian soldier George Gordon to organize defenses, the Mahdi Muhammad Ahmad travelled huge distances to recruit the warriors needed to fight his holy war. The story of how Gordon died on January 24, 1884, along with the whole Egyptian garrison and many Khartoum residents, soon travelled around the world. With the whole Upper Nile and wide areas of hinterland now under his control, the Mahdi closed the river to trade and travel and established an Islamic state, which practiced full sharia law.

According to the received End-Time narrative, the Mahdi would reign for just eight years, before the Dajjal emerged to defeat him in battle. At that point, Jesus would descend from the skies to destroy the Dajjal and bring on the Last Judgment. In the event, Muhammad Ahmad died in June 1885, four years after proclaiming his mission and just five months after capturing Khartoum. His appointed successor Abdallahi ibn Muhammad then ruled for another 13 years, until 1898, when the Mahdi's disciples were destroyed by a joint British and Egyptian army's greatly superior firepower. As army chaplains thanked their Christian God for victory just two days later, it has been estimated that some 10,800 Muslim warriors of the jihad still lay either dead or dying on the battlefield of Omdurman. At the cost of just 45 Anglo-Egyptian dead, the Nile valley once again lay open to administrators, missionaries, traders, and other bearers of the Western civilization that was so deeply loathed by all faithful followers of Mahdi Muhammad Ahmad.

11

No Other Goal than Palestine: Zionists and Politicians

In 1894, journalists from many countries gathered in a Paris courtroom to cover the highly charged trial of Jewish army officer Alfred Dreyfus, who had been accused of leaking secret military information to the German embassy. Among those who bundled into the press seats, Jewish journalist Theodore Herzl represented the Austrian liberal newspaper *Neue Frie Presse*. As a secular Jew, Herzl had no patience for dreams of messianic redemption or for promises of land that had been delivered to ancient forefathers by a remote deity.

I consider religion indispensible for the weak. There are those who, weak in willpower, mind or emotions, must always be able to rely on religion. The others, the normal run of mankind, are weak only in childhood and old age; for them religion serves as an educational instrument or a source of comfort.[1]

Herzl's concerns lay with the realities of oppression and discrimination his people faced in the routine course of everyday life. After growing up in Budapest and Vienna at the time of the pogroms, he had firsthand experience of anti-Semitism, but Dreyfus was being tried in the very birthplace of *liberté*, *egalité*, and *fraternité*, and the Paris mob was now crying "*mort à les juifs*" in the streets outside the courthouse. As Herzl covered this unashamedly racist trial, he concluded that "the death of a Jew involves more than a judicial error; it embodies the desire of the vast majority to condemn a Jew, and to condemn all Jews in this one Jew."[2] His seminal book presented *Der Judenstaat—The Jewish State*—not as harbinger of a messianic age, but as a place of safety for his own persecuted race. "Shall we end by having a theocracy?" he asked. "No, indeed.... We shall keep our priests within the confines of their temples in the same way in which we shall keep our professional army within the confines of its barracks."[3] Hebrew, Yiddish and local Jewish dialects would have no place in this forward-looking environment. For the first time since the Babylonian exile, Theodore Herzl planned to transform his scattered people into an effective political force.

197 delegates converged on his First Zionist Congress in Basel, Switzerland in August 1897. With *Der Judenstaat* banned in their home country, members of the large Russian delegation were largely ignorant of the proposals that they had assembled to debate. To further complicate matters, Eastern Europeans, who lacked democratic experience, expected that rabbis would take ultimate responsibility for all issues of policy. Frustrated by his band of followers, Herzl admitted, "the fact—and one that I am keen to keep from everyone—is that all I have is an army of sknorrers. I am leading a bunch of boys, beggars and smucks."[4] Still, with his imposing head framed by a huge beard like some Assyrian king, Herzl dominated the congress and delegates did agree a final motion. With the word *state* omitted in deference to Ottoman sensibilities, the Congress demanded "the creation of a home for the Jewish people in Palestine, secured by public law."[5] For all the obstacles, Herzl believed that the job had been well done. "In Basle I founded the Jewish state . . .," he declared. "Maybe in five years, certainly in fifty, everyone will realize it."[6]

As delegates returned home, Herzl directed his own energies toward the task of negotiating for land. Since the region lay within Ottoman territory, he first tried to talk directly with the Sultan. In five visits to Istanbul, he floated the idea that rich international Jews might take responsibility for managing the inflated Turkish national debt in exchange for a grant of settlement land, but any chance of progress evaporated when the Sultan realized that this Jew was offering financial expertise rather than hard cash. If nothing could be achieved by direct talks, Herzl need to recruit the assistance of at least one of Europe's Great Powers.

While Christian Zionists still flourished in Britain, they were rare creatures in continental Europe. German national and Anglican priest William Hechler had developed his eccentric version of end-time expectation while working as chaplain to the British consulate in Vienna. Reverting to Mede's discredited formula of adding 1,260 years to a chosen date in antiquity—which, in Hechler's case, was Caliph Umar's conquest of Jerusalem in 637 CE—he was astonished to discover that Jesus' Second Coming could be no more than a few months away. While there was no vacancy at the time, Hechler fantasized that he would be suddenly invested Bishop of Jerusalem so that he could stand to meet his Lord when Jesus arrived at the city gates. Although an unlikely ally to Herzl's new brand of secular Zionism, Hechler had worked as tutor in the Grand Duke of Baden's house, and there was a chance that he could organize a meeting with the united Germany's new Kaiser Wilhelm II.

When Herzl and Hechler met, the clergyman set about delivering a crash course in biblical prophecy. According to his reading of scripture, "the Palestine of David and Solomon" had once stretched from the present site of the Suez Canal, along the Mediterranean Sea, to the mountains of Cappadocia in Central

Turkey and inland to Baghdad.[7] Wildly overestimating the scale of immigration, Hechler suggested that the Jewish population of Palestine could already have reached 20 million (as against the widely accepted estimate of 800,000). "Palestine belongs to them by right," he announced, "for it is the only country in the whole world of which God has himself said to whom it should belong."[8] Although Herzl had now concluded that this strange clergyman was mentally deranged, he still hoped he might manage arrange the meeting with Wilhelm II, but, in the event, the Kaiser treated the whole process as something of a joke. Wilhelm's own evangelical court chaplain Adolf Stoecker had recently founded the stridently anti-Semitic Christian Social Movement and, while Zionism might one day be a useful device for deporting Jews, it was unthinkable that the Kaiser himself should link the German crown with such aspirations. After cutting Hechler adrift, Herzl crossed the channel to London with confidence that "the still existing happy position of English Jews, their high standard of culture, their proud adherence of the old race caused them to appear to me as the right men to realize the Zionistic idea."[9]

Shaftesbury had now been dead for some 17 years and, with nobody coming foreword to take his place, fully fledged Christian Zionism was now confined to a fundamentalist Anglican fringe. Still, after centuries of obsession with Old Testament stories, the British retained vestiges of that complex relationship with Hebrew history that had persisted since Francis Kett met his death in the moat of Norwich Castle. Indoctrination began in early childhood. Originally started as a place for teaching literacy to the working poor, ubiquitous Sunday Schools were now places of retreat for churchgoers' children at times when their elders were sitting through the more indigestible parts of church services. Gathered in their classes from the age of five, the little ones learned simplified versions of key Bible stories. Truncated teachers' notes provide an insight into the lessons they imbibed. First the little ones needed to know of God's earliest promises to Abraham.

All repeat. I will make thee a great nation and I will bless thee.
Would not Abraham be in danger in poverty? No. God will take care of him.
Make him great and rich. . . .
Abraham's children to be a great nation. The Jews proud of Abraham's name.
To give his children the land of Canaan. Think of Abraham at his tent door. All this land will be mine! All came to pass.

Then they must know how Joshua's Israelites undertook the business of conquest.

Weary dusty traveller. Has had a long tedious journey. But now home in sight, How glad he is! Rest at last! Yonder the hills of the Promised Land. Their home.
But stay—how could this be? Others living in it. What to be done? Home to be won. Work to be done. Inhabitants to be dislodged.[10]

As those children grew to become politicians, soldiers, administrators, teachers, and doctors, both at home and in remoter outposts of the empire, half-remembered Old Testament stories coalesced into the imperial myth of a virtuous British people who had been had chosen by God to rule over lesser breeds. At the same time, at least in Britain's upper classes, excessive respect for a long-dead Hebrew people could coexist with a pervasive anti-Semitism, according to which living Jews were categorized under those familiar stereotypes—as anarchists who were set on importing revolution into well-ordered British society or as money-obsessed financiers who would direct their ample resources toward controlling the world.

*

Arch-imperialist Colonial Secretary Joseph Chamberlain had never been squeamish about dislodging indigenous people—and the process was all the more straightforward when their land was used for nomadic grazing rather than settled forming. While Chamberlain was in no position to distribute Ottoman territory, he did invite Herzl to "show him a spot in the British dominions where there was no white population yet, then we could talk."[11] Egyptian Sinai was considered a possible "foot in the door" to Palestine, but the peninsula was adjudged too small and arid to support the anticipated number of immigrants, and the desert land was also unpromising for farming. At just this time, however, workers on the new East African Railway were coming close to its first terminus at Nairobi, and the line would vey soon be open to passengers. Beyond Nairobi, an extension was planned that would take the railway around the northern bank of Lake Victoria to Uganda. Since White settlers were still showing little interest in taking up farming concessions that were on offer along the route, the land seemed suitable for Jewish settlement. What became known in Zionist circles as the Uganda project was, more accurately, a proposal to promote Jewish settlement in the region that would become known as the White Highlands of Kenya. One Foreign Office official recorded that he anticipated no problems with the scheme—just as long as it remained under direct British control, "but if the promoters want a petty state of their own, I fear there would be great exception."[12]

Herzl appears to have been taken aback to encounter implacable opposition from delegates at the Sixth Zionist Conference of 1903. Desperately trying to salvage something from the wreck, he admitted that the proposal for a national home in East Africa was unsatisfactory, but he asked delegates to consider how much had been achieved.

The Jewish people can have no other goal than Palestine and.... our views as to the land of our fathers are unalterable and must remain unchanged, yet the congress will recognize what an extraordinary advance our movement has made through the negotiations with the British government.[13]

Although a motion to send a commission of enquiry to Africa did pass with a slim majority, the party never sailed, and the exhausted Theodore Herzl died within the year at the age of 44. Zionist leadership passed to other secular Jews, who had now learned that they could never disassociate the aspiration for a Jewish homeland from the concept of a God-given Promised Land.

*

As soon as Free Churchman C. P. Scott took financial control of the *Manchester Guardian* in 1905, he launched the paper into a campaign of support for the Zionist ideal. When Prime Minister and Conservative leader Arthur Balfour arrived in his city to fight the 1906 general election, Scott saw an opportunity to introduce him to Chaim Weizmann, a Russian-born Jew who was rising to prominence as a local Zionist leader. Balfour was not known for his fondness for Jews. Just the previous year, growing alarm at the number of of Jewish refugees that were arriving from Eastern Europe had prompted his government to pass an Aliens Act, which imposed strict restrictions on immigration. But Balfour was personally shocked by the pogroms, and he recognized it as an anachronism that Britain should be closing its borders at just the time that life in Russia and the Pale was becoming intolerable for Jews. Still in Weizmann Balfour found a Jew who shared his own conviction that immigration had "reached saturation point," and who believed that the problem could not be settled until the Jews had a state of their own. Weizmann would later recall how the prime minister had been impressed by his reminder that Jerusalem had belonged to the Jews at a time when London was only a swamp.[14] Before the meeting ended Balfour expressed his personal sympathy with Zionist aspirations, and from that time on he would sometimes describe himself as a Zionist.

In the event, the 1906 general election turned into a Liberal landslide, and the two men did not meet again for more than a decade. As Weizmann stepped aside from front-line Zionism to follow a chemist's career, the task of lobbying Parliament passed to others. With the Dreyfus case now consigned to history, Zionism dropped off the political agenda. To Prime Minister (after 1908) Herbert Asquith, the very concept of relocating some nine million Jews into an area the size of Wales did not even deserve critical examination. Foreign Secretary Edward Grey, who had long promoted Irish home rule, also did not readily understand why nationalistic Jewish claims should be given precedence over those of the majority population, which had possessed the land for so many centuries. Only Welsh Chancellor of the Exchequer David Lloyd George showed sympathy with Zionist aspirations. Though he had cut ties with the narrow sect within which he had been raised, he still called himself a Baptist and laced his speeches with Old Testament quotations.

The fact that two leading Jews—first cousins Herbert Samuel and Edwin Montague—rose to cabinet rank in those prewar years did not necessarily make the task of lobbying in the Zionist cause any easier. The fundamental division between Zionists and assimilated Jews lay in whether they chose to describe themselves as Britons who happened to be Jews or Jews who happened to live in Britain. As a member of Britain's elite, Lord Montague feared that any accusation of dual loyalty could jeopardize not only the social status but even the physical security of successfully assimilated Jews.

When war broke out in August 1914, combatants waited to see whether the Ottomans would enter the conflict and, if so, which side they would join. After the Sultan chose to declare war on the Allies, France and Britain felt free to begin cautious talks over how the Middle East might be divided when the war ended. With negotiations delegated to diplomats Sir Mark Sykes and Georges Picot, a plan surfaced early in 1916 that divided areas of influence between France in Syria and the north and Britain in Mesopotamia and Egypt. The two diplomats suggested that the sensitive territory of Palestine should be brought under international control.

Meanwhile—to widespread surprise—Herbert Samuel had revealed his true colors as a Zionist. After discussing drafts with Jewish leaders, he presented a memorandum to the cabinet, proposing that Palestine should become a Jewish state within a larger British Protectorate.

It is hoped that under British rule facilities would be given to Jewish organizations to purchase land, to found colonies, to establish educational and religious institutions, and to cooperate with the economic development of the country, and that Jewish immigration, carefully regulated, would be given preference, so that, in the course of time, the Jewish people, grown into a majority and settled in the land, may be conceded such a degree of self-government as the conditions of the day might justify.[15]

Samuel made the point that a pronouncement in favor of Zionism would win wide support for the Allied cause across worldwide Jewry. "Help given now towards the attainment of the ideal which great numbers of Jews have never ceased to cherish through so many centuries of suffering cannot fail to secure, into the far-distant future, the gratitude of a whole race, whose goodwill, in time to come, may not be without value."[16] Montague bitterly opposed every word his cousin wrote, and Prime Minister Asquith dismissed the very idea that scattered Jews of the world "could in time swarm back from all quarters of the globe and in due course obtain Home Rule (What an attractive community!)"[17] But Asquith's Liberal government fell in December 1916 and was replaced by a coalition administration in which Zionist sympathizers Lloyd George and Balfour were Prime Minister and Foreign Secretary.

Just four months later, America entered the war on the Allied side. Until that time, Supreme Court Justice and Zionist leader Louis Brandeis had held back from aligning American Zionists with either combatant, but now he received a message from his British counterpart, Baron Rothschild, suggesting that American Zionists should urge "son of the manse" President Woodrow Wilson to support Samuel's program for creating a Jewish homeland within a Middle Eastern British protectorate. When Brandeis met Wilson two weeks later, he urged the high-minded President to consider the humanitarian benefits that would flow from such a move. Wilson's sympathies with the idea of a Jewish return to the Promised Land were tempered with reservations. As a committed supporter of national self-determination, he was deeply suspicious of European—and particularly British—imperialism, which was so blatantly exposed by the Sykes-Picot proposals. Also, although America was now at war with the Central Powers, it was still at peace with the Ottomans. He therefore, continued to reserve his position.

*

After unseating Asquith, David Lloyd George established a system of emergency personal rule unknown in Britain since the days of Oliver Cromwell. With his decisions effectively scrutinized by just two Conservative colleagues— ex-prime minister Arthur Bonar Law and grandee Lord George Curzon—he maintained a tight personal grip over the direction of Britain's war effort. His attention turned early to the Middle East. Even as the Sykes-Picot Agreement was being secretly ratified by both governments, he decided to mount an offensive into Palestine, which would ensure that "British boots were on the ground" when the war was over. Questioning the Sykes-Picot proposal for the international control of Palestine, he declared that it would not be worth winning the Holy Land, "only to hew it in pieces before the Lord. ... Palestine, if recaptured, must be one and indivisible to renew its greatness as a living entity."[18] At the same time, conflicting assurances of future independence encouraged the Hashemite rulers of Mecca to launch a guerilla assault against Ottoman control of the region.

Although Arthur Balfour did not belong to the inner war cabinet, he did often attend meetings. In the dark autumn days of 1917, as rival armies were fighting to exhaustion at Passchendaele, Prime Minister, Foreign Secretary, and Middle East specialist Mark Sykes made time to revisit Samuel's proposal that the British government should make an open declaration of support for a Jewish homeland in Palestine. At a time, when final defeat on the European battlefield appeared to be a real possibility and Communist revolution was diverting Russia's war effort, cabinet members would grasp at any means of recruiting support for the tottering Allied cause. With Jews fighting on both sides of the conflict, Lloyd George was concerned that the Central Powers might steal a march by issuing their own their own Zionist declaration. "A friendly Russia," he declared, "would mean not only more food and raw material for Germany ... but also fewer German troops on the Eastern front, and therefore more available for the west."[19] The bizarre idea that a pro-Zionist declaration could even bring America into the war had circulated in the Foreign Office the previous year; now these three policy makers grasped a wild hope that such an action could impact enough on Communist Jewish opinion to avert Russian surrender on the Eastern Front.

One further hurdle needed to be overcome: Woodrow Wilson was in a position to bankrupt Britain, and no statement could be issued without his approval. Since he would never endorse any suggestion that a new Jewish homeland would fall within a British Protectorate, the idea was neither stated nor denied in the declaration's final draft. But the Ottoman grasp on its Middle Eastern possessions was now terminally slipping and Wilson was less concerned about giving offense. The message that President Wilson would support the Declaration was transmitted to London and the text passed to the War Cabinet for formal approval. With Sykes, Balfour, and the Prime Minister speaking warmly in support, only Lord Curzon lodged three serious objections. Could Palestine sustain the projected number of immigrants? Of the three ancient faiths that venerated Jerusalem as a holy city, would the other two "timidly accept" the fact that the Jews would surely take it as their capital? And would Palestine's current inhabitants, who had lived in the region for 1,500 years, be content to serve as "hewers of wood and drawers of water" for those who would effectively be their imperial masters? But Lloyd George was no longer in doubt and, when Curzon's questions were brushed aside, he did not pursue them further.

The Balfour Declaration was released to the world on November 2, 1917.

His Majesty's government view with favor the establishment in Palestine of a national home for the Jewish people, and will use their best endeavors to facilitate the achievement of this object, it being clearly understood that nothing shall be done which may prejudice the civil and religious rights of existing non-Jewish communities in Palestine, or the rights and political status enjoyed by Jews in any other country.

The brief document lacked detail, and there was no discussion on how aspiration would be converted into action. Indeed, the text appears to have carried different meanings for different participants. Just three months later, Balfour was asked whether the Declaration was "a charter for ultimate sovereignty in Palestine." Choosing his words carefully, he replied; "My personal hope is that is that the Jews make good in Palestine and eventually found a Jewish State. It is up to them now; we have given them their great opportunity." Just a year later, Lloyd George told his private secretary, "If the Zionists claim that the Jews are to have domination over the Holy Land under a British Protectorate, then they are certainly putting their claims too high."[20] Cabinet member and Secretary of State for India Edwin Montagu immediately lodged a protest against the implied assertion that all Jews—in wherever country they might be living—belonged to a distinct nationality He predicted that "every country will desire to get rid of its Jewish citizens, and you will find a population in Palestine driving out its present inhabitants, taking all the best country."[21] At the same time, British Chief Rabbi Joseph Hertz addressed a meeting of fellow Jews packed into London's Opera House.

Twenty five hundred years ago Cyrus issued his edict of liberation to the Jewish exiles in Babylon.... Theirs was a similar feeling of joy and wonder.... That caused them to exclaim "We have seen it done and done consummately, the thing so many have thought could never be done. (Cheers)"[22]

If the Balfour Declaration was, first and foremost, a desperate attempt to keep the new Russia involved in World War I, it turned out to be a catastrophic failure when Russia's revolutionary leaders signed a peace treaty with Germany at Brest Litovsk in February 1918. Still, against all the evidence, British statesmen continued to debate whether the whole disastrous Revolution might have been averted if the Declaration had only been issued a year earlier.

In December 1917, cavalryman General Allenby led his triumphant British army into Jerusalem. As a gesture of respect for the city's three religions, he dismounted and finished the journey on foot. Yet in popular culture, this would be remembered as the moment when a crusader knight returned to the holy city in conquest. In the following September, Allenby's army won a decisive victory—fought on that apocalyptic plain of Megiddo—that marked the end of Ottoman rule in the Middle East. Germany surrendered to the allies just two months later; on November 11, 1918, and the ghastly slaughter was over. Although the Sykes-Picot plan that the Middle East should be partitioned between Britain and France had found no place in the Balfour Declaration, Zionists and members of the newly formed League of Nations agreed that the imposition of French and British mandates might be the best way of bringing stability to a troubled region.

*

Through all the Zionist debates and discussions, the Arab residents of Palestine had never been consulted over the future of their own land. When newly appointed Colonial Secretary Winston Churchill visited the region in 1921, he did agree to receive an Arab delegation. After protesting at the loss of land that had been theirs for more than a thousand years, they warned of Zionist plans to appropriate all the region's natural resources. Although Churchill had no mandate to change cabinet policy, he did make some effort to calm Arab anxiety. He told members of the Arab delegation that the Jews did need a national home where "some of them would be reunited" and he even suggested that Jewish immigration would bring benefits to people of all races.

We think it will be good for the world, good for the Jews and good for the British Empire. But we also think it will be good for the Arabs who live in Palestine, and we intend that it shall be good for them, and that they shall not be sufferers or supplanted in the country in which they shall dwell or denied a share in all that makes for its progress and prosperity.[23]

Even after the British mandate was formally approved by the League of Nations in 1922 and Zionist Sir Herbert Samuel was installed as the first Jewish ruler of Palestine since Herod, the promised Jewish homeland still had no flag, no parliament, and no law courts. While, by Zionist interpretation, the Balfour Declaration committed the British administration to a policy of open Jewish entry into Palestine, immigration policy was controlled in practice by unsympathetic administrators. When Weizmann was granted a meeting with Lloyd George, Balfour, and Churchill to protest that the Declaration's provisions were already being eroded, Churchill was surprised to hear his two older colleagues offer fulsome reassurance. The Balfour Declaration, they assured him, had always meant that there would ultimately be a Jewish majority and that Palestine would have "an eventual Jewish state."[24] Shortly afterward, Balfour went so far as to express expectations for the future in guardedly apocalyptic language. "The reconstitution of a Jewish Kingdom would be an interesting experiment," he concluded, "and if a King of the Jews really meant the end of the world, that would be even more interesting."[25]

After Samuel returned home in 1925, the Palestine administration became increasingly staffed by broadly pro-Arab colonial servants. Solitary premillennial member of the Palestine administration Lord Eustace Percy protested that "certain Englishmen ... who do not like the Zionist policy ... have inspired them (the Arabs) with ideas that they never dreamed of before."[26]

At Zionist meetings across America, supporters placed contributions dedicated to the purchase of land across Palestine into blue boxes. Apart from being generally poor, the existing Jewish population of Palestine tended to be elderly—largely made up of those who had returned to the Holy Land to die. The first kibbutz for younger people had been established at Degania as far back as 1910; now, in the early 1920s, young people began to set up communities as models of socialist communal living. Here, it was planned that divisions would wither away as the individual became absorbed into the larger classless community. In 1923, the Zionist-Socialist Union passed a resolution that "the chief basis and instrument of our economic activity in Palestine—whether concerned with agriculture, industry or public works—is the kibbutz, where ideology and practice have been merged and which is ready to embark on a collective life under the auspices of the society of workers."[27] Pooling resources to buy land that none could have afforded individually, they set about establishing self-sufficiency by learning the arts of farming and tending citrus groves. Although early kibbutzim eschewed millenarianism—and, indeed, often religion itself—all were dedicated Zionists who located fortified settlements ever deeper in Arab territory and, by necessity, learned those military skills that would qualify them to become the shock troops of later Israeli fighting units.

As Arab unrest rose, British High Commissioners ever more urgently pressed the home government to abandon the policy of open immigration. Matters came to a head over the long-standing issue of access to the Western Wall. A provocative illustration, copied from an American Zionist publication, that showed Herzl looking down benignly as huge streams of immigrants poured into Jerusalem, was then circulating around Arab settlements. The picture also showed an imaginary Third Temple on the Mound and a Zionist flag flying over a building that looked suspiciously like the Dome of the Rock. On August 23, 1929, village Arabs carried sticks and knives as they streamed into Jerusalem to mount a mass devotion at the place where Muhammad had been taken up for his night journey to heaven. Soon tension erupted into violence and 116 Arabs and 133 Jews died in Jerusalem, Hebron, and Safed during the following week of riots. When an administration enquiry studied the causes, no sign of premeditation could be found on either side. However, as communal tension continued to spiral out of control, the British felt obliged to issue a document that provided further detail on how the Balfour Declaration would be administered in practice. Prime Minister Ramsay Macdonald sent a long reply to Weizmann's protest that the document marked a retreat from earlier commitments:

Under the terms of the mandate his Majesty's Government are responsible for promoting the establishment of a national home for the Jewish people, it being clearly understood that nothing shall be done which might prejudice the civil and religious rights of existing non-Jewish communities in Palestine or the rights and political status enjoyed by Jews in any other country. A double undertaking is involved, to the Jewish people on the one hand and to the non-Jewish population of Palestine on the other; and it is the firm resolve of his Majesty's Government to give effect, in equal measure, to both parts of the declaration and to do equal justice to all sections of the population of Palestine. That is the duty from which they will not shrink and to discharge of which they will apply all the resources at their command....

In carrying out the policy of the mandate the mandatory cannot ignore the existence of the differing interests and viewpoints. These, indeed, are not in themselves irreconcilable, but they can only be reconciled if there is a proper realization that the full solution of the problem depends upon an understanding between the Jews and the Arabs. Until that is reached, considerations of balance must inevitably enter into the definition of policy.[28]

Still, immigration continued, and the Jewish population of Palestine more than doubled in the years between 1931 and 1936. The three violent years of 1936 to 1939 are known at the time of the Arab Revolt. Morally bound by the Declaration's terms, the British now felt obliged to defend Jewish lives and property and it has been estimated that some 10 percent of all Arabs between the ages of 20 and 60 were killed, wounded, imprisoned, or exiled during these years.

Even as British troops tried to defend Zionist settlements against Arab attack, personal relationships between Briton and Jew continued to deteriorate. Then, in 1936, British army captain Orde Wingate (later to command the Burma Chindits in World War II) was assigned to special duties, training Jewish irregulars and leading forays into Arab territory. After growing up in a Plymouth Brethren family, he adopted the Zionist cause with unusual fervor—"like a man devoured by a kind of inner fire addicted to a single idea that had devoured his imagination."[29] Wingate's methods in the field could be brutal, as he freely distributed whippings and even execution. He was even recorded employing communal punishment; when 15 Jews were left dead after one Arab raid, he retaliated by killing 10 Arabs villagers, who were chosen at random. He confided motives to his Jewish irregulars:

I count it as my privilege to help you fight your battle. To that purpose I want to devote my life. I believe that the very existence of mankind is justified when it is based on the moral foundation of the Bible. Whoever lifts a hand against you or your enterprise here should be fought against. Whether it is jealousy, ignorance or perverted doctrine such as have made your neighbors rise against you, or "politics," which made some of my countrymen support them, I shall fight with you against any of these influences.[30]

Then, in 1939 (even as Jewish refugees were pouring out of German-speaking countries), the British government reversed its policy and decided that Jewish immigration to Palestine could no longer be imposed on the Arabs by force of arms. After Orde Wingate received instructions to leave Palestine, he addressed a celebration called in his honor. Speaking in Hebrew, he addressed those fighters he had trained in irregular warfare.

I am sent away from you and the country I love. I suppose you know why. I am transferred because we are too great friends. They want to hurt me and you. I promise that I will come back, and if I cannot do it in the regular way, I shall return as a refugee.[31]

*

In 1923, German writer Arthur Muller van den Bruck published a book he called *Das Dritte Reich (The Third Reich)*. In this, he divided German history into Joachim of Fiore's three ages. The first—the Age of the Father—had lasted from the coronation of Charlemagne in 800 CE to the rise of the Hohenzollerns in the late twelfth century. This was followed by the second Age of the Son, which had ended with defeat in 1918. As he wrote, the German people were living through the interim despised Weimar period of liberal democracy, out of which would shortly erupt the third great age of the Holy Ghost. In the year before publication, van den Bruck met the young Austrian Adolf Hitler, who was making a name in right-wing politics. Repelled by this rabble rouser's "proletarian primitiveness," van den Bruck did not join Hitler's party and committed suicide in 1930. Nevertheless, the Nazi party would borrow his book title to describe the thousand-year Third Reich, which opened when Hitler acceded as Chancellor of Germany in 1933.

In that same year of 1922, aptly named ex-army officer and journalist Josef Hell made careful notes of a conversation with the same young politician. Hell recorded how Hitler boasted that his first task when he came to power would be to annihilate the Jews.

I shall have gallows erected, in Munich, for example, in the Marienplatz, as many as traffic permits. Then the Jews will be hanged one after another, and they will stay hanging until they stink. As soon as one is untied, the next will take his place and that will go on until the last Jew in Munich is obliterated. Exactly the same thing will happen in other cities until Germany is cleansed of its last Jew.

When Hell asked why he would choose the Jews, Hitler replied that, after suffering so much humiliation, the German people needed a target for hatred. "On the basis of all relevant factors, I have come to the conclusion that a battle against the Jews will be as popular as it will be successful."[32] North German evangelical Christians from the Adolf Stoecker tradition, flocked in particularly large numbers to Hitler's messianic banner and remained loyal to the bitter end. As Hitler offered belief in "Aryan blood"—*ein Vőlk; ein Reich; ein Fürher*. Jehovah's Witnesses were consigned to concentration camps for the sin of awaiting the wrong Messiah. Filmmaker Leni Riefenstahl employed heightened messianic language to describe the emotional impact of a Nuremburg rally.

> I was too far away to see Hitler's face, but after the shouts died down I heard his voice: "Fellow Germans!" That very same instant I had an almost apocalyptic vision that I was never able to forget. It seemed as if the earth's surface was spreading out in front of me, like a hemisphere that suddenly split apart in the middle, spewing out an enormous jet of water, so powerful that it touched the sky and shook the earth . . . I sensed that the audience was in bondage to this man.[33]

While Hitler professed no coherent Christian faith, his speeches were replete with apocalyptic language and inference. Viewing himself as the agent of "Providence" and "the Creator," he prided himself on leading a "historic struggle which, for the next 500 or 1,000 years, will be described as decisive, not only for the history of Germany, but for the whole of Europe and indeed the whole world."[34] In the event, the Thousand-Year Reich survived for just 12 years. Most terribly, during this time, the Jewish Holocaust proved to be the apotheosis of every torture, burning, and mass killing of Jews that had continued throughout a millennium of Christian civilization. Apart from causing unspeakable suffering in his own time, Hitler's shadow would continue to darken events in the Middle East until the present day.

*

At the war's end, British Prime Minister Clement Attlee and Foreign Secretary Ernest Bevin contemplated the consequences of this huge humanitarian disaster. As refugees of all nationalities moved across Europe, many Jews would contemplate no other home than Palestine. At the same time, Atlee and Bevin were receiving clear messages from Arab nations that they must not reverse the British government's 1939 decision to clamp down on immigration. Arabs, after all, had played no part in the Holocaust, and the Balfour Declaration did oblige the mandatory power to ensure "that nothing shall be done which may prejudice the civil and religious rights of existing non-Jewish communities in Palestine." In 1946, Britain angered Jews by granting effective independence to the new Hashemite kingdom of Jordan on the river's east bank. Militant Zionists argued that, since this was an integral part of Palestine, the action breached the newly written United Nations Charter, which laid down that nothing "shall be construed in or of itself to alter in any manner the rights whatsoever of any states or any peoples of the terms of existing international instruments to which the Members of the United Nations may respectively be parties."[35] By this interpretation, the Balfour

Declaration had been transformed from a statement of intent, which was hedged by matching obligations to existing populations, into a binding treaty obligation to allow free immigration into Palestine, and the establishment of a majority Jewish state.

On April 12, 1945, American Vice President Harry Truman received news that his predecessor, the great FDR, was dead and he had acceded to the position of President. Chaim Wiseman chose just this time to plead the case of Zion. "The choice for our people, Mr. President, is between statehood and extermination. History and providence have placed this issue in your hands and I am confident that you will yet decide in the spirit of the Moral law."[36] Within two weeks Truman had assured Zionist leader Stephen Wise that he would remain committed to implementing the the Balfour Declaration.

In common with Woodrow Wilson before him, Truman had been born into an evangelical household, and he always remained a devout Southern Baptist.

I have always done considerable reading of the Bible. I had read it twice before I went to school ... The stories in the Bible ... were to me stories about real people, and I felt I knew them better than the *actual* people I knew. But it wasn't just the biblical part about Palestine that interested me. The whole history of that area of the world is just about the most complicated and interesting of any area anywhere, and I have always made a careful study of it.[37]

Beyond personal religious commitment, Truman came under increasing political pressure at a time when his own Democratic party bosses were anxious to maximize Jewish votes and donations, and Republican opponents were equally watchful for any chance to launch their own bid for Zionist support.

In early 1946, Britain and America set up a joint Palestine Mandate Convention, charged with making recommendations for the region's future. While proposing the immediate acceptance of 100,000 refugees, the report also insisted that the constitution would be so structured that no Jew could dominate Arab or Arab Jew. On receiving the report Truman pressed that those 100,000 new immigrants should be admitted swiftly, but rejected the proposed constitutional safeguards against future Jewish domination. Just three months later, in July 1946, Irgun paramilitaries under future Prime Minister Menachem Begin succeeded in blowing up the wing of the King David Hotel that housed both the British Mandate secretariat and military headquarters—killing a mixed-race collection of officials, soldiers, and civilian passersby. Unable to maintain the peace or impose a balanced settlement, the British government announced that it would renounce the mandate on May 15, 1948, and hand over all decisions about Palestine's future to the United Nations. Setting aside the idea of a single federal state, the secretariat prepared plans to partition all the land west of the Jordan River into two independant states.

As the date for British withdrawal approached, Zionists used the good offices of Truman's old Jewish friend and business partner Eddie Jacobsen to pass messages to the President. At the same time the influence of Zionist staffers inside the White House was increasing, while senior cabinet members took up the Arab case. Secretary of State George C. Marshall and Secretary of Defense James Forrestal were keenly aware that American companies had discovered oil in Arabia before World War II, and the region's strategic importance was rapidly increasing. They now argued that the Arab nations would not stop fighting until the hated Zionist state had been destroyed.

On May 14—just one day before Britain's mandate was due to end—David ben Gurion stood under a large picture of Theodore Herzl in the Tel Aviv Museum to read Israel's unilateral declaration of independence. United States delegates to the United Nations were just then negotiating terms for the city of Jerusalem's trusteeship agreement, but, without contacting either hostile Secretary of State, Truman took just 11 minutes to issue *de facto* recognition of the new state of Israel. As the United Nation descended into turmoil, it seemed that the president might face a mass walkout by members of members of his own UN delegation as well as the resignation of two Secretaries of State as well as senior members of their staff. Political adviser Robert Lovett expressed his frustration:

My protests against the precipitate action and warnings as to the consequences with the Arab world appear to have been outweighed by considerations unknown to me, but I can only conclude that the President's political advisers...having failed to make the President the father of a new state, have determined at least to make him the mid-wife.[38]

In the event, Marshall and Forrestal placed loyalty above judgment, and UN diplomats obeyed instructions to lobby non-Arab nations to vote in favor of recognizing the *fait accompli*. Throughout the Cold War, the Soviet Union aligned its satellites with the United States on this one issue, while Britain broke ranks with her ally just this once. On May 15, seven Arab nations declared war as Egyptian, Syrian, Jordanian, Iraqi, and Lebanese troops crossed into Israeli-occupied territory. By late September, Israel had lost Jerusalem's old city to Jordanian troops serving under British officers, but had won control over as much territory again as had been allocated under the UN partition proposals. While the new state was early accepted as a member of the United Nations, ownership of conquered land on the West Bank of the Jordan River has never been recognized.

The number of Palestinian Arabs who were displaced from their homes in the 1948 Arab–Israeli War is a matter of dispute; Israeli sources place the number at somewhere between 400,000 and 650, 000; contemporary British totals ran at 600,000 to 750,000, while UN and Arab computations rise to more than 900,000.[39] Three generations on—after further dispossession and population increase—this Arab diaspora is estimated to encompass around 5 million generally very poor people.

*

Meanwhile, within the United States, Christian premillennialism was losing ground to more liberal definitions of the faith. After being consigned to the periphery of their own denominations, dispensationalists also lost what little political influence they might have had in Blackstone's days. Yet the shadow of religion continued to steer political decisions. Although neither Balfour and Lloyd George in Britain nor Woodrow Wilson and Harry Truman in the United States would have described themselves as either fundamentalists or end-time believers, their early indoctrination in Old Testament narrative had a profound influence on political outcomes. Had Herbert Asquith continued to occupy 10 Downing Street through World War I, no declaration in support of a Jewish homeland would have reached the War Cabinet's table and Palestine could have remained a predominantly Islamic region within the wider Middle East. However, when Arthur Balfour declared that "the case of the Jews is absolutely exceptional and must be treated by exceptional methods," he was already defining Palestine's future in terms that would not be applicable to any other state.[40]

Soon after Harry Truman left office in November 1953, old friend and business colleague Eddie Jacobsen introduced the retired President to a meeting in a New York Jewish theological college. "This is the man who helped create the State of Israel," declared Jacobsen. "What do you mean helped to create?" retorted Truman. "I am Cyrus. I am Cyrus."[41]

12

Signs of the Times: A Troubled World

When news spread on August 6, 1945, that U.S. B-29 *Enola Gay* had dropped an atomic bomb on the Japanese city of Hiroshima, few doubted that the event would mark a turning point in human history. As the secular-minded contemplated this new precarious world within which humans had acquired awesome power to destroy both their own species and their environment, biblical literalists reminded themselves of prescient words from Peter's Second Epistle. "The day of the Lord will come like a thief, and then the heavens will pass away with a loud noise, and the elements will dissolve with fire, and the earth and the works that are upon it will be burned up."[1] Any evil ruler who looked to assume the mantle of Antichrist could now exercise control by means of a terrifying weapon of destruction. "When he is sitting there with his finger on the button," asked one Los Angeles preacher, "what will the nations of the world do? They will do exactly what he wants them to do. He will be an absolute dictator."[2] Even liberal Christians began to ask those hard questions fundamentalists insisted that they had ignored for too long. "A function of Christianity is to make preparation for the world's end," wrote one. "For generations this fundamental aspect of the Christian faith has been ignored or relegated to the unconscious. But now eschatology confronts us at the very center of consciousness."[3]

As the Iron Curtain descended across Europe, Cold War contestants, the United States and Soviet Russia, invested ever-larger proportions of their budgets in stockpiling the very weapons that threatened humanity's future. While many liberal Christians aligned themselves with freethinkers in opposing nuclear proliferation, conservative dispensationalists prepared to greet the apocalyptic events that were surely approaching ever closer. By this view, Christian America needed to stand resolute against the godless communism, which was threatening to consume weaker nations across the globe.

After reacting violently against Mennonite parents (who later defected to the Jehovah's Witnesses), Dwight Eisenhower always nursed a deep suspicion of religious extremism. As general in command of Allied troops, he felt deep sympathy for the Jews he helped liberate; as Army Chief of Staff, he joined with Marshall and Forrestal in opposing Truman's plan to create an independent Zionist state in Palestine. Still, once the step was taken and he succeeded as President, he could only accept the situation he had inherited. When Gamal Abdel Nasser nationalized the Suez Canal in 1956, the British, French, and Israelis kept Eisenhower in the dark on plans for retaliation. If they had banked on receiving American support, they were quickly disillusioned. In the face of fierce opposition in the United Nations and threats of financial sanctions from Washington, Britain and France pulled their troops out of the Canal zone, while the Israelis withdrew from Gaza and Sinai. Since very few American Jews voted Republican and the Middle East was still beyond the horizon for most conservative Christians, Dwight Eisenhower's electoral prospects remained undamaged and, just months later, he secured re-election by a landslide. On the other side, however, Nasser proved to be an unreliable ally. Nursing ambitions of creating an Arab super-state under Egyptian leadership, he became increasingly dependent on the Soviets' continued supply of armaments. With the region now sucked into Cold War politics, Americans could see no other ally in the Middle East but Israel.

Democrat Lyndon Johnson was in the White House on June 5, 1967, at the time when Israeli Air Force planes launched the "preemptive strikes," which destroyed the Egyptian and Syrian air forces before they even left the ground. With Arab pilots killed and runways torn up, Israel enjoyed full control of the air for just six days of land fighting. By the end Israel had won control of a heavily populated Arab area on the West Bank of the River Jordan, as well as Sinai, Gaza, and the tactically significant Golan Heights. Now Israel controlled twice the area that the United Nations had allocated as a Jewish homeland in 1948. As fresh waves of Arab refugees went on the move, the prime minister's office confirmed the fact of conquest.

This land is ours. We have learned to understand that land is bought with three things: tears, blood and sweat. We have shed our tears. We have spilled our blood. Today we have begun pouring out our sweat, to betroth this land to us forever . . . It is ours and we shall not leave it.[4]

The immediate problem was that settlement on conquered land was prohibited under international law. Israel's own legal officer secretly delivered the opinion that, by Article 49 of the Fourth Geneva Convention, no Israeli citizen could settle in occupied territory. However he suggested that this restriction might be circumvented if any new settlement was dressed up to look like a temporary army camp.[5]

Nursing the crushing humiliation of defeat in 1967, Egypt and Syria made secret preparations for a counterattack. On the Jewish feast of Yom Kippur 1973, Egyptian forces threw themselves on Israeli defenses along the Suez Canal and broke into the Sinai Peninsula, while Syrian troops assaulted the Golan Heights. As ammunition and supplies soon threatened to run out, there was serious risk that Israel would experience the same humiliation that it had imposed on Arabs in 1967. But President Nixon's government managed to resupply its Israeli allies more rapidly than General Secretary Brezhnev's did the Arabs, and the tide of fighting turned. By the time peace was imposed, Israeli forces had recaptured Sinai and were a bare 63 miles from Cairo and 20 from Damascus. The initial victories restored Arab pride, and much of Sinai was returned to Egypt. On the Israeli side, possession of the West Bank seemed all the more secure, as a powerful settler movement claimed divine authority for sweeping aside the Geneva Convention's provisions on settlement in occupied territory.

*

As far back as 1929, Hasidic philosopher Martin Buber had laid out alternative paths for a future Jewish state.

The first view, the view of the so-called non-Zionists, argues that Israel is less than a nation in the modern sense. The second view argues that Israel is identical with a nation. And the third argues that Israel is more than a nation; in other words, the national characteristics of the modern concept of a nation apply also to the reality of Israel but do not suffice. Israel is a unique creation that includes all characteristics of a nation in the modern sense, without being defined by them; rather it carries its own laws.[6]

Theodore Herzl and those secular leaders who followed were very clear that they planned to create a Zionist state that was "identical with a nation." But religious Jews were also settling in Palestine during those inter-war years and first Ashkenazi Chief Rabbi of Jerusalem Abraham Kook (Kook the Elder) had no doubt that Israel must be "more than a nation." As the only state that had been established by divine decree rather than historical accident, she had a duty to follow her messianic destiny, without regard to outside pressure. Although past and present secular leaders may not have understood God's purposes, Kook insisted that they were still agents of a great heavenly strategy; while not themselves the Messiah, they had perhaps been the donkeys who were destined to carry the Messiah back to the Holy Land. The first religious kibbutz, founded in 1935, was quickly supplemented by others, which built their settlements in clusters so that they could educate their children without risk of contamination by irreligious neighbors.

Abraham Kook's son, 76-year-old Rabbi Avi Yehudah Kook (Kook the Younger), celebrated Independence Day with some 300 students on the evening of May 14, 1967. Suddenly he showed signs of deep distress and began to shout in anger. He recalled how, 19 years earlier, when the entire nation flowed into the streets to celebrate the creation of a Jewish state, he alone had sat in silence as biblical words spun in his head: "They have divided my land," he repeated.

Yes, where is our Hebron—have we forgotten it? And where is our Sechem... And our Jericho—will we forget them? And the far side of Jordan—it is ours every clod of soil... every region and bit of earth belonging to the Lord's land. Is it in our hands to give up even a millimeter?[7]

As passion eased, Kook admitted that independence had marked the beginning of that redemption the prophets had forecast when they spoke of the End of Days.

Just three weeks later, many of the young people who had heard this outburst found themselves caught up in the Six Day War. When the fighting was over, all agreed that such swift and comprehensive victory had to be the work of God.

Extreme-Orthodox Judaism had now divided into two sharply contrasting groups. On one side, traditionalist (*Haredim*) believers retained the familiar black garments, lived in close urban communities—largely on state benefits—shunned military service, and educated large broods of children from the narrowest possible religious curriculum. In contrast, followers of Kook the Younger and like-minded rabbis formed themselves into an organization that became known as *Gush Emunim* (Block of the Faithful), with a key objective of extending Israel's frontiers by driving settlements ever deeper into Arab-occupied territory. These militant people lived very differently from the quietist Haredim. In times of conflict, Gush Emunim activists sought out places in the front line of battle; in times of peace, they commuted from their settlements to regular jobs in urban centers, wearing regular clothing—only distinguishable from others by a distinctive knitted skullcap.

Gush Emunim rabbis were anxious to change the vocabulary of Zion. By their criteria, secular leaders had overemphasized the memory of return from exile. Until God promised them new land, Abraham's family had lived in the Mesopotamian city of Ur, Rights of occupancy in Palestine were, therefore, more properly based on the act of "coming in" to a Promised Land rather than "returning" to territory they had once owned. Scripture confirmed that this could not be achieved without violence and conquest. According to a favorite passage from the Book of Numbers:

In the plains of Moab by the Jordan at Jericho, the Lord spoke to Moses saying, "Speak to the to the Israelites and say to them: When you cross over the Jordan into the land of Canaan, and you shall drive out all the inhabitants of the land before you... You shall take possession of the land and settle in it, for I have given you the land to possess.... But if you do not drive out the inhabitants of the land from before you, those of them whom you let remain shall be as barbs in your eyes and thorns in your side, and they will trouble you in the land where you are settling."[8]

This claim to the land was both historical and "metahistorical": The nation of Israel was not only the product of history—it also creates history. Settlers were therefore released from any obligation to respect indigenous land rights. "We did not invite the Palestinians to come and reside in our land; they penetrated it and invaded it, as foreign nomads, when we were not at home."[9] Jewish myth could even claim possession of traditional Arab culture. "The *darbuka* (drum) and flute are not Arab instruments. Patriarch Abraham and Miriam the prophet played on them, and they belong to the culture of the Land of Israel... Now we return to the roots that once were ours."[10] Replacing the term *West Bank* with the ancient names of Judea and Samaria, the new settlers redefined those occupied territories as well as the Golan Heights and Sinai as integral parts of Israel, from which—in Rabbi Kook the Younger's words—not "even one millimeter" could be alienated. The government's decision to return most of Sinai to Egypt at the end of the Yom Kippur War was therefore simple blasphemy.

Jewish settlements spread out along West Bank hilltops that overlooked Arab communities in the fertile valleys below. Whatever the Knesset might decree, these represented *de facto* possession of the land and testified to wider Israeli society that the messianic era had arrived. In the words of extremist rabbi Azri'el Ariel:

The religious settlements were established not only to create facts on the ground but also to affect the hearts and minds of the Jewish people. We believed that, by encountering the holy parts of the land as if they were alive, the hearts of the Jewish masses would be united with the heart of the land. We envisaged the process as reconnecting the national Jewish consciousness with its spiritual roots.[11]

Still, Israel's boundaries remain much smaller than the territory had been originally promised to Abraham and no pronouncement by the United Nations or even the Israeli Knesset could alter God's word. To the horror of many secular-minded Israelis, Gush Emunim rabbis took it on themselves to define the boundaries of *Eretz* (the land of) *Israel*. As Hechler had spotted, Israel's biblical boundaries should properly stretch from the Nile in the south to the Euphrates in the east; on the west they should follow the Mediterranean coast into modern Lebanon or even Turkey.[12] The fact that no ancient Hebrew ruler ever controlled such wide stretches of land was not the issue; as long as God's promise remained unfulfilled, the boundaries of contemporary Egypt, Jordan, Lebanon, Syria, and Iraq would remain illegitimate.

Under the Israeli system of election by proportional representation, neither the Labor nor the Likud parties can command a working majority in the Knesset without the support of smaller political groups. Gush Emunim members, who overwhelmingly voted for the right-wing National Religious Party, can therefore exercise a political influence disproportionate to their numbers when ruling in coalition with the conservative Likud Party. In practice therefore, no Likud administration can restrain the advance of settlement in occupied lands. Indeed, successive Israeli governments have massively supported illegal settlements by providing dedicated roads, finance, education and military protection.

The full intensity of communal hatred was demonstrated when Brooklyn-born and—bred army doctor Baruch Goldstein entered a mosque and started firing on the worshipers, killing 29 and injuring 125, before he was himself beaten to death by worshippers. In the disturbances that followed, another 19 Arabs were killed by Israeli "peacekeepers." Murderous attacks by deranged gunmen may be a worldwide phenomenon, but the manner in which many ultranationalist Jews reacted to the event gives serious cause for concern. While addressing Goldstein's funeral, one rabbi announced that the lives of a million Arabs were not worth a single Jewish fingernail, while a teacher announced that, of all Jews, only Goldstein could be considered 100 percent perfect. The assassin's tomb then became a place of pilgrimage, where extremists could embrace and kiss the stone, while Hasidic parties danced around in joy. As late as 2010, the Internet carried pictures of East Jerusalem settlers celebrating in full sight of their Arab neighbors as they sang; "Dr. Goldstein, there is none other like you in the world, Dr. Goldstein we all love you ... he aimed at terrorists' heads, squeezed the trigger hard, and shot bullets, and shot, and shot."[13] Meanwhile, on the West Bank hilltops, a new breed of even younger people defy statute law by planting token settlements in ever more barren places, from where they raid Arab farmers as they try to harvest their olive crops. Eight separate attempts were made to control this antisocial behavior and only after the last had ended in failure was the government forced to confess (in words from the Talmud) "My children have defeated me. My children have defeated me."[14]

Some settlers believe that the Messiah is yet to come, others that the messianic age has already arrived. The expected savior can be defined in communal terms either as the body of learned orthodox rabbis or, indeed, as the whole community of settlers who have committed their lives to Zion. Israel may be properly held up as the only democracy in the Middle East, but, this would cease to be true if some extreme rabbis had their way. Having virtuously fulfilled their task of bringing the people back to Palestine and establishing a viable state, they urge that political leaders must now restore a theocratic state under a monarch of David's line. In this divinely ordered world, different levels of punishment for the same offence would be meted out to Jews and non-Jews, and modernist concepts like equality for all and universal respect for human rights would be abandoned forever.[15] Dismissing such messianic ideas as ravings of the lunatic fringe does not inhibit their apparently inexoable spread within Israeli society

*

In the South East corner of the Old City of Jerusalem is the site Jews know as the Temple Mount and Muslims as Sacred Noble Sanctuary *(al-Haram ash-Sharif)*. This is a place redolent of both myth and history.

> The Temple mount that matters is built out of stories not stones ... Some say the world began here. Some say the Holy of Holies ... was a rock known as the Foundation Stone because the creation of the world began there.[16]

Maimonides taught that "not only was Adam born where the altar stood, but Cain and Abel made their sacrifices there; so did Noah after the flood; so did Abraham."[17] Solomon's First Temple stood on this site for more than 400 years before Nebuchadnezzar razed the building in 587 BCE. A Second Temple, constructed by those returning from Babylonian exile (and later much expanded by Herod the Great), was finally destroyed by the Romans in 70 CE. Here, too, Jesus of Nazareth preached and threw moneylenders out of the precinct. Since the Muslim conquest, the site has been dominated by two magnificent Islamic buildings: the Al Aqsa Mosque and the larger Dome of the Rock. After Jewish troops recovered the whole city in the Six Day War, the Knesset (as Lord Curzon had forecast) did set about converting Jerusalem into Israel's inalienable capital city. While foreign countries refused to move their embassies from Tel Aviv, Arab residents came under growing pressure from aggressive settlers. Still, by a strange twist of ancient purity law, the conquerors still have no access to the Temple Mount itself. According to that legalistic *Book of Numbers*, Jews become unclean after having any contact with a dead body and "all who touch a corpse ... and do not purify themselves, defile the tabernacle of the Lord."[18] Since dead bodies lie buried in all kinds of unknown places, rabbis decreed that everybody must live in a state of impurity. In fear that somebody might unwittingly desecrate the unidentified site of the Holy of Holies, Jews are still prohibited from passing through the Temple gate. The ban offered the practical benefit of segregating worshippers; while Jews pray outside the Temple gate at the Western Wall, Muslims pass through to worship in their ancient mosques. The *Book of Numbers* offers just one opening to those extremists who remain determined to gain access to the Temple Mount in order to destroy the Dome.[19] If an unblemished red heifer is sacrificed, those marked by the beast's ashes will become purified and so able to pass through the gate. Still, even after an apparently suitable beast named Melody was identified, rabbis preserved the Middle East from looming Armageddon by discovering a few white strands of hair on the beast's tail.[20]

Opinion divided when an extremist plot to blow up the Dome of the Rock was exposed in 1984. While mainstream Jews feared that such an action would trigger a united Arab assault on Israel, extreme Messianic believers responded that risks of warfare must pale into insignificance beside the fact that the Messiah would not return to his city until a Third Temple stood on the Temple Mount; believers had a duty to "shatter the world to make it whole." Three years later, ultra-orthodox Rabbi Yisrael Ariel founded a Temple Institute, charged with the task of preparing public opinion for the great moment when Israel would be ready to address the task. Although the Institute displays faithful replicas of the sacred robes and vessels that will be required when ancient rituals (including animal sacrifice) are revived, majority public opinion remains stubbornly hostile to any suggestion that the Dome of the Rock might be destroyed an the Temple rebuilt. Rabbi Ariel laments this breakdown of national purpose.

Every day when I see the people's estrangement and alienation, I look with disbelief upon what is happening. A generation will come and say that there was a great failure. The religious Judaism, which calls itself Zionist—and Zion is the Temple—has to look in the mirror. A person needs to ask himself where he is and what he is doing with "and they shall build me a Temple and I shall dwell within them" and many other commandments (*mitzvot*). If, after 40 years, all religious Zionism has to show for its efforts is another flag-dance march on Jerusalem Day, we are in critical condition.[21]

*

In 1948, Egyptian scholar Sayyid Qutb travelled to America to study contemporary trends in Western education. After completing a Master's degree, he was allowed the experience of attending a Christian church service in the town of Greeley, Colorado. When worship had finished, young people left the building for a hall that was set up for dancing. The scene became branded on Qutb's memory.

The dance hall was lit with red and blue flashes and a few white lamps. While listening to the tones of a gramophone, dancing intensified, the dance floor started swarming with legs, hands embraced waists and lips touched. Suddenly (the clergyman) noticed that the white lamps were getting brighter, which might spoil the romantic atmosphere ... (and) turned off the lights one by one ... Actually the place appeared more romantic. Then he went to pick out another dance record suitable to the atmosphere, and encouraged those who were sitting to take part in the dance. He picked out a famous song called "But Baby It's Cold Outside."[22]

In Qutb's defense, popular dancing had become unusually sensuous during those years before the eruption of rock and roll, and, even within the "smooch" genre, "But Baby It's Cold Outside" was a notoriously erotic number. After experiencing that sexually charged atmosphere, Qutb returned to complete his studies at Cairo's Al-Azhar University with a fixed conviction that America had deteriorated into a promiscuous and spiritually empty consumer society. Having experienced some kind of religious conversion, he joined the radical Muslim Brothers and became editor in chief of the organization's weekly journal.

After mobilizing the Brothers' support in seizing power, new president Gamal Abdel Nasser came to recognize that these religious enthusiasts could threaten his own hold on power. He therefore banned the Brotherhood and executed some of its leading members. Although sentenced to 25 years' imprisonment and repeatedly tortured, Qutb managed to spend long hours in study and writing. Alongside a 30-volume commentary on the Qur'an, he also produced a brief manifesto for militant Islam, which became known in English as *Milestones* (although the Arabic word might also be transliterated as *Signposts*).

End-time themes are less easily identified within Sunni Islam than they are in Christianity, Judaism, or the Shi'a. Apart from Muhammad's night journey to heaven and hell, the Qur'an carries no apocalypse, and predictions for the arrival of a Mahdi are rejected by some Sunni scholars as inauthentic. At the same time, belief in the Last Days remains a central tenet of faith, and Sunni teachers have always urged the faithful prepare for that event. Those early Muslims who carried the jihad across the Levant and North Africa had interpreted victory in millennial terms; now, thirteen centuries later, Muslims looked back across decades of humiliation at the hands of western imperialists and "Crusader/Zionists." Judging that true Islamic society had been extinct for many centuries, Qtub directed *Milestones* at that "vanguard" of believers who could help restore the faith to its primitive purity. While these Muslim activists are today widely known as *jihadists*, most prefer the term *salafi*—those who follow the model set in the days of the first three "rightly guided" caliphs. Since Islam had a message for all mankind, true believers needed to confront all godless regimes that kept their people in ignorance and idolatry. Sayyid Qutb accepted that this must involve violence.

Anyone who understands this particular character of this religion will also understand the place of *jihad bis saif* (striving through fighting), which is to clear the way for striving through preaching in the application of the Islamic movement. He will understand that Islam is not a "defensive movement" in the narrow sense which today is technically called a "defensive war."[23]

Since all authority lay with the one indivisible God, it was blasphemous to suggest that any secular ruler possessed sovereignty. Christians might accept that they should "render to Caesar the things that are Caesar's and to God the things that are God's";[24] within Islam, the secular and the religious were one and no such distinction could be made. The sole duty of worldly rulers was to submit their own will to God and create a society that was wholly obedient to God's will. In the real world, where every Muslim ruler clung fiercely to personal sovereignty, all had to be legitimate targets for jihad. Qtub looked forward to a time when individual rulers would be replaced by a millennial caliphate, that would restore true faith and even reconquer the lost Iberian Peninsula. Islam would then be recognized as a faith for all humanity. While no Christian or Jew would be forced to accept the faith, all would have to pay the poll tax and accept the fact that they were second-class citizens within a Muslim society.

Gamal Abdel Nasser had Qutb hanged in 1966, but, even after the author was dead, his violent message continued to gather supporters. When Anwar Sadat made peace with Israel in exchange for massive American subsidies, jihadists announced that he had signed his own death warrant. Activist Abdel Salam Faraj defended those army officers who performed the deed in October 1981.

The rulers of the age are in apostasy from Islam. They were raised at the tables of imperialism, be it Crusaderism, or Communism, or Zionism. They carry nothing from Islam but their names, even though they pray and fast and claim to be Muslim. It is a well-established rule of Islamic Law that the punishment of an apostate will be heavier than the punishment of someone who is by origin an infidel.[25]

In retaliation for this contribution, Faraj was also hanged alongside Sadat's four killers.

In late 1979, the Soviet Union launched a major land and air assault on Afghanistan. Palestinian cleric Abdullah Azzam had drawn close to the Muslim Brothers while studying at Cairo's Al-Azhar university; now he summoned jihadists from across the Muslim world to strengthen Afghan resistance to the invaders. Calling his followers *mujahidin* (holy warriors), he revived Qutb's message that every Muslim had a duty to wage jihad against the faithless and apostate. Following standard American policy of treating all Russia's enemies as friends of the United States, President Carter provided Azzam's *mujahidin* with armaments, which included destructive ground-to-air missiles. With salafi recruits pouring in from across the Islamic world, Azzam's Islamic fighters soon outnumbered the invading Russians. Military morale was broken and the Soviet state approaching bankruptcy by the time that the Russians finally withdrew from Afghanistan in 1988. The Berlin Wall fell just one year later.

One notorious recruit had joined Azzam's mujahidin in the course of this Afghan war. Saudi national Osama bin Laden recorded how he become radicalized during Israel's First Lebanon War.

The events that affected me personally began in 1982, when America gave Israel the green light to invade Lebanon and the American Sixth Fleet helped them. When the bombardment began, many were killed and injured, and others were terrorized and displaced. I cannot forget those terrible scenes of blood and severed limbs, the corpses of children strewn everywhere, houses destroyed with their occupants and high-rise buildings burying their residents.[26]

Bin Laden took command of the mujahidin after Azzam was blown up in suspicious circumstances and he was busy creating jihadist al-Qaeda (*the base*) at just the time when Westerners were celebrating the fall of communist governments across Eastern Europe. The organization's manifesto protested that the American government had colluded with puppet rulers to gain control of Middle Eastern politics and natural resources. It was particularly intolerable that the Saudi royal house had permitted the Americans to establish a Christian bridgehead on the sacred peninsula, "plundering its riches, overwhelming its rulers, humiliating its people, threatening its neighbors." Apart from providing cover for massive oil workings, "crusader" military bases now threatened the independence of Muslim nations across the Middle East. Anxiety proved justified in 1990, when Saudi-based air superiority determined the outcome of the First Iraq War and then allowed the victors to enforce harsh United Nations sanctions.

In spite of the appalling number of dead, exceeding a million, the Americans nevertheless, in spite of all this, are trying to repeat the dreadful slaughter. It seems that the long blockade following after a fierce war, the dismemberment and the destruction are not enough for them. So they come again to destroy what remains of this people and to humiliate their Muslim neighbors.[27]

By destroying Iraq and weakening the buffer states that bordered on Israel, America had managed to shore up the "petty state of the Jews" and divert attention from "the occupation of Jerusalem and their killing of Muslims in it." Al Qaeda was now aware of Gush Emunim's longer-term dreams of creating a Greater Israel, with borders that reached to the Umayyad capital city of Baghdad. All this activity was a "clear declaration of war by the Americans against God, his Prophet and the Muslims ... When enemies attack the Muslim lands," declared the manifesto, "Jihad becomes the personal duty of every Muslim."[28] As jihadi terrorist attacks were mounted across different continents, democratic governments continued to support those authoritarian and, all too often, corrupt governments, which could, at least, provide some kind of buffer against Al Qaeda and its sympathizers.

*

After leading the opposition to Iranian Shah Mohammed Reza and suffering periods of imprisonment, the Ayatollah Ruhollah Khomeini was finally forced into exile in 1964. Settling across the Iraqi frontier in the Shi'a city of Najaf, he continued to teach Islamic studies to eager students from his own community. Khomeini took particular issue with those Shi'a scholars who argued that members of the clergy should stand back from political controversy until the day when the Twelfth Imam would finally come out of hiding. In response he declared that any member of the clergy who shunned active involvement had made a clear decision to side with tyrant oppressors.

This mullah is political. The Prophet was a political person. This evil propaganda was spread by the agents of imperialism to cause you to shun politics, to prevent you from intervening in the affairs of society, and struggling against treacherous governments and their anti-nationalistic and anti-Islamic policies. They want to do whatever they please without anybody trying to stop them.[29]

Khomeini argued that, as long as the Twelfth Imam remained hidden, his authority must be exercised by a "vice-regency of theologians," who would install a full Islamic state and govern according to rules laid down in the sharia.

The fundamental difference between Islamic government and constitutional monarchies and republics is this: whereas the representatives of the people or monarch in such regimes engage in legislation, in Islam the legislative power and competence to establish laws belongs exclusively to God Almighty.[30]

On January 16, 1979, after months of civil unrest, His Imperial Majesty Shah Mohammed Reza and his wife Farah fled from Tehran. Just two weeks later,

Ayatollah Khomeini returned from the Paris suburb where he had spent the last year of exile. The cry of *Allahu Akbar* arose as some 5 million thronged the streets of Tehran, while, across the country, "young and old exchanged sweets and swept the streets as they told each other that *Aqa* (the holy man) was about to arrive." Understandably, many less learned folk drew the conclusion that the Hidden Imam had returned at last from his long occultation.

At the end of March, the Iranian people approved (at least officially, by 98.2% of the popular vote) that an Islamic republic should replace the 2,500-year-old Persian monarchy. Under Khomeini's guidance, a constitution emerged that made some attempt to reconcile the competing concepts that the state should be ruled by God, and that the people should also be allowed to contribute through a democratic process. While a president and parliament (*majlis*) would be elected by a Western-style secret ballot, the most senior cleric or Supreme Leader (initially, of course, Khomeini himself) would have day-to-day executive control over the civil service, army, and police. A Council of Guardians, appointed by the Supreme Leader, would also have power to strike off unsuitable parliamentary candidates and veto "un-Islamic" legislation passed down by the majlis. In practice, Khomeini had surrounded the president's office with so many checks and balances that any future reforming politician would struggle to get legislation onto the statute book. In the event, first President Banisadr quickly fell foul of the mullahs and was impeached by his own majlis. He only managed to escape into exile after three of his closest associates had been summarily executed. The next president and prime minister were both murdered just a month after taking office.

Meanwhile, Khomeini concentrated on directing anger outward towards the "Great Satan" (the United States) and "Little Satan" (Israel). As crowds shouted "Death to America" and "Death to Israel," students broke into the American embassy and took the whole staff hostage. Thirteen women and African Americans were later released, but the remaining 52 white males were held prisoner for 444 days. As messianic emotions ran high in Iran, Sunni rulers of other Arab states became increasingly concerned that revolutionary contagion would infect their own minority populations. From its base in war-torn Lebanon, Shi'a jihadist organization Hezbollah (the Party of God) aroused international alarm by hijacking aircraft and launching suicide attacks on Jewish and Western targets. As a Sunni Muslim who ruled over a population that was 65 percent Shi'a, Iraq president Saddam Hussein felt particularly threatened. At the same time, he was also developing plans to exploit upheaval across the border to grasp some of Iran's oil wealth and expand Iraq's coastline on the Persian Gulf. After disbanding the Shah's army and executing many of its officers, Khomeini no longer commanded any professional fighting force and, when all factors were taken into account, it seemed likely that Saddam would achieve his objectives within a few months. In the event, the Iranian population remained loyal to its revolution, and citizen armies turned the Iraqi invaders back. The war would then last for almost eight years, cost around a million lives, and inflict great damage on both economies.

Locked in stalemate, the Iranian mullahs took command out of the military men's hands and settled down to wage a war of attrition in which Iran would exploit its larger population to absorb human loss. While they anticipated no magical intervention by the hidden Twelfth Imam, Khomeini and his mullahs revived the traditional Shi'a belief that martyrdom would bring instant salvation. Pious volunteers now arrived at the front carrying the shrouds in which they expected to be buried. Reports also described how young boys moved in human waves across no-man's-land exploding landmines under their feet as they advanced towards the Iraqi guns. Each potential martyr carried a metal key that assured him entrance to the gardens of paradise. Then, as public opinion turned, families began to find ever more creative ways of shielding their children from front-line service. The United Nations managed to enforce a cease-fire in 1988, with nothing of significance achieved on either side. The 86 year-old Ayatollah died just a year later.

The thousand-year old myth that Twelfth Imam Muhammad ben Hasan would return to bring true Islam and justice to a troubled world still lived on among the more impoverished and oppressed members of Iranian society. In the desert town of Jamkaran, near the Shi'a holy city of Qom, was a small mosque, where—at least according to popular tradition—the Twelfth Imam had once walked. Behind could be found the dried-up "well of the Lord of the Age" (later increased to two wells—one for men and the other for women), which was said to be immediately above the underground cellar where the Twelfth Imam still waited for the moment of return. Every day, believers dropped thousands of messages, which kept the hidden one informed of their anxieties and achievements. In 2005, "Twelver" devotee Mahmud Ahmadinejad stood for election as president of Iran and, in the final run-off, was elected by more than 60 percent of the votes. "Today is the beginning of a new era," he announced. "I am proud of being the Iranian nation's little servant and street sweeper."[31] It was said that, at his inauguration, Ahmadinejad let Supreme Leader Ayatollah Ali Hoseyni Khamenei know that he expected to hand his position over to the Mahdi within two years. "What if he doesn't appear by then?" asked the bemused Ayatollah. "I really believe this," replied the new president. "He will come soon."[32]

Ahmadinejad's millennial speeches became a familiar feature of UN General Assembly meetings. In the first year, he told how,

From the beginning of time, humanity has longed for the day when justice, peace equality and compassion envelop the world.... When that day comes, the ultimate promise of all religions will be fulfilled with the emergence of a perfect human being who is heir to all prophets and pious men.

Next year, his address ended with a version of the prayer for deliverance:

O, Almighty God, all men and women are your creatures and you have ordained their guidance and salvation. Bestow upon humanity that thirsts for justice, the perfect human being promised to all by you, and make us among his followers and among those who strive for his return and his cause.

Back in Iran, Ahmadinejad told how the atmosphere had changed when the "Imam of the Age" enveloped him in a halo of light.

For those twenty-seven or twenty-eight minutes, none of the leaders of the world blinked—and I say this without exaggeration. They were looking as if a hand was holding them there, and had just opened their eyes.[33]

As Ahmadinejad's cabinet voted funds for expansion, the Jamkaram mosque grew to be a huge edifice of five courtyards and 12 minarets, set on a 600-acre (250-hectare) site, which was designed to accommodate 250,000 people at any one time. A small man—identified as the country's president—could sometimes be spotted among the crowds that now thronged the shrine. Rightly or wrongly, it was even whispered that this president dropped cabinet minutes down the well so the hidden imam could keep abreast of state affairs and offer guidance for the future.

There is considerable evidence that voters—even some believers—are reluctant to vote for politicians whose decisions might be driven by religious faith rather than political expediency. Since Jewish, Christian, and Islamic scriptures all predict that the End Time will bring warfare and tribulation, suspicions linger that religious enthusiasts might be tempted to hasten the process. Although many Iranians find their government's addiction to myth and millennial speculation deeply embarrassing, Shi'ite millennialism does not stand out as uniquely eccentric. While the Iranian president awaits his hidden imam, apparently sane Jews try to breed pure red heifers, whose ashes will allow the destruction of ancient Muslim shrines—and likely trigger a Third World War. At the same time, even rich and influential American Christians can look to the moment when God will lift them bodily into the air so that they can rise above the fray as Jesus of Nazareth gathers his forces for that final battle of Armageddon that will presage the death and destruction of humankind.

*

Richard Nixon could not foresee the scale of problems that lay ahead when he took the oath of office as thirty-seventh president of the United States in January 1969. Anti-war protests increased after news of the massacre of hundreds of women and children in the Vietnam village of Mai Lai leaked into the public arena. When four protesting students at Kent State University were shot dead by the Ohio National Guard in May of the following year, it seemed as if the nation was about to tear itself apart. As liberal Christians took their places on the picket lines, veteran conservative clergyman Karl McIntyre was organizing triumphant Vietnam victory parades in cities across the country. Since the end of World War II, this New Jersey pastor had campaigned against every liberal innovation within church and state. After placing his weight behind Senator Joe McCarthy's anticommunist witch hunt, he pressed that liberally minded church leaders should be investigated along with other suspect members of society. In common with other conservative Christians, McIntyre hated all supranational bodies. Proclaiming that the Antichrist would emerge from the United Nations, he forecast that the organization's "marble tower" would bring destruction to New York City. Wherever the World Council of Churches held its meetings, members could not avoid his demonstrations against its religious and political apostasy. While McIntyre's abrasive style achieved publicity, Billy Graham's more softly spoken message gained the president's ear. As Cold War politics forced Eisenhower closer to the Israeli cause, Graham was able to conduct regular prayer meetings in the White House. Discontinued during Catholic Kennedy's presidency, Virginia minister Jerry Falwell re-established these White House meetings under Republican successors Nixon, Ford, and Reagan. Working from the same agenda that would define the "moral majority," they opposed abortion, homosexuality, and expenditure on welfare programs while promoting increased spending on armaments.

In the early 1970s, dispensationalist Protestants began to draw unflattering comparisons between Israel's clinically efficient conduct of the Six Day War and their own ignominious withdrawal from Vietnam.

As Americans we were made acutely aware of our own diminished authority, of no longer being able to police the world or perhaps even our own neighborhoods. Many Americans ... turned worshipful glances towards Israel, which they viewed as militarily strong and invincible. They gave their unstinting approval to the take-over of Arab lands because they perceived this conquest as power and righteousness.[34]

The dangers for Jewish survival in the Holy Land came into focus during the perilous early days of the Yom Kippur War. After this shock had been absorbed, dispensationalist writers felt increasing need to chart the future progress of humanity toward the tribulation and final judgment. Although many set their hand to the task, it would be Hal Lindsey's *The Late Great Planet Earth* that scooped the popular market. "I believe," he pronounced, "that God gave me a special insight, not only how John described what he actually experienced, but also how this whole phenomenon encoded the prophecies so that they could only be fully understood when their fulfillment drew near."[35] Bound in an eye-catching cover and displayed by booksellers alongside New Age titles on the Knights Templar and the Holy Grail, this work sold in multi-millions across North America and the wider world. Lindsey took pride in showing the watch presented by his German publisher in gratitude for high sales of the translation that had saved his company from bankruptcy.

This book told how the long-expected countdown toward the world's end had begun and the 1980s would probably be the last decade of history "as we know it." Events in the Holy Land had set the apocalyptic clock ticking.

To be specific about Israel's great significance as a sign of the time, there are three things that were to happen. First, the Jewish nation would be reborn in the land of Palestine. Second, the Jews would repossess Old Jerusalem and the sacred sites. Thirdly, they would rebuild the ancient temple of worship upon its historic site.[36]

Concerns about the Dome of the Rock were irrelevant. "Obstacle or no obstacle, it is certain that the Temple will be rebuilt. Prophecy demands it."[37] Conflating John's Revelation with Ezekiel's bloody battle, Lindsey predicted that the last three years before Christ's return would "make the regimes of Hitler, Mao and Stalin look like Girl Scouts weaving a daisy chain by comparison."[38] It had long been accepted that Gog and Magog would descend on Israel from the North, and "Bible scholars" now agreed that this fearsome enemy could only be the Soviet Union. Gathering its allies together, this "Confederacy of the North" would plunge the world into its final great war, which Christ will return to end.[39] Anticipating that the whole of Africa would soon turn to communism, Lindsey predicted that all that continent's nations would ally with the Arabs to form the "army of the Kings of the South." The huge force would be completed by the hordes of Communist China. Another writer provided the challenge that sent them on their way.

We will conquer all of Asia, we will conquer the Middle East, we will conquer Africa. Tomorrow 200 million warriors will march. We will not be stopped until the whole world kneels at our feet. We will be victorious. The ovation was spontaneous and tremendous as citizens raised their familiar Red Book and shouted . . . "VICTORY—VICTORY—VICTORY."[40]

When these "200 million soldiers from the Orient, with millions more from the West" gathered in Israel, Jesus would return to strike first at those who were attacking Jerusalem before moving to destroy many millions more who were massed on the plain of Megiddo. After the Messiah Christ had done his work, the whole valley would be filled with war materials, animals, bodies of men, and blood.

Lindsey described the end-time holocaust with unholy zest, hypnotically piling catastrophe on catastrophe: "multiplied millions" of soldiers are incinerated; civilian casualties mount into the billions amid nuclear horrors including a "quadrillion megaton explosion"; a mass poisoning of water results as water turns to blood. ("There's going to be a big run on Coca-Cola, but even this will run out after a while").[41]

By the time that Lindsey came to update his predictions in *The 1980s: Countdown to Armageddon*, the European Union had just admitted Greece as its tenth member. With membership equating to the 10 horns on Daniel's fourth Beast, it was clear that a new Roman Empire had finally emerged. While the European Union's program was superficially peaceful, Lindsey unmasked its secret plan to create a world empire. Since prophecy demanded that that Antichrist should come from Rome, Lindsey forecast that this ultimate destroyer might already be a member of the European parliament. "This charismatic leader will receive his powers from himself and will appear to devote his life to world peace. But in reality he will lead us to final holocaust."[42]

Every time some part of Lindsey's forecast fails to materialize, he somehow manages to argue awkward facts away. Even as the Soviet empire crumbled, he was still insisting:

the reality is that the "collapse of Communism" is part of a masterful game of deceit engineered by Mikhail Gorbachev and the Soviet KGB. It is part of an elaborate strategy to secure Western aid and technology, but time, persuade the West to unilaterally disarm and, at the same time, continue a covert but nevertheless dramatic military build-up of its own.[43]

Today in his 80s, Hal Lindsey still produces a daily "news analysis of current events from the perspective of Bible prophecy." On the day this paragraph is being written,[44] he chides a lady for growing bored with the whole process.

A viewer e-mailed me this week and told me to "Give it a rest." Zoe wrote, "Hal, your (sic) a charlatan. You've been prophesying the Lord's return in the 1970s 80s 90s and 2000s ... We're sick of you." Ouch! Would she say the same thing to Jesus Himself? I'm only repeating His words and the words of the ancient prophets He spoke through ... As I see it, my failure ... and that of many of my like-minded ministry colleagues, has been that we underestimated the growing "frequency and intensity" of the "birth pangs" we have witnessed the last several years. But even as I write this, a massive tsunami from an undersea earthquake has hit Japan and threatens Hawaii and the entire Pacific Rim. Early reports are that this may be one of the biggest earthquakes in history! Another intense birth pang? ... Only Father God knows when the birth pangs have run their course and the time for "delivery" has arrived.[45]

During the same period, ultra right-wing activist Tim LaHaye has sold many millions of copies of the *Left Behind* series of novels along with multimedia spin-offs. After professional ghostwriter Jerry Jenkins has written the book's text, LaHaye reportedly checks his work for apocalyptic authenticity. Across the series, the narrative conducts the reader from Rapture to Armageddon. After telling how passengers on a transatlantic flight suddenly disappear, leaving possessions piled on their seats, the authors take up the story of those who are "left behind" to survive seven years of Tribulation as best they can. Leading the forces of evil is brilliant Rumanian Nicolae Carpathia. After being appointed Secretary-General of the United Nations during the chaos that follows the Rapture, Carpathia sets about inflating that organization into an authoritarian Global Community, within which he rises to the position of Supreme Potentate. Since the Tribulation is divided into two periods of 3½ years, in which the second half is very much more violent than the first, the narrative becomes more gruesome as the series progresses. After moving the Community's headquarters to Babylon, Carpathia reveals that he is the Antichrist and the last great battle for Jerusalem is joined.

And Jesus said, in a voice like a trumpet and the sound of rushing eaters. "I AM WHO I AM." At that instant the Mount of Olives split in two from east to west ... All the firing and the running and the galloping and the rolling stopped. The soldiers screamed and fell, their bodies bursting open from head to toe at every word that proceeded out of the mouth of the Lord.[46]

While dispensational believers lose no opportunity to complain about portrayals of sex and violence in the public media, they appear to have endless tolerance for this pornography of violence when presented in an apocalyptic setting. A young fan is recorded as saying; "the best thing about the *Left Behind* books is the way the non-Christians get their guts pulled out by God."[47] A more skeptical critic can only agree with the evil Carpathia that "if there is a God, I respectfully submit that this is not the capricious way he would operate."[48]

*

While all Christian Zionists agree that the Jews will have a central role in the coming apocalyptic drama, the question of how they will fare in the Final Judgment remains a matter for debate. Many dispensationalists anticipate a "greater holocaust" in which two-thirds of the Jewish race will face destruction. Others argue that the God has given two covenants—one for the Jews and another for the Christians—and that he will accept all those who remain faithful to their own dispensation. Either way, there is wide consensus that the 144,000 converted Jews described in Revelation will take up the final task of evangelizing all those everyone who has survived the Tribulation.

In the meantime, end-timers quote Bible texts to prove that America must support Israel uncritically: "I will bless those who bless you" said the prophet, "and him who curses you I will curse."[49] Israel's enemies can therefore expect to suffer more than her friends in the time of Tribulation.

And this shall be the plague with which the Lord will smite all the peoples that wage war against Jerusalem; their flesh shall rot while they are still on their feet, their eyes shall rot in their sockets and their tongues shall rot in their mouths.[50]

It followed that the American government must not seek to find compromise between Israel and Arab interests. In 1977, Christian Zionists were shocked when supposedly born-again President Jimmy Carter negotiated the Camp David agreement between Israel and Egypt, which involved recognizing "the legitimate rights of the Palestinian people" and withdrawing from settlements in the Sinai Peninsula. Sixteen years later, Falwell employed every device to frustrate Bill Clinton's Oslo Accords. The negotiators had high-minded objectives.

The Government of the State of Israel and the PLO team ... agree that it is time to put an end to decades of confrontation and conflict, recognise their mutual legitimate and political rights, and strive to live in peaceful coexistence and mutual dignity and security and achieve a just, lasting and comprehensive peace settlement and historic reconciliation through the agreed political process.[51]

Working toward a two-state solution, there would be "direct, free and general elections" for a self-governing Palestinian authority, and Israel would withdraw from both Gaza and "the Jordan area." Any suggestion that the tide of West Bank settlement should be reversed aroused fierce opposition from ultra-Zionists and Israeli Prime Minister Yitzhak Rabin was assassinated by a right-wing extremist. As Likud leader Benjamin Netanyahu set about undermining the agreement at home, his American mouthpiece, Jerry Falwell, threatened to mobilize the lobbying power of 200,000 evangelical pastors and church leaders to frustrate any practical attempt to enforce the Accords' provisions.[52]

After reading Hal Lindsey's *The Late Great Planet Earth*, Ronald Reagan became convinced that the end-times were indeed closing in. "The Messiah has taken me by the hand," he once declared, "to lead me to victory in the great battle of Armageddon."[53] Leading cabinet members shared his views. At his confirmation hearing, Interior Secretary-designate James Watt publicly questioned the value of environmental conservation, "I do not know how many generations we can count on before the Lord returns." During the eight years of Reagan's presidency Falwell and Lindsey ran regular White House seminars on prophecy; but Reagan's relations with Israel would remain uneasy and he was particularly distressed by the massacres in refugee camps during the 1982 Israeli invasion of Lebanon. Falwell might ask why Israel should carry the blame for atrocities committed by others; an eyewitness gave the answer:

If the Israelis had not taken part in the killings, they had certainly sent militia into the camp. They had trained them, given them uniforms, handed them U.S. army rations and Israeli medical equipment. Then they had watched the murderers in the camps, they had given them military assistance—the Israeli airforce had dropped all those flares to help the men who were murdering the inhabitants of Sabra and Chatila.[54]

While Reagan's Cold War rhetoric remained loaded with ancient images of conflict between good and evil, his actions did retain some measure of pragmatism. In the face of bitter dispensationalist opposition, it was he and Soviet President Mikhail Gorbachev who concluded the first bilateral Strategic Arms Reduction Treaty.

As Reagan's second term neared its end, premillennial TV evangelist Pat Robertson launched a determined attempt to win the Republican presidential nomination. Letting it be known that he intended to run the country according to strict scriptural principles, he made a strong showing in early state counts before dropping back to end a poor third behind George H. W. Bush. Always confident in his personal mission, Robertson could only wonder at the mysterious ways of Providence:

My supporters were devastated. It was as if they mourned for the dead. Because they felt as I did, that God had called me to win, not run third, . . . they were asking and I was asking one simple question—did God call me to run for president or not? And if He did call me to run, why did I lose?[55]

The apocalypse appeared to draw very close on the morning of September 11, 2001, when airliners flown by Al Qaeda terrorists destroyed Manhattan's Twin Towers and severely damaged Washington's Pentagon building. But for the presumed courage of passengers, the White House was likely to have been the fourth target. Confronted by disaster and bereavement on such a scale, George W. Bush reverted to dualistic language of conflict between good and evil. His call for a "crusade" against terrorism created wide alarm across Europe. "That was very unfortunate," commented a British cabinet member. "I'm sure he didn't mean it. When you read back into the history of the Crusades, the behavior of the crusaders was much less civilized than Saladin's."[56] Certainly the word still inflames many of the region's Muslims, who hold passionately that their people and lands have been the victims of "crusader" aggression. While anger at perceived national humiliation is thought to be the dominant motivation for terrorism, Islamic politics and religion are never far apart and many (though not perhaps all) suicide bombers die in confidence that they will awake in the beautiful gardens of paradise

A decade after 9/11, there may be early signs that the movement so vigorously promoted by Sayyid Qutb and Osama bin Laden is beginning to lose impetus. When Tunisians decided that they wished to be rid of President Zine El Abidine and his corrupt family, they did not act in the name of violent jihad. Spurred on by anger at rising food prices and high unemployment, they simply took to the streets until the ruling family fled abroad. This proved to be the spark that would ignite discontent across much of the Arab world. While nobody could forecast that pro-Western regimes will emerge from the continuing upheaval, protesters are looking towards secular virtues of honest and participatory democratic government rather than the death of unbelievers and revival of the caliphate. Still—even after the killing of Osama bin Laden—few can doubt that violent jihadism will survive until some resolution can be found to the intractable problems of Israeli settlement on Arab land and Palestinian human rights. When security experts warn that it is not a question of whether but when Western populations will experience further terrorist assaults, perversely, it is ordinary Muslims, going about their daily business in Iraq and Pakistan, who suffer most from jihadist extremism.

*

While dispensationalist pastors fed conservatively-minded congregations with tales of rapture, tribulation, and Armageddon, in fashionable California charismatic but unstable prophets were delivering every kind of New Age fantasy—stirred in with varying quantities of Christian and Eastern religious belief. Results were disastrous.

Shortly after civil rights icon Martin Luther King was murdered in April 1969, Californian long-term criminal and self-styled prophet Charles Manson forecast that America was on the brink of an Armageddon of interracial strife. Naming the event after Beatles song *Helter Skelter*, he forecast that conflict would be triggered by the sound of his own pop music. Then, while his, largely female, "family" found shelter in a subterranean land of milk and honey, the desert above would be soaked with human blood. Sadly, the Manson family dealt in more than fantasy; on the night of the August 8 to 9, his young followers roamed through prosperous Los Angeles homes. Announcing that they were there to do the devil's business, on that night alone, they left seven residents either shot or knifed to death. Two other murders brought the family's total number of killings up to nine

Founded as a social outreach of the mainstream Disciples of Christ, James Warren (Jim) Jones' People's Temple set out to work multiracially among some of the most vulnerable people in the city of Indianapolis. While still in the Midwest, the operation already showed signs of developing into an inward-looking cult. Operating on socialist principles drawn from both the Acts of the Apostles and works of Karl Marx, everything centered around Jim Jones' charismatic figure. As he grew increasingly certain that nuclear war was about to bring civilization to an end, he began to search for a place where his own people would be able to survive the coming holocaust and then assume a place of leadership as the world awaited Jesus' Second Coming. After first searching in Brazil, he settled on a remote location in Northern California, and members of his Indiana congregation sold their possessions to make the journey with him. As more temples sprang up across the state in the 1970s, headquarters moved to Los Angeles. Anticult activists became increasingly alarmed as Jones declared himself to be above the moral law and refugees from the cult reported that he was using mind-control techniques thought to be based on those employed by the North Vietnamese on American prisoners of war. As hostility grew, Jones decided to plant an agricultural community deep in the Guyana rainforest, and hundreds of Temple members joined the enterprise.

The story of how Congressman Leo Ryan flew out to investigate allegations of human rights abuses and was then shot dead, alongside three reporters and a cult member, as he left on November 18, 1978, has often been told—likewise how, later the same day, 638 adults and 276 children—914 People's Temple members in total—either committed suicide with poison or were murdered. While conspiracy theories abound, this was the largest-scale cultic killing since thousands of Russian Old Believers burned themselves to death in seventeenth-century Russia.

Jonestown would not be the last such event. In March 1997, 39 bodies were discovered in a house within the exclusive gated community of Rancho Santa

Fe near San Diego. Following leader Marshall Applewhite, members of the Heaven's Gate cult had pursued the ascetic life within their own semimonastic community. Applewhite taught that human bodies were mere containers of the soul. "The final act of metamorphosis or separation from the human kingdom," he declared, "is the disconnect or separation from the human container or body in order to be released from the human environment."[57] At some time during the week before the discovery of their bodies, these devotees had killed themselves, believing that they would board a spaceship that was supposedly concealed in the tail of the Hale-Bopp comet, which would then transport them to a new and blissful heaven.

Still, apocalyptic violence was not confined to the state of California or to New Age speculation. Having grown up within the fractured world of Seventh Day Adventism Vernon Howell developed a consuming interest in both guns and the Bible. After being excluded from the main Adventist body on a charge of immorality, he joined a subsect known as the Branch Davidians. In the course of a grotesque contest to show which of them could raise the dead, Howell wounded the previous leader and took charge of the group. He then changed his name to David Koresh, which conflated the two messianic Old Testament figures of King David and the Emperor Cyrus—which transliterated into Hebrew as Koresh. In this new role he saw himself as apocalyptic mediator between God and humans.

> The ones who believe the seventh seal believe in Cyrus to deliver them from captivity. The message of Cyrus, the angel that ascends from the east . . . that same person is going to be able to stand before Christ and explain to Christ why we are so bad the way we are.[58]

After annulling the marriages of all his followers, Koresh claimed sexual rights over all female followers—including many who were below the age of consent.

Four federal agents and six Davidians died when the Bureau of Alcohol, Tobacco and Firearms raided the sect's headquarters of Mount Carmel, Waco, on February 28, 1993, and the ensuing 49-day standoff attracted a worldwide television audience. Violence reached its climax on April 19 when the federal agents bombarded the heavily armed compound with tear gas and "flash-bang" grenades. The gun battle and fire that consumed the compound and its occupants killed some 78 Branch Davidians—including more than 20 children. Whether this tragedy at Waco, Texas, was another case of communal suicide or a return to state oppression of end-time groups remains a matter of dispute.

*

New Age violence also spread beyond North America. During the 1980s, lecturer Joseph di Mambro began to gather like-minded people into a sect, which he named The Order of the Solar Temple. Declaring himself to be a reincarnation of Moses and the Pharaoh Akhnaton, he recruited members in Switzerland, France, and Francophone Canada. When the authorities began to investigate the Temple as a cult, di Mambro gathered followers onto a remote Swiss farm. On

October 5, 1994, police found 25 bodies neatly arranged in a circle, along with a further 23 at a neighboring farm. Most had been either strangled or shot. An additional 26 Solar Temple members would then lose their lives to either suicide or murder over the next three years.

Meanwhile, in distant Tokyo, a group of high-achieving science and technology graduates had succeeded in refining the destructive poison sarin within a compound owned by their Aum Shinrikyo cult. They first tested the drug's effects by releasing it in clouds near the homes of judges who were trying a property case in which the cult was involved. Seven died and some 500 needed hospital treatment after that trial run. The longer plan was to create an apocalyptic event on such a scale that the government would fall and cult leader Shako Asahara would be pronounced Emperor of Japan. On March 20, 1995, 10 young men mounted attacks on five branches of the city's metro system. But the anticipated mass mortality did not materialize; while hundreds packed the hospitals, only 17 unfortunate people died.

Partly as a result of racist attitudes and partly through poor communications, events in Africa never receive the same publicity as those in more developed countries. In the southwestern corner of Uganda, near the Rwandan border, Catholic prostitute Credonia Mwerinde discovered that she could make out the image of the Virgin Mary in a hillside rock. Anxious to atone for her sinful life, she shared the vision with prominent local politician Joseph Kibweteere, and together they decided to promote religious reform by establishing "the Movement for the Restoration of the 10 Commandments of God." After assigning prominent positions to excommunicated priests and nuns, the two founders promised that all who joined the order would be able to communicate directly with Jesus. On joining, new entrants were expected to lay all their possessions at Kibweteere's feet; once inside the order, all sex and (inexplicably) the use of soap were strictly prohibited. Lest anyone should break the commandment by bearing false witness, even talking was discouraged. According to one eyewitness:

> The whole cult revolved around a belief that some selected people communicated with God through visions and had received warnings from the Blessed Virgin Mary about the end of the world by the year 2000 ... They preached ... about how on that "last day," snakes as fat as tractor wheels and big blocks of cement will fall from heaven onto the sinners. They preached of three days of consecutive darkness that will engulf the entire earth and how only their camps would be safe havens.[59]

As January 1, 2000, passed without incident, members of the community began to grow restless, and some demanded the return of their possessions. Announcing that the world would end on March 17, Kibweteere then called a great banquet in which three bulls and many crates of Coca-Cola were consumed. After whole families had gathered in the church, the doors were bolted and the windows boarded up. Then the building began to blaze. The suggestion that this was a case of collective suicide was undermined when the Ugandan police began to recover hundreds of bodies, buried in pits across the country. All had died before March 17, 2000, and all showed clear evidence of murder. The total death toll was finally estimated at 778. Although international arrest warrants have been issued for cult leaders, no evidence has emerged that any are still alive and they probably died along with humbler members of the group in the March 17 immolation.

Since then, murderous bands of Joseph Kony's Lord's Resistance Army have continued to bring chaos and death to that area of Central Africa. Supposedly an apocalyptic body, it is reported to have "no political program or ideology, at least none that the local population has heard or can understand."[60] Notoriously supplementing its fighting force with thousands of kidnapped and abused child soldiers, these bandits still rape and kill—supposedly in Jesus' name—across northern Uganda, the southern Sudan, and eastern parts of the Central African Republic and Democratic Republic of Congo.

The impact of destructive cults cannot be measured by mortality statistics alone. With official services unaffordable, children and the vulnerable become increasingly exposed to abuse as premillennial churches disclaim responsibility for "worldly" issues of social justice. On occasion, the church itself can become the persecutor. According to widespread African tradition, nobody dies of natural causes; human mortality is therefore ascribed to witchcraft. In the troubled lands of the Niger Delta, indigenous church pastors, who mix African with Christian belief, too often accuse defenseless children of practicing witchcraft.

Five-year-old Utitofong can never go home. She has a loving family and has committed no crime, but her neighbors want her dead ... When her father died, Utitofong was blamed for having caused his death by witchcraft. Her mother spent more than four months' wages on exorcisms, fearing that her daughter would be killed by hostile villagers. But when the money ran out and a pastor proclaimed her a lost cause, Utitofong had to leave home for ever.[61]

Having come to the notice of a journalist, this child may have found help in an NGA shelter; most must fend for themselves within a hostile environment.[62]

*

While Jewish, Islamic, and Christian millennialism start from far different places, all unite in rejecting Western enlightenment methods and values root and branch. Jewish fundamentalists base their structure on a Bronze Age myth, which has no basis in archaeology, contemporary inscriptions, or scholarly biblical studies. Fundamentalist Muslims—who claim to possess scriptures directly dictated by God's angel—will anathemize any believer who dares to question whether first man Adam was literally formed out of clay or even whether Zulqurnain truly constructed a great wall against the forces of Gog. Meanwhile literalist Christians reject vast areas of scientific discovery and impose tenuously constructed apocalyptic patterns on a wide variety of contemporary events.

Some 3,000 years after the prophet Zarathustra first contemplated how the earth will be consumed by fire and earthquake in the last days, disciples of 89-year-old Californian Christian broadcaster, Harold Camping started distributing leaflets across North America. According to the old man's calculations, Judgment Day would arrive exactly 7,000 years—to the day—after Noah closed the door of the ark that separated the elect few who were saved from the mass of humanity that was left outside to perish. By esoteric interpretation of biblical clues, he calculated that this day would fall on May 21 2011. On that very day, he declared, there could be no doubt that thousands of God's elect would be 'raptured' up to heaven, while billions of their fellow humans were left behind to meet a terrible fate. Five months later, on October 21, the world would be consumed by earthquake and fire. More than a century and a half had passed since Walter Miller learned the danger of fixing a single date for end-time events and skeptics celebrated with boisterous "survival parties" as May 21 passed once again without incident. Still, humanity has yet to survive Camping's revised date of October 21, 2011 as well as the fate anticipated by the end of the Inca calendar on December 21, 2012. With these hurdles overcome, the credulous must then nurse concerns over Isaac Newton's less specific prophesies for the 2060s.

All science is interrelated, and the implications of rejecting the Enlightenment system of reaching truth by observation and experiment stretch far beyond the conventional battleground of Darwinian evolution. While it might have appeared reasonable to measure the time elapsed since creation in thousands of years in the early seventeenth century, it is only perverse to cling to such calculations four centuries later. The statement that our universe began 13.7 billion years ago in a "creation" event known as the Big Bang is no longer mere hypothesis. Far from having been created in BCE 4004, Planet Earth is approximately 4.6 billion years old. It is no longer an issue of dispute that the first single-celled forms of life appeared some 3 billion years ago, and species *homo sapiens* is a latecomer—little more than 100,000 years old. Far from facing imminent extinction—Planet Earth will survive for unknown billions of years to come. Whatever environmental calamities may arrive (as, in the past, at the close of the Permian and Cretaceous eras), total extinction of life on earth is unlikely, as the great survivors, such as sponges, beetles, and crocodiles, keep the cycle of life turning.

However the immediate fate of our own species remains much less certain. Even as end-time believers of all three Abrahamic faiths take alarming risks that could ignite a nuclear holy war in the Middle East, astronomers range across space, listening for messages from distant planets. Some ask whether continued silence indicates that advanced technological life is ultimately unsustainable. In just four generations between 1900 and 2010 CE the human population of the world has increased from around 1.8 billion to 6.9 billion, and it is expected to rise to 9 billion by around 2045–50. At the time when British cities were burgeoning in the Industrial Revolution, Anglican clergyman Thomas Malthus put forward three propositions: that population is limited by the means of subsistence, that population will grow as the means of subsistence expands, and that unsustainable increase will be controlled by famine and misery. Although his most dismal predictions have been frustrated by those agriculturalists who have succeeded in increasing food production far beyond expectations, ominous indications have already appeared that the necessary increase in output will not be delivered. Challenges that now face humanity can be grouped within four categories: the destructive power of advanced weapons, be those atomic, chemical, biological, cyber, or any other that might be devised in times to come; depletion of those limited natural resources on which technological life is based; failure to produce enough food to sustain a spiraling population; and climate change—specifically global warming—generated by industrial and consumer activity. Secular doomsday prophets look with anxiety toward a "perfect storm" when all the factors could come together. In a worst-case scenario, food prices increase as changed climate reduces farming output at just the time when population is increasing most rapidly. As food, fuel and water supplies become ever more depleted, nations and tribes armed with advanced technological weapons could contest ownership of key natural resources. While specialists become increasingly concerned, for the future, many apocalyptic believers continue to insist that environmental and social degradation is none of their concern. Still, in real life, believers and nonbelievers share the same planet and depend on the same resources and—if that is what humankind chooses to bring upon itself—will finally share the same environmental and very earth-bound Tribulation.

Notes

PREFACE

1. Secker and Warburg, London, 1957.
2. Yale University Press, 1993.
3. Cohn's *Guardian* obituary, (New Haven, CT: Yale University Press, 1993).

CHAPTER 1

1. While no evidence exists from antiquity, the inference can be drawn from structures of hunter-gatherer groups within historical times.
2. Stephanie Dalley, *Myths from Mesopotamia. Creation, the Flood, Gilgamesh and others* (Oxford: Oxford University Press, 1998), 156.
3. *The Epic of Gilgamesh; An English Version*. Intro: Nancy K. Sandars (London: Penguin, 1960), 99.
4. Benjamin J. Foster, "Mesopotamia and the End of Time," in *Imagining the End: Visions of the Apocalypse from the Ancient Middle East to Modern America*, A. Amanat and M. Bernhardsson, p. 17 (London and New York: Tauris, 2002).
5. Dalley, 20n2.
6. Hesiod, *Theogany* (ll. 507 ff). http://www.sacred-texts.com/cla/hesiod/theogony.htm.
7. M. Barnshad et al., Evidence on the Origins of Indian Caste Populations. In *Genome Research 11* (2001), 994–1004.
8. Jeanine Miller, *The Vision of Cosmic Order in the Vedas* (London and Boston: Routledge Kegan Paul, 1985), 12.
9. David M. Knipe, *Hinduism, Experiments in the Sacred* (San Francisco: Harper, 1991), 172–75.
10. Most immediately, the Eurasian, Arabian, and Anatolian faults, but the larger African and the Indo-Australian also influence the region's western and eastern ends.

11. Mary Boyce, "The Antiquity of Zoroastrian Apocalyptic," *Bulletin on the School of Oriental and African Studies*, Vol. 47 (London: University of London, 1984), 57.

12. Philip G. Kreyenbroek, "Millennialism and Eschatology in the Zoroastrianism Tradition," in *Imagining the End: Visions of the Apocalypse from the Ancient Middle East to Modern America*, A. Amanat and M. Bernhardsson, p. 41 (London and New York: Tauris, 2002).

13. Ibid., 36–37. Kreyenbroek argues that scholars who say that the total period can be 9,000 years omit the 3,000 years of Creation from the calculation.

14. Mary Boyce, *Textual Sources for the Study of Zoroastrianism* (Manchester: Manchester University Press, 1984), 82.

15. Ibid., 83.

16. Anders Hultgård, "Persian Apocalypticism," from *The Encyclopaedia of Apocalypticism Vol. 1.* by John J. Collins (New York: Continuum, 1998), 49–50.

17. Mary Boyce, *Zoroastrians. Their Religious Beliefs and Practices* (Routledge, Kegan Paul: London, 1979), 28.

CHAPTER 2

1. Deuteronomy 32:8–9. (Revised Standard Version). Unless noted otherwise, all biblical quotations are taken from the New Revised Standard Version. The RSV is preferred here because the NRSV inserts "the Lord's *own* portion," to imply that, after distributing other peoples to his sons, "the Most High" kept Israel for himself. Scholars consider this incorrect. Yahweh also sits as a member of El's council in Psalm 82:1.

2. Hosea 1, Jeremiah 16:1–3 and 23:10; Ezekiel 23.

3. Isaiah 10:1–2.

4. Isaiah 36:18–20.

5. For the "deuteronomic hypothesis" see Martin Noth, *The Deuteronomic History*. JSOT Press, Department of Divinity, University of Sheffield, Sheffield, UK, 1991.

6. Joshua 11:20; Deuteronomy 20:16–18; 1 Samuel 15:17ff.

7. Joshua 10:12–13.

8. Joshua 23:14–16.

9. Zehpaniah 2:9.

10. Psalm 137:1–6.

11. Ezekiel 1:25–26.

12. Based on the assumption that Isaiah 26:19 is a postexile addition.

13. Ezekiel 37:13–27.

14. Ezekiel 39:17–20.

15. Leslie C. Allen, *Ezekiel*. Word Biblical Commentary (Dallas: Word Books, 1990), 210.

16. Isaiah 43:6–9.

17. Isaiah 44:28–45:1.

18. James D. Smart, *History and Theology of Second Isaiah. A Commentary on Isaiah 35, 40–66* (London: Epworth Press, 1967), 24.

19. Haggai 1:9.

20. Isaiah 58:6–7. Zachariah 9–16, with its rejection of the temple and priests, is ascribed to a member of second Isaiah's prophetic group. This section cannot be accurately dated.

21. Isaiah 66:10–13 (New English Bible).

22. Zechariah 8:22, 9:1–9.

23. Hans Jonas, *The Gnostic Religion. The Message of an Alien God and the Beginnings of Christianity* (Boston: Beacon Press, 1958), 25.

24. Acts 2:9–11.

25. James C. VanderKam, *Enoch and the Growth of an Apocalyptic Tradition*, Catholic Biblical Quarterly Monograph Series No. 18 (Washington, DC, 1984), 180–81.

26. Norman Cohn, *Cosmos, Chaos and the World to Come* (Yale University Press, New Haven, 1993), p. 177.

27. Revelation 11:4.

28. 1 Enoch 1:6.

29. Genesis 6:1.

30. Ezekiel's Chapter 28 tirade against the King of Tyre has been interpreted as a description of Satan's fall, but there is no suggestion here that this event contaminated humans with sin.

31. 1 Enoch 8:1–8.

32. 1 Enoch 10:4–8.

33. 1 Enoch 80, 98. George Widengren, "Iran and Israel in Parthian Times with Special Reference to the Ethiopic Book of Enoch," in *Religious Syncretism in antiquity: Essays in Conversation with George Widengren*, Berger Pearson, pp. 113–14 (Santa Barbara, CA: Scholars Press, 1975).

34. Book of Jubilees 11:4.

35. Daniel 7:2.

36. Daniel 1:2–3, 7–8.

37. 2 Maccabees 5:11–14.

38. Daniel 7:9–10.

39. The NRSV translates this more literally as "one like a human being," but, for familiarity, we keep the traditional "one like the son of man."

40. 1 Enoch 57:7–9.

41. Daniel 12:8–13.

42. Qumran. For the Essene thesis see e.g., www.jewishvirtuallibrary.org/jsource/Archaeology/Qumran.html, Fullarcheological references are provided in http://en.wikipedia.org/wiki/Qumran#Recent_archaelogical_analysis.

43. John J. Collins, *Apocalypticism in the Dead Sea Scrolls* (London: Routledge, 1997), 39.

44. William Horsbury, *Jewish Messianism and the Cult of Christ* (London: SCM Press,. 1998), Chapters 1 and 2.

45. Jeremiah 23:5–6.

46. Collins, John J. *The Communnity Rule*, above 75n34.

47. Dale G. Allison, "The Eschatology of Jesus," in *The Encyclopedia of Apocalypticism. Vol. 1*, edited by John J. Collins, p. 289 (New York: Continuum, 1998).

48. Matthew 3:12.

CHAPTER 3

1. Albert Schweitzer, first published as *Geschichte der Leben-Jesu-Forschung* (Mohr: Tubigen, 1906).
2. Albert Schweitzer, *The Quest of the Historical Jesus* (London: SCM Press, 2000), 485.
3. Dale C. Allison, "The Eschatology of Jesus," in *Encyclopaedia of Apocalypticism, Vol. 1, The Origins of Apocalypticism in Judaism and Christianity*, edited by John J. Collins (New York: Continuum, 1998), 281.
4. Mark 11:25–6.
5. Mark 4:10–12.
6. Matthew 4:1–11; Mark 1:12–13; Luke 1:1–13; Matthew 17:1–9; Mark 9:2–3; Luke 8:28–36.
7. Matthew 13:12–13; 21–22.
8. The "Q" hypothesis is widely accepted by scholars.
9. Matthew 10:9–10, 14–15, 23.
10. Schweitzer, 331n2.
11. Matthew 16:13–20.
12. Zechariah 9:9.
13. Albert Schweitzer, *The Quest of the Historical Jesus* (New York: Dover, 2006), 369.
14. Stephen Neill and Tom Wright, *The Interpretation of the New Testament 1861–1988* (Oxford: Oxford University Press, 1988), 203–16.
15. Rudolph Bultmann, *Theology of the New Testament, Vol. 1* (London: SCM Press, 1952), 33–34, 20.
16. Schubert Ogden, ed. and trans., *New Testament and Mythology and Other Basic Writings of Rudolf Bultmann* (London: SCM Press, 1985), 3.
17. C. H. Dodd, *The Founder of Christianity* (London: Fontana, 1973), 115.
18. Neill and Wright, 213n13; N. T. Wright, *Jesus and the Victory of God* (London: SPCK Society for Promoting Christian Knowledge, 1996), 80–82.
19. N. T. Wright, *Mark for Everyone* (London: SPCK, 2001), 112.
20. Crossan, John Dominic. *The Historical Jesus. The Life of a Mediterranean Jewish Peasant* (Edinburgh, UK: T & T Clark, 1991), 229. Gospel of Thoman 3:151, 113
21. Allison, Dale C. *Jesus of Nazareth. Millenarian Prophet* (Minneapolis, MN: Fortress Press, 1998), p. 35.
22. Acts 1:6–7.
23. Acts 2:1–36.
24. Acts 5:1–3.
25. Flavius Josephus, *Jewish Antiquities*. 20: 97–98. Josephus was a well known Jewish historian who was a contemporary of these events. www.livius.org/men-mh/messiah/messianic_claimants08.html.
26. 1 Thessalonians 4:16–17.
27. Romans 3:28.
28. James 2:14.
29. James 5:8; Hebrews 10:37; 1 Peter 4:17.
30. 1 John 2:18.
31. Flavius Josephus, *The Wars of the Jews or History of the Destruction of Jerusalem*, Book VII. Chapter 1.1. http://www.ccel.org/j/josephus/works/war-7.htm.
32. Revelation 2:9.

33. Acts 21:25.
34. Revelation 1:9.
35. Compare, for instance, the very similar use prophetic images from Isaiah and Ezekiel in Revelation and the contemporary Jewish *Apocalypse of Abraham*.
36. Revelation 9:7–11.
37. Bernard McGinn, *Two Thousand Years of Human Fascination with Evil* (San Francisco: Harper, 1996), pp. 45–54. Also John J. Collins. *The Sibylline Oracles of Egyptian Judaism* (Atlanta, GA: Society of Biblical Literature, 1972), 73–84.
38. Revelation 1:8, 9–10.
39. Revelation 19:21.
40. Revelation 16:20.
41. Revelation 20:1–3, 10.
42. Revelation 21, 21:2, 22:20.
43. Revelation 17:9–13.
44. Brian E. Daley, *The Hope of the Early Church. A Handbook of Patristic Eschatology* (Cambridge, UK; Cambridge University Press, 1991), 26–27. The author reports that these Gnostic documents had then not received full scholarly analysis.
45. Jaroslav Pelikan, *The Christian Tradition. A History of the Development of Doctrine, Vol. 1.* (Chicago: University of Chicago Press, 1971), 48.
46. Hugh M. Riley, *Christian Initiation: A Comparative Study of the Interpretation of the Baptismal Liturgy in the Mystagogical Writings of Cyril of Jerusalem, John Chrysostom, Theodore of Mopsuestia, and Ambrose of Milan* (Washington, DC: The Catholic University of America Press, 1974), 200.
47. Rex D. Butler, *The New Prophesy and New Visions. Evidence of Montanism in the Passion of Perpetua and Felicitas* (Washington, DC: The Catholic University of America Press, 2006), 36.
48. Ibid., 88.
49. George Widengren, *Mani and Manichaeism* (London: Weidenfeld and Nicolson, 1961).
50. Ibid., 51.
51. Church Fathers. On the Morals of Manichaeans (Augustine.) Chapter 1 www.newadvent.org › Fathers of the Church. Online University of Saint Mary.
52. J. R. King, *Writings in Connection with the Donatist Controversy*, Vol. 3 of *The works of Aurelius Augustine. A new translation.* Ed Marcus Dods. Edinburgh T. & T. Clark, 1871–1876, 484–89.
53. Ibid., 499–500.
54. Theodore, E. Mommsen, "St. Augustine and the Idea of Progress. The Background of The City of God," in *The City of God. A Collection of Critical Essays*, edited by Dorothy F. Donnelly, p. 357 (New York: Peter Lang, 1995).
55. St. Augustine, *The City of God Vol. 2*, edited by Gerald G. Walsh and Daniel J. Hogan (Washington, DC: The Catholic University of America Press, 1954), 261–63.
56. Ibid., 294.
57. Ibid., 269–70.

CHAPTER 4

1. Quotations are from the Online Quran Project. http://al-quran.info/?x=y, p. 112.

2. S. 22:1–4, 7.
3. S. 56:4, 82:1–4.
4. David Cook, *Muslim Apocalyptic and Jihad*. Jerusalem Studies in Arabic and Islam. 20, 1996, p. 75.
5. S. 39:68–70.
6. Amir Arjomand, "Islamic Apocalypticism in the Classic Period," in *The Encyclopedia of Apocalypticism, Vol. 2. Apocalypticism in Western History and Culture*, edited by Bernard McGinn, p. 242 (New York: Continuum, 2000).
7. Birger A. Pearson, ed., *Religious Syncretism in Antiquity. Essays in Conversation with George Widengren* (Santa Barbara, CA: Scholars Press, 1975), 113–14.
8. Signs of the Appearance of the Dajjal and his Destruction. http:/www.turntoislam.com/foru,/showthread.php?p=505669.
9. S. 18:29, 21:47.
10. Abu Hamid Muhammad Al-Ghazali, *The Remembrance of Death and the Afterlife* (Cambridge, UK: Islamic Texts Society, 1989), 223.
11. From Mrs. C. F. Alexander's Christmas hymn *Once in Royal David's City*.
12. Jane I. Smith and Yvonne Y. Haddad, *The Islamic Understanding of Death and resurrection* (Albany: State University of New York Press, 1981), 162.
13. A. Guillaume, *A Life of Muhammad. A Translation of b Hisham's Recession of the Sirat rasul Allah* (Karachi: Oxford University Press, 1987), 182–83.
14. Ibid., 185–86.
15. George Widengren, *Muhammad: The Apostle of God, and his Ascension (King and Saviour V)* (Uppsala, Sweden: Lundequistska bokhandeln, 1955), 10.
16. S. 92–97. S 18:92–94.
17. S. 21:96–97.
18. S. 3:124.
19. Living Islam. Haadith on the Present Fitna. v. 28 mac.abc.se/~onesr/ez/hdth/hpf_e.html
20. Cook, 83n4.
21. Patricia Crone, *The First Century Concept of Higra*. Arabica 41, 1994, p. 383.
22. S. 4:95, 8:72.
23. Cook, 69–70n4.
24. Ibid., 78.
25. Bernard McGinn, *Visions of the End. Apocalyptic Traditions in the Middle Ages* (New York: Columbia University Press, 1979), 73.
26. Paul, J. Alexander, *The Byzantine Apocalyptic Tradition* (Berkeley: University of California Press, 1985), 44.
27. Islam and Iran: A Historical Study of Mutual Services. Murtada Mutahhari Trs. Wahid Akhtar. www.al-islam.org/al-tawhid/iran/mutual.htm.
28. Bernard Lewis, *The Origins of Ismailism. A Study on the Historical Background of the Fatimid Caliphate* (Cambridge: Heffer, 1940), 26.
29. S. 39, 30–31.
30. Wilferd Madeburg and Paul E. Walker, *An Ismaili Heresiography. The Bab al Shaytan from Abu Jammam's Kitab al Shajara* (Leiden: Brill, 1998).
31. Jafar was sixth Imam by most Shi'a reckoning but fifth to Ismailis, who do not accept Hasan.
32. "Taken from Kitab al Irshad by Sheik al Mufid." Imam Ja'far b. Muhammad al Sadiq. http://en.al-islam.org/masoom/bios/6thimam.html.

33. The Qarmatians in Bahrain. http://ismaili.net/histoire/history05/history 510.html.
34. See John Voll, "The Sudanese Mahdi. Frontier Fundamentalist," *International Journal of Middle East Studies* 10 (1970): 145–66.
35. Paul E. Walker, *Early Philosophical Platonism: The Ismaili Neo-Platonism of Abu Yaguls al-Sijistani* (Cambridge, UK: Cambridge University Press, 1993), 33.
36. Reynold Nicholson, trans., Al-Ma'arri. www.humanistictexts.org/al_ma'arri.httm.
37. Idries Shah, *The Sufis* (London: Jonathan Cape, 1964), xxv.
38. Iysa A. Bello, *The Medieval Islamic Controversy between Philosophy and Orthodoxy* (Leiden: Brill, 1989), 60. (This book defends al-Ghazali's views from the orthodox standpoint.)
39. Ibn Rushd (Averroes), *Tahafut al-tahafut, The Incoherence of the Incoherence, Vol. 1*. Simon van der Bergh, trans. (Oxford, UK: Oxford University Press, 1954), 72.
40. Barry S. Kogan, *Averroes and the Metaphysics of Causation* (Albany: State University of New York Press, 1985), 205.
41. Ibn Rashud (Averroes), 359.
42. Ali Alawi. The Four Stones of the Albaicin. http://www.nuradeen.com/contributions/ali-alawi/the-four-stones-of-the -albaicin.

CHAPTER 5

1. Bernard McGinn, *Visions of the End. Apocalyptic Traditions in the Middle Ages* (New York: Columbia University Press, 1979), 101–2.
2. Andrew C. Gow, *The Red Jews. Antisemitism in an Apocalyptic Age. 1200–1600* (Leiden: Brill, NV. 1995), 40.
3. Matthew 16:18–20.
4. Dante Alighieri, *The Divine Comedy*, trans. C. H. Sissons (Oxford: Oxford University Press, 1993), *Inferno*. XIX:88–9; 115–16.
5. Michael Foss, *People of the First Crusade* (London: Caxton Editions, 1997), 38.
6. Ibid., 39.
7. Norman Cohn, *The Pursuit of the Millennium. Revolutionary Millenarians and Mystical Anarchists of the Middle Ages* (London: Pimlico, 2004), 76.
8. Robert Chazan, *European Jewry and the First Crusade* (Berkeley: University of California Press, 1987), 68.
9. Ibid., 65.
10. Edward Peters. *The First Crusade. The Chronicle of Fulbert of Chartres and Other Source Materials* (Philadelphia: University of Pennsylvania Press, 1971), 130.
11. Robert Chazan, *In the Year of 1096. The First Crusade and the Jews* (Jerusalem: Jewish Publication Society, 1996), ix.
12. Ibid., 106.
13. Steven Runciman, *A History of the Crusades, Vol. 1 The First Crusade* (London: Penguin, 1971), 133.
14. Lewis Sumberg, "The Tarfurs and the First Crusade." *Medieval Studies* 21 (1959): 241.
15. Runciman, 287n13.
16. Robert Ian Moore, *The Birth of Popular Heresy* (Google Books, n.d.), 3.
17. John 15:6.

18. Moore, 9n17.
19. Malcolm Lambert, *The Cathars* (Oxford: Blackwell, 1998), 22.
20. A group of proto-Cathars, known as Bogomils, has been identified in contemporary Bulgaria.
21. New World Encyclopedia. The Albigensian Crusade. www.newworldencyclopedia.org/entry/Albigensian_Crusade.
22. Michael Costen, *The Cathars and the Albigensian Crusade* (Manchester, UK: Manchester University Press, 1997), 123.
23. William of Tudela and successor, *The Song of the Cathar Wars*, trans. Janet Shirley (Aldershot, UK: Scholar Press, 1996), 117.
24. Walter L. Wakefield and Austin P. Evans, *Heresies of the High Middle Ages. Selected Sources Translated and Annotated* (New York: Columbia University Press, 1969), 267.
25. Bernard McGinn, *The Calabrian Abbot. Joachim of Fiore in the History of Western Thought* (New York: Macmillan, 1985), 26.
26. Marjorie Reeves, *Joachim of Fiore and the Prophetic Future* (Stroud: Sutton, 1999), 24.
27. Revelation 16:10–11.
28. Curtis V. Bostick, *The Antichrist and the Lollards. Apocalypticism in Late Medieval and Reformation England* (Leiden: Brill, 1998), 89.
29. Revelation 14:6.
30. Saint Dominic. Telling the Stories that Matter. www.ttstm.com/2010/08/august-8-st-dominic-friar-preacher.html.
31. Marjorie Reeves, *The Influence of Prophesy in the Later Middle Ages: A Study in Joachimism* (Oxford, UK: Oxford University Press, 1969), 146.
32. McGinn (1985) 209n25.
33. Paul Halsall, Medieval Sourcebook: The Testament of St. Francis. 1996 www.fordham.edu/halsall/source/stfran-test.html.
34. McGinn, Bernard. ed. *Apocalyptic Spirituality. Treatises and letters of Lactantius, Adso of Montier-en-Der, Joachim of Fiore, the Franciscan Spirituals, Savonarola* (London: SPCK Publishers, 1980), 165.
35. Robert E. Lerner, *The Heresy of the Free Spirit in the Later Middle Ages* (Berkeley: University of California Press, 1972), 68.
36. McGinn (1985) 207n25.
37. Dante Alighieri, *Paradiso* XXVII:220–6.
38. Dante Alighieri, *Inferno* XIX:52–7; 73.
39. Dante Alighieri, *Paradiso* XII:139–42.
40. Wakefield, 411–39n24.
41. Lerner, 39n35.
42. Robert Pasnau. Peter John Olivi *Stanford Encyclopaedia of Philosophy*. Online . *Peter John Olivi* Note 31. http://plato.stanford.edu/entries/olivi/ 2008.
43. Cohn, 154n7.
44. Wakefield, 259n24. Also see McGinn (1979), 226–29n3.
45. Margaret Porete, *The Mirror of Simple Souls*, trans. Ellen L. Babinsky (New York: Paulist Press, 1993), 201. Quoted in home.infionline.net/~ddisse/porete.html.
46. Meister Eckhart, *The Essential Sermons, Commentaries, Treatises, and Defence*, trans. Edmund Colledge and Bernard McGinn (London: SPCK, 1981), 75. Also John 17:21.
47. Titus 1:15.
48. Cohn, 177n7.

49. *Chronica fratris Salimbene*, in *Monumenta Germaniae scriptores*, XXXVII, I, 255. Quoted in www.notbored.org/resistance-33.html.
50. Wakefield, 405–6n44.
51. L. Mariotti, *A Historical Memoir of Fra Dolcino and his Times* (London: Longman, Brown, Green, 1853), 268.
52. Ibid., 236.
53. Lerner, 224n35.

CHAPTER 6

1. Philip Zeigler, *The Black Death* (London: Collins, 1969), 41.
2. M. Meiss, *Paintings in Florence and Sienna after the Black Death* (Princeton, NJ: Princeton University Press, 1951), 66.
3. See, for instance, *St. Sebastian Protecting the City from the Plague*. Painting by Benozzo Gozzoli. Old Cathedral, San Gimignano, Tuscany.
4. Zeigler, 67n1.
5. Ibid., 91.
6. Ibid., 108–9.
7. John Wycliffe, *Tracts and Treatises* (London: Blackburn and Pardon, 1845), 196.
8. Ibid., 141.
9. Ibid., 61.
10. Lilian M. Swinburn, ed., *The Lanterne of Liyt* (London: Kegan, Paul, Trench, Trubner, 1917), ix.
11. Curtis V. Bostick, *The Antichrist and the Lollards. Apocalypticism in Late Medieval and Reformation England* (Leiden: Brill, 1998), 72.
12. Norman Cohn, *The Pursuit of the Millennium. Revolutionary Millenarians and Mystical Anarchists of the Middle Ages* (Pimlico: London, 2004), 200.
13. Margaret Aston, *Lollards and Reformers. Images and Literacy in the Late Middle Ages* (London: Hambledon, 1984), 50.
14. John A. Thomson, *Sir John Oldcastle. Dictionary of National Biography* (Oxford: Oxford University Press, 1990).
15. Matthew Spinka, *John Huss at the Council of Constance* (New York: Columbia University Press, 1965), 295.
16. H. Kaminsky, *A History of the Hussite Revolution* (Berkeley: University of California Press, 1967), 279.
17. Bernard McGinn, *Visions of the End. Apocalyptic Traditions in the Middle Ages* (New York: Columbia University Press, 1979), 261.
18. Martin Luther, *Luther's Works. Vol. 54. Table Talk* (St. Louis, MO: Concordia Publishing House, 1967), 220.
19. Kaminsky, 311n16.
20. Roberto Ridolfi, *Life of Girolamo Savonarola* (New York: Knopf, 1959), 19.
21. Girolamo Savonarola, *A Guide to Righteous Living and Other Works*. Edited by Konrad Eisenbichler (Toronto: Victoria University, 2003), 63.
22. Peter Amelung, Koninklijke Brill NV, 2011. www.primarysourcesonline.nl/c6/background.php.

23. Katherine R. Firth, *The Apocalyptic Tradition in Reformation Britain* (Oxford, UK: Oxford University Press, 1979), 8.
24. See note 11 above.
25. Heinko A. Oberman, *Luther. A Man Between God and the Devil* (New Haven, CT: Yale University Press, 1989), 188.
26. Romans 13:2.
27. Eric W. Gritsch, *Thomas Müntzer. A Tragedy of Errors* (Minneapolis, MN: Fortress Press, 1989), 26. James Hastings, *Encyclopedia of Religion and Ethics Vol. 1* (Edinburgh, Scotland: T & T Clark, 1908–26), 406.
28. P. Matheson, ed., *The Collected Works of Thomas Müntzer* (Edinburgh, Scotland: T & T Clark, 1988), 358.
29. Gritsch, 71n27.
30. Ibid., 90.
31. Ibid., 99.
32. Theodore Tappert, *Selected Writings of Martin Luther* (Philadelphia, PA: Fortress Press, 1967), 353, 349.
33. George H. Williams, *The Radical Reformation* (Kirksville, MO: Sixteenth Century Journal Publishers, c1992), 1077.
34. Anthony Arthur, *The Tailor-King. The Rise and Fall of the Anabaptist Kingdom of Münster* (New York: St. Martin's Press, 1999), 10.
35. Hans-Jürgen Goertz, *The Anabaptists* (London and New York: Routledge, 1988), 7.
36. Ibid., 105.
37. Cohn, 266n12.
38. Arthur Anthony, 40n34.
39. Ibid., pp. 55–57. c.f. George H. Williams, *The Radical Reformation* (Kirksville, MO: Sixteenth Century Journal Publishers, c1992), 564.
40. Arthur, 76n34.
41. Hermann von Kerssenbrooch, *Narrative of Anabaptist Madness: The Overthrow of Münster, the Famous Metropolis of Westphalia* (Leiden: Brill, NV, 2007), 579.
42. Cohn, 272n12.
43. Kerssenbrooch, 593n41.
44. Arthur, 171n34.

CHAPTER 7

1. Henry Corbin, *Alone with the Alone. Creative Imagination in the Sufism of Ibn Arabi* (Princeton: Princeton University Press, 1997), 119.
2. S. A. Q. Husaini, *The Pantheistic Monism of Ibn Al-Arabi* (Lahore: Ashraf, 1970), 179.
3. Jean-Pierre Filiu, *L'Apocalypse dans l'Islam* (Paris: Fayard, 2008), 58.
4. Mahmoud al-Misri. Multaqa Ahl al Hadeeth. The Battle of Ain Jalout. 2009, www.youtube.com/watch?v=9y5Su8HcRfk.
5. Filiu, 69n3.
6. Daniel 12:2; 13.

7. Genesis 49:10 KJV.

8. Aviezer Ravitzky, *Messianism, Zionism, and Jewish Religious Radicalism* (Chicago: University of Chicago Press, 1996), 20.

9. Yitzhak Baer, *The History of the Jews in Christian Spain*, vol. 1 (Philadelphia: The Jewish Publication Society of America, 1960), 263.

10. Naomi R. Frankel. Maimonidean Controversy and the Story of Creation. www.aishdas.org/articles/rambam_creation.htm.

11. Pinchas Giller, *Reading the Zohar* (Oxford, UK: Oxford University Press, 2001), 163.

12. Sefer Ha-Bahir, Sec 3 184. www.servantsofthelight.org/QBL/Books/Bahir_1.html.

13. Jacob Yuval Israel, "Jewish Messianic Expectation towards 1240 and Christian Reactions," in *Toward the Millennium: Messianic Expectations from the Bible to Waco*, edited by Peter Schäfer and Mark R. Cohen, p. 107 (Leiden: Brill, 1998).

14. Moshe Idel, "Jewish Apocalypticism 670–1670," in *The Encyclopedia of Apocalypticism, Vol. 2. Apocalypticism in Western History and Culture*, edited by Bernard McGinn (New York: Continuum, 1979), 212.

15. Abraham Abulafia (1240–1295). Rabbi Avraham Abdul Abulafia, www.alefreiki.com/Dev2Go.web?id=199373&rnd=1.

16. Giller, 104n11.

17. Quoted in *Secrets of Kabbalah*, History Channel, *Decoding the Past*, 2006.

18. Giller, 12n11.

19. Ibid., 1.

20. Stephen Sharot, *Messianism, Mysticism and Magic. A Sociological Analysis of Jewish Religious Movements* (Chapel Hill: University of North Carolina Press, 1982), 99.

21. Gershom Scholem, *The Messianic Idea in Judaism and Other Essays on Jewish Spirituality* (London: Allen and Unwin, 1971), 40.

22. Julius H. Greenstone, *The Messiah Idea in Jewish History* (1906; repr., Westport, CT: Greenwood, 1972), 162.

23. Norman Roth, *Conversos, Inquisition and the Expulsion of Jews from Spain* (Madison: University of Wisconsin Press, 1995), 226.

24. Moses Cordovero, *Tomer Devorah: The Palm Tree of Deborah* 1:3, brilliance.com/kab/deborah/deborah.htm.

25. Gershom Gorenberg, *End of Days. Fundamentalism and the Struggle for the Temple Mount* (Oxford, UK: Oxford University Press, 2002), 41.

26. This is the widely held view. Some scholars prefer to push influences on Sabbatti Sevi further back to early kabbalists such as Abraham Abulafi.

27. Raphael Patai, *The Messianic Texts* (Detroit, MI: Wayne State University Press, 1979), 277.

28. Pauline M. Watts, "Prophesy and Discovery. On the Spiritual Origins of Christopher Columbus' Enterprise of the Indies," *American Historical Review*, 90 (Supplement, 1985): 86–90. Columbus's prime source, Cardinal Pierre d'Ailly's *Imago Mundi*, relied heavily on the eschatological predictions of thirteenth-century English Franciscan Roger Bacon.

29. Ibid., 89.

30. Ibid., 96.

31. Ibid., 102.

32. William Housley, "The Eschatological Imperative. Millennialism and Holy War in Europe. 1260–1556," in *Toward the Millennium: Messianic Expectations from the Bible to Waco*, edited by Peter Schäfer and Mark R. Cohen, p. 123 (Leiden: Brill, 1998).

33. John L. Phelan, *The Millennial Kingdom of the Franciscans in the New World* (Berkeley: University of California Press, 1970), 24.

34. Ibid., 47.

35. Ibid., 57.

CHAPTER 8

1. *Geneva Bible. Annotated New Testament 1599 Edition* (New York: Pilgrim Press, 1989). *Binding of Satan*. Revelation 20:1–3 c.f. *Geneva Bible. Facsimile of the 1560 Edition* (Peabody, MA: Hendreckson Bibles, c. 2007).

2. Daniel 12:7.

3. Le Roy Edwin Froome, *The Prophetic Faith of our Fathers* (Washington, DC: Review and Herald, 1948), 492–94.

4. Peter Toon, "The Latter Day Glory," in *Puritans, the Millennium and the Future of Israel*, edited by Peter Toon, p. 27 (Cambridge: James Clark, 1970).

5. Revelation 3:8–16.

6. Avihu Zakai, *Exile and Kingdom, History and Apocalypse in the Puritan Migration to America* (Cambridge: Cambridge University Press, 1992), 57.

7. e.g., Numbers 14:34; Ezekiel 4:6.

8. Voltaire's essay on Isaac Newton. 1998, lyman/english233/Voltaire/Newton.htm.

9. Christopher Hill, *Antichrist in 17th Century England* (London: Oxford University Press, 1971), 81.

10. Christopher Hill, *The World Turned Upside Down* (London: Temple Smith, 1972), 31.

11. A. S. P. Woodhouse, *Puritanism and Liberty. Being the Army Debates (1647–9) from the Clarke Manuscripts* (London: Dent, 1938), 53–54.

12. George H. Sabine, *The Works of Gerrard Winstanley. With an Appendix of Documents Relating to the Digger Movement* (Ithaca, NY: Cornell University Press, 1941), 57.

13. Gerrard Winstanley, et al., *The True Levellers Standard Advanced—April, 1649*, www.bilderberg.org/land/diggers.htm.

14. Daniel 7:17–18; 2:44.

15. Hilary Hinds, ed., *The Cry of a Stone by Anna Trapnel* (Tempe, AZ: Center for Medieval and Renaissance Studies, 2000), 18.

16. Austin Woolrych, *Commonwealth to Protectorate* (London: Oxford University Press, 1982), 165.

17. Norman Cohn, *The Pursuit of the Millennium. Revolutionary Millenarians and Mystical Anarchists of the Middle Ages* (London: Pimlico, 2004), 290.

18. Ibid., 309–10; 312–13.

19. July 1620. Pilgrim Hall Museum. Plymouth, MA. http:/pilgrimhall.org/Robinson FarewellSermon.htm.

20. Avilia Zakai, *Exile and Kingdom. History and Apocalypse in the Puritan Migration to America* (Cambridge: Cambridge University Press, 1992), 124.

21. Genesis 16:35; Revelation 12:1–6.

22. Perry Miller, *Errand into the Wilderness* (Cambridge, MA: Harvard University Press, 1976), 11.

23. Zakai, 117n20.

24. Larzer Ziff, *The Career of John Cotton. Puritanism and the American Experience* (Princeton, NJ: Princeton University Press, 1962), 60–62. The wording of the text differs significantly from that in NRSV II Samuel 7:10.

25. Ibid., 81.

26. Rachel Walker. Cotton Mather. Documentary Archive and Transcription Project. www2.iath.virginia.edu/salem/people/c_mather.html.

27. Peter White and Harrison Meserole, eds., *Puritan Poets and Poetics: Seventeenth Century American Poetry in Theory and Practice* (University Park: Pennsylvania State University Press, 1985), 46–47.

28. Douglas J. Culver, *Albion and Ariel. British Puritanism and the Birth of Political Zionism* (New York: Peter Lang, 1995), 72.

29. Victoria Clark, *Allies for Armageddon. The Rise of Christian Zionism* (New Haven, CT: Yale University Press, 2007), 32.

30. Thomas Brightman, "A most comfortable exposition: of the last and most difficult part of the prophecie of Daniel..." (1644), 964.

31. Sir Henry Finch (pseud. William Gouch), *The World's Great Restoration or the Calling of the Jews. A Present to Judah and the Children of Israel* (London, 1621), 6.

32. Genesis 12:2–7; 13:14–17; 15:18; 17:8; 26:1–5; 28:3–18; 35:10–12.

33. Isaiah 11:11.

34. Romans 11:26–29.

35. Gershom Scholem, *Sabattai Sevi. The Mystical Messiah* (Princeton, NJ: Princeton University Press, 1973), 336.

36. D. S. Katz, *Philo-Semitism and the Readmission of Jews to England. 1603–1655* (Oxford, UK: Clarendon Press, 1982), 103.

37. Scholem, 201n35.

38. Stephen Sharot, *Messianism, Mysticism and Magic. A Sociological Analysis of Jewish Religious Movements* (Chapel Hill: University of North Carolina Press, 1982), 88.

39. Scholem, 549n35.

40. Increase Mather, *An Account of the Life and Death of the Rev. Increase Mather DD* (Boston, 1692), 64–65.

41. Sharot, 122–24n38.

42. C. Douglas Nicoll, "Old Believers," in *The Modern Encyclopedia of Russian and Soviet History*, vol. 25, 228–237. www.synaxis.info/old-rite/0_oldbelief/history_eng/nicoll.html.

43. G. Michels, *Apocalypse on Lake Onega. The Destruction of an Island Monastery.* http://www.recherches-slaves.paris4.sorbonne.fr/Cahier7/Michels.htm. Robert O. Crummey, *The Old Believers & the World of Antichrist. The Vyg Community & the Russian State 1694–1855* (Madison: University of Wisconsin Press, 1970), 46–47.

44. Ibid., 2.

CHAPTER 9

1. Matthew 28:19–20.

2. Moses Lowman, *Paraphrase and notes on The Revelation of St. John, 2nd ed.* (London: Noon, 1745), vi–vii (First edition 1737). *Works of Jonathan Edwards Online, Volume 5, Apocalyptic Writings* (Jonathan Edwards Center at Yale University, 2008), 55–58.

3. Jonathan Edwards, (author). Edited by J. F. Wilson. *A History of the Work of Redemption* (New Haven, CT: Yale, 1989), 458–59, 471.

4. Acts 2:17.

5. James H. Moorhead, "Apocalypticism in Mainstream Protestantism. 1800 to the Present Day," in *The Encyclopedia of Apocalypticism Volume 3, Apocalypticism in the Modern Period and the Present Day*, edited by Stephen J. Stein, p. 76 (New York: Continuum, 1998).

6. Ibid., 44.

7. Martin Ballard, *White Men's God. The Extraordinary Story of Missionaries to Africa* (Westport, CT: Greenwood, 2008), 11.

8. Elhanan Winchester, *A Course of Lectures on the Prophesies that Remain to be Fulfilled*, Vol. II (I Garner et al.: London, 1789), 15.

9. Ibid., 25–27.

10. Edward King, *Remarks on the Signs of the Times* (London: Nicol, 1798), 18.

11. James Hatley Frere, *The Combined View of the Prophesies of Daniel, Esdras and St. John, shewing that all the prophetic writings are formed of one plan* (London: Hatchard, 1815), 189.

12. John A. Q. Brown, *The Jew. The Master key of the Apocalypse. In answer to Mr. Frere's General Structures and the dissertations of Mr. Irving* (London: Hatchard, 1827), 9, xi.

13. W. H. Oliver, *Prophets and Millennialists. The Uses of Biblical Prophecy in England from the 1790s to the 1840s* (Auckland, NZ: Auckland University Press, 1978), 109.

14. Henry Drummond, *Dialogue on Prophesies* (London: Nisbet, 1827), 93.

15. Edward Irving, *Missionaries of the Apostolic School* (London: Hamilton Adams, 1825), 22.

16. Ibid., 108–9.

17. Edward Irving, *The Rev. Edward Irving's Preliminary Discourse to the Work of Ben Ezra entitled the Coming of Messiah in Glory and Majesty* (London: Seeley, 1827), li.

18. Ernest R. Sandeen, *The Roots of Fundamentalism. British and American Millenarianism. 1800–1930* (Chicago: University of Chicago Press, 1970), 42.

19. Ronald L. Numbers and Jonathan M. Butler, *The Disappointed. Millerism and Millenarianism in the 19th Century* (Bloomington: Indiana University Press, 1989). The charts are reproduced on pp. 44–45.

20. Eric Anderson, "The Millerite Use of Prophesy. A Case Study of a 'Striking Fulfilment,'" in Numbers, 78; 86n17.

21. Luther Boutelle; "Reminiscence," in Numbers, 210–11n17.

22. Jonathan D. Burnham, *The Story of Conflict. The Controversial Relationship between Benjamin Wills Newton and John Newton Darby* (Carlisle, UK: Paternoster, 2004), 116–17.

23. Sandeen, 32n18.

24. W. Kelly, *Collected Writings of John Nelson Darby. Vol. 1. Notes on Revelation* (London: Morish, 1867–1883), 251.

25. F. Roy Coad, *A History of the Brethren Movement. Its Origins, Worldwide Development and its Significance for the Present Day* (Exeter, UK: Paternoster, 1968), 106.

26. Paul R. Wilkinson, *For Zion's Sake: Christian Zionism and the Role of John Nelson Darby* (Milton Keynes, UK: Paternoster Press, 2007), 100–101.

27. 2 Peter 3:10. Revelation 8.7. Mark 13.

28. The seven-year Tribulation (twice 3½) is also reached by an abstruse interpretation of "twenty weeks of years" in Daniel 9:24. This converts biblical *weeks* to *years*, which are then set to run from Artaxerxes' decision to rebuild the Jerusalem Temple to the crucifixion of Jesus—leaving an unused seven years for the Tribulation.

29. Jeremiah 25:27, 33.

30. Matthew 24:19–21.

31. Manuel Lacunza (pseud. J. J. Ben-Ezra), *The Coming of the Messiah in Glory and Majesty*, vol. 2, trans. Edward Irving (London: Seeley, 1827), 101.

32. Burnham, 155n22.

33. Coad, 130n25.

34. E.g., Leviticus 20:9; 25: 44–46; Exodus 21:7–11; Judges 18:27–28. The word *fundamentalist* would be introduced as a term of commendation in 1918.

35. Sandeen, 77n18.

36. Ibid., 73–74.

37. Yaakov Ariel, *On Behalf of Israel. American Fundamentalist Attitudes towards Jews, Judaism and Zionism* (Brooklyn, NY: Carlson, 1991), 71; W. E. Blackstone, *Letter to President Harrison. March 5. 1991*, 13–14.

38. Delavan A. Pierson, *Arthur T. Pierson. A Spiritual Warrior. Mighty in the Scriptures. A Leader in the Modern Missionary Crusade* (New York: Garland, 1988), 195.

39. Arthur T. Pierson, *Crisis of Missions or the Voice out of the Cloud* (London: Nisbet, 1886), 294.

40. Ibid., 4.

41. Albert B Simpson. Hymn Lyrics. http://www.allthelyrics.org./mostpopular hymns/yesterday_today_forever.php.

42. T. K. Thomas and Ken Draper. A. B. Simpson and World Evangelizatism online.ambrose.edu/alliancestudies/ahtreadings/ahtr_s72.html.

43. Ruth M. Slade, *English Speaking Missions in the Congo Independent State. 1878–1908* (Brussels: Académie royale des sciences colonials, 1959), 227.

CHAPTER 10

1. Tzvi Howard Adelman, *History of the Hasidic Movement*, www.hebroots.org/hebrootsarchive/9902/9902_o.html.

2. Gloria Weiderkehr-Pollack, *Eliezer Zweifel and the Intellectual Defence of Hasidism* (Jersey City, NJ: KTAV, 1995), 172–73.

3. Elijah J. Scochet, *The Hasidic Movement and the Gaon of Vilna* (Northvale, NJ: Aronson, 1994), 4.

4. Ibid., 7.

5. Ibid., 18–19.

6. L. Lowe, ed., *Diaries of Sir Moses and Lady Montefiore*, Vol. 1 (London: Griffeth, Rarren, Ogden and Welsh, 1890), 167.

7. Leviticus 25:2–4.
8. Psalm 127:1.
9. Aviezer Ravitzky, *Messianism, Zionism, and Jewish Religious Radicalism* (Chicago: University of Chicago Press, 1996), 18.
10. Yosef Salmon, *Religion and Zionism: First Encounters* (Jerusalem: Hebrew University Magnes Press, 2002), 60.
11. Lewis Way, *Poems. Isaiah Chapter lxii* (Stansted, UK: Private Press, 1822).
12. Lewis Way, *Letter to the Rt. Rev. the Lord Bishop of St. David* (London: Hatchard, 1818).
13. Geoffrey Finlayson, B. A. M. *The Seventh Earl of Shaftesbury* (London: Eyre Methuen, 1981), 14.
14. Ibid., 444–45.
15. Donald M. Lewis, *The Origins of Christian Zionism. Lord Shaftesbury and Evangelical Support for a Jewish Homeland* (Cambridge, UK: Cambridge University Press, 2010), 150.
16. Ibid., 129.
17. Michael Polowetzky, *Jerusalem Recovered, Victorian Intellectuals and the Birth of Modern Zionism* (Westport, CT: Praeger, 1995), 17.
18. Paul Charles Merkley, *The Politics of Christian Zionism. 1891–1948* (London: Frank Cass, 1998), 41.
19. Finlayson, 115n13.
20. W. H. Hechler, *The Jerusalem Bishopric. Documents with Translations* (London: Trübner, 1883), 116, 129.
21. Samuel Gobat, *Address to the Friends of Zion* (London: J. Hatchard and Son, 1848), 7.
22. Lewis, 151n15.
23. Shaykh Ahmad al-Ahsa'i. en.wikipedia.org/wiki/Shaykh_Ahmad
24. John Walbridge, ed., *Translations of Shaykhi, Babi and Baha'i Texts*, Vol. 2, 1998. www.h-net.org/~bahai/trans.htm.
25. Baha'u'llah to Prof. E. G. Browne of Cambridge University. www.northill.demon.co.uk/bahai/index.htm.
26. Edward Granville Browne, ed., "Editor's Introduction," in *A Traveller's Narrative Written to Illustrate the Episode of the Báb*, p. xxxix (Los Angeles, CA: Kalimat Press, 2004).
27. Iain Anderson, *Ahmad, the Guided one. A Life of the Holy Founder of the Movement to Unite all Religions* (Baltimore MD: Islamic International Publishers, 1998), 113.
28. For an analysis of Ahmad's claims to prophesy, see Simon Ross-Valentine, *Islam and the Ahmadiyya Jana'at: History, Belief, Practice* (New York: Columbia University Press, 2008), 133–37.
29. Ibid., 67.

CHAPTER 11

1. Paul C. Merkley, *The Politics of Christian Zionism. 1891–1948* (London: Cass, 1998), 7.
2. Based on the work of Alex Bein, "Theodor Herzl: A Biography," in *The Jewish State*, Theodor Herzl, p. 34. (New York: Dover, 1988).

3. Theodor Herzl, *The Jewish State* (New York: Dover, 1988), 146.

4. E. Pawel, *The Labyrinth of Exile. The life of Theodore Herzl* (London: Collins Harvill, 1990), 329.

5. Ibid., 335.

6. Theodor (Binyamin Ze'ev) Herzl Jewish Virtual Library. http://www.jewishvirtuallibrary.org/jsource/biography/Herzl.html.

7. Merkley, 22n1.

8. R. Palai (ed.), *Herzl, Hechler, the Grand Duke of Baden and the German Emperor, 1896–1904* (Tel Aviv: Ellem's Bank, 1961), 3.

9. Leonard Stein, *The Balfour Declaration* (London: Valentine Mitchell, 1961), 18.

10. John Watson, *A Course of Sunday School Lessons on the Gospel in the Old Testament* (London: National School Society, 1885), 24, 93.

11. Barbara Tuchmann, *Bible and Sword. England and Palestine from the Bronze Age to Balfour* (London: Phoenix, 2001), 298.

12. Ibid., 305.

13. Oskar, K. Rabinowicz, *Herzl, Architect of the Balfour Declaration* (New York: Herzl Press, 1958).

14. Chaim Weizmann, *Trial and Error: The Autobiography of Chaim Weizmann* (London: Hamish Hamilton, 1949), 99.

15. Sachar, Howard H. *History of Israel: From the Rise of Zionism to the Present Time.* (New York: Knopf, 1979), 136.

16. James Renton, *Zionist Masquerade. The Birth of the Anglo-Zionist Alliance. 1914–18* (New York: Palgrave Macmillan, 2007), 44–45.

17. Ibid., 145.

18. David Fromkin, *A Peace to End all Peace* (London: Phoenix, 2000), 268.

19. Ran Marom, "The Bolsheviks and the Balfour Declaration," in *The Left Against Zion. Communism, Israel and the Middle East*, edited by Robert S. Wistrich, p. 16 (London: Valentine Mitchell, 1979).

20. Renton, 153n16.

21. Ami Isseroff. The Anti-Zionism of Edwin Montagu and his opposition to the Balfour Declaration, http://www.zionism-israel.com.hdoc/Montague_balfour.htm.

22. Renton, 87n16.

23. Martin Gilbert, *Winston Churchill. World in Torment. 1917–22* (London: Minerva, 1975), 565.

24. Ibid., 621.

25. Jason Tomes, *Balfour and Foreign Policy* (Cambridge, UK: Cambridge University Press, 1997), 200.

26. Jill Hamilton, *God, Guns and Israel: Britain, the First World War and the Jews in the Holy Land* (Stroud, UK: Sutton, 2004), 212.

27. Ya'akov Hurwitz, "The Kibbutz—Its Socialist and National Roots," in *The Left Against Zion. Communism, Israel and the Middle East*, edited by Robert S. Wistrich, p37n19 (London: Valentine Mitchell, 1979).

28. Jacqueline Shields. Arab Riots of the 1920s. Jewish Virtual Library. www.jewishvirtuallibrary.org/jsource/History/mcdonald.html.

29. Tom Segev, *One Palestine Complete. Jews and Arabs under the British Mandate* (London: Abacus, 2005), 429.

224 Notes

30. Dan Cohn-Sherbok, *The Politics of Apocalypse. History and the Influence of Christian Zionism* (Oxford, UK: Oneworld, 2006), 129.

31. Ibid., 130.

32. Robert Wistrich, *Hitler's Apocalypse. Jews and the Nazi Legacy* (London: Weidenfeld and Nicolson, 1985), 31. Hell's notes are deposited in the Institut für Zeitgeschichte, Munich.

33. Robert Elwood, "Nazism as a Millennial Movement," in *Millennialism, Persecution and Violence*, edited by Catherine Wessinger, p. 246 (Syracuse, NY: Syracuse University Press, 1999).

34. Jim Walker. The Christianity of Hitler revealed in his speeches and proclamations. 1997/2006. Speech to the Reichstag in 1941. www.nobeliefs.com/speeches.htm.

35. United Nations Charter Chapter 80(1). www.un.org/en/documents/charter/index.shtml -

36. Paul C. Merkley, *American Presidents, Religion and Israel. The Heirs of Cyrus* (Westport, CT: Praeger, 2004), 8.

37. Ibid., 2.

38. Robert J. Donovan, *Conflict and Crisis. The Presidency of Harry S. Truman* (New York: Norton, 1977), 384.

39. http//en.wikipedia.org/wiki/Estimates_of_the_Palestinian_flight_of_1948.

40. R. J. Q. Adams, *Balfour. The Last Grandee* (London: J. Murray, 2007), 333.

41. Merkley, 191–92n1.

CHAPTER 12

1. 1 Peter 3:10.

2. Paul Boyce, *When Time Shall Be No More. Prophecy Belief in Modern American Culture* (Cambridge, MA: Harvard University Press, 1992), 125.

3. Ibid., 117.

4. Tom Segev, *1967. Israel, the War and the Year that Transformed the Middle East* (New York: Metropolitan Books, 2007), 575.

5. Ibid., 576.

6. Martin Buber, *Reader* (New York: Palgrave Macmillan, 2007), 277.

7. Gershom Gorenberg, *The Accidental Empire. Israel and the Birth of Settlements. 1967–1977* (New York: Holt, 2007), 22–23.

8. Numbers 33:50–56.

9. Michael Feige, *Settling the Hearts. Jewish Fundamentalism in the Occupied Territories* (Detroit MI: Wayne Sate University Press, 2009), 122.

10. Ibid., 242.

11. Israel Shahak and Norton Mezvinsky. *Jewish Fundamentalism in Israel* (London: Pluto Press, 1999), 87.

12. Joshua 1:4

13. Sheikh Jarrah Jews praise Baruch Goldstein on Purim, www.ynetnews.com › Ynetnews › New.

14. Harretz Israeli News. 29.3.2007. www.jewishvirtuallibrary.org/jsource/Judaism/Halakha_&_aggadata_&_midrash.htm.

15. E.g., David Hirst, "Pursuing the Millennium," *The Nation*, February 2, 2004, http://www.ifamericansknew.org/download/hirst_booklet.pdf.

16. Gershom Gorenberg, *The End of Days. Fundamentalism and the Struggle for the Temple Mount* (Oxford, UK: Oxford University Press, 2002), 60.

17. Ibid., p. 60.

18. Numbers 19:13.

19. Numbers 19:1–10.

20. William Dankenbring, Red Heifer Born in Israel—Harbinger of Messiah. www.triumphpro.com/red? heifer-harbinger.pdf. and many other internet sites.

21. Ofra Lax. Ariel's Jerusalem: An Interview with Rabbi Yisrael Ariel. www.israelnationalnews.com/News/News.aspx/122460.

22. Ahmad S. Moussalli, *Radical Islamic Fundamentalism. The Ideological and Political Discourse of Sayyid Qutb* (Beirut, Lebanon: University of Beirut University Press, 1992), 28.

23. Sayyid Qutb, "Milestones," in *The Sayyid Qutb Reader. Selected Writings on Politics, Religion and Society*, edited by Albert J. Bergesen, pp. 35–42 (New York: Routeledge, 2008).

24. Mark 12:17.

25. Jansen, Johannes, J. G. The Neglected Duty. *The Creed of Sadat's Assassins and Islamic Resurgence in the Middle East.* Appendix contains Muhammad Faraj's translation of Al-Faridah al-Gha'ibah (New York: Macmillan, 1986), 159.

26. Abdal Bari Atwan, *The Secret History of al-Qa'ida* (London: Abacus, 2007), 72.

27. Bernard Lewis, *Crisis of Islam. Holy War and Unholy Terror* (London: Weidenfeld and Nicolson, 2003), xxii–xxiii.

28. Ibid., xxiii.

29. Baqer K. Moin, *Khomeini. The Life of the Ayatollah* (London: Tauris, 1989), 153.

30. Ibid., 155.

31. Kasra Naji, *Ahmadinejad. The Secret History of Iran's Radical Leader* (London: Tauris, 2008), 85.

32. Ibid., 92.

33. Abbas Amanat, *Apocalyptic Islam and Iranian Shi'ism* (London: Tauris, 2009), 241–42.

34. Grace Halsell, *Prophesy and Politics. Militant Evangelicals on the Road to Nuclear War* (Veritas, WA: Bulbrook, 1987), 72–73.

35. Stephen Sizer, *Christian Zionism. Road Map to Armageddon* (Leicester, UK: Inter Varsity Press, 2004), 91. This book criticizes Christian Zionism from an alternative conservative evangelical viewpoint.

36. Hal Lindsey, *The Late Great Planet Earth* (Grand Rapids, MI: Zonderman, 1970), 50.

37. Ibid., 56.

38. Ibid., 11.

39. Ibid., 59.

40. Paul Boyer, *When Time Shall Be No More. Prophecy Belief in Modern American Culture* (Cambridge, MA: Harvard University Press, 1992), 169.

41. Ibid., 128.

42. Hal Lindsey, *The 1980s. Countdown to Armageddon* (Basingstoke, UK: Lakeland, 1986) 99.

43. Stephen D. O'Leary, *Arguing the Apocalypse. A Theory of Millennial Rhetoric* (New York: Oxford University Press, 1994), 191.

44. March 17, 2011.
45. The Hal Lindsey Report, www.hallindsey.com.
46. Tim LaHaye and Jerry Jenkins. *Glorious Appearing. The End of Days* (Wheaton, IL: Tyndall House, c 2004), 286.
47. Jason G. Bivins, *The Religion of Fear. The Politics of Horror in Conservative Evangelicalism* (Oxford, UK: Oxford University Press, 2008), 208.
48. Joan Didion, *New York Review of Books*, November 6, 2003.
49. Genesis 12:3.
50. Zechariah 14:13.
51. Oslo Accords Text: 1993 Declaration of Principles, news.bbc.co.uk/1/hi/in_depth/middle_east?israel_and_the_politicians/key?doc/.
52. Dan Cohn-Sherbok, *The Politics of Apocalypse. The History and Influence of Christian Zionism* (Oxford, UK: Oneworld, 2006), 162.
53. Jean-Pierre Filiu, *L'Apocalypse dans l'Islam* (Paris: Fayard, 2008), 129
54. Robert Fisk, *Sabra and Shatila*, www.countercurrents.org/pa-fisk180903.htm.
55. Pat Robertson Official Website. A Presidential Bid Analyzed. www.patrobertson.com/statsman/PresidentialBidAnalyzed.
56. Andy McSmith. Short attacks Bush for "crusade" quote. 21 Sep 2001, www.telegraph.co.uk/worldnews/short-attacks-Bush-for –crusade.quote.html.
57. Heaven's Gate. http:/www.religioustolerance.org/de_highe.htm
58. Eugene V. Gallagher, "Theology is Life and Death. David Koresh on Violence, Persecution and the Millennium," in *Cults, Religion and Violence*, edited by David G. Bromley and J. Gordon Melton, p. 87 (Cambridge, UK: Cambridge University Press, 2002).
59. Gerald Businge, Seven Years Since the Kanungu Massacre, www.ugpulse.com › People, "People – Seven years since the Kanungu massacre," www.ugpulse.com.
60. Robert Gerson, *The Anguish of Northern Uganda. Results of a Field-Based Assessment of the Civil Conflicts in Northern Uganda.* http:/pdf.usaid.gov/pdf_docs/.
61. Emily Dugan. Scandal of the children killed for "witchcraft." www.independent.co.uk › News › World › Africa. scandal-of-the-children-killed-for-witchcraft-1003968.html.
62. *Saving Africa's Witch Children*, BBC Dispatches, December 4, 2008.

Select Bibliography

Abanes, Richard. *End Time Visions. The Road to Armageddon*. New York: Four Walls Eight Windows, 1998.
Adair, John. *Puritans, Religion and Politics in 17th Century England and America*. Glous: Stroud, UK Sutton, 1998.
Adams, R. J. Q. *Balfour. The Last Grandee*. London: J. Murray, 2007.
Adelman, Tzvi Howard. *History of the Hasidic Movement*. www.hebroots.org/hebroots archive/9902/9902_o.html.
Afnan, Habib Allah. *The Genesis of the Babi-Baha'I Faith in Shiraz and Fars*. Leiden: Brill, 2008.
Alexander, Paul J. *The Byzantine Apocalyptic Tradition*. Berkeley: University of California Press, 1985.
Alexander, Paul J. *The Oracle of Baalbek. The Tiburtine Sibyl in Greek Dress*. Washington, DC: Center for Byzantine Studies, 1967.
Allen, Leslie, C. *Ezekiel 1–19 and Ezekiel 20–48*. Dallas: Word Books, c. 1990 and 1994.
Allison, Dale C. *Jesus of Nazareth. Millenarian Prophet*. Minneapolis, MN: Fortress Press. 1998.
Allison, Dale C. "The Eschatology of Jesus," in *Encyclopaedia of Apocalypticism*, vol. 1, *The Origins of Apocalypticism in Judaism and Christianity*, vol. 1, edited by John J. Collins, 267–302. New York: Continuum, 1998.
Alvyn, Austin. *China's Millions. The CIM and late Qing Society*. Grand Rapids, MI: Eardmans, 2007.
Amanat, Abbas. *Apocalyptic Islam and Iranian Shi'ism*. London: Tauris, 2009.
Amanat, Abbas. "Shi'a Legal Authority into Political Power," in *Political Islam from Muhammad to Ahmadinejad*, edited by J. M. Skelly, 230–64. Santa Barbara, CA: Praeger ABC-CLIO, 2010.
Amanat, Abbas, and Bernhardsson, Magnus, eds. *Imagining the End. Visions of the Apocalypse from the Ancient Middle East to Modern America*. London and New York: Tauris, 2002.

Anderson, Eric. "The Millerite Use of Prophesy. A Case Study of a 'Striking Fulfilment,'" in *The Disappointed. Millerism and Millenarianism in the 19th Century*, edited by Ronald L. Numbers and Jonathan M. Butler, pp. 78–91. Bloomington: Indiana University Press, 1989.

Anderson, Iain. *Ahmad, the Guided One. A Life of the Holy Founder of the Movement to Unite all Religions*. Tilford: Islamic International Publishers, 1998.

Andrew, George. *The Epic of Gilgamesh*. London: Penguin, 1999.

Ariel, Yaakov. *On Behalf of Israel. American Fundamentalist Attitudes toward Jews, Judaism and Zionism*. New York: Carlson, 1991.

Arjomand, Amir. "Islamic Apocalypticism in the Classic Period," in *The Encyclopedia of Apocalypticism*, vol. 2, *Apocalypticism in Western History and Culture*, edited by Bernard McGinn, pp. 238–86. New York: Continuum, 2000.

Arjomand, Said Amir. "Messianism, Millennialism and Revolution in Early Islamic History," in *Imagining the End. Visions of the Apocalypse from the Ancient Middle East to Modern America*, edited by A. Amanat and Magnus Bernhardsson, 106–25. London and New York: Tauris, 2002.

Arthur, Anthony. *The Tailor King. The Rise and Fall of the Anabaptist Kingdom of Münster*. New York: St. Martin's Press, 1999.

Aston, Margaret. *Lollards and Reformers. Images and Literacy in Late Medieval England*. London: Hambledon Press, 1984.

Attridge, Harold, W. "The Messiah and the Millennium. The Roots of Two Jewish Christian Symbols," in *Imagining the End. Visions of the Apocalypse from the Ancient Middle East to Modern America*, edited by Abbas Amanat and Magnus Bernhardsson, pp. 90–105. London and New York: Taurus, 2002.

Atwan, Abdal Bari. *The Secret History of al-Qa'ida*. London: Abacus, 2007.

Augustine, St. *The City of God*, vol. 2. Walsh, Gerald G. and Hogan, Daniel J., eds. Washington, DC: The Catholic University of America Press, 1954.

Aune, David E. "The Apocalypse of John and the Problem of Genre." *Semeia* 36 (1986): 65–96.

Azmeh, A. Al. "Rhetoric for the Senses. A Consideration of Muslim Paradise Narratives." *Journal of Arabic Literature* 26, no. 3 (1995): 215–31.

Baer, Yitzhak. *The History of the Jews in Christian Spain*, vol. 1. Philadelphia: The Jewish Publication Society of America, 1966.

Ball, Bryan W. *A Great Expectation. Eschatological Thought in English Protestantism to 1660*. Leiden: Brill, 1975.

Barnshad, M., et al. "Evidence on the Origins of Indian Caste Populations," in *Genome Research 11*. Online journal, 2001.

Barr, David L. "The Apocalypse as a Symbolic Transformation of the World." *Interpretation* 38 (1984): 34–50.

Barr, James. *Fundamentalism*. London: SCM Press, 1981.

Bivins, Jason G. *Religion of Fear. The Politics of Horror in Conservative Evangelicalism*. Oxford, UK: Oxford University Press, 2008.

Bleeker, C. J., and G. Widengren, eds. *Historia Religionium. Handbook for the History of Religions*, vol. 1. Leiden, NV: Brill, 1969.

Bloom, H. I. *The Economic Activities of the Jews in Amsterdam in the 17th and 18th Centuries*. Williamsport, PA: Bayard Press, 1937.

Boccaccini, Gabriele, ed. *Enoch and Qumran Origins*. Grand Rapids, MI, and Cambridge: New Light on a Forgotten Collection, 2005.

Bostick, Curtis, V. *The Antichrist and the Lollards. Apocalypticism in Late Medieval and Reformation England*. Leiden: Brill, NV, 1998.

Bousset, W. *The Antichrist Legend*. Atlanta, GA: Scholars Press, 1999.

Boyce, Mary. "On the Antiquity of Zoroastrian Apocalyptic." *Bulletin of the School of Oriental and African Studies. University of London* 47 (1984): 57–75.

Boyce, Mary. *History of Zoroastrianism*, vol. 1. Leiden: Brill, 1975.

Boyce, Mary. *Textual Sources for the Study of Zoroastrianism*. Manchester: Manchester University Press, 1984.

Boyce, Mary. *Zoroastrians, Their Religious Beliefs and Practices*. London: Routledge Kegan Paul, 1979.

Boyer, Paul. "The Growth of Fundamentalist Apocalyptic in the United States," in *The Encyclopedia of Apocalypticism*, vol. 3, *Apocalypticism in the Modern Period and the Present Day*, edited by Stephen J. Stein. New York: Continuum, 1998.

Boyer, Paul. *When Time Shall Be No More. Prophecy Belief in Modern American Culture*. Cambridge, MA: Harvard University Press, 1992.

Brightman, Thomas. *A Most Comfortable Exposition of the Last and Most Difficult Part of the Prophesie of Daniel*. London, 1644.

Brown, Carl. "The Sudanese Mahdiya," in *Protest and Power in Black Africa*, edited by Robert I. Rotberg and Ali A. Mazrui, 145–68. New York: Oxford University Press, 1970.

Brown, John A. Q. *The Jew. The Master key of the Apocalypse. In answer to Mr. Frere's General Structures and the dissertations of Mr. Irving*. London: Hatchard, 1827.

Bultmann, Rudolph. *Theology of the New Testament*. London: SCM Press, 1952.

Bumgartner, F. T. *Longing for the End*. New York and London: Palgrave and St. Martin's Press, 1999.

Burnham, Jonathan D. *The Story of Conflict. The Controversial Relationship between Benjamin Wills Newton and John Newton Darby*. Carlisle, UK: Paternoster, 2004.

Burr, David. *The Spiritual Franciscans. From Protest to Persecution in the Church after St. Francis*. University Park: Pennsylvania State University Press, 2001.

Butler, Rex, D. *The New Prophesy and New Visions. Evidence of Montanism in the Passions of Felicitas and Perpetua* Washington, DC: Catholic University of America Press, 2006.

Cancik, Hubert. "The End of the World, of History and of the Individual in Greek and Roman Antiquity," in *The Encyclopaedia of Apocalypticism*, vol. 1, edited by John J. Collins, 84–125. New York: Continuum, 1998.

Capp, B. S. *The Fifth Monarchy Men. A Study in 17th Century Millennialism*. London: Faber, 1972.

Chatterji, Jagadish C. *The Wisdom of the Vedas*. Wheaton, IL: Theosophical Publishing House, 1980.

Chazan, Robert. *European Jewry and the First Crusade*. Berkeley: University of California Press, 1987.

Chazan, Robert. *In the Year of 1096. The First Crusade and the Jews*. Jerusalem: Jewish Publication Society, 1996.

Clark, Victoria. *Allies for Armageddon. The Rise of Christian Zionism*. New Haven, CT: Yale University Press, 2007.
Coad, F. Roy. *A History of the Brethren Movement. Its Origins, Worldwide Development and its Significance for the Present Day*. Exeter, UK: Paternoster, 1968.
Cohn-Sherbok, Dan. *The Politics of Apocalypse. History and the Influence of Christian Zionism*. Oxford, UK: Oneworld, 2006.
Cohn, Norman. *Cosmos, Chaos, and the World to Come: The Ancient Roots of Apocalyptic Faith*. New Haven, CT, and London: Yale University Press, 1995.
Cohn, Norman. *The Pursuit of the Millennium. Revolutionary Millennarians and Mystical Anarchists of the Middle Ages*. London: Secker and Warburg, 1957.
Collins, A. Yarbro. *Cosmology and Eschatology in Jewish and Christian Apocalypticism*. Leiden: Brill, 1996.
Collins, A. Yarbro. *The Combat Myth in the Book of Revelation*. Missoula, MT: Scholars Press, 1976.
Collins, John J. *Apocalypticism in the Dead Sea Scrolls*. London: Routledge, 1997.
Collins, John J. *Daniel with an Introduction to Apocalyptic Literature*. Grand Rapids, MI: Wm. B. Eerdmans, 1984.
Collins, John J. *The Apocalyptic Vision of the Book of Daniel*. Missoula, MT: Scholars Press, 1977.
Collins, John J., Bernard McGinn, and Stephen J. Stein. *The Encyclopaedia of Apocalypticism*, vols. 1–3. New York: Continuum, 1998.
Cook, David. "Muslim Apocalyptic and Jihad." *Jerusalem Studies in Arabic and Islam*. 20 (1996): 66–104.
Cook, David. *Understanding Jihad*. Berkeley: University of California Press, 2005.
Cook, Stephen, L. *Prophesy and Apocalypticism*. Minneapolis, MN: Fortress Press, 1995.
Corbin, Henry. *Alone with the Alone. Creative Imagination in the Sufism of Ibn Arabi*. Princeton, NJ: Princeton University Press, 1997.
Costen, Michael. *The Cathars and the Albigensian Crusade*. Manchester, UK: Manchester University Press, 1997.
Crone, Patricia. *The First Century Concept of Higra*. Arabica 41, 352–87. Leiden, NV: Brill, 1994.
Crummey, Robert O. *The Old Believers & the World of Antichrist. The Vyg Community & the Russian State 1694–1855*. Madison: University of Wisconsin Press, 1970.
Culver, Douglas J. *Albion and Ariel. British Puritanism and the Birth of Political Zionism*. New York: Peter Lang, 1995.
Daftary, F. *A Short History of the Ismailis. Traditions of a Muslim Community*. Edinburgh, UK: Edinburgh University Press, 1998.
Daftary, F. *Medieval Isma'ili History and Thought*. Cambridge, UK: Cambridge University Press, 1996.
Daftary, F. *The Isma'ili. Their History and Doctrines*. Cambridge, UK: Cambridge University Press, 2007.
Dalley, Stephanie. *Myths from Mesopotamia: The Flood, Gilgamesh and Others*. Oxford: Oxford University Press, 1998.
Dante Alighieri, *The Divine Comedy*, trans. C. H. Sissons. Oxford, UK: Oxford University Press, 1993.
Darby, John Nelson. "Apostacy of the Successive Generations" in *Collected Writings of John Nelson Darby*, vol. 1., ed Kelly W. Morish. London, pp. 189–19, 1867.

Darby, John Nelson. *Irvingism: Its Root Principle Examined in the Light of Scripture.* London: James Carter, 1895.

De Boer, M. C. "Paul and Apocalyptic Eschatology," in *Encyclopaedia of Apocalypticism*, vol. 1, *The Origins of Apocalypticism in Judaism and Christianity*, vol. 1, edited by John J. Collins, 385–43. New York: Continuum, 1998.

Deppermann, Klaus. *Melchior Hoffman. Social Unrest and Apocalyptic Visions in the Age of Reformation.* Edinburgh, Scotland: T & T Clark, 1979.

DiDomizio, Daniel. "Jan Hus's De Ecclesia. Precursor of Vatican II." *Theological Studies* 60 (June 1999): 247–60.

Dillon, Francis. *A Place of Habitation. The Pilgrim Fathers and their Quest.* London: Hutchinson, 1973.

Doan, Ruth A. *The Miller Heresy, Millennialism and American Culture.* Philadelphia, PA: Temple University Press, 1987.

Dodd, C. H. *The Founder of Christianity.* London: Fontana, 1973.

Dodd, C. H. *The Parables of the Kingdom.* London: Nisbet, 1935.

Dodds, Marcus, ed. *Aurelius Augustine. Bishop of Hippo*, vol. 3. *Writings in Connection with the Donatist Heresy.* Edinburgh, Scotland: T & T Clark, 1872.

Donovan, Robert J. *Conflict and Crisis. The Presidency of Harry S. Truman.* New York: Norton, 1977.

Drax, Tomas. *The Worlde's Resurrection and the General Calling of the Jews.* Coventry, UK, 1608.

Drummond, Henry. *Dialogue on Prophesies.* London: Nisbet, 1827.

Dunn, D. G., and McKnight, Scot. *The Historical Jesus in Recent Research.* Winona Lake, IN: Eisenbraus, 2005.

Eckhart, Meister: *The Essential Sermons, Commentaries, Treatises, and Defence*, trans. Edmund Colledge and Bernard McGinn. London: SPCK, 1981.

Edwards, Jonathan. Ed. Wilson J. F. *A History of the Work of Redemption.* New Haven, CT: Yale, 1989.

Edwards, Jonathan. *Works of Jonathan Edwards Online*, vol. 5, *Apocalyptic Writings.* Jonathan Edwards Center at Yale University, 2008.

Eisen Bichler, Konrad, ed. *Savonarola Girolamo. A Guide to Righteous Living and Other Works.* Toronto, Canada: Victoria University, 2003.

Ellison, H. L. *The Prophets of Israel from Ahijah to Hosea.* Exeter, UK: Paternoster Press, 1969.

Elwood, Robert. "Nazism as a Millennial Movement," in *Millennialism, Persecution and Violence*, edited by Catherine Wessinger, 241–60. Syracuse, NY: Syracuse University Press, 1999.

Emerson, R. S. *Antichrist in the Middle Ages. A Study of Medieval Apocalypticism in Art and Literature.* Seattle: University of Washington Press, 1981.

Emerson, R. S., and R. S. Herzman. *The Apocalyptic Imagination in Medieval Literature.* Philadelphia, PA: University of Philadelphia Press, 1992.

Enoch, The Book of. Online http://heaven.net.nz/writings/thebookofenoch.htm.

Evans, G. R. *John Wyclif. Myth and Reality.* Oxford: Lion, 2005.

Faber, George Stanley. *Remarks on the Effusion of the Fifth Apocalyptic Vial.* London: Rivington, 1815.

Fadiman, James, and Robert Frager. *Essential Sufism.* San Francisco: Harper, 1997.

Feige, Michael. *Settling the Hearts. Jewish Fundamentalism in the Occupied Territories.* Detroit, MI: Wayne State University Press, 2009.
Filiu, Jean-Pierre. *L'Apocalypse dans l'Islam.* Paris: Fayard, 2008.
Finch, Sir Henry (pseud. Gouch, William). *The World's Great Restoration or the Calling of the Jews. A Present to Judah and the Children of Israel.* London, 1621.
Finger, Thomas A. *A Contemporary Anabaptist Theology.* Downers Grove, IL: InterVarsity Press, 2004.
Finlayson, Geoffrey, B. A. M. *The Seventh Earl of Shaftesbury.* London: Eyre Methuen, 1981.
Firth, Katherine R. *The Apocalyptic Tradition in Reformation Britain. 1530–1645.* Oxford, UK: Oxford University Press, 1979.
Focillon, Henri. *The Year 1000.* New York: Ungar, 1969.
Foss, Michael. *People of the First Crusade.* London: Caxton Editions, 1997.
Foster, Benjamin R. "Mesopotamia and the End of Time," in *Imagining the End. Visions of the Apocalypse from the Ancient Middle East to Modern America*, edited by Abbas Amanat and Magnus Bernhardsson, 23–32. London and New York: Tauris, 2002.
Frankel, Naomi R. *The Maimonidean Controversy and the Story of Creation* www.aishdas.org/articles/rambam_creation.htm.
Frankfurter, David. "Early Christian Apocalypticism," in *Encyclopaedia of Apocalypticism*, vol. 1, *The Origins of Apocalypticism in Judaism and Christianity*, vol. 1, edited by John J. Collins, 421–53. New York: Continuum, 1998.
"The Free Spirit in Cromwell's England: The Ranters and their Literature." Appendix in Norman Cohn, *The Pursuit of the Millennium. Revolutionary Millenarians and Mystical Anarchists of the Middle Ages*, 289–332. London: Pimlico, 2004.
Frere, James Hatley. *The Combined View of the Prophesies of Daniel, Esdras and St. John, shewing that all the prophetic writings are formed of one plan.* London: Hatchard, 1815.
Friedmann, Yohanan. *Prophesy Continuous.* Oxford, UK: Oxford University Press, 2003.
Friesen, Abraham. *Thomas Muentzer a Destroyer of the Godless. The Making of a 16th Century Revolutionary.* Berkeley: University of California Press, 1990.
Fromkin, David. *A Peace to End all Peace.* London: Phoenix, 2000.
Froom, LeRoy Edwin. *The Prophetic Faith of Our Fathers.* Washington, DC: Review and Herald, 1948.
Fudge, Thomas, A. *The Magnificent Ride. The First Reformation in Hussite Bohemia.* Adlershot UK: Ashgate, 1998.
Fudge, Thomas, A., ed. *The Crusade Against the Heretics in Bohemia, 1416–1437. Sources and Documents for the Hussite Crusade.* Adlershot, UK: Ashgate, 2002.
Furnish, Timothy R. "The Modern Impact of Mahdism and the Case of Iraq," in *Political Islam form Muhammad to Ahmadinejad*, edited by J. M. Skelly, 182–92. Santa Barbara, CA: Praeger ABC-CLIO, 2010.
Ghazali-Al, Abu Hamid Muhammad. *The Remembrance of Death and the Afterlife Heaven and the Varieties of Bliss.* Cambridge, UK: Islamic Texts Society, 1989.
Gidney, W. T. *The History of the London Society for the Promotion of Christianity among the Jews.* London: London Jews Society, 1908.
Gignoux, Philippe M. "Nouvaux Regards sur l'Apocalyptique Iranienne." *Comptes Rendus de l'Academie des Inscrtiptions et belles letters* XX: 334–36.
Gilbert, Martin. *Winston Churchill. World in Torment. 1917–22.* London: Minerva, 1975.
Giller, Pinchas. *Reading the Zohar.* Oxford, UK: Oxford University Press, 2001.

Gobat, Samuel. *Address to the Friends of Zion*. London: J. Hatchard and Son, 1848.
Goertz, Hans-Jurgen. *Thomas Müntzer. Apocalyptic Mystic and Revolutionary*. Edinburgh, UK: T & T Clark, 1993.
Gorenberg, Gershom. *The Accidental Empire. Israel and the Birth of Settlements. 1967–1977*. New York: Holt, 2007.
Gorenberg, Gershom. *The End of Days. Fundamentalism and the Struggle for the Temple Mount*. Oxford, UK: Oxford University Press, 2002.
Gosnell, Harold F. *Truman's Crises. A Political Biography of Harry S. Truman*. Westport, CT: Greenwood, 1980.
Gow, Andrew C. *The Red Jews. Antisemitism in an Apocalyptic Age. 1200–1600*. Leiden: Brill, 1995.
Gray, John. *Black Mass. Apocalyptic Religion and the Death of Utopia*. London: Allen Lane, 2007.
Greenstone, John H. *The Messiah Idea in Jewish History. 1906*. Westport, CT: Greenwood, 1972.
Greenstone, Julius H. *The Messiah Idea in Jewish History*. 1906. Reprint, Westport, CT: Greenwood, 1972.
Gritsch, Eric, W. *Thomas Müntzer. A Tragedy of Errors*. Minneapolis, MN: Fortress Press, 1989.
Guillaume, A. *A Life of Muhammad. A Translation of b Hisham's Recession of the Sirat rasul Allah*. Karachi: Oxford University Press, 1987.
Hall, John R. "Mass Suicide of the Branch Davidians," in *Cults, Religion and Violence*, edited by David G. Bromley and J. Gordon Molton, 149–69. Cambridge, UK: Cambridge University Press, 2002.
Halm, Heintz. "The Cosmology of the Pre-Fatimid Ismailiyya," in *Medieval Isma'ili History and Thought*, edited by F. Daftary, 73–89. Cambridge: Cambridge University Press, 1996.
Halsell, Grace. *Prophesy and Politics. Militant Evangelicals on the Road to Nuclear War*. Veritas, WA: Bulbrook, 1987.
Hamilton, Jill. *God, Guns and Israel: Britain, the First World War and the Jews in the Holy Land*. Stroud, UK: Sutton, 2004.
Hanson, Paul, D. *Prophesy and Apocalypticism. The Post-exilic Social Setting*. Minneapolis, MN: Fortress Press, 1995.
Haude, Sigrun. *In the Shadow of "Savage Wolves." Anabaptist Munster and the German Reformation During the 1530s*. Boston: Humanities Press, c2000.
Hawting, G. R. *The First Dynasty of Islam. The Umayyad Caliphate*. London: Taylor and Francis, 2005.
Hegghammer, Thomas. "Global Jihadism after the Iraq War." *Middle East Journal* 1 (2005): 11–32.
Herzl, Theodor, ed. *The Jewish State*. New York: Dover, 1988.
Hill, Christopher. *Antichrist in 17th Century England*. London: Oxford University Press, 1971.
Hill, Christopher. *The World Turned Upside Down. Radical Ideas During the English Reformation*. London: Temple Smith, 1972.
Holt, P. M., A. K. S. Lambton, and Lewis Bernard. *The Cambridge History of Islam*, vol. 1. *The Central Islamic Lands*. Cambridge: Cambridge University Press, 1970.
Horbury, William. *Jewish Messianism and the Cult of Christ*. London: SCM Press, 1998.

Horsley, Norman. "The Eschatological Imperative. Messianism and the Holy War in Europe. 1260–1556," in *Towards the Millennium. Messianic Expectations from the Bible to Waco*, edited by Peter Schäfer and Mark Cohen, 123–50. Leiden: Brill, 1998.
Hultgård, Anders. "Persian Apocalypticism," in *The Encyclopaedia of Apocalypticism*, vol. 1, edited by John J. Collins, 39–83. New York: Continuum, 1998.
Hurwitz, Ya'akov. "The Kibbutz–Its Socialist and National Roots," in *The Left Against Zion. Communism, Israel and the Middle East*, edited by Robert S. Wistrich, 35–49. London: Valentine Mitchell, 1979.
Husaini, S. A. Q. *The Pantheistic Monism of Ibn Al-Arabi*. Lahore: Ashraf, 1970.
Idel, Moshe. "Jewish Apocalypticism 670–1670," in *Visions of the End. Apocalyptic Traditions in the Middle Ages*, edited by Bernard McGinn, 204–37. New York: Columbia University Press, 1979.
Idel, Moshe. *Messianic Mystics*. New Haven, CT: Yale University Press, 1998.
Idel, Moshe, and Mortimore Ostow. *Jewish Mystical Leaders and Leadership in the Thirteenth Century*. Northvale, NJ: Jason Aronson, 1998.
Irving, Edward. *Missionaries of the Apostolic School*. London: Hamilton Adams, 1825.
Irving, Edward. *The Rev. Edward Irving's Preliminary Discourse to the Work of Ben Ezra entitled the Coming of Messiah in Glory and Majesty*. London: Seeley, 1827.
Israel, Menasseh ben. *Bound Together. Hope of Israel*. London, 1652.
Jacobsen, Thorkild. *Treasures of Darkness. A History of Mesopotamian Religion*. New Haven, CT: Yale, 1978.
Jansen, Johannes, J. G. *The Neglected Duty. The Creed of Sadat's Assassins and Islamic Resurgence in the Middle East*. Appendix contains Muhammad Faraj's translation of Al-Faridah al-Gha'ibah, 159–230. New York: Macmillan, 1986.
Jenkins, Roy. *Truman*. London: Collins, 1986.
Johnson, Luke T. *The Acts of the Apostles*. Collegeville, MN: Liturgical Press, 1992.
Jonas, Hans. *The Gnostic Religion. The Message of an Alien God and the Beginnings of Christianity*. Boston: Beacon Press, 1958.
Jubilees, The Book of. Online. www.pseudepigrapha.com/jubilees/index.htm.
Kaiser, Otto. *Isaiah 1–12. A Commentary and Isaiah 13–39 a Commentary*. London: SCM Press, 1974 and 1983.
Kaminsky, H. *A History of the Hussite Revolution*. Berkeley: University of California Press, 1967.
Katz, D. S. *Philo-Semitism and the Readmission of Jews to England. 1603–1655*. Oxford, UK: Clarendon Press, 1982.
Katz, David S. *Philo-Semitism and the Readmission of the Jews to England*. Oxford, UK: Oxford University Press, 1982.
Kieser, Hans-Lukas. *Nearest East. American Millennialism and Mission to the Middle East*. Philadelphia, PA: Temple University Press, 2010.
King, Edward. *Remarks on the Signs of the Times*. London: Nicol, 1798.
King, J. R., ed. *Aurelius Augustine. Bishop of Hippo*, vol. 5. *Writings in Connection with the Manichean Heresy*. Edinburgh, Scotland: T & T Clark, 1872.
Kiracofe, Clifford, A. *Dark Crusade. Christian Zionism and US Foreign Policy*. London: Tauris, 2009.
Kogan, Barry S. *Averroes and the Metaphysics of Causation*. Albany, NY: State University of New York Press, 1985.

Kramer, S. N. *Sumerian Mythology. A Study of Spiritual Achievement in the Third Millennium BC*. Philadelphia, PA: University of Pennsylvania Press, 1972.

Kreyenbroek, Philip G. "Millennialism and Eschatology in the Zoroastrianism Tradition," in *Imagining the End: Visions of the Apocalypse from the Ancient Middle East to Modern America*, edited by A. Amanat and M. Bernhardsson, 33–55. London and New York: Tauris, 2002.

Lacunza, Manuel (pseud. Ben-Ezra, J. J.). *The Coming of the Messiah in Glory and Majesty*. Trans. Edward Irving. London: Seeley, 1827.

Lalleman-de Winkel, H. *Jeremiah in the Prophetic Tradition*. Leuven, NV: Peeters, 2000.

Lambert, Malcolm. *The Cathars*. Oxford, UK: Blackwell, 1998.

Landes, Richard, Richard A. Gow, and David C. Van Mester. *The Apocalypse Year of 1000. Religious Expectation and Social Change*. New York: Oxford University Press, 2003.

Lerner, Robert E. "Frederick II, Alive, Aloft and Allayed in Franciscan-Joachite Eschatology," in *The Use and Abuse of Eschatology in the Middle Ages*, edited by W. Verbeke, D. Verheist, and A. Welkenhuysen, 359–80. Leuven: Leuven, NV. Leuven University Press, 1988.

Lerner, Robert E. "Millennialism," in *The Encyclopaedia of Apocalypticism*, vol. 2, edited by Bernard McGinn, 326–60. New York: Continuum, 1998.

Lerner, Robert E. *The Heresy of the Free Spirit in the Later Middle Ages*. Berkeley: University of California Press, 1972.

Lewis, Bernard. *The Crisis of Islam. Holy War and Unholy Terror*. London: Weidenfeld and Nicolson, 2003.

Lewis, Bernard. *The Origins of Ismailism. A Study on the Historical Background of the Fatimid Caliphate*. Cambridge: Heffer, 1940, p. 26.

Lewis, Donald M. *The Origins of Christian Zionism. Lord Shaftesbury and Evangelical Support for a Jewish Homeland*. Cambridge, UK: Cambridge University Press, 2010.

Lindsey, Hal. *The 1980s. Countdown to Armageddon*. Basingstoke, UK: Lakeland, 1986.

Lindsey, Hal. *The Late Great Planet Earth*. Great Rapids: Zonderman, 1970.

Lowe, L., ed. *Diaries of Sir Moses and Lady Montefiore*, vol. 1. London: Griffeth, Rarren, Ogden and Welsh, 1890.

Lowman, Moses. *Paraphrase and Notes on The Revelation of St. John*, 2nd ed. London: Noon, 1745.

Madeburg, Wilferd. "The Fatimids and the Qarmatis of Bahryn," in *Medieval Isma'ili History and Thought*, edited by F. Daftary, 21–74. Cambridge, UK: Cambridge University Press, 1996.

Madeburg, Wilferd, and Paul E. Walker. *An Ismaili Heresiography. The Bab al Shaytan from Abu Jammam's Kitab al Shajara*. Leiden: Brill, 1998.

Madeburg, Wilferd, and Toby Mayer. *Struggling with the Philosopher. A Refutation of Avicenna's Metaphysics*. London: Tauris, 2001.

Marcus, Jacob Rader. *The Jews in the Medieval World. A Source Book*. Cincinnati, OH: Hebrew Union College Press, 1999.

Mariotti, L. *A Historical Memoir of Fra Dolcino and his Times*. London: Longman, Brown, Green, 1853.

Marom, Ran. "The Bolsheviks and the Balfour Declaration," in *The Left Against Zion. Communism, Israel and the Middle East*, edited by Robert S. Wistrich. London: Valentine Mitchell, 1979.

Mather, Increase. *An Account of the Life and Death of the Rev. Increase Mather DD*. Boston, 1692.
McDannell, Colleen, and Bernhard Lang. *Heaven: A History*. New Haven, CT: Yale University Press, 1988.
McGee, Gary B. "Shortcut to Language Preparation? Radical Evangelicals, Missions and the Gift of Tongues." *International Bulletin of Missionary Research*, July 2001. www.agts.edu/faculty/faculty-publications/articles/shortcut-mcgee.pdf.
McGinn, Bernard, ed. *Meister Eckhart and the Beguine Mystics*. New York: Continuum, 1994.
McGinn, Bernard. *Antichrist: Two Thousand Years of the Human Fascination with Evil*. San Francisco: Harper, 1996.
McGinn, Bernard. "Apocalypticism and Church Reform," in *The Encyclopaedia of Apocalypticism*, vol. 2, edited by Bernard McGinn, 74–109. New York: Continuum, 1998.
McGinn, Bernard. *Apocalypticism in the Western Tradition*. Aldershot, UK: Variorium, 1996.
McGinn, Bernard. *The Calabrian Abbot. Joachim of Fiore in the History of Western Thought*. New York: Macmillan, 1985.
McGinn, Bernard. *Visions of the End. Apocalyptic Traditions in the Middle Ages*. New York: Columbia University Press, 1979.
McKim, Donald K., ed. *The Cambridge Companion to Martin Luther*. Cambridge, UK: Cambridge University Press, 2003.
Meiss, M. *Paintings in Florence and Sienna after the Black Death*. Princeton, NJ: Princeton University Press, 1951.
Merkley, Paul C. *American Presidents, Religion and Israel. The Heirs of Cyrus*. Westport, CT: Praeger, 2004.
Merkley, Paul C. *The Politics of Christian Zionism. 1891–1948*. London: Cass, 1998.
Merkley, Paul Charles. *The Politics of Christian Zionism. 1891–1948*. London: Frank Cass, 1998.
Michels, G. *Apocalypse on Lake Onega. The Destruction of an Island Monastery*. http://www.recherches-slaves.paris4.sorbonne.fr/Cahier7/Michels.htm.
Middlekauff, Robert. *The Mathers. Three Generations of Puritan Intellectuals 1596–1728*. Berkeley: University of California Press, 1999.
Miller, Jeanine. *The Vision of Cosmic Order in the Vedas*. London and Boston: Routledge Kegan Paul, 1985.
Miller, Perry. *Errand into the Wilderness*. Cambridge, MA: Harvard University Press, 1956.
Moin, Baqer K. *Khomeini. The Life of the Ayatollah*. London: Tauris, 1989.
Momen, Moojan. *Babi and Baha'i Religions. 1844–1944. Some Contemporary Western Accounts*. Oxford, UK: Ronald, 1981.
Mommsen, Theodore, E. "St. Augustine and the Idea of Progress. The Background of The City of God," in *The City of God. A Collection of Critical Essays*, Dorothy F. Donnelly, pp. 353–72. New York: Peter Lang, 1995.
Moorhead, James, H. "Apocalypticism in Mainstream Protestantism. 1800 to the Present Day," in *The Encyclopedia of Apocalypticism*, vol. 3, *Apocalypticism in the Modern Period and the Present Day*, edited by Stephen J. Stein, 72–107. New York: Continuum, 1998.
Morgan, Alison. *Dante and the Medieval Other World*. Cambridge, UK: Cambridge University Press, 1990.

Moussalli, Ahmad, S. *Radical Islamic Fundamentalism. The Ideological and Political Discourse of Sayyid Qutb.* Beirut: University of Beirut University Press, 1992.
Naji, Kasra. *Ahmedinejad. The Secret History of Iran's Radical Leader.* London: Tauris, 2008.
Nasr, S. H., H. Dabashi, and S. V. R. Nasr. *Expectation of the Millennium. Shi'ism in History.* New York: University of New York Press, 1989.
Nickelsburg, George W. E. *1 Enoch: A Commentary on the Book of 1 Enoch.* Minneapolis, MN: Fortress Press, 2001.
Nicoll, C. Douglas. "Old Believers," in *The Modern Encyclopedia of Russian and Soviet History*, vol. 25, 228–37. Gulf Breeze, Florida: Academic International Press, 1976.
Nomani, Mohammad Manjoor. *Khomaini, Revolution and the Shi'ite Faith.* Lucknow, Uttar Pradesh, India: Al-Furqan, 1988.
Numbers, Ronald L., and Jonathan M. Butler. *The Disappointed. Millerism and Millenarianism in the 19th Century.* Bloomington: Indiana University Press, 1989.
Numbers, Ronald L., and Janet S. Numbers. "Millerism and Madness. A Study of Religious Insanity in Nineteenth Century America." In Ronald L. Numbers and Jonathan M. Butler, *The Disappointed*, 92–118. Bloomington: Indiana University Press, 1989.
Oberman, Heinko A. *Luther. A Man between God and the Devil.* New Haven, CT: Yale University Press, 1989.
Ogden, Schubert, ed. and trans. *New Testament and Mythology and Other Basic Writings of Rudolf Bultmann.* London: SCM Press, 1985.
O'Leary, Stephen, D. *Arguing the Apocalypse. A Theory of Millennial Rhetoric.* New York: Oxford University Press, 1994.
Oliver, W. H. *Prophets and Millennialists. The Uses of Biblical Prophecy in England from the 1790s to the 1840s.* Auckland, NZ: Auckland University Press, 1978.
Olster, David. "Byzantine Apocalypses," in *The Encyclopaedia of Apocalypticism*, vol. 2, edited by Bernard McGinn, 48–73. New York: Continuum, 1998.
Palai, R., ed. *Herzl, Hechler, the Grand Duke of Baden and the German Emperor, 1896–1904.* Tel Aviv, Israel: Ellern's Bank, 1961.
Paris, Erna. *The End of Days. A Story of Tolerance, Tyranny, and the Expulsion of the Jews from Spain.* Amherst, MA: Prometheus Books, 1995.
Parrinder, G. *Jesus in the Qur'an.* London: Sheldon Press, 1965.
Passan, Pierre. *A Crown of Fire. The Life and Times of Savonarola.* London: Hutchinson, 1961.
Patai, Raphael. *The Messianic Texts.* Detroit, MI: Wayne State University Press, 1979.
Pawel, E. *The Labyrinth of Exile. A Life of Theodore Herzl.* London: Collins, 1990.
Pelikan, Jaroslav. *The Christian Tradition. A History of the Development of Doctrine*, vol. 1. *The Emergence of the Catholic Tradition.* Chicago: University of Chicago Press, 1971.
Perry, Yaron. *British Mission to the Jews in 19th Century Palestine.* London: Cass, 2003.
Phelan, John, L. *The Millennial Kingdom of the Franciscans in the New World.* Berkeley: University of California Press, 1970.
Pierson, Arthur T. *Crisis of Missions or the Voice out of the Cloud.* London: Nisbet, 1886.
Pierson, Delavan L. *Arthur T. Pierson. A Spiritual Warrior. Mighty in the Scriptures. A Leader in the Modern Missionary Crusade.* New York: Garland, 1916.
Plöger, Otto. *Theocracy and Eschatology.* Oxford: Blackwell, 1968.
Plooij, D. *Pilgrim Fathers from a Dutch Point of View.* New York: New York University Press, 1932.

Polowetzky, Michael. *Jerusalem Recovered, Victorian Intellectuals and the Birth of Modern Zionism*. Westport, CT: Praeger, 1995.

Porete, Margaret. *The Mirror of Simple Souls*, trans. Ellen L. Babinsky. New York: Paulist Press, 1993.

Potestà, Gian, L. "Radical Apocalyptic Movements in the Late Middle Ages," in *The Encyclopaedia of Apocalypticism*, vol. 2, edited by Bernard McGinn, 110–42. New York: Continuum, 1998.

Qutb, Sayyid. "Milestones," in *The Sayyid Qutb Reader. Selected Writings on Politics, Religion and Society*, edited by Albert J. Bergesen, 35–42. New York: Routeledge, 2008.

Rabinowicz, Oskar K. *Herzl, Architect of the Balfour Declaration*. New York: Herzl Press, 1958.

Ravitzky, Aviezer. *Messianism, Zionism, and Jewish Religious Radicalism*. Chicago: University of Chicago Press, 1996.

Reeves, Marjorie. *Joachim of Fiore and the Prophetic Future*. Stroud, UK: Sutton, 1999.

Reeves, Marjorie. *The Influence of Prophesy in the Later Middle Ages: A Study in Joachimism*. Oxford, UK: Oxford University Press, 1969.

Renton, James. *Zionist Masquerade. The Birth of the Anglo-Zionist Alliance. 1914–18*. Basingstoke, UK Palgrave Macmillan, 2007.

Rex, Richard. *The Lollards*. Basingstoke, UK: Palgrave Macmillan, 2002.

Riley-Smith, Jonathan. *The First Crusaders*. Cambridge, UK: Cambridge University Press, 1997.

Ringren, H. "The Religion of Ancient Syria," in *Historia Religionium. Handbook for the History of Religions*, vol. 1, edited by C. J. Bleeker and Widengren, 195–222. Leiden: NV Brill,1969.

Robbins, Thomas. "Apocalyptic Persecution and Self-Immolation. Mass Suicides among Old Believers in Late 17th Century Russia," in *Millennialism, Persecution and Violence*, edited by Catherine Wessinger, 205–19. Syracuse, NY: Syracuse University Press, 1999.

Roberts, Dana L. "The Crisis of Missions. Premillennial Mission Theory and the Origins of Independent Evangelical Missions," in *Earthen Vessels. American Evangelicals and Foreign Missions. 1880–1980*, edited by Joel A. Carpenter and W. R. Shank. Grand Rapids: Eerdmans, 1990.

Rőmer, W. H. "The Religion of Ancient Mesopotamia," in *Historia Religionum*, vol. 1, edited by C. J. Bleeker and G. Widengren, 115–94. Leiden, NV: Brill, 1969.

Ross-Valentine, Simon. *Islam and the Ahmadiyya Jana'at: History, Belief, Practice* New York: Columbia University Press, 2008.

Roth, Norman. *Conversos, Inquisition and the Expulsion of Jews from Spain*. Madison: University of Wisconsin Press, 1995.

Runciman, Steven. *A History of the Crusades*, vol. 1, *The First Crusade*. London: Penguin, 1971.

Sabine, George H. *The Works of Gerrard Winstanley. With an Appendix of Documents Relating to the Digger Movement*. Ithaca, NY: Cornell University Press, 1941.

Sachar, Howard H. *History of Israel: From the Rise of Zionism to the Present Time*. New York: Knopf, 1979.

Salmon, Yosef. *Religion and Zionism: First Encounters*. Jerusalem: Hebrew University Magnes Press, 2002.

Sandeen, Ernest R. *The Roots of Fundamentalism. British and American Millenarianism. 1800–1930.* Chicago: University of Chicago Press, 1970.

Schäfer, Peter, and Mark R. Cohen, eds. *Toward the Millennium: Messianic Expectations from the Bible to Waco.* Leiden: Brill, 1998.

Scholem, Gershon. *Sabattai Sevi. The Mystical Messiah.* London: Routledge Kegan Paul, 1973.

Scholem, Gershon. *The Messianic Idea in Judaism and Other Essays on Jewish Spirituality.* London: Allen and Unwin, 1971.

Schweitzer, Albert. *Paul and His Interpreters: A Critical History.* London: A & C Black, 1912.

Schweitzer, Albert. *The Quest of the Historical Jesus.* London: SCM Press, 2000; New York: Dover, 2006.

Scochet, Elijah J. *The Hasidic Movement and the Gaon of Vilna.* Northvale, NJ: Aronson, 1994.

Segev, Tom. *1967. Israel, the War and the Year that Transformed the Middle East.* New York: Metropolitan Books, 2007.

Segev, Tom. *One Palestine Complete. Jews and Arabs under the British Mandate.* London: Abacus, 2005.

Shah, Idries, *The Sufis.* London: Jonathan Cape, 1964.

Shahak, Israel, and Mezvinsky. *Jewish Fundamentalism in Israel.* London: Pluto Press, 1999.

Silver, Abba Hillel. *The World Crisis and Jewish Survival.* Reprinted from Yearbook. XLIX Central Conference of American Rabbis, 1939.

Simons, Walter. *City of Ladies. Beguine Communities in the Medieval Low Countries, 1200–1565.* Philadelphia: University of Pennsylvania Press, 2001.

Sizer, Stephen. *Christian Zionism. Road Map to Armageddon.* Leicester, UK: Inter Varsity Press, 2004.

Smart, James, D. *History and Theology of Second Isaiah. A Commentary on Isaiah 40–66.* London: Epworth Press, 1967, p. 24.

Smith, Jane I., and Yvonne Y. Haddad. *The Islamic Understanding of Death and Resurrection.* Albany, NY: State University of New York Press, 1981.

Smith, Peter. *Babi and Baha'i Religions. From Messianic Shi'ism to a World Religion.* Cambridge, UK: Cambridge University Press, 1987.

Soggin, J. Alberto. *Israel in the Biblical Period.* Edinburgh, Scotland: T & T Clark, 2001.

Spinka, Matthew. *John Huss at the Council of Constance.* New York: Columbia University Press, 1965.

Stayer, James, M. *The German Peasants' War and Anabaptist Community of Goods.* Montreal, QB: McGill-Queens University Press, 1991.

Stein, Leonard. *The Balfour Declaration.* London: Valentine Mitchell, 1961.

Stein, Stephen J. "Apocalypticism Outside the Mainstream," in *The Encyclopedia of Apocalypticism*, vol. 3, *Apocalypticism in the Modern Period and the Present Day*, edited by Stephen J. Stein, 108–139. New York: Continuum, 1998.

Stein, Stephen J., ed. *Jonathan Edwards' Apocalyptic Writings.* New Haven, CT: Yale University Press. 1977.

Stein, Stephen, J. *Alternative American Religions* Oxford, UK: Oxford University Press, 2000.

Stone, Jon R., ed. *Expecting Armageddon. Essential Readings in Failed Prophesy.* New York: Routledge, 2000.

Strachan, Gordon. *The Pentecostal Theology of Edward Irving*. London: Darton Longman Todd, 1973.
Strenlan, Rick. *Strange Acts. Studies in the Cultural World of the Acts of the Apostles*. Berlin and New York: Walter de Gruyer, 2004.
Sumberg, Lewis. *The Tarfurs and the First Crusade*. In Medieval Studies. Vol. 21, 224–46, 1959.
Sweet, Leonard I. "Christopher Columbus and the Millennial Vision of the New World." *Catholic Historical Review*, 72 (1986): 396–82.
Swinburn, Lilian M., ed. *The Lanterne of Liyt*. London: Kegan, Paul, Trench, Trubner, 1917.
Tappert, Theodore G., ed. *Selected Writings of Martin Luther*. Philadelphia, PA: Fortress Press, 1967.
Thomson, John A. *Sir John Oldcastle. Dictionary of National Biography*. Oxford, UK: Oxford University Press, 1990.
Tomes, Jason. *Balfour and Foreign Policy*. Cambridge, UK: Cambridge University Press, 1997.
Toon, Peter. *Puritans, the Millennium and the Future of Israel. Puritan Eschatology 1600–1660*. Cambridge: James Clark, 1970.
Trevett, Catherine. *Montanism. Gender, Authority and the New Prophesy*. Cambridge, UK: Cambridge University Press, 1996.
Tudela, William of, and successor. *The Song of the Cathar Wars*, trans. Janet Shirley. Aldershot, UK: Scholar Press, 1996.
VanderKam, James C. "Messianism and Apocalypticism," in *The Encyclopaedia of Apocalypticism*, vol. 1., John J. Collins, 193–228. New York: Continuum, 1998.
VanderKam, James C. *Enoch and the Growth of an Apocalyptic Tradition*. Washington, DC: Catholic Biblical Quarterly Monograph Series No. 18, 1984.
Vermès, Géza. *Jesus the Jew: A Historian's Reading of the Gospels*. London: Collins, 1973.
Vingeas, Louis André. "St. Thomas. Apostle of America." *Hispanic American Historical Review*, 57 (1977): 82–90.
Voll, John. "The Sudanese Mahdi. Frontier Fundamentalist." *International Journal of Middle East Studies*, 10 (1979): 145–66.
Wakefield, Walter L., and Austin P. Evans. *Heresies of the High Middle Ages. Selected Sources Translated and Annotated*. New York: Columbia University Press, 1969.
Walbridge, John, ed. *Translations of Shaykhi, Babi and Baha'i Texts*, vol. 2 1998. www.h-net.org/~bahai/trans.htm.
Walker, Paul E. *Early Philosophical Platonism. Abu Ya'guls Sijistani*. Cambridge, UK: Cambridge University Press, 1993.
Walls, Gerry L. *The Oxford Handbook of Eschatology*. Oxford, UK: Oxford University Press, 2008.
Watson, John. *A Course of Sunday School Lessons on the Gospel in the Old Testament*. London: National School Society, 1885.
Watt Pauline. "Prophesy and Discovery. On the Spiritual Origins of Christopher Columbus' Enterprise of the Indies." *American Historical Review*, 90 (supplement, 1983): 73–102.
Watt, W. Montgomery. *Early Islam. Collected Articles*. Edinburgh, UK: Edinburgh University Press, 1990.

Watt, W. Montgomery. *Free Will and Predestination in Early Islam*. London: Luzac, 1948.
Way, Lewis. *Poems. Isaiah Chapter lxii*. Stansted: Private Press, n.d.
Weber, E. *Apocalypses, Prophesies, Cults and Millennial Beliefs through the Ages*. London: Hutchinson, 1999.
Weiderkehr-Pollack, Gloria. *Eliezer Zweifel and the Intellectual Defence of Hasidism*. Jersey City, NJ: KTAV Publishing House, 1995.
Weizmann, Chaim. *Trial and Error: The Autobiography of Chaim Weizmann*. London: Hamish Hamilton, 1949.
Wessinger, Catherine, ed. *Millennialism, Persecution and Violence*. Syracuse, NY: Syracuse University Press, 1999.
Widengren, Geo. *Muhammad: The Apostle of God, and his Ascension (King and Saviour V)*. Uppsala, Sweden: Lundequistska bokhandeln, 1955.
Williams, George H. *The Radical Reformation*. Kirksville, MO: Sixteenth Century Journal Publishers, 1993.
Wilson, Robert R. "The Biblical Roots of Apocalypticism," in *Imagining the End: Visions of the Apocalypse from the Ancient Middle East to Modern America*, edited by A. Amanat and M. Bernhardsson, 56–66. London and New York: Tauris, 2002.
Winchester, Elhaman. *A Course of Lectures on the Prophesies that Remain to be Fulfilled*. London, 1789.
Wise, Stephen. *Challenging Years. The Autobiography of Stephen Wise*. London: East and West Library, 1951.
Wistrich, Robert S., ed. *The Left Against Zion. Communism, Israel and the Middle East*. London: Valentine Mitchell, 1979.
Wistrich, Robert. *Hitler's Apocalypse. Jews and the Nazi Legacy*. London: Weidenfeld and Nicolson 1985.
Wolf, Lucien. *Menasseh ben Israel's Mission to Oliver Cromwell. Being a Reprint of the Pamphlets Published by Menasseh ben Israel to Promote the Readmission of the Jews*. London: Macmillan, 1901.
Woodhouse, A. S. P. *Puritanism and Liberty. Being the Army Debates (1647–9)*. London: Dent, 1938.
Woolrich, Austin. *Commonwealth to Protectorate*. Oxford, UK: Oxford University Press, 1982.
Wycliffe, John. *Tracts and Treatises*. London: Blackburn and Pardon, 1845.
Yaval, Israel J. "Jewish Messianic Expectations towards 1240 and Christian Reactions," in *Towards the Millennium. Messianic Expectations from the Bible to Waco*, edited by Peter Schäfer and Mark Cohen, 105–21. Leiden: Brill, 1998.
Zakai, Avihu. *Exile and Kingdom, History and Apocalypse in the Puritan Migration to America*. Cambridge, UK: Cambridge University Press, 1992.
Zeigler, Philip. *The Black Death*. London: Collins, 1969.
Ziff, Larzer. *The Career of John Cotton. Puritanism and the American Experience*. Princeton, NJ: Princeton University Press, 1962.

Index

Abbas, Abdul, Caliph, 55
Abbasid assassins, 55–56
Abbasid caliphate, 58
Abd al-Malik, Caliph, 51
Abdulafia, Abraham, 105
Abdulafia, Meir, 103
Abi Talib, 52
Abu Bakr, Caliph, 52
Abu Hamid, 59
Acts of the Apostles (Luke), 18, 31–32, 201
Adam and Eve, fall of, 19
Addison, Joseph, 133
Afghanistan, Soviet war in, 190
Ahmadinejad, Mahmud, 193–94
Ahmadiyya movement, 161–62
Ahmad, Mirza Ghulam, 161–62
Ahmad, Shaykh, 158–59, 161
Ahura Mazda, 5–8, 26
Ain Jalut, Battle of, 101
Albigensian Crusade, 67–69
Alexander, Michael Solomon, 157–58
Alexander II, Tsar of Russia, 154
Alexander VI, Pope, 88
Alexander of Macedon, 16, 17, 21, 48; bronze gates of, 51–52, 109
Alexios I, Byzantine Emperor, 63, 65
Alexis II, Tsar of Russia, 129

Al-Ghazali (The Spinner), 59, 60
Al Hassan, Abu Sa'id, 57
Allah, 44, 45, 54
Allenby, General, 173
Allison, Dale, 31
Al-Mahdi, Abdullah, 57
Al-Ma'um, Caliph, 58
Al-Qaeda, 190, 191, 200
Al Sadiq, Jafar, 55, 56
Alsted, Johann, 114–15
Amillennarian, 141
Amos, 10, 11, 12
Anabaptists, 94–98, 111, 122
Anat, 10
Angra Mainyu, 6, 7, 8, 16, 26
Antichrist, 33, 100, 101, 139, 198; corrupt popes as, 73–74, 78, 79, 84–86, 89–90, 112, 113, 114; Crusades and, 63–70; European Jews as, 64–65, 113; in Europe (before 1346), 61–70; Free Spirit movement and, 76–78; heretics as, 66–69; Holy Roman emperor as, 71–72, 78, 79, 95; Joachim of Fiore and, 69–71, 72, 74, 76, 78; Napoleon as, 137; nuclear weapons and, 181; Roman emperor as, 36, 52; Russian tsar as, 129–31; in United Nations, 195, 197
Antiochus IV, Epiphanes, 21, 22

Apocalypse, 20, 24, 31; Black Death and, 81–83; English fervor for, 112; four horsemen of, 35; in Judaism, 32. *See also Book of Revelation* (John of Patmos)
Apostolic Brethren, 78–79, 82, 86
Applewhite, Marshall, 202
Arab-Israeli conflicts, 179, 182–88, 195
Arab Revolt (1936–1939), 175–76
Arabs, 43, 52, 109, 200; Zionism and, 174, 175–76, 179
Ariel, Azri'el, 185
Ariel, Yisrael, 187–88
Aristotelian revival, 58–60, 70, 72, 102
Armageddon, 24, 35, 114, 115, 144, 194
Arnauld-Amalric, 68
Aryan migrations, 4–5, 6
Ashkenazi Jews, 151, 153
Ashley Cooper, Anthony, 156, 157, 158
Asquith, Herbert, 169, 170, 171, 180
Assyria, threat to Israel from, 11, 12
Attlee, Clement, 177
Augustine, Bishop of Hippo, 39–41, 89
Aum Shinrikyo cult, 203
Averroes. *See* Ibn Rushd (Averroes)
Avestan language, 6
Avicenna. *See* Ibn Sina (Avicenna)
Avignon papacy, 79, 82, 83
Ayan blood, in Nazi Germany, 177
Azâzêl, 19
Azrael, 45
Azzam, Abdullah, 190

Ba'al, 10, 11
Baal Shem Tov (Besht), 151–52
Babists, in Islam, 159–60
Babylonian exile, 13, 15, 20, 102
Baghdad, 100, 191; House of Wisdom in, 58
Bahá'u'lláh, 160–61
Balfour, Arthur, 169, 170, 171, 180
Balfour Declaration (1917), 172–75, 177–78
Begin, Menachem, 178
Belarmine, Cardinal, 113
Belial, 23
Bevin, Ernest, 177

Bible, the, 25, 72; authenticity of, 136; authority of, 147; Calvinist, 111–12; interpretation of, 141; literalist view of, 143, 145–46; Protestantism and, 92. *See also* Hebrew Bible; New Testament
Bin Laden, Osama, 190, 200
Black Death, in Europe, 81–83
Blackstone, William, 147–48
Bockelson, Jan, 97–98
Bonaventure, 72, 73
Boniface VIII, Pope, 74, 78, 79
Book of Revelation (John of Patmos), 34–37, 40–41, 69, 87, 112–16; *Book of Daniel* and, 35, 113–14; Ezekiel in, 35, 36, 44; Frere and, 137–38; Geneva Bible and, 112; Lowman on, 134–35; wilderness in, 121
Botticelli, Sandro, 88–89
Branch Davidians, 202
Brandeis, Louis, 170
Brightman, Thomas, 114, 115, 125
Brooks, James, 146
Buber, Martin, 183
Bubonic plague. *See* Black Death, in Europe
Bullinger, Heinrich, 112
Bultmann, Rudolph, 28–29
Byzantine Empire, 51

Calling of the Jews, The (Finch), 125
Calvin, John, 89, 92
Calvinists, 114; Puritans, 111–12, 120–24, 125, 126
Camping, Harold, 205
Canaanites, 11, 12, 18; gods of, 9–10
Carter, Jimmy, 198
Cathars, in France, 67–69
Catherine I, Tsarina of Russia, 151
Catholic Church: counterreformation in, 113; schism in, 84, 85. *See also* Popes and papacy
Celestine V, Pope, 74
Chamberlain, Joseph, 168
Charles I, King of England, 116
Charles II, King of England, 120
Charles V, Holy Roman Emperor, 95
Charles VII, King of France, 87–88

Index

China Inland Mission (CIM), 148–49
Christ. *See* Jesus of Nazareth
Christ, Second Coming of. *See* Second Coming, of Christ
Christian end-time, 25–41; Augustine and, 39–41; *Book of Revelation* and, 34–37, 40–41; Cold War and, 181–82; eschatology, 25, 29, 30–31; Gospel of Mark and, 27, 29, 30; heaven and hell, 46; Montanism and, 38–39; Nicene Creed and, 38, 41; Roman Empire and, 33–36; Schweitzer and, 25–26, 27, 29–30, 31; Trinitarian doctrine in, 51
Christian Missionary Alliance, 149
Christian Zionism, 124–28, 147, 166, 198; conversion of Jews and, 148, 158; Old Testament stories and, 167–68
Churchill, Winston, 173–74
Church of England, 114
Circumcellions, 39
City of God (Augustine), 40, 41
City-states, hierarchical structure in, 1–2
Clarkson, Lawrence, 119
Clement VI, Pope, 82, 83
Clement VII, Pope, 84
Clermont, Council of (1095), 63
Cold War, 181–82, 195, 199
Columbus, Christopher, 109–10
Coming of the Messiah in Glory and Majesty, The (Ribera), 140
Conrad of Marburg, 68–69
Constance, Council of (1415), 85
Constantine, Roman Emperor, 39, 114
Constantinople, 51, 65–66, 100, 101
Cordovero, Moses, 108
Cotton, John, 122–23
Cromwell, Oliver, 116–20, 126–67; death of, 120
Crossan, John Dominic, 30
Crusades, 63–70, 99–100; against Albigensians, 67–69; against Apostolic Brethren, 78–79; against terrorism, 200
Curzon, Lord, 172
Cyrus II, Emperor of Persia, 12, 14, 15, 202
Cyrus the Great, Emperor of Persia, 8

Daniel, Book of, 12, 20–22, 102, 118, 136, 140; *Revelation* and, 35, 113–14
Dante Alighieri, 63, 74
Darby, John Nelson, 143–47
Darwinian evolution, 145–46, 205
David, King of Israel, 10, 23
Day of Doom (Wigglesworth), 123–24
Dead Sea Scrolls, 22–23
Defenestration of Prague (1419), 86
De Guzmán, Dominic, 71
De Montfort, Simon the Elder, 68
Diggers, in England, 117–18
Di Mambro, Joseph, 202–3
Dispensationalists, 143, 145, 146, 148, 180, 181; endtime novels and, 195–97, 198, 199
Dodd, Charles, 29–30
Dolcino of Novara, 78–79, 86
Dome of the Rock (Jerusalem), 51, 174, 187, 196
Dominican order, 71, 72, 90
Donation of Constantine, 62–63, 84
Donatist movement, 39–40
Donne, John, 122
Doomsday prophets, 206
Dreyfus, Alfred, 165, 169
Drummond, Henry, 139, 140
Du Jon, François, 112
Dutch United Provinces, 120–21

East Africa, Jewish settlement in, 168
Edwards, Jonathan, 136, 138, 141, 148, 149; Great Awakening and, 133–34, 135
Egranus, John, 91
Egypt, 163; Mamlukes in, 100–101; Suez Crisis and, 182; underworld of, 2, 3; war with Israel, 183
Eisenhower, Dwight, 182, 195
El Abidine, Zine, 200
El (Elohim), 9, 18, 21
Elijah, 10, 18, 35
Elizabeth I, Queen of England, 111, 124
Emicho, Count of Leningen, 65
England: Church of England, 114; under Cromwell, 116–20; Diggers in, 117–18; heretics in, 83–85, 86; Jewish

community in, 126–27; Levelers in, 116–17; Puritans, 111–12, 124; Ranters in, 119–20
Enlightenment thinkers, 133, 134, 205
Enlil, 3
Enoch, Book of, 18–20, 21–22, 35
Erasmus, 89
Eschatology, 25; realized, 29, 30
Europe: (1346–1588), 81–98; Anabaptists in, 94–98; Antichrist in (before 1346), 61–70; Black Death in, 81–83; English heretics, 83–85, 86; Hus and Hussites in, 85–86, 87, 92; Luther in, 89–94; Müntzer in, 91–93; Pale of Settlement in, 151, 153, 154–55, 169; Savonarola in, 87–89; Taborites in, 86–87, 91. *See also specific country*
European Union, 196–97
Exodus, Book of, 121
Ezekiel, 12, 13–14, 15, 16, 21, 24; in *Book of Revelation*, 35, 36, 44

Falwell, Jerry, 195, 198–99
Faraj, Abdel Salam, 189–90
Fatima of Cordova, 99
Female sexuality, fear of, 75, 76
Ferdinand of Aragon, 107
Finch, Henry, 125
Finney, Charles Gradeson, 135
First Fitna, in Islam, 53–54
First Zionist Congress (1897), 166
Flagellants, Black Death and, 82, 83
Flood myths, 3–4
Forrestall, James, 179, 182
Fourth Geneva Convention, 182, 183
Foxe, John, 112
France: Cathars of, 67–69; Dreyfus affair in, 165, 169; massacre of Jews in, 82–83
Franciscan order, 71–72, 73, 74–75, 88; in Americas, 110
Francis of Assisi, 71, 72–73
Frank, Jacob, 151
Frederick II, Holy Roman Emperor, 71–72, 78, 82
Frederick III, Elector, 90
Free Spirit movement, 76–78

Free will, 76
Frere, James Hatley, 137–39
Funk, Robert, 30

Gathas, 6
Genesis, Book of, 3, 103
Geneva Bible, 111–12
Gerard of Borgo san Donninio, 72, 73
Germany, Nazi rule in, 176–77
Gilgamesh, epic of, 3
Gnosticism, 37, 47, 58, 67, 76; kabbalah and, 104; Protestantism and, 92; resurrection and, 102; in Shi'a Islam, 159; Sufism and, 99; syncretism and, 17; *Zohar* and, 106
Gobat, Samuel, 156, 158
God, challenge to existence of, 133. *See also* Allah; Yahweh
Gog and Magog, 48, 52, 89, 114; Ezekiel and, 16, 44; Muslim empire of, 110, 141
Goldstein, Baruch, 186
Good *vs.* evil, 37; in Jewish end-time, 19–20, 23, 24; in Zoroastrian faith, 6–8
Gordon, David, 154
Gordon, George, 163
Great Awakening, 133–35
Great Disappointment, 142, 146. *See also* Miller, William
Greece: culture of, 21; philosophy of, 17, 58 (*See also* Aristotelian revival); underworld of, 2. *See also* Hellenistic age
Gregory IX, Pope, 71, 73
Gregory VII, Pope, 62, 112
Gregory XI, Pope, 83, 84
Grosseteste, Robert, Bishop of Lincoln, 66–67
Gui, Bernard, 75, 78
Guide to the Perplexed, A (Maimonides), 102, 103
Gurion, David ben, 179
Gush Emunim (Block of the Faithful), 184, 185, 191

Hadith, 44, 47, 49, 50. *See also* Islamic end-time
Haggai, 16

Harrison, Thomas, 118, 119, 120
Hasan, Muhammad ben, 193
Hasidism, 151, 152, 186
Heaven's Gate cult, 202
Heber, Reginald, 136
Hebrew Bible, 104, 106; Enoch, 18–20; Exodus, 121; Genesis, 3, 103; Leviticus, 153; Numbers, 184, 187; Old Testament, 36, 167–68, 180; prophets of, 10–16. *See also specific* prophets; Yahweh and, 9, 10, 11, 13–14. *See also Daniel, Book of*
Hechler, William, 166–67, 185
Hell, Josef, 176
Hell, Muslim vision of, 46–47
Hellenistic Age, 16, 18, 20–21, 22
Hertz, Joseph, 172
Herzl, Theodore, 165–67, 168, 174, 183
Hesiod, 4
Hidden imams, in Islam, 55, 56, 57; in Iran, 191, 192, 193, 194
Hildegard of Bingen, 61
Hiroshima, atomic bombing of, 181
History of the Work of Redemption, A (Edwards), 135
Hitler, Adolf, 176–77
Hoffman, Melchior, 95–96
Holy Roman Emperor, as Antichrist, 71–72, 78, 79, 95
Hooker, Thomas, 123
Hosea, 10, 11, 12
Hulagu, Khan, 100
Hume, David, 133
Hus, Jan, 85–86, 92
Husayn, 53, 56
Hussein, Saddam, 192
Hussites, 87, 92
Hut, Hans, 94–95
Hutter, Jacob, 95
Hyrcanus, John, 23–24

Ibn Abu, Mukhtar, 54–55
Ibn al-Hanafiyya, Muhammad, 55
Ibn Arabi, 99–100, 101
Ibn Kathir, 101
Ibn Rushd (Averröes), 59–60, 99, 102
Ibn Sina (Avicenna), 58–59, 72

Ignatii, Father, 130
Inanna (Ishtar), 2
Incoherence of the Philosophers, The (Al-Ghazali), 59
Indo-European languages, 4, 5
Innocent III, Pope, 67, 68, 71, 72
Inquisition, 67, 68, 73, 75, 76–77, 78; in Spain, 107, 109
Iran, 191–93; hidden imam in, 191, 192, 193, 194; Islamic Revolution in, 191–92; war with Iraq, 192–93
Iraq Wars, 190–91, 192–93
Ireton, Henry, 116–17
Irving, Edward, 138–40, 148
Isabella of Castile, 107
Isaiah, Book of, 10–11, 14–15, 26, 125
Islamic end-time: 43–60, 158–63, 188–94; Aristotelian revival and, 58–60; Babists and, 159–60; Bahá'u'lláh and, 160–61; First Fitna, 53–54; heaven and hell in, 46–47; holy war in. *See* Jihad; Messianism in (Mahdi), 45, 53–54, 101 (*See also* Mahdi [Islamic Messiah]); Muhammad and, 43, 44–48, 50, 161, 162, 174; *Pseudo Methodius* and, 51–52; Shi'a Islam, 53–54, 55, 158–59, 161–62, 192, 193; Sufism and, 58, 59, 99, 162; Sunni Islam, 53–54, 55, 57, 188–89; Wahabi Muslims and, 162
Islamic republic, in Iran, 192
Ismaili Severners, in Islam, 56, 70
Israelites, 2, 9. *See also* Hebrew Bible; Jewish end-time
Israel (modern state), 192, 199; Arab-Israeli hostilities, 179, 182–85, 195. *See also* Zionism
Istanbul, 141. *See also* Constantinople

Jacobsen, Eddie, 178, 180
James, Bishop of Jerusalem, 33
James II, King of England, 120
Jan of Leiden, 97–98
Jerusalem, 10, 11, 16, 27; Antichrist in, 113; bishop of, 157; Christian Zionism and, 124; Crusades to, 63–64, 66, 70; Dome of the Rock in, 51, 174, 187, 196; early Christians in, 32; Roman siege of,

33; Temple Mount in, 49, 174, 186–87; Zionism and, 169, 179
Jesuits, 113, 140
Jesus of Nazareth, 25–28, 51; Great Commission of, 134, 139; second coming of (*See* Second Coming of Christ); Sermon on the Mount, 26; Transfiguration of, 26–27, 86. *See also* Christian end-time
Jewish end-time, 9–24; Assyrian threat and, 11, 12; Babylonian exile and, 13, 15, 20, 102; Hellenistic age and, 16, 18, 20–21; kabbalah and, 104; Maimonides and, 101–4, 106; Messiah in, 15, 23–24, 32, 103, 104–6, 127; prophets of, 10–16; underworld of, 2; Yahweh and, 9, 10, 11, 13–14, 24; *Zohar*, 105–6, 108; Zoroastrian concepts and, 14, 15, 18. *See also* Hebrew Bible; Jewish Messianism
Jewish Holocaust, 177
Jewish Messianism, 15, 23–24, 32, 103; Besht and, 151–52; Kabbalah and, 104–6, 108–9, 127, 151; Zionism and, 186; *Zohar* model and, 105–6, 108, 152
Jewish rebellion (66 CE), 33–34
Jews: as Antichrist, 64–65, 113; conversion of, 138, 158; expelled from Spain, 106–8; Hasidism and, 151, 152, 186; massacre of, 82–83; Nazi Germany and, 176–77. *See also* Jewish end-time; Zionism
Jihad, 50, 57, 159, 163, 189, 200; Al Qaeda and, 190, 191; Hezbollah and, 192
Joachim of Fiore, 69–71, 74, 87, 104; Third Ages doctrine of, 70, 71, 72, 73, 76, 78
Job, Book of, 19
John of Patmos, 52, 70. *See also Book of Revelation* (John of Patmos)
Johnson, Lyndon, 182
John the Baptist, 24, 138
John XXII, Pope, 79
Jones, James Warren (Jim), 201
Josephus, 32, 33–34
Joshua, Book of, 11–12

Judaism, 32, 184. *See also* Hebrew Bible; Jewish end-time
Judenstaat, Der (Herzl), 165–66
Judgment Day, 67, 69, 92, 205; Black Death and, 82; in Islam, 44; in Jewish end-time, 19, 21–22, 24; in parables of Jesus, 26, 27; in Zoroastrian faith, 6, 7, 33
Justinian I, Roman Emperor, 49

Ka'bah shrine, in Mecca, 43, 57
Kabbalah, 104–6, 108, 126, 151, 152
Kabbalism, 108–9, 125, 127
Karbala, Battle of, 53, 159
Kenya, Jewish settlement in, 168
Kett, Francis, 124
Keys of the Revelation Searched and Demonstrated (Mede), 115
Khamenei, Ayatollah, 193
Kharijite Islam, 54
Khomeini, Ayatollah Ruhollah, 191–92, 193
Kibbutz, 174, 183
Kibweteere, Joseph, 203
King, Edward, 136–37
Knox, John, 112
Kony, Joseph, 204
Kook, Abraham (Kook the Elder), 183
Kook, Avi Yehudah (Kook the Younger), 183–84, 185
Koresh, David, 202

Lacunza, Manuel, 140, 144
Last Judgment. *See* Judgment Day
Last Testament (Francis of Assisi), 73
Late Great Planet Earth, The (Lindsey), 195–97, 199
League of Nations, 172
Left Behind series (Jenkins and LaHaye), 197–98
Leo X, Pope, 90
Levelers, in England, 116–17
Leviticus, Book of, 153
Liliburne, John, 116
Lloyd George, David, 169, 170, 171, 172
Loew, Judah, 126
Lollards, 84, 85, 86

London Jews' Society (LJS), 155, 156, 157
London Missionary Society (LMS), 138–40, 148
Lord's Resistance Army, 204
Lovett, Robert, 179
Lowman, Moses, 134–35
Luria, Isaac, 108–9
Lurianic Kabbalism, 125, 127. *See also* Kabbalah
Luther, Martin, 87, 89–94; Müntzer and, 91–93; Two Kingdoms doctrine of, 91, 93

Maccabee revolt, 21, 23
Macdonald, Ramsay, 175
Magog. *See* Gog and Magog
Mahdi (Islamic Messiah), 45, 53–54, 55, 193; Ahmadiyya movement, 161–62; Antichrist and, 100, 101; Babists and, 159–60; jihad and, 57, 159, 163; occultation of, 54, 56, 57. *See also* Hidden Imam
Maimon, Moses ben (Maimonides), 101–4, 106, 187
Malthus, Thomas, 205–6
Mamlukes, in Egypt, 100–101
Manichaean faith, 39
Manson, Charles, 201
Marduk, 2
Margaret of Trent, 78–79
Mark, Gospel of, 27, 29, 30
Mark for Everyone (Wright), 30
Marshall, George C., 179, 182
Mather, Cotton, 123
Mather, Increase, 123, 127–28
Mather, Richard, 123
Matthijs, Jan, 96–97, 98
McIntyre, Karl, 194–95
Mecca, pilgrimage to, 50; Ka'bah shrine in, 43, 57
Mede, Joseph, 125, 141, 142, 166; millennial dating of, 115, 137, 144
Mehemet Ali, 141–42
Meister Eckhart, 77
Messianism, 27, 28, 36, 98; in Zoroastrian faith, 6, 7. *See also* Jewish Messianism; Mahdi (Islamic Messiah)

Methodius of Olympus, 51. *See also Pseudo Methodius*
Michael the Archangel, 23
Milestones (Qutb), 188, 189
Millenarianism, 24, 85
Millennialists, 91, 94, 118, 137, 141; Columbus and, 109; Mede and, 115; secularists and, 122; in Shi'ite Islam, 194
Miller, Walter, 144, 146, 205
Miller, William, 141–42
Milton, John, 19, 115
Mirror of Simple Souls (Porete), 76–77, 106
Mithra, 7, 8
Möngke, Great Khan, 100, 101
Mongol Empire, 100
Montague, Edwin, 169–70, 172
Montanism, 38–39
Montefiore, Moses, 153
Most Comfortable Exposition . . . (Brightman), 125
Muawiyah, Caliph, 51, 53, 54
Muhammad Ali Pasha, 156, 163
Muhammad (Prophet), 43, 44–48, 50, 161, 162; death of, 48; Night Journey of, 47–48, 174. *See also* Islamic end-time
Mujahidin (holy warriors), 190
Müntzer, Thomas, 91–93
Muslim Brotherhood, 188, 190

Napoleon, as Antichrist, 137
Nasser, Gamal Abdul, 182, 188, 189
Nathan of Gaza, 127
Native Americans, 134; as lost tribes, 110, 126
Naylor, James, 120
Nero, Roman Emperor, 33, 34, 35–36
Netherlands, 120–21
New England, 142; Great Awakening in, 133–35; Puritans of, 122–24
New Jerusalem, 38, 40, 70, 93, 136; Anabaptists and, 95, 96, 98; Crusades and, 63–64; in Geneva Bible, 112; Luther on, 91; Müntzer on, 92
New Testament, 25, 89; Acts of the Apostles, 18, 31–32; Epistles of Paul,

32–33, 91, 125–26, 139, 144; Gospel of Mark, 27, 29. *See also* Christian end-time
Newton, Benjamin Wills, 143, 145
Newton, Isaac, 115, 205
Niagra Conference (1888), 146–47, 148, 149
Nicene Creed, 38, 41
Nicholas III, Pope, 74, 105
Niger Delta, witchcraft in, 204
Nikon, Patriarch of Russia, 128, 129
1980s, The: Countdown to Armageddon (Lindsey), 196
Nixon, Richard, 183, 194
North America: Great Awakening in, 133–35; Puritans in, 121–24
Notes on the Revelation of St. John (Lowman), 134–35
Numbers, Book of, 184, 187

Occultation, 74, 128
Occultism, in Islam, 55, 56, 57, 192. *See also* Hidden Imam
Old Believers, in Russia, 128–31
Old Testament, 36, 167–68, 180. *See also* Hebrew Bible
Olivi, Peter John, 73, 74, 75–76
Order of the Solar Temple, 202–3
Origen of Alexandria, 37–38, 40, 59, 141
Orthodox Christianity, in Russia, 128–31
Ottoman Empire, 137, 141, 142, 156; Zionism and, 166, 168, 170, 172

Pale of Settlement, Jews in, 151, 153, 154–55, 169
Palestine, return of Jews to. *See* Zionism
Palestine Mandate Convention, 178
Palmerston, Lord (Henry Temple), 157
Parliament (England), 116
Paul of Tarsus, letters of, 32–33, 91, 125–26, 139, 144
Peasants' Revolt (1381), 85
Peasants' War (1524–1525), 93–94
Pentecost, 31, 148
People's Crusade, 64, 65–66
People's Temple, 201
Persian Empire, 16

Peter, the Apostle, 31–32, 33, 74, 144, 181
Peter the Great, Tsar of Russia, 129, 130–31
Peter the Hermit, 64, 65–66
Pierson, Arthur T., 148
Plato, 17, 58
Plymouth Brethren, 143–47
Polygamy, 97
Popes and papacy: as Antichrist, 73–74, 78, 79, 84–86, 89–90, 112, 113, 114; in Avignon, 79, 82, 83, 84, 85; Crusades and, 63–64, 67–68; *Donation of Constantine* and, 62–63, 84; Inquisition and, 67, 68; Savonarola and, 88; secular power of, 115; Wyclif and, 83–84. *See also specific* pope
Porete, Margaret, 76–77, 106
Postmillennarians, 141, 154, 160
Powerscourt, Lady (Theodosia Wingfield), 142–43
Premillennarians, 140–41, 147, 148, 155, 160, 180
Protestantism, 91; apocalypse and, 114. *See also* Dispensationalists; *See also specific* sect
Pseudo-Methodius, 51–52, 61, 63, 71
Puritans: in England, 111–12, 124; in Netherlands, 120–21; in North America, 121–24; Zionism and, 125, 126
Pythagoras, 17

Qajar dynasty, of Persia, 158
Quakers (Society of Friends), 120
Quest of the Historical Jesus, The (Schweitzer), 25–26, 28, 29
Qumran community, 23
Qur'an, 44, 47, 48, 49, 50, 162, 188. *See also* Islamic end-time
Qurmatians, 57
Qutb, Sayyid, 188, 189, 190, 200
Qutuz, Sultan, 100–101

Ra, 2, 3
Rabin, Yitzhak, 199
Rainsborough, Colonel, 116–17
Ranters, in England, 119–20

Rapture, 144–45, 197
Reagan administration, 199
Resurrection, 37–38, 102
Revelation. See Book of Revelation (John of Patmos)
Reza, Mohammed, Shah of Iran, 191–92
Ribera, Francisco, 113–14, 115, 140, 144
Richard I (the Lionhearted), King of England, 69, 70, 99–100
Riefenstahl, Leni, 177
Rig Veda, 5
Robertson, Pat, 199–200
Roman Empire, 35–36; Jewish rebellion and, 33–34
Roman Inquisition, 67, 68, 73, 75, 76
Romans, Epistle to (Paul of Tarsus), 125–26
Rome, Visigoth sack of, 40
Rothschild, Baron, 170
Runciman, Steven, 66
Russia, 169; Old Believers in, 128–31, 201; tsars of, 129–31, 151

Sadat, Anwar, 189, 190
Safed, 108, 153
Saladin, 69, 102, 200
Salmon, Joseph, 119
Samuel, Herbert, 169, 170, 173, 174
Saoshyant, 6, 7
Savonarola, Girolamo, 87–89, 91
Schweitzer, Albert, 25–26, 27, 29–30, 31
Second Coming, of Christ, 38, 40, 93, 140, 141, 150; Islamic end-time and, 44, 101; Mede and, 115; in Paul's epistle, 32; Zionism and, 126, 148, 155, 156, 158, 166
Segarelli, Gherardo, 78
Seljuk Turks, Crusades against, 63, 65–66
Sennacherib, King of Assyria, 11
Sephardic (Spanish) Jews, 106–8
September 11 (2001) terrorism, 200
Sevi, Sabbattai, 127, 128, 151
Shaftesbury, Earl of (Anthony Ashley Cooper), 156, 157, 158
Shi'a Islam, 53–54, 55, 158–59, 192; Ahmadiyya movement, 161–62; Gnostic tradition in, 159; martyrdom in, 193

Simon, Menno, 98
Simpson, Arthur, 149
Six Day War, 184, 195
Sixth Zionist Conference (1903), 168
Siyyid Ali Muhammad, 159, 160
Socrates, 17, 58
Solomon, Benjamin, 155
Son of Man, 21–22; Jesus as, 25, 28
Soviet Union, 190, 196
Suez Canal crisis (1956), 182
Sufism, 58, 59, 99, 162
Suicide bombers, 200
Suicide cults, 129, 130, 201–4
Sumerians, underworld of, 2, 3
Sunni Islam, 53–54, 55, 57, 188–89
Sykes-Picot Agreement, 170, 171, 173
Syncretism, 17, 55

Taborites, 86–87, 91
Talmud, 26
Tarfurs, 66
Taylot, James Hudson, 148–49
Temple Mount (Jerusalem), 49, 174, 186–87
Tetzel, Johannes, 90
Thessalonians, Epistles to (Paul), 32–33, 144
Third Age of the Holy Spirit, 70, 71, 72, 73, 76, 78
Third Reich, The (van den Bruck), 176
Thomas, Gospel of, 30
Thomas Aquinas, 72, 74
Timur the Lame (Tamburlaine), 101
Torquemada, Tomás de, 107
Transfiguration, of Jesus, 26–27, 86
Trapnel, Anna, 118
Tribulation, time of, 27, 53, 134, 141, 197–98
Truman, Harry, 178–79, 180
Turner, Nat, 141

Uganda, 168; suicide cult in, 202–4
Umayyad caliphate, 53, 55
Underworld, 2, 3
United Nations, 177, 178, 179, 182, 190, 193; Antichrist in, 195, 197

Urban II, Pope, 63–64
Uthman ibn Affan, 53

Van den Bruck, Arthur Muller, 176
Vedas, 5
Vilna Gaon (sage of Vilna), 152–53
Virgin Mary cult, 35, 51, 82, 203
Voltaire (François-Marie Arouet), 115–16, 133

Wahabi Muslims, 162
Way, Lewis, 155
Weizmann, Chaim, 169, 173, 175, 178
Whitefield, George, 133–34
Whore of Babylon, 35, 113
Wigglesworth, Michael, 123–24
Wilhelm II, Kaiser of Germany, 166, 167
Wilhelm IV, King of Prussia, 157, 158
Wilson, Woodrow, 170–71, 172, 178
Winchester, Elhaman, 136, 137
Wingate, Orde, 175–76
Winstanley, Gerrard, 117–18, 120
Wright, Tom, 30
Wyclif, John, 83–85, 86, 114

Yahweh, 9, 10, 11, 13–15, 24, 121. *See also* Jewish end-time
Yazid, Caliph, 53, 54
Yohai, Shimon ben, 105, 108
Yom Kippur War (1973), 183, 185, 195

Zarathrustra, 5, 6, 7, 205. *See also* Zoroastrian faith
Zechariah, Book of, 15, 16, 28, 115
Zionism, 125–26, 153–54; Arab response to, 174, 175–76, 179; Balfour Declaration (1917), 172–75, 177–78; Christian, 124–28, 147, 148, 158, 166, 167–68, 198; Herzl and, 165–67, 168, 174, 183; Hitler and, 176–77; Ottoman response to, 166, 168, 170, 172; politicians and, 165–80
Zizka, Jan, 87
Zohar (Yohai), 105–6, 108, 152
Zoroastrian faith, 5–8, 26, 33, 67; Arabs and, 43; Jewish end-time and, 14, 15, 18; Manichaeanism and, 39; occultism in, 55
Zwickau Prophets, 91–92, 94
Zwingli, Ulrich, 89, 92, 94, 112

About the Author

MARTIN BALLARD won scholarships at St. Paul's School London and Jesus College Cambridge, where he read history. He also studied theology at Ridley Hall Cambridge. After a career in teaching and publishing, he has spent an active retirement in local politics and writing books that draw from both of his academic disciplines. He has written *White Men's God: The Extraordinary Story of Missionaries in Africa* (Praeger) and edited *New Movements in the Study and Teaching of History.* In earlier years, he was also a prolific author of novels and factual books for younger readers. He is also a novelist whose work has been published in Britain and the United States and translated into several languages.